HOME OFFICE

DEPARTMENT OF HEALTH AND SOCIAL SECURITY

Report of the Committee on Mentally Abnormal Offenders

*Presented to Parliament by the Secretary of State for the Home Department
and the Secretary of State for Social Services
by Command of Her Majesty
October 1975*

LONDON
HER MAJESTY'S STATIONERY OFFICE
£3.95 net

Cmnd. 6244

Committee on Mentally Abnormal Offenders
20 Grosvenor Hill
London W1X 0HX

14 August 1975

From The Chairman

To the Rt Hon Roy Jenkins MP, Secretary of State for the Home
Department and the Rt Hon Mrs Barbara Castle MP, Secretary
of State for Social Services.

I have the honour to submit to you the Report of the Committee on Mentally
Abnormal Offenders which was set up by the Home Secretary and the Secretary
of State for Social Services jointly in September 1972.

Except for reservations expressed by some members on particular points in
the course of the text, the Report is unanimous.

Yours very sincerely

(Signed) BUTLER
Chairman

TABLE OF CONTENTS

CHAPTER 3—PROBLEMS OF THE PRESENT TREATMENT ARRANGEMENTS

I. Treatment by the Health and Social Services

II. The Mentally Disordered in the Prisons

CHAPTER 4—DANGEROUS MENTALLY DISORDERED OFFENDERS

CHAPTER 5—PSYCHOPATHS

CHAPTER 20—CO-OPERATION AMONG THE PROFESSIONS: FORENSIC PSYCHIATRIC SERVICES

APPENDICES

GLOSSARY OF TERMS USED IN THE REPORT

Aarvold Committee | Committee set up under the Chairmanship of Sir Carl Aarvold OBE TD in June 1972 to advise whether any changes, within the existing law, were required in the procedures for the discharge and supervision of patients subject to special restrictions under section 65 of the Mental Health Act 1959. The Committee reported in January 1973 (Cmnd. 5191).

Automatism | Discussed in paragraph 18.22.

Conditional discharge | Discharge of a restricted patient subject to conditions of supervision and the possibility of recall: see paragraph 2.31.

Dangerousness | See paragraphs 4.9 and 4.10. We equate dangerousness with a propensity to cause serious physical injury or lasting psychological harm.

Day training centres | See paragraph 8.20.

Day treatment units | See paragraph 8.21.

DHSS | Department of Health and Social Security.

Disability in relation to the trial | See paragraph 10.2, and Chapter 10 generally.

"Durham" formula | See paragraph 18.14.

Forensic psychiatry | See paragraph 20.13 (footnote).

Guardianship orders | See paragraph 15.2, and Chapter 15 generally.

"Hazardous or irreversible" medical procedures | See paragraph 3.54 (footnote).

Hospital order | Order under section 60 of the Mental Health Act for a mentally disordered person to be admitted to and detained in hospital: see paragraphs 2.29–2.30.

Inadequates | See paragraph 6.1.

"Irreversible" medical procedures | See paragraph 3.54 (footnote).

Juvenile | See paragraph 2.25 (footnote).

Medical treatment | See paragraph 1.19.

Mental disorder | See paragraph 1.12 and, for the statutory definition, paragraph 1.13.

Mental element in crime | See paragraph 18.5 (footnote).

Mental handicap	Mental retardation: subnormality or severe subnormality.
Mental Health Act	Mental Health Act 1959.
Mental Health Review Tribunal	See paragraph 7.4.
Mental illness	Not defined in the Mental Health Act but refers to a disorder which has not always existed in the patient but has developed as a condition overlying the sufferer's usual personality.
Mental welfare officers	See paragraph 9.1 (footnote).
M'Naghten Rules	See paragraph 18.4.
Model Penal Code (American Law Institute)	See paragraph 18.14.
NHS	National Health Service.
Personality disorder	See paragraph 5.17.
Place of safety	As defined in the Mental Health Act: see paragraph 9.1. In connection with our proposals for emergency recall of condition-dally discharged patients, see paragraph 14.31.
Psychiatric probation order	See paragraph 16.1, and Chapter 16 generally.
Psychopathic disorder	See paragraph 1.13(c).
Regional Health Authorities Regional Hospital Boards	See paragraph 2.3 (footnote).
Regional secure [hospital] units	See paragraphs 1.3–1.4.
Restriction order	Order under section 65 of the Mental Health Act reserving to the Home Secretary certain powers in connection with patients detained under hospital orders: see paragraphs 2.31–2.32.
Restricted patient	Patient subject to a restriction order.
Royal Commission of 1954–57	Royal Commission on the Law Relating to Mental Illness and Mental Deficiency, 1954–57 (Cmnd. 169).
Royal Commission on Capital Punishment	Royal Commission on Capital Punishment, 1949–53 (Cmnd. 8932).
Severe mental illness	As defined in connection with our special verdict proposals, see paragraph 18.35.

Severe subnormality	See paragraph 1.13(*b*).
Special hospitals	See paragraphs 2.14–2.15.
Special verdict	As provided at present, see paragraphs 18.2–18.3. As we propose, see paragraphs 18.17–18.18.
Subnormality	See paragraph 1.13(*b*).
The 1959 Act	The Mental Health Act 1959.
Treatment	See paragraph 1.19.
Youth treatment centres	See paragraph 2.40.

CHAPTER 1

INTRODUCTORY REMARKS

I. CONSTITUTION AND PROCEEDINGS OF THE COMMITTEE

1.1 The Committee was set up on 21 September 1972 with the membership shown in Appendix 1 and the following terms of reference:—

   (a) To consider to what extent and on what criteria the law should recognise mental disorder or abnormality in a person accused of a criminal offence as a factor affecting his liability to be tried or convicted, and his disposal;

   (b) To consider what, if any, changes are necessary in the powers, procedure and facilities relating to the provision of appropriate treatment, in prison, hospital or the community, for offenders suffering from mental disorder or abnormality, and to their discharge and aftercare; and to make recommendations.

1.2 Our first meeting was held on 4 October 1972. In full Committee we have met on 31 days, and there have been 62 meetings of sub-committee or *ad hoc* groups. We have received written evidence from a large number of organisations and individuals, many of whom we invited to give oral evidence also. Lists of those who gave evidence are set out in Appendix 2. We are grateful to all those who have helped us by submitting their views or supplying information on the subjects we have considered. We have paid a number of visits either in groups or individually to establishments whose work is relevant to the scope of our inquiry both in this country and in Sweden, Denmark and Holland. A list of these visits is also at Appendix 2. Wherever we went we were made welcome and we found the staff of all the establishments most willing to discuss their work with us and intensely concerned about the problems requiring to be resolved. We wish to record our gratitude for this assistance. We should also like to express our thanks to all other persons who have helped us in numerous invaluable ways in the course of our deliberations; our particular thanks are due to the Home Office and the Department of Health and Social Security for their resourcefulness and unfailing patience in supplying us with information and responding to our many inquiries. We have also appreciated the assistance given us by Mr D J Cowperthwaite of the Scottish Home and Health Department who attended our meetings in the role of observer and adviser on Scottish law and practice.

II. ACTION ON OUR INTERIM REPORT

1.3 On 20 April 1974 we submitted an Interim Report[1] the purpose of which was to recommend the provision, as a matter of urgency, of secure hospital units in each Regional Health Authority area. To avoid local financial difficulties we proposed that this provision should be financed by a direct allocation of central Government funds to the Regional Health Authorities.

1.4 The units are required for those mentally disordered persons, offenders and non-offenders alike, who do not require the degree of security offered by the

---
[1] Cmnd. 5698.

special hospitals, which in any event are overcrowded, but who, nonetheless, are not suitable for treatment under the open conditions obtaining in local psychiatric hospitals. At present no adequate provision is made for these people and indeed, as we pointed out, although recommendations by a Working Party for the provision of secure units were commended to Regional Hospital Boards by the Ministry of Health as long ago as July 1961 not a single secure unit materialised. Consequently courts sometimes have no option but to impose sentences of imprisonment on offenders who are in need of treatment in hospital but for whom, whether for their own safety or for the protection of the public, secure containment is essential. A recent Judgment of the Court of Appeal (*Regina* v. *Parker, Griffiths and Rainbird*)[2] has provided three examples of such cases. Delivering the Judgment of the Court, Lord Justice James supported our call for the provision of secure hospital accommodation in each region:

> "The interim report of the Committee under the Chairmanship of Lord Butler of Saffron Walden . . . stresses the difficulties of the present situation in the special hospitals and urges the provision of suitable accommodation within the region, and we can only add the court's voice to the wishes expressed in that interim report . . .".

1.5. An internal Working Party of the Department of Health and Social Security had also been considering the need for secure accommodation of this kind over the whole range of provision for the mentally disordered, offenders and non-offenders, and they too found that the need was established.

1.6 We were glad that, as announced in Parliament on 18 July 1974, the Government was able to accept our recommendations and those of the Working Party. A circular[3] was issued to Regional and Area Health Authorities, and Boards of Governors, emphasising the desirability of urgent action and requesting that suitable interim arrangements should be made for treating patients in conditions of security until such time as the new units were provided.

1.7 The proposals were widely well received. An editorial in the British Medical Journal (27 July 1974) expressed the opinion that "the general case made for facilities for these patients is overwhelming". But criticisms have been expressed in the correspondence columns of that Journal, particularly of lack of precision about the type of patient for whom the new units should cater, and about the relationship of the units to the special hospitals. Some doubt has been expressed about the possibility of patients being transferred from the special hospitals to the units, on the assumption that, because they are in the special hospitals, they are dangerous, violent or criminal so that they would inevitably be an immediate danger to the public if they absconded, and therefore are in the category of patients we have recommended should not be accommodated in the units. This assumption, however, is false. Some patients admitted to the special hospitals are then found not to require the degree of security they provide; others respond to treatment and become suitable for less secure conditions. We explicitly stated that many patients in the special hospitals need not be there for reasons of security. Some are

---

[2] Not reported. Judgment given 21 March 1975.

[3] HSC(IS)61 of July 1974.

ransferred to local psychiatric hospitals, as has always been the practice. It is difficult to see why it should be thought that others, possibly not yet suitable for completely open conditions, could not be transferred to the regional units. It is true, as has also been said, that we have recommended against keeping long-term patients in the units, but there is a difference between, as we put it, "the accumulation of more or less permanent residents", and the accommodation for a time of patients on their way to recovery and likely to be acceptable before long in an open hospital or in the community. It will be seen that later in this Report (paragraphs 4.28–4.29) we propose that there should be ready re-admission to the special hospitals of any transferred patients who subsequently give cause for anxiety. We also describe in Chapter 20, the role of the units in the development of co-ordinated forensic psychiatric services, which we believe may answer some of the other questions that have been raised about the functions of the units, including the important matters of staff training and the need for developing improved methods of treatment of psychiatric patients with the help of "built-in" research.

1.8 As for the types of patient to be catered for, in our view the Department of Health and Social Security Working Party adequately cover the ground in paragraphs 36–43 of their revised Report.[4] As they have said, it is easier to identify categories of patient who should not be admitted than to identify those who should, but in general the units are required for "patients who present severely disruptive behaviour, who may be mentally ill or mentally handicapped or those who suffer from psychopathic or severe personality disorder, whether alone or in conjunction with mental illness or handicap.". Whether admission is appropriate can be decided only after clinical assessment taking into account the circumstances of each individual case. "Broadly speaking the need for admission to a secure unit should be decided on a multi-disciplinary basis bearing in mind the nature or the degree of risk to the patient himself, other patients, staff or the public if he is treated elsewhere, and the prospects of his responding to treatment in a secure National Health Service hospital setting, as opposed for example to an open hospital, a special hospital, a penal establishment or, for younger persons, a community home or a borstal.". We find no conflict between the Working Party's remarks on the intended population of the secure units and our own recommendations.

1.9 In the face of the widely acknowledged and urgent need, we have been disturbed to learn that little progress has as yet been made in establishing units, or even in providing temporary arrangements, as the Departmental circular requested. We recognise the difficulties of finding sufficient suitable staff, and it is satisfactory to note that financial recognition for nurses who will work in the units has now been negotiated which we hope will encourage many of them to accept this specialised and demanding work. What causes us concern is that in some parts of the country there have been indications of unwillingness either to formulate plans at all, or to give our proposals the priority which we thought and the Government agreed to be necessary. It appears that in most of the Regions consultations are proceeding, but in some clear affirmations of intent are lacking. Although the Government has undertaken to provide the requisite capital for the units we recognise that Regional Health Authorities will be obliged to meet future running costs from revenue.

[4] DHSS: "Revised Report of the Working Party on Security in NHS Psychiatric Hospitals". London, DHSS, 1974.

The prospects of this additional burden on Regions' resources may serve to discourage speedy progress with projects and we therefore recommend that the costs of running the units should also be met by central Government funds.

1.10 Later in this Report (paragraph 3.7) we argue the case for treating offenders and non-offenders together in the hospital system. The overriding need is to provide the best possible treatment for the patient's mental disorder and he should have full access to treatment in the best location to suit his needs. Ultimately in individual cases this must depend on clinical judgment, but in general policy we hope that humane counsels will prevail, and that considerations of the patient's background will not be allowed to obscure this basic principle. We urge that hospital units should be set up as quickly as may be practicable for offenders and non-offenders alike, and interim arrangements made in the meantime.

III. DISCUSSION OF TERMS OF REFERENCE

1.11 Our terms of reference have given rise to a number of questions about the proper limits to be set to our field of inquiry and we think it necessary at the outset to indicate these problems and how we have dealt with them.

(1) "Mental disorder" and "mental abnormality"

1.12 We have considered what significance if any should be attached to the distinction apparently drawn between "mental disorder" and "mental abnormality". We assume that together these terms were intended to be comprehensive. The inconvenience of not having available a single expression covering all forms of mental ill health (and, one might add, mental disability) was pointed out by the Royal Commission on the Law Relating to Mental Illness and Mental Deficiency 1954–1957 in their Report.[5] The term "abnormality of mind" had been used in the provision for diminished responsibility in section 2(1) of the Homicide Act 1957. The Royal Commission thought that "abnormality" implied a permanent condition; they preferred "mental disorder" as a comprehensive term and this was the term used in the Mental Health Act 1959. The use of the phrase "mental abnormality" as more or less a synonym for "mental disorder" is in our view unfortunate, since there are people who can be said to be mentally abnormal, in the sense of diverging from the statistical norm of mental functioning, although not necessarily disordered. Examples are religious fanatics, occasional drunks and people with unusual mental capacities such as "photographic memories". The use of the term "abnormality" as synonymous with "disorder", implying that the condition in question should if possible be remedied, is liable to lead to misunderstanding. Throughout our Report, therefore, we shall avoid the term "mental abnormality". Nevertheless, the use of both phrases in our terms of reference has been an advantage, since it has enabled us to discuss the problems raised by offences committed under the influence of alcohol and other drugs without begging the question whether such offences involve mental *disorder*. (See our further remarks on alcohol and drugs at paragraph 1.14.)

(2) Categories of mental disorder

1.13 The term "mental disorder" is the most comprehensive available to describe abnormal mental states that require medical treatment or care or are

---

[5] Cmnd. 169, paragraph 74.

4

otherwise of interest to the medical practitioner. Section 4(1) of the Mental Health Act 1959 defines "mental disorder" as meaning "mental illness, arrested or incomplete development of mind, psychopathic disorder, and any other disorder or disability of mind". More than one of these conditions may afflict a patient at one time. Some of the problems we discuss in our Report relate more particularly to psychopathic disorder than to the other conditions referred to. Taking the conditions listed in the statutory definition in turn, the following comments may be helpful:

(a) The Act does not define "mental illness", but this expression denotes a disorder which has not always existed in the patient but has developed as a condition overlying the sufferer's usual personality.

(b) "Arrested or incomplete development of mind" is sub-divided by the Act into "severe subnormality" and "subnormality", the former condition being defined in section 4(2) of the Act as "of such a nature or degree that the patient is incapable of living an independent life or of guarding himself against serious exploitation, or will be so incapable when of an age to do so". Severe subnormality and subnormality (together generally referred to as mental handicap) are permanent disabilities; care and training may, over a long period of time, to some extent improve the patient's level of performance, but the disabilities are not, in the present state of medical knowledge, susceptible of cure.

(c) The expression "psychopathic disorder" is defined in section 4(4) of the Act as "a persistent disorder or disability of mind (whether or not including subnormality of intelligence) which results in abnormally aggressive or seriously irresponsible conduct on the part of the patient, and requires or is susceptible to medical treatment". We discuss in Chapter 5 the problems involved in the concept of psychopathy and in paragraphs 5.19–5.26 we consider the case for excluding the term from the Mental Health Act. At this stage, for the purposes of these introductory remarks and the occasional references in the early chapters of the Report, it will suffice to say that the term is used to refer to a range of personality disorders. We discuss in paragraphs 5.27–5.42 the difficulties of dealing with these offenders, and in particular the doubts which arise as to whether they are aptly regarded as cases for treatment within the National Health Service.

(d) "Any other disorder or disability of mind" was said in the Parliamentary Proceedings on the Bill to have been intended by the draftsman to cover conditions such as disabilities arising from head injuries or encephalitis or mental enfeeblement as the aftermath of mental illness.[6] But of course there are many other disorders or disabilities

---

[6] On the Committee stage of the Mental Health Bill, speaking on an amendment to remove "any other disorder or disability of mind", the Minister, Mr Derek Walker-Smith said:

"The sort of disorder and disability which would not be covered by any of the other categories are the sort of disabilities which are more akin, taking a physical analogy, to those of a crippled person than to those of an ill person; for example, disabilities arising from head injuries or encephalitis or mental enfeeblement as the aftermath of mental illness. Many of these disabilities may require services and care, but would not be appropriate for compulsory treatment".

House of Commons Official Report, Standing Committee on the Mental Health Bill, 12 February 1959, Cols. 65–66.

of mind which would be included under this description. If the International Classification of Diseases (8th Revision) (1968) is followed, the category would include neuroses, personality disorders, sexual deviation, alcohol or drug dependence, the behaviour disorders of children and many other minor mental disorders, such as transient situational mental disturbances, those associated with medical diseases and certain specific disorders of learning, speech or motility which are not of the type likely to require the provisions of the Mental Health Act. There is no power under the Act to detain a person for treatment, either as a non-offender, under Part IV, or as an offender, under Part V, unless he is suffering from one of the four conditions specified in (a) to (c) above, namely mental illness, severe subnormality, subnormality or psychopathic disorder. A person who is suffering from any other disorder or disability of mind may be admitted to hospital compulsorily only for observation for up to 28 days under the provisions of section 25 (or, in emergency, for up to 72 hours under section 29).

(3) Alcohol and drugs

1.14 We have considered to what extent the effects on the mind of drink or drugs might come within the meaning of mental disorder for the purposes of our terms of reference. It seems clear that a normal person who commits an offence during an isolated bout of uncomplicated intoxication should not be considered as "a mentally disordered offender"; but we have regarded ourselves as having some concern with, on the one hand, mentally disordered people who commit offences after taking drink or drugs, and, on the other hand, alcoholics and drug addicts who commit offences, their mental condition having been impaired by their addiction. Provision for the treatment of alcoholics has in recent years been very fully considered by the Working Party on Habitual Drunken Offenders,[7] whose recommendations have been accepted by the Government and are in course of implementation. The Government have also recently announced the establishment of an Advisory Committee on Alcoholism.[8] Provision for drug addicts is within the purview of the Advisory Council on the Misuse of Drugs. We have therefore not regarded it as appropriate for ourselves also to review the generality of such arrangements. On the other hand, if a person's mental condition has been affected by drink or drugs the question arises to what extent he should be held responsible for his acts or omissions, and what powers are required by the courts for the protection of society. These are subjects to which we have given considerable attention in relation to mentally disordered offenders as such, and on which we have made recommendations. We have thought it right to consider the relevance of these recommendations to people suffering from the effects of drinks and drugs, and we make certain supplementary proposals to cover these cases (see paragraphs 18.51–18.59).

(4) Starting point—police action

1.15 The next point about the scope of our inquiry is that the terms of reference speak at part (a) of "a person accused of a criminal offence" and at

[7] HMSO, 1971: see further reference at paragraph 6.7.
[8] One of our members, Dr D I Acres, has been appointed to this Committee.

part (*b*) of "offenders". It therefore appears that strictly we have not been required to concern ourselves with what happens before a criminal charge is preferred. But whether a person who has committed an anti-social act is charged and brought before a court, and so is brought within the formal scope of our concern, often depends upon preceding decisions taken by the police and other agencies and authorities in the exercise of their discretion and professional judgment. These decisions bear directly on how the cases of mentally disordered offenders are dealt with; they may strongly influence the whole course of their future treatment, including, in particular, whether they end up in prisons, or hospitals, or the community. We have received a substantial amount of evidence on various aspects of this issue—principally about the exercise of police powers and about decisions whether to prosecute. It has seemed to us no less important to consider the circumstances in which mentally disordered persons should be protected from involvement in the judicial processes altogether than to consider how they should be dealt with once they have come within the system. Accordingly, we take as our starting point in time the first involvement with the police as a result of the anti-social act of the mentally disordered person. We should not be justified in going further back, to consider the influences within the community, the family or the individual himself[9] which may go to produce the mentally disordered offender, and which might be the target of preventive measures.

(5) Exclusion of general health service and general penal system questions

1.16 A number of problems in interpreting our remit have arisen from the fact that mentally disordered offenders comprise but a proportion of the whole population of offenders on the one hand, most of whom are within the range of mental normality, and of all mentally disordered people on the other, most of whom have not committed offences. The problem can be seen in proper perspective when we realise that in 1973 there were some 197,000 admissions[10] to all hospitals which receive mentally disordered patients (see table in paragraph 2.33), but that less than one per cent of these came from criminal courts or penal establishments. Even if only compulsory admissions are counted—about 14 per cent of all admissions—only about 11 per cent of these came from criminal courts, penal establishments or the police: the rest came from family doctors or the social services. As for the throughput of the criminal courts, psychiatric disposals accounted for less than half of one per cent of the 736,860 convictions[10] for non-motoring offences[11]. In the prisons the proportion of prisoners displaying signs of mental disorder is considerably higher (see the research findings cited in paragraph 3.19) and in the four special hospitals—Broadmoor, Rampton, Moss Side and Park Lane—which provide treatment in conditions of security, offenders comprise about 70 per cent of all the patients. Our terms of reference obviously require us to be concerned

---

[9] Throughout our Report we refer to offenders as male except where specific reference to women is appropriate. Apart from convenience, this is justified by the statistics, for women are a small minority of offenders.

[10] These are the totals not of separate individuals but of admissions or convictions as the case may be: the same person may be admitted or convicted more than once in the same year.

[11] The fraction is smaller still if we count also motoring offences, thus bringing the throughput of the courts up to nearly 2 million convictions a year. But motoring offences seldom lead to psychiatric methods of disposal.

with how the courts, prisons, hospitals and the community deal with mentally disordered offenders but they would not justify us in carrying out a detailed review of everything to do with these institutions and services and recommending changes in their arrangements for dealing with all their clients. We have therefore sought to exclude from consideration arrangements within the penal system and the health service which are of general application, and not specially provided for mentally disordered offenders, but we have not always found it easy to draw the line between our legitimate area of inquiry and those arrangements which we should regard as being beyond our intended competence.

(6) The special hospitals

1.17   It has been particularly difficult to do so in relation to the special hospitals, where mentally disordered offenders predominate to the extent stated above. Nevertheless, although the special hospitals happen to accommodate more offenders than non-offenders, they are provided under statute not for the treatment of offenders in preference to non-offenders but for any persons subject to detention under the Mental Health Act 1959 "who, in the opinion of the Secretary of State, require treatment under conditions of special security on account of their dangerous, violent or criminal propensities".[12]   Our interest is substantial because of the number of offenders actually being treated in the special hospitals and the importance of their secure facilities for this purpose, but the statute does not give us an overriding interest.   We have not, therefore, regarded ourselves as authorised to consider, for example, questions relating to the general administration or regime of the special hospitals, where no special point about offenders is involved.

(7) Acceptance of existing framework

1.18   In general, mentally disordered offenders must continue to be dealt with within the established framework of the existing legal, penal, health and community systems.   This does not mean that we have felt precluded from proposing special provision for mentally disordered offenders where the existing arrangements do not suitably provide for them.   But we have not expected that the existing systems of law, penal custody, medicine and social care or control could be completely or substantially re-shaped or re-orientated solely in the interests of this special group.   Nor have we thought it our business to become involved in the current controversies about the concept of mental disorder itself, although we are well aware of them.   Such issues could not be resolved by this committee; their resolution can come about only by the gradual formulation of professional and public opinion during a long period of time.   We have had to make an exception of psychopathic disorder (see Chapter 5) because a large part of the evidence put to us has been concerned with the nature of psychopathic disorder, the possibility or impossibility of its treatment by various methods, and whether psychopaths should be dealt with in prisons or in hospitals.   These questions have occupied so much of the ground within our remit that it has been necessary for us to examine and reach conclusions on them in order to make recommendations on some of the main practical problems arising with the present arrangements.

---

[12] National Health Service Reorganisation Act 1973, section 40.

(8) Meaning of "treatment"

1.19 With the foregoing reservations in mind, we have considered the interpretation to be given to the expression "appropriate treatment" in the second part of our terms of reference. "Treatment" is an ambiguous term. It may perhaps be generally understood to mean a measure calculated to cure or ameliorate a disorder, but for our purposes it has to be given a wider meaning so as to cover all measures employed in the management of a case. Section 147(1) of the Mental Health Act defines "medical treatment" in the following way:—

> "Medical treatment" includes nursing, and also includes care and training under medical supervision."

Not everyone who referred to treatment under the Act, in giving evidence to us, had appreciated that care and training come within the statutory definition. We take it for granted that in the context of our remit the "appropriate treatment" for an offender suffering from mental disorder will always be to deal with him in whatever way gives him the best prospects of recovery from his condition, or the most substantial improvement possible if full recovery cannot be attained, subject to considerations of public safety. If even a modest degree of improvement cannot be attained the person concerned should nevertheless be within the scope of treatment in the sense of nursing or care and training under professional supervision provided that the required facilities are available. These have been our primary objects in considering each stage of the procedures for dealing with mentally disordered offenders, and when we refer to a treatable condition, or to treatment, we intend this wide interpretation, unless we explicitly say otherwise.

1.20 Treatment of a psychiatric disorder requires the willingness of the patient, and failure of treatment measures may be caused by a deliberate refusal of co-operation. This is more common with offender-patients than with non-offenders, and is one reason why hospitals are not always willing to accept offenders. Our views about the rights of patients to refuse medical treatment are set out in paragraphs 3.50–3.62.

IV. OTHER PRELIMINARY REMARKS

(1) Guiding principles

1.21 The recommendations we have made in pursuance of the treatment objectives mentioned above are based upon the following principles:

(a) that everything practicable should be done to ensure that the occurrence of mental disorder is recognised at the appropriate stage in the legal process;

(b) that there should be the greatest possible flexibility in disposal;

(c) that arrangements should safeguard the mentally disordered person whom it would be unjust to try;

(d) that the mentally disordered offender should be placed in the treatment situation which is best for him consistent with the requirements of public safety;

(e) that treatment should be made available as soon as possible.

9

With reference to (a) we would add that the appropriate stage in the legal process will normally be the earliest possible stage, subject to the need to avoid prejudicing the defence case where a defence is being put forward which does not involve reliance on mental disorder. The successive stages to be considered are:

(i) When the police first have cognizance of the case. Paragraphs 9.1– 9.14 discuss the arrangements under section 136 of the Mental Health Act governing police action when they find someone in a public place apparently suffering from mental disorder and in immediate need of care or control.

(ii) When the question whether to charge or prosecute is made by the police or the Director of Public Prosecutions. Paragraphs 9.15–9.25 discuss the circumstances in which prosecution might be avoided.

(iii) When the case first comes into court. Before the case is tried there may be grounds for deciding that the defendant is not fit to stand trial, and new arrangements on this are recommended in Chapter 10. It is of the utmost importance that the courts should have adequate information about the mental condition of the defendant and in Chapters 11 and 12 we recommend improvements in this connection.

(iv) When the case is tried. In addition to the recommendations in Chapter 10 on the finding of disability in relation to the trial, and in Chapters 11 and 12 on remands for medical reports or for hospital care, or under interim hospital orders, we examine in Chapter 18 the provisions relating to the trial of persons who were suffering from mental disorder at the time of committing the offence and we propose new provisions with regard to the finding of the jury and the disposal of the defendant. In Chapter 19 we deal with the defence of diminished responsibility in homicide cases, and the provisions of the Infanticide Act 1938. The disposal options open to the courts are discussed in Chapters 13–17.

(2) Research

1.22 The need for more research was stressed by many of our witnesses, and at many points in our discussions we ourselves were acutely conscious of the need for precise answers to questions of the kind which only research could provide.

1.23 Sometimes our questions could be answered with varying degrees of precision by reference to published statistics or research reports. Sometimes it was possible for the Home Office or the Department of Health and Social Security to provide answers by producing new tabulations of information in their possession. References to such statistics, reports, articles or tables will be found at various points in our Report. In connection with after-care arrangements for patients discharged from the special hospitals useful information has been provided by a research project carried out by one of our members (Dr Acres), a summary of which is found at Appendix 3.

1.24 At other points, however, we found we were asking questions to which no satisfactory answer could be produced without specially commissioned research of a kind which would have taken a considerable time. For example, we do not know of any comprehensive and thorough survey of the way in which guardianship under Parts IV and V of the Act is working, or again of the operation and effectiveness of psychiatric probation orders (although we refer in Chapter 16 to Mrs Woodside's study of what happened in Edinburgh in 1966–68). The chapter on dangerous offenders demonstrates how patchy is factual knowledge in this area also. We know, for example, that certain diagnoses are associated with certain types of law-breaking: subnormality with sexual offences, paranoid schizophrenia with personal violence. But this association has been properly established only in samples of disordered persons. We do not know to what extent a subnormal or paranoid male is more likely than members of his age-group in general to commit such offences, or whether the probability of his being hospitalised makes him less likely to do so than free males.

1.25 We have not undertaken a comprehensive review of research, past and present, concerning mentally disordered offenders, nor have we thought it appropriate to make specific proposals for the future. Having drawn attention to the general deficiency of knowledge in this field we shall content ourselves with the following general comments. First, we emphasise the need to plan evaluative studies as soon as any new regime or form of treatment has been decided upon. Unless evaluation is "built in", and research workers are taken into consultation from the outset, evaluation is likely to run up against methodological difficulties. Secondly, we observe that it seems generally to be left to potential research workers to identify profitable areas of research, and it is only rarely that those responsible for the operation of the Mental Health Act (including the Government Departments), or the criminal courts, or the various services, do so. Yet except with regard to aetiological research, where the research worker is best at formulating the right questions, it is usually the administrators, doctors, lawyers and social workers who are in a position to formulate the most relevant questions and so to elicit useful answers. This is especially so where operational research is concerned, although the research worker may be able to help the administrator, doctor, lawyer or social worker to formulate a question in a way that makes it possible to produce a useful answer.

(3) Implementation of the Report

1.26 It will be seen that the terms of reference give no indication of any financial or other resource limitations (including manpower) within which our recommendations should be confined. Some of our proposals, if accepted, will involve increased expenditure and the provision of additional resources and services. There are four reasons why we have decided not to restrict our recommendations on economic grounds. The first is simply that we have not been asked to do so. The second is that we are in no position to assess how the economic ice-cap may advance or recede in the next few years, and could not tailor our Report to fit unknown variables. Thirdly, it is and must be for the Government of the day to decide how much of the national resources can be afforded for mentally disordered offenders. Finally, the question is not merely one of expenditure but also of the priority to be accorded to this sector of the public interest in comparison with other sectors, and this again must be for the Government to decide. We have therefore come to the conclusion that our right course is to recommend what we think necessary or desirable, in the light of the evidence we have received and the information we have obtained, recognising that our Report must be considered by responsible Ministers in due course in relation to the general financial situation, the scarcity or availability of resources, and other competing demands at the time. It is perhaps necessary to make the point, which was put to us by a number of witnesses, that it would be most undesirable for any of our recommendations which require resources for their effective implementation (including, in particular, sufficient numbers of adequately trained staff) to be formally introduced before those resources are available.

1.27 We are aware of the difficulties for the central Government in maintaining both impetus and co-ordination in the implementation of recommendations such as ours which are necessarily long-term and which in some cases involve action by bodies to whom responsibility is delegated for the planning of services. It has seemed to us that it would be a constructive step if a national advisory body were constituted with representation from all the interests involved, to keep under review the progress made in carrying through such of our recommendations as are accepted, to report where problems are arising and to assist towards solutions. We recommend that consideration be given to the feasibility of arrangements on these lines.

INTRODUCTORY REMARKS

SUMMARY OF CONCLUSIONS

1. We recommend that the running costs as well as the capital costs of the regional secure hospital units proposed in our Interim Report should be met from central Government funds. (Paragraph 1.9.)

2. We draw attention to the need for more research in connection with mentally disordered offenders, and the importance of planning evaluative studies to be "built in" to any new regime or form of treatment. The initiative in identifying profitable areas of research should more often come from those responsible for the operation of the system, including the Government Departments, the criminal courts and the various services, especially where operational research is concerned. (Paragraphs 1.22–1.25.)

3. We recommend that consideration be given to the feasibility of establishing a national advisory body with representation from all the interests involved to oversee the implementation of those of our recommendations which are accepted, to report where problems are arising and to assist towards solutions. (Paragraph 1.27.)

EXISTING FACILITIES

I. HISTORICAL INTRODUCTION

(1) Origins and early development

2.1   Before we discuss the problems arising in the treatment of mentally disordered offenders, we propose briefly to describe the historical origins, range and organisation of the existing facilities for the treatment of mentally disordered people.   Legislation for the provision by public authorities of care and treatment specifically for the mentally disordered, and for special arrangements for mentally disordered offenders, dates from the early 19th century. Services for the mentally ill (then called "lunatics") and the severely subnormal (then called "idiots") developed during that century throughout the country, and provision for "criminal lunatics" developed under separate legislation. These services were largely institutional and custodial.   Criminal lunatics were received both into local lunatic asylums and into the special criminal lunatic asylum (Broadmoor) which opened in 1863.

2.2   Towards the end of the century the social problems and need for care presented by those with less pronounced mental subnormality (then called "feeble-minded") received increasing attention, and following the Report of the Royal Commission on the Care and Control of the Feeble-minded 1904–1908 the Mental Deficiency Act 1913 was passed.   This required local authorities to provide both institutions and supervision in the community for the feeble-minded and the severely subnormal, including those committed to care under this Act by the courts after commission of an offence.   State institutions for defectives of dangerous and violent propensities, whether offenders or not, were to be managed by the Board of Control; two such institutions (Rampton and Moss Side) were provided in the 1920s and 1930s.

2.3   The administration of the mental health services was fundamentally changed with the introduction of the National Health Service.   All local authority institutions (and many private ones) for the mentally ill and mentally defective were transferred to the new hospital authorities.[1]   Community services for defectives not in institutions (who have always outnumbered those in institutions) remained the responsibility of the health departments of the local authorities.   At the same time responsibility for the administration of the only criminal lunatic asylum (Broadmoor) was transferred, under the Criminal Justice Act 1948, from the Home Office to the Ministry of Health, its management being placed in the hands of the Board of Control, who

---

[1] Under the National Health Service Act 1946 the Minister of Health became responsible for providing hospital and specialist services.   Regional Hospital Boards, Hospital Management Committees and (for teaching hospitals) Boards of Governors were given responsibility under the Act for the administration of the hospitals.   In November 1968 the functions of the Minister of Health were transferred to the Secretary of State for Social Services and in April 1969 his functions in respect of Wales were transferred to the Secretary of State for Wales.   Under the National Health Service Reorganisation Act 1973 the functions of Hospital Boards and Management Committees, together with other health functions, passed, with effect from 1 April 1974, to new Regional Health Authorities (except in Wales) and Area Health Authorities (including Area Health Authorities (Teaching)).   Like the former Boards and Committees, these Authorities carry out their functions subject to regulations, directions and general guidance from the Secretaries of State.

continued also to manage Rampton and Moss Side. Broadmoor continued to receive offenders only, while Rampton and Moss Side (like all other mental deficiency institutions) continued to receive both offenders and non-offenders.

(2) The Mental Health Act 1959

2.4 These arrangements (apart from those for Broadmoor patients) and the procedures for the admission to, detention in and discharge from hospitals and institutions of individual patients were reviewed by the Royal Commission on the Law Relating to Mental Illness and Mental Deficiency 1954–57.[2] Their recommendations were substantially accepted and those which required legislation were incorporated in the Mental Health Act 1959, which repealed and replaced most of the nineteenth century legislation on criminal lunatics as well as the Lunacy and Mental Treatment Acts and the Mental Deficiency Acts. Implementation of the recommendations for the provision of more residential and other services outside hospitals has been proceeding but is still far from complete.

2.5 Major elements in the philosophy underlying the 1959 Act were the principles that no one should be admitted to hospital if care in the community would be more appropriate, and that where admission was required compulsion should if possible be avoided. At the time of the Royal Commission's report about 75 per cent of admissions to mental illness hospitals in the National Health Service were of voluntary patients, and all patients in mental deficiency hospitals were compulsorily detained (other than those admitted for periods of less than three months). Since the 1959 Act informal admissions (to all psychiatric hospitals and units in the National Health Service) have risen to over 86 per cent in 1973; informal patients now constitute over 90 per cent of the total population of in-patients at any one time. When the provisions of the 1959 Act came into effect Broadmoor started taking non-offenders as well as offenders.

(3) Legislation since 1959

2.6 In 1971, responsibility for the education of the severely subnormal was transferred from local health and hospital authorities to the local education authorities, and all other local health authority responsibilities for services for the mentally disordered passed to the local authority social services departments set up under the Local Authority Social Services Act 1970. The National Health Service Reorganisation Act 1973, which reformed the administrative structure of the National Health Service, has been referred to in the footnote to paragraph 2.3. This year legislation has been enacted to secure the continued detention of dangerous patients whose disorder has been reclassified as subnormality or psychopathic disorder, conditions subject to age limits for initial admission for hospital treatment. A High Court judgment in 1972[3] was thought to have uncovered a loophole in the Mental Health Act 1959, rendering unlawful the detention of certain patients, however dangerous, whose original order for detention had specified other forms of mental disorder. The Mental Health (Amendment) Act 1975 now ensures that a patient so reclassified shall continue to be liable to be detained if he is likely to act in a manner dangerous to other persons or to himself.

[2] Cmnd. 169.
[3] *In re* V.E. (Mental Health Patient) (1972) 3 WLR 669.

II. EXISTING HEALTH AND PERSONAL SOCIAL SERVICES

2.7   The services now available for mentally disordered offenders as well as for non-offenders under these statutory arrangements include general practitioner services, community health and general hospital services, and local authority child care and personal social services.   Health services specifically for the treatment of mental disorder include hospitals for the mentally ill (providing in-patient, day-patient and some out-patient services), psychiatric out-patient clinics at general hospitals, psychiatric units in general hospitals providing services for in-patients and day-patients, child guidance clinics, hospitals for the mentally handicapped, and the special hospitals.   Offenders are a small minority of those using these services, which we describe in greater detail below.

(1) General Practitioners

2.8   A large number of patients with minor mental disorders are treated by general practitioners often working closely with other members of the community health and social services.   It is also usually general practitioners who refer the more seriously disordered patients to psychiatrists for diagnosis or treatment, and general practitioners are also involved in the care and treatment of patients discharged from hospital.

(2) Hospitals

(i)   *The range of hospital provision*

(a)   *Hospitals for the mentally ill*

2.9   Hospital services for the mentally ill are provided on an in-patient, out-patient and day-patient basis for patients of all ages; some provision is made for children and adolescents but most hospital treatment is for adults.   Out-patient clinics for the mentally ill were started in the 1930s, but before the mid-1940s hospital treatment was provided mainly on an in-patient basis for the more serious forms of mental illness.   The hospitals were based on a mainly custodial tradition, within which various forms of treatment had been established.

2.10   The onset of the more serious illnesses (such as schizophrenia) frequently occurs between the ages of 20 and 40, and before the mid-1950s it was usual for some categories of patients, once admitted, to remain in hospital for very long periods, often for the rest of their lives.   In the early 1950s, new methods of treatment (particularly drugs) as well as new attitudes to custodial care were developed.   This led to a reduction in the time needed for in-patient treatment and to a substantial increase in out-patient and day treatment; moreover, whereas in the past patients normally remained in hospitals during periods of remission of their illness, the normal practice now is for the patient to be discharged and if necessary re-admitted later.   In 1972 half the patients leaving mental illness hospitals had stayed for less than one month and 80 per cent had stayed for less than three months.   Partly as the result of these developments in treatment, and partly owing to changing public attitudes towards mental illness and greater willingness to accept treatment, there has been a large increase in the last 20 years in the number of attendances at out-patient clinics and day-hospitals and of in-patient admissions (including re-admissions), though there are indications that in-patient admissions are now levelling out. In spite of the increase in admissions, the shorter length of stay has led to a steady reduction in the number of in-patients in the hospitals at any one time. However, most mental illness hospitals still contain large numbers of patients who have been in the hospitals for many years, and there is still some over-crowding and understaffing, with staff often working under great pressure because of increasing out-patient and day-patient work, and the high rate of in-patient admissions and discharges.

2.11 During the last 30 years further developments of great importance, which are now well established, have been the replacement of locked doors and other physical restrictions by greater freedom, and more active rehabilitation. Many hospitals now have no locked wards; most of the rest have only one or two, and some of these are locked only occasionally.

2.12 Since the Mental Health Act 1959 removed the previous prohibition on the reception of "persons of unsound mind" in hospitals other than designated mental hospitals the development of psychiatric in-patient units in general hospitals has been gathering momentum. We have been informed that the present policy[4] is to develop a network of health and social services facilities locally in each district instead of having services based on large distant specialist hospitals. Specialist treatment facilities would be based on psychiatric depart-ments in general hospitals, with additional facilities for the longer term care of the elderly severely mentally infirm. These facilities would be complemented by a considerable expansion in the scale and range of personal social services provided for the mentally ill by local authorities and by developments in the community health and employment services. (See paragraph 2.34 below.) When this comprehensive range of facilities has been developed, the Department of Health and Social Security envisage that the number of occupied beds in the large mental hospitals will gradually decline to the point at which, ultimately, most of these hospitals can be closed. Nationally this is a long-term programme and we have been informed that the overall strategy will be the subject of a White Paper which is expected to be published in the autumn of this year.

(b) Hospitals for the subnormal and severely subnormal

2.13 Most of the present hospitals for the mentally handicapped were originally provided by local authorities under the Mental Deficiency Acts 1913–38 for the long term residential care and treatment of mental defectives. Although there has been some improvement in recent years, many are overcrowded and under-staffed, and some seriously so. In the light of the recommendations of the Royal Commission of 1954–57 the policy is that greater reliance should be placed on the provision of residential and other services by the local authorities. (We refer further to these services at paragraphs 2.34–2.45 below.) When these are fully developed it is expected that there will be a need for only a little over half the present number of beds. It is also envisaged that the hospital services should be brought closer to the populations served, mostly in smaller units than at present, closely co-ordinated with local authority services.

---

[4] Cf. paragraphs 6.4 *et seq* where we express certain reservations about this policy, with particular reference to the loss of accommodation for "inadequates".

(c) The special hospitals

2.14 The Secretary of State for Social Services is responsible under section 40 of the National Health Service Reorganisation Act 1973 for providing and maintaining "establishments for persons subject to detention under the Mental Health Act 1959, who in his opinion require treatment under conditions of special security on account of their dangerous, violent or criminal propensities". These are known as "special hospitals" and are provided and managed directly by the Department of Health and Social Security. There are at present three long established special hospitals serving the whole of England and Wales, with a fourth under construction and partly in use. In June this year, their total population stood at just over 2,150 patients. The existing hospitals are:

> *Broadmoor Hospital*, at Crowthorne, Berkshire, which treats mainly mentally ill and psychopathic patients. Broadmoor opened in 1863 as the first state asylum for criminal lunatics in England and continued to receive criminal lunatics exclusively[5] until the Mental Health Act 1959 permitted it to receive non-offenders under Part IV of that Act as well as offenders. At present it contains about 630 male patients and about 120 female, but the accommodation is old and is seriously overcrowded on the male side.

> *Rampton Hospital*, near Retford, Notts. At present there are about 780 male patients and 250 female; there is considerable overcrowding in parts of the hospital.

> *Moss Side Hospital*, at Maghull, Lancs. At present there are about 310 male patients and 100 female.

The fourth hospital, Park Lane, is being built on land adjoining Moss Side, to take about 400 male patients, mainly mentally ill or psychopathic. The new hospital is to be completed in phases and the Department expect that the first phase will be completed in 1980, the second about one year later. An advance unit has been opened which has received 70 patients from Broadmoor. Broadmoor is to be rebuilt and reduced in size to take about 400 male and 100 female patients. This will allow a net increase of about 100 places for male patients. On 31 December 1974 about 25 per cent of the patients in each of the three established special hospitals were suffering from psychopathic disorder. In Broadmoor all the other patients, with the exception of three suffering from subnormality, were suffering from mental illness. In Rampton and Moss Side the other patients were fairly evenly distributed between mental illness, subnormality and severe subnormality; in other words, about half of the patients in these two hospitals were mentally handicapped.

2.15 The limitation in the statute quoted above to "persons subject to detention" prevents the special hospitals from accepting patients informally. Otherwise, there is now no category of patient who may be admitted to a special hospital but not to a local psychiatric hospital, or vice versa. Special hospitals are not restricted to patients who have committed offences. The distinction between patients treated in special hospitals and those treated in local

---

[5] Some patients, however, who had been transferred from prisons and who ceased to be regarded technically as "criminal lunatics" when their sentences expired were nevertheless retained in Broadmoor.

psychiatric hospitals is solely that the former require treatment under conditions of special security. Patients may be transferred between local National Health Service and special hospitals, in either direction, when their condition justifies it; in practice there are sometimes difficulties in arranging these transfers, which we discuss in paragraphs 4.26–4.29.

(d) Secure hospital accommodation in the regions

2.16 It is the responsibility of the Regional Health Authorities to provide as part of the psychiatric services in their regions the necessary facilities for patients who do not require the security of a special hospital but nevertheless cannot suitably be treated in an open psychiatric ward. We have drawn attention in our Interim Report to the failure of the former Regional Hospital Boards to make adequate secure provision in their regions despite guidance issued by the then Ministry of Health in 1961, and we have recommended that secure hospital units should be provided as a matter of urgency, with central Government finance. We have discussed in paragraphs 1.3–1.9 above the progress that has been made in implementing our recommendations.

(ii) Methods of admission to hospital and powers of discharge

2.17 The Royal Commission of 1954–57 described in paragraph 317 of their Report[6] the circumstances in which they considered the use of compulsory powers for admission to and detention in hospital justified, and indeed desirable; and the application of these principles to offenders was discussed in paragraphs 511–537. With some changes of detail, the Royal Commission's recommendations were incorporated in the Mental Health Act 1959. The present methods of admission to psychiatric hospitals and units (including the special hospitals) and powers of discharge therefrom are described in the following paragraphs.

(a) Admission to the special hospitals

2.18 In accordance with the terms of section 40 of the National Health Service Reorganisation Act 1973 quoted in paragraph 2.14 above the admission of patients to the special hospitals is controlled by the Department of Health and Social Security, who apply fairly stringent criteria for admission, based on the wording of the section. The Department attach due weight to the considerations that admission to a special hospital entails subjecting patients to very close supervision and restriction of movement and taking them far from their homes and families. Admissions to other hospitals are at the discretion of the local hospital authorities (with regard to offenders see paragraph 2.29 below).

(b) Informal admission to hospital

2.19 Except to the special hospitals,[7] the great majority of in-patients are admitted without any legal formality. If they wish to leave hospital before their treatment is complete they are free to do so, but most patients complete their treatment and are then discharged by the doctor in charge of their treatment; those who have been treated for mental illness often continue to see him

---

[6] Cmnd. 169.

[7] See paragraph 2.14 above: the statute restricts the special hospitals to "persons subject to detention".

at an out-patient clinic after discharge. In 1973, 169,856 of the 196,817 admissions to local psychiatric hospitals in the National Health Service were informal. Offenders who agree to receive in-patient medical treatment as a condition of a probation order, under the provisions of section 3 of the Powers of Criminal Courts Act 1973 (formerly section 4 of the Criminal Justice Act 1948), are admitted to hospital informally: we deal with "psychiatric probation orders" in Chapter 16.

(c) *Persons in public places in immediate need of care or control* (*section* 136 *of the* 1959 *Act*)

2.20 This section empowers a constable to remove to "a place of safety" (which includes a hospital) a person found in a public place who appears to be suffering from mental disorder and to be in immediate need of care or control. A person may be detained in the place of safety to which he is taken for up to 72 hours for medical examination and interview by a local authority social worker, so that any necessary arrangements can be made for care or treatment in the community or in hospital. In 1973, 1,555 persons were recorded as being admitted to hospital under section 136; the majority of those who needed to remain for treatment did so informally. We discuss this provision at greater length in Chapter 9.

(d) *Admission and discharge under Part IV of the* 1959 *Act* (*non-offender procedures*)

For observation

2.21 A patient may be compulsorily admitted for observation under section 25 of the 1959 Act on an application made by a local authority social worker or the nearest relative. The application must be supported by two medical recommendations stating that the patient is suffering from mental disorder of a nature or degree that warrants detention in hospital and that the patient should be detained in the interests of his own health or safety or for the protection of others. Patients may be detained for a period of up to 28 days. They may receive medical treatment in addition to observation while detained. Of those who require treatment for more than 28 days many remain on an informal basis; others may be compulsorily detained if the conditions of section 26 apply (see paragraphs 2.24 and 2.25).

2.22 In cases of urgent necessity a patient may be admitted for observation under section 29 on an application made by any relative or a local authority social worker and supported by only one of the medical recommendations mentioned above. The patient may not be detained compulsorily for more than 72 hours unless the second medical recommendation required under section 25 is given within that period. Many patients remain for treatment on an informal basis.

2.23 Under sections 25 and 29 no precise diagnosis of the form of mental disorder is required. Psychopathic and subnormal patients of any age, as well as mentally ill and severely subnormal patients, may be admitted and detained for up to 28 days.

For treatment

2.24 Under section 26, a patient may be compulsorily admitted for treatment on the application of his nearest relative or of a local authority social worker supported by two medical recommendations. If the application is to be made by a local authority social worker he must consult the nearest relative, if this is reasonably practicable, and may not make an application if the nearest relative objects. An application under section 26 may be made in respect of a patient already in hospital under section 25 or 29 or as an informal patient.

2.25 An application under section 26 must be founded on medical recommendations specifying the form(s) of mental disorder from which the patient is suffering, and may not be made in respect of a psychopathic or subnormal patient over the age of 21 (unless he is also suffering from mental illness or severe subnormality). The disorder must be of a nature or degree which warrants detention in hospital, and admission must be regarded as necessary in the interests of the patient's health or safety or for the protection of others.

2.26 Patients admitted under section 26 may be detained indefinitely (subject to the powers of discharge referred to below) if the authority for detention is renewed at certain statutory intervals, except that patients suffering from subnormality or psychopathic disorder (and not from mental illness or severe subnormality) may not be detained beyond the age of 25 unless at that time the doctor in charge of their treatment considers that they would be likely to act in a manner dangerous to other persons or to themselves if discharged.

2.27 The patient may be discharged at any time by the doctor in charge of his treatment or by the managers of the hospital. His nearest relative may also order his discharge at any time; such an order does not take effect if the responsible doctor records an opinion that the patient is likely to act in a manner dangerous to other persons or to himself if discharged. In addition, the patient (and his nearest relative if his power to order discharge has been countermanded) has a right to apply at statutory intervals to a Mental Health Review Tribunal consisting of legal, medical and lay members. The Tribunal has power to direct discharge in any case if it thinks fit, and in certain circumstances it has an obligation to do so. (See further at paragraphs 7.4–7.5.)

2.28 A patient liable to be detained in hospital under Part IV of the Act who is absent from the hospital without leave may be returned to the hospital within the following time limits: in the case of a patient over the age of 21 who is suffering from psychopathic disorder or subnormality, six months; in any other case 28 days. (We discuss the implications of this provision as it affects offenders at paragraphs 14.13–14.16 below.)

(e) *Admission and discharge under Part V of the* 1959 *Act* (*offenders and remand cases*)

2.29 Part V of the Act applies to offenders (and certain other persons detained in prisons). It contains in section 60 powers for courts in certain circumstances to order mentally disordered offenders to be admitted to and detained in hospital. The conditions which must be fulfilled before a hospital order can be made and other matters in connection with hospital orders are dealt with in Chapter 14. Among these conditions, the effect of section 60(3) of the Act is that admission to hospital in pursuance of a hospital order requires in practice the consent of the hospital in which the offender will be treated.[8] Sections 72 and 73 provide powers for the Home Secretary to direct the transfer of mentally

---

[8] As to the control of admissions to the special hospitals, see paragraph 2.18 above.

20

disordered offenders to hospital from prison. We have been informed that although there is no statutory requirement under section 72 equivalent to section 60(3) mentioned above, the Home Secretary observes the practice of seeking the consent of the hospital before directing transfers from prison. These powers of transfer are further described and discussed in paragraphs 3.37–3.49 below.

2.30 Patients detained under Part V who have not been made subject to restrictions under section 65 (see paragraph 2.31) are in exactly the same position in relation to duration and renewal of the authority for detention, powers of discharge and rights to apply to a Mental Health Review Tribunal as patients admitted under section 26 (see paragraphs 2.24–2.28) with the following exceptions:—

(i) the age-limits for admission and detention of psychopathic and subnormal patients (see paragraphs 2.25 and 2.26) do not apply;

(ii) the nearest relative has no power of discharge; instead he or she has a right to apply to a Mental Health Review Tribunal at stated intervals.

As we explain in paragraph 14.8, in making a hospital order without restrictions the court places the patient in the hands of the doctors, foregoing any question of punishment and leaving his discharge to the normal hospital processes except as noted above.

2.31 Where the courts order admission to hospital under section 60 they may (except for magistrates' courts) also make a "restriction order" under section 65, of either limited or unlimited duration, if they think this necessary for the protection of the public. When a patient has been made subject to restrictions under section 65, he may not be given leave of absence, transferred to another hospital or discharged, except with the consent of the Home Secretary. Section 66(2) of the Act empowers the Home Secretary at any time, if he thinks fit, to effect the discharge from hospital, either absolutely or subject to conditions, of a patient who is subject to restrictions, and section 66(3) enables him to recall to hospital a restricted patient who has been conditionally discharged. Under section 66(1) he may terminate the restrictions if he is satisfied that they are no longer required for the protection of the public; if the restrictions are removed before the patient is discharged from hospital, by virtue of section 65(5) he is regarded, from the date of the ending of the restrictions, as being subject to a hospital order made on that date and the provisions about hospital orders apply to him.

2.32 By virtue of section 65(3)(b) of the Act restriction order cases are not subject to the general provisions in the Act (see paragraph 2.27 above) enabling patients or their nearest relative to apply to a Mental Health Review Tribunal to order their release. No restricted patient can apply to a Mental Health Review Tribunal, nor may his nearest relative do so. Instead, section 66(6) of the Act enables the Home Secretary at any time to refer to a Mental Health Review Tribunal for their advice the case of a patient who is for the time being subject to a restriction order; and he must so refer the case within two months if such a patient requests this in writing, which he is allowed to do not sooner than one year after the making of the hospital order and subsequently once in each period of two years (sections 66(7) and 43(6) of the Act). Patients recalled from conditional discharge have an additional right to make an application for reference to a Tribunal between six and twelve months following the date of recall (section 66(8)). The decision whether to accept the advice of the Tribunal remains with the Home Secretary.

(iii) Statistics of hospital admissions

2.33 The following table gives the numbers[9] of psychiatric patients of all types admitted to local National Health Service hospitals and special hospitals in England and Wales during 1973:—

	Informal[10]	Detained				
		Under Part IV	Under Part V without restrictions	Under[11] Part V with restrictions	Other	Totals
Local NHS hospitals	169,856	24,038	956	191	1,776[12]	196,817
Special hospitals	1[13]	88	62	193	27	371
Patients[14] in all hospitals	169,857	24,126	1,018	384	1,803	197,188
	(86·1%)	(12·3%)	(0·7%)		(0·9%)	

Of the patients resident in the special hospitals at the end of 1973 30 per cent were detained under Part IV of the 1959 Act (or corresponding provisions of earlier Acts) and 70 per cent under Part V of the 1959 Act or the Criminal Procedure (Insanity) Act 1964 (or corresponding provisions of earlier Acts). Similar figures are not available for patients resident in local psychiatric hospitals, but it is estimated that about 95 per cent were informal and 5 per cent subject to detention under Parts IV and V of the Act combined.

(3) Local authority social services for the mentally disordered

(i) General

2.34 The social services available for the care and after-care of the mentally disordered include social work support, other domiciliary services (for example, home helps for the elderly mentally infirm living at home), a wide range of different types of residential care (short-stay hostels providing care and rehabilitation for a limited time to help people return to their own homes;

[9] These are not numbers of separate individuals but of admissions; the same person may be admitted more than once in the same year.

[10] In 1973 over 60 offenders were made subject to probation orders requiring them to undertake psychiatric treatment as hospital in-patients: these are included in the informal admissions in the above Table. In addition 1,347 others received treatment outside hospitals under similar orders. (See also Chapter 16: Psychiatric Probation Orders).

[11] Includes admissions under the Criminal Procedure (Insanity) Act 1964: 8 of those who entered local NHS hospitals and 13 of those entering special hospitals were admitted under this Act. (See also Chapter 14 Section II: Hospital Orders with Restrictions).

[12] Mainly section 136.

[13] Temporary re-admission while suitable accommodation was found.

[14] Figures also expressed as percentages of the total.

22

longer-stay homes for people who need support for a longer period, perhaps even indefinitely; group homes, sheltered housing or lodgings) and day centres providing suitable occupations and rehabilitation. In Part V of their Report the Royal Commission of 1954–57 recommended that local authorities should assume responsibility for providing residential accommodation for mentally disordered persons who require some supervision but do not need, or no longer need, hospital in-patient care or treatment; and that there should also be a considerable expansion of the services provided by local authorities for the training and occupation of mentally handicapped people not in hospital who cannot be catered for within the general services for the disabled, and an expansion of social work to support such people and their families. There was a considerable expansion of local authority services during the 1960s and early 1970s, but these are still very far from fully developed.[15] The health and local authority services need to be closely co-ordinated both at the planning and operational levels. The Joint Consultative Committees established with the reorganisation of the National Health Service will provide a forum for the agreement of joint plans. At the operational level an inter-disciplinary approach is being developed whereby medical, nursing and other health service staff and social workers from the local authority social services department work together in primary care or specialist therapeutic teams. We discuss some of the problems facing local authority social service departments in paragraphs 3.12–3.15.

(ii) *Children and Young Persons*[16]

2.35 Juveniles[16] who cannot, for whatever reason, look to their parents or guardians for care and control are provided with a wide range of services by local authorities. Of these services, the most important in the present context is residential care. Residential establishments for juveniles in need of care or control have been reorganised in pursuance of the Children and Young Persons Act 1969. An integrated system of establishments ("community homes") has superseded and absorbed three previously separate systems. Previously, approved schools were set aside for those juveniles who were the subject of an approved school order, remand homes for those awaiting a court appearance or transfer to an approved school, and children's homes and hostels for those who had been received into local authority care under a "fit person" order or, more commonly, without any court order at all. On 1 January 1971, a single form of order—the care order—took the place of orders of committal to an approved school, to a remand home, and to the care of a local authority as a "fit person".

2.36 This account concentrates on residential care; but it is important to bear in mind that less than half of the total of some 96,000 juveniles in the care of local authorities in 1974 were in residential institutions, and that many juveniles not in care, and their families, are supervised, guided or assisted in various ways

---

[15] See, for example, *Better Services for the Mentally Handicapped* (Cmnd. 4683).

[16] For the purpose of court proceedings the definition of a child in the Children and Young Persons Act 1969 is someone under the age of 14, a young person someone between 14 and 16. For the purpose of accommodation and certain other specific purposes the statutory definition of a child extends to persons up to the age of eighteen and persons who have attained that age and are the subject of care orders. In this section we use the word "juvenile" to include all children and young persons within the meaning of the Act.

by local authority social services departments. These non-residential services play an important part in keeping juveniles out of trouble and in the prevention and early recognition of mental disorder.

2.37 The majority of juveniles in the care of local authorities are received into care without any court order under section 1 of the Children Act 1948, and their parents are free to resume care unless the local authority have assumed parental rights as provided by section 2 of that Act. The remainder are the subject of care orders under section 1 of the Children and Young Persons Act 1969. A care order may be based on the court finding that a juvenile is ill-treated or neglected or in moral danger, or is guilty of an offence and that he is also in need of care or control which he is unlikely to receive unless the court makes a care order. A care order remains in force, unless earlier discharged by the court, until the subject is 18 or, if made when he is 16, until he is 19. A care order makes it the duty of the local authority to keep the juvenile in their care while the order is in force notwithstanding any claim by his parent or guardian, vests in them the same powers and duties as the subject's parent would have apart from the order, and authorises them to restrict his liberty to such extent as they consider appropriate.

2.38 The general duty of a local authority as respects a juvenile in their care (whether the subject of a care order or not) is to further his best interests and to afford him opportunity for proper development, but notwithstanding this to have regard for the protection of the public; and the Secretary of State for Social Services may, if he considers it necessary for the protection of the public, give directions to a local authority as to the exercise of their powers in relation to a particular juvenile in care (Children and Young Persons Act 1969, section 27). It follows that the form of care employed for a particular juvenile is determined by the local authority's view (subject to any directions given by the Secretary of State) of his needs for care, treatment, and control as they stand at the particular time. For example, a juvenile in care whose disturbed or damaged personality or behaviour problems call for close control in a residential setting, possibly in physically secure conditions, and the employment of special professional skills will be provided with that treatment—so far as resources permit—whether or not he came into care as an offender, and whether or not his offence (if any) was considered to be associated with some form of mental disorder. Conversely, the fact that a juvenile has been committed to care as an offender does not prevent the authority from employing, in his case, a milder form of control, such as boarding him out with foster-parents or allowing him to be in the charge of his own parents on a trial basis, if in the authority's judgment his needs for care, treatment, and control can best be met in that way.

2.39 If residential care is considered necessary, the local authority will usually place the juvenile in a community home. Plans providing *inter alia* for a comprehensive system of community homes were prepared by the Children's Regional Planning Committees for all the planning areas in England and for Wales and came into operation on 1 April 1973. These plans are kept under review by the Planning Committees and their constituent local authorities.

2.40 The intention is that community homes should be supplemented by "youth treatment centres", that is homes provided by the Secretary of State for Social Services under section 64 of the Children and Young Persons Act 1969, to accommodate the small minority of boys and girls in care who are too severely disturbed and disruptive for community homes, and for whom in-patient hospital treatment is not appropriate. It is proposed to provide three centres with about 60 places each. The first, St Charles Youth Treatment Centre, Brentwood, was opened in July 1971 and by the end of 1974 had a capacity of 38, providing 12 places in a secure unit and 13 each in a semi-secure and an open unit, with plans for a further 12 places in a secure unit. In addition some accommodation will be available in staff maisonettes for juveniles in the last stage of their stay to go out to work in the locality. The plans for the next two centres, at Birmingham and Wakefield, have been prepared in the light of the experience gained at St Charles. We understand that the first of these two additional centres, which will provide between them some 140 places, may be ready by about 1977. We discuss further these provisions for mentally disordered juveniles in Chapter 17.

(iii) *Guardianship*

2.41 A few mentally disordered persons who require care in the community also require some degree of control in their own interests or for the protection of others. Section 33 of the 1959 Act provides for such persons in certain circumstances to be received into the guardianship of the local authority or of any other person who the local authority is satisfied is able and willing to undertake the duties involved. A guardianship application under section 33 must be supported by two medical recommendations and may be made in respect of a person of any age suffering from mental illness or severe sub-normality, and in respect of a person under 21 suffering from psychopathic disorder or subnormality, if the disorder is of a nature or degree which warrants his reception into guardianship and if it is necessary in his interests or for the protection of other persons that he should be so received. Guardianship lapses at the age of 25 for psychopathic and subnormal persons. These powers are virtually unused for children under 16.

2.42 Under section 60 of the Act a court may make a guardianship order for a mentally disordered offender in the circumstances described in paragraph 13.4 below. In contrast to guardianship orders made under section 33 there are no age limits under this provision for psychopathic or subnormal patients. There are no powers to apply restrictions on discharge under section 65 in relation to persons under guardianship.

2.43 Persons may be discharged from guardianship at any time by the responsible doctor, the local authority or (except for persons admitted to guardianship under section 60) the nearest relative. They (and the nearest relative if admission to guardianship has been under section 60) may apply to a Mental Health Review Tribunal at statutory intervals; the Tribunal's powers are the same as in relation to patients detained in hospital (see paragraphs 7.4–7.5).

2.44 The powers of guardians are equivalent to the powers of a father over a child under the age of 14. The guardian must appoint a medical attendant and provide as far as practicable for the occupation, training or employment and general welfare and recreation of the person under his guardianship. The local authority maintains overall supervision by visiting and giving such directions as appear appropriate. The local authority must assist the guardian with the advice of its own staff and the other facilities which it is its own duty to provide for mentally disordered persons in the community.

2.45 There has been a dramatic reduction in the use made of the guardianship order provisions of the Mental Health Act 1959 since they came into force in 1960. In 1961, the first full year of the operation of the new provisions, 220 people (non-offenders and offenders) were admitted to guardianship. In the 12 months up to 31 March 1974 only 37 guardianship orders were made. Offenders account for a small percentage of the total of those admitted to guardianship, and the compulsory guardianship powers under section 60 have been used steadily less over the years: 21 such orders were made in 1961; in 1974, only seven. We comment further on the use of guardianship orders in Chapter 15.

(4) The probation and after-care service

2.46 Unlike the social workers in the local authority social service departments members of the probation and after-care service, which is administered by Committees of magistrates, are officers of the courts, and are primarily concerned with offenders. In relation to offenders suffering from mental disorders they have an important role to play at various stages of the criminal process: in particular, they prepare social inquiry reports for the courts, and, whether from contact with the defendant himself or from information derived from other sources, their investigations for this purpose may well bring to light indications of mental disorder in the defendant. The probation officer is, therefore, well placed to suggest to the court the possible need for remand for psychiatric assessment.

2.47 In the light of the medical evidence the court may decide that the defendant should be admitted to hospital for treatment, either by means of a hospital order under section 60 of the Mental Health Act 1959 or by means of a probation order with a requirement to undergo psychiatric treatment under section 3 of the Powers of Criminal Courts Act 1973. In the event of admission to hospital under a section 60 order after-care may be provided either by the local authority social service departments or by the probation and after-care service. (We deal with the assignment of responsibility in paragraph 8.7.) Where a psychiatric probation order has been made, supervision of the patient after his discharge from hospital is the responsibility of the probation and after-care service (see Chapter 16). In the event of the offender being committed to prison, the members of the prison welfare departments who are seconded probation officers, provide a link with the probation and after-care service in the offender's home area and are responsible for doing what they can to establish arrangements for the satisfactory re-settlement of the offender in the community, and for providing supervision where this is required—particularly within the parole system (see paragraph 8.8).

2.48 The assistance of the probation and after-care service is available to all offenders on a voluntary basis, and the service does a great deal to support the inadequate and the homeless and the many who are handicapped by drink or drug taking. The service is closely associated with the support of offenders

26

resident in hostels provided by voluntary organisations, and has power, since the Criminal Justice Act 1972,[17] to establish hostels of its own (see paragraphs 8.15–8.19).

(5) The Prison Medical Service

2.49 Significant numbers of mentally disordered offenders are located in prisons and, to complete this summary of the caring and medical resources available for dealing with the mentally disordered, a brief account is now given of the Prison Medical Service which may fairly claim to be the oldest civilian medical service in the country. It owes its inception to the influence of John Howard and an Act of 1774 "for preserving the health of prisoners" whereby "an experienced surgeon or apothecary" had to be appointed to every prison. Originally medical officers were part-time and, indeed, many still are. 1877, when the Prison Commission was established, saw the beginning of an organised full-time medical service. The Hospital Officer (male) grade was established in 1899 and Female Nursing Sisters were introduced in 1919. In 1906 the Home Office sent a circular to magistrates' courts drawing attention to the services of medical officers in providing "state of mind" reports upon prisoners remanded in custody.

2.50 When the National Health Service was introduced in 1948 the Prison Medical Service continued as a separate, autonomous service, its full-time medical officers being civil servants. However, in the light of the complexity of modern medicine, it is not, nor can it be, a self-sufficient service. Full use is made of the specialist services of the National Health Service, and in accordance with a recommendation of a working party on the Organisation of the Prison Medical Service which reported in 1964 some appointments of consultants in forensic psychiatry are made jointly between the Home Office and Regional Health Authorities. (See our comments on the joint appointments in the section on forensic psychiatric services in Chapter 20 below.)

2.51 The tasks of the Prison Medical Service may be listed as:
  (a) to care for the physical and mental health of all inmates in Prison Department establishments;
  (b) to advise governors and the Prison Department upon all matters relating to the health of inmates, eg hygiene at establishments, work, dietary, etc;
  (c) to advise governors, the Prison Department and other Departments of the Home Office and the Parole Board upon individual cases;
  (d) to provide a service to the courts by assessing and reporting upon the health—particularly mental health—of untried prisoners remanded in custody.

The two main effects of the National Health Service on the work of the Prison Medical Service were that it removed from Prison Medical Officers the responsibility for the general medical care of prison staff and their families (with the result that since that time the Prison Medical Service has become a very specialised service) and it gave greater access to the use of the National Health Service hospital and specialist services.

---

[17] The provision has now been consolidated in paragraph 11 of Schedule 3 to the Powers of Criminal Courts Act 1973.

2.52 Organisationally the Prison Medical Service is under the immediate direction of a Director of Prison Medical Services who is also a member of the Prisons Board. To facilitate the administration of the medical services Regional Principal Medical Officers are appointed to each of the four Regions in which the prison service is at present organised. Senior Medical Officers, appointed to the more important establishments, also supervise groups of smaller establishments to which they act as consultants.

2.53 Every prison service establishment has a number of special rooms set aside for the sick. At the larger establishments there are separate hospitals with up to 100 beds. Many are now equipped with apparatus for special investigations but can provide only limited laboratory services. The older hospitals—and this means most of those at the larger establishments—were built for the care of the chronic physically sick. These are not really adapted to present needs, particularly in the psychiatric field.

2.54 Although attending to the physical health of the inmates is still the principal concern of the Prison Medical Service it has represented a declining proportion of the Prison Medical Officers' work during the past 25 years. All inmates are physically examined on first reception into custody. This is necessarily usually a brief examination and is intended to assess the fitness of prisoners for various forms of work, to screen for infectious disease, and to identify those who need more detailed physical or psychiatric examination. While the Prison Medical Service makes full use of the specialist services and hospitals of the National Health Service it still has a need for its own four Surgical Units at Wormwood Scrubs, Grendon, Parkhurst and Liverpool. A fifth is to be provided in the new Holloway Prison.

2.55 During the last 25 years psychiatric work has become increasingly important. More than half the full-time Prison Medical Officers are involved to some extent in assessments of pre-trial remand prisoners for the courts. The demand for this service has steadily increased and in the past seven years the Parole Board too has been making a steady demand for more psychiatric reports. The demand for psychiatric care and treatment of sentenced inmates has also increased, particularly with regard to alcohol and drugs users. Treatment is provided both by full-time Prison Medical Officers who are psychiatrically qualified and by visiting psychotherapists. There are now 43 establishments with psychiatric units, 36 prisons, six borstals and one remand centre, to which inmates from other establishments may be referred. The earliest psychiatric unit was started at Wormwood Scrubs in 1936, but the largest, and most important, is now Grendon Psychiatric Prison, opened in 1962. (We comment on the work of Grendon Prison in paragraphs 5.44–5.48.) However, none of these psychiatric units is equipped to deal with acute or severe mental illness; such cases require transfer to a National Health Service local psychiatric hospital or a special hospital under the powers given to the Home Secretary by sections 72 and 73 of the Mental Health Act 1959 as described in paragraphs 3.37–3.39 below.

CHAPTER 3

PROBLEMS OF THE PRESENT TREATMENT ARRANGEMENTS

I. TREATMENT BY THE HEALTH AND SOCIAL SERVICES

(1) Experience of the Mental Health Act 1959

3.1   In general the 1959 Act has been successful in relation to the treatment of mentally disordered offenders, and we have no criticism of the underlying principles.   The provisions of the Act have enabled many such offenders to be treated in hospital or in the community, in accordance with their medical needs, like any other patients, without undue risk to other people.   This is not to say that there have been no problems.   The situation was summed up in the memorandum of evidence submitted to us by the Home Office and the Department of Health and Social Security jointly in the following terms:

> "No problems arise in a large proportion of cases; but in those cases where difficulties are experienced they are liable to occasion particular concern, sometimes because they relate to the containment and appropriate treatment of dangerous and it may be notorious offenders, or disruptive offenders who cause trouble wherever they are, or to the release of offenders whose return to the community whenever it occurs may be followed by fresh offences which may give rise to criticism of the system by the public and the courts.   Some of the problems derive from certain features of the present system . . . but some derive from the increasing numbers of people in our modern society who are recognised as suffering from mental abnormality and particularly from psychopathic conditions.   Some reference has already been made . . . to the increasing numbers seeking treatment.   Whether this increase is attributable to the stresses of modern life, or to improvements in techniques of diagnosis, prognosis and treatment, or to changes in social attitudes which nowadays make it more acceptable and natural than it once was for people to seek psychiatric advice, there is no doubt that the social services in the community, the National Health Service and the penal system are all having to cope with rising numbers of people requiring help, support and treatment for mental conditions.   There is a general insufficiency of resources of all kinds to deal with this situation and strains in the operation of the system are bound to make themselves felt".

It is not in any event surprising if, after 15 years, some strains have appeared in the operation of the provisions of the Act.

3.2   A major problem is the lack of satisfactory co-ordination of the various services involved in the treatment[1] of the mentally disordered offender (or, for that matter, for the treatment of the mentally disordered in general).   These services have continued largely to work independently, each to some extent following its own objectives and limiting its responsibilities and involvement according to its own judgment.   In particular areas of the country progress is

---

[1] We remind the reader of our definition in paragraph 1.19; we are referring here to treatment in the widest sense including the provision of a caring situation.

being made towards more effective co-operation, or at least towards reaching common understandings about objectives and the ways and means of attaining them, but there is still a considerable task to be done. Later in this Report (Chapter 20) we make proposals for the development of forensic psychiatric services which would be based on the proposed regional secure units. Their successful introduction will depend not only on the determination, in discussion between all bodies concerned, of carefully worked out policies but also on close inter-disciplinary co-operation at the level at which the treatment programme is carried out. At this level it is essential to resolve the difficult problems connected with safeguarding the confidentiality of personal information about the patient which is obtained in the course of professional relationships with him, while making it sufficiently available to those who need it for the purpose of their own treatment of the patient. This matter also is discussed in Chapter 20. We now go on to consider the present position and problems of the various treatment services after 15 years' operation of the Act.

(2) Treatment of offenders in local hospitals

3.3 Some witnesses have urged that offenders should never, or only exceptionally, be treated in National Health Service local hospitals. This point of view has sometimes been based on the belief that it is morally wrong to mix offenders with non-offenders in any hospital. Again, the local "image" of the hospital has been said to be adversely affected by the presence of offender-patients; other patients do not expect to have to rub shoulders with an anti-social minority and might even discharge themselves prematurely to avoid it. We have been told also of the problems and hazards which arise for the staff in hospitals where offenders are admitted; it is said that there may be no suitable special provisions for dealing with offenders and the nursing staff may have no special training. The Confederation of Health Service Employees expressed the view that the effect was to reduce the standard of care and the progress in treatment of the other patients. No doubt the situation must depend to some extent on the numbers involved and the characteristics of the offenders, including the nature of their mental disorder.

3.4 However, we have had other evidence which has supported the treatment of offenders in local hospitals and special hospitals alongside non-offenders (whether compulsorily detained or voluntary patients). The National Association of Chief and Principal Nursing Officers told us that in the special hospitals mixing offenders and non-offenders gave rise to no problems and indeed, as an issue, was hardly discussed at all, patients being distinguished according to the security risk which they presented. Witnesses have also commented on the beneficial effects for the offender of avoiding separate treatment systems which might give rise to stigma, in effect reviving the old concept of the criminal lunatic asylum. In reply to suggestions made to us that relatives of some non-offender patients may feel there is stigma in their admission to the special hospitals because of the association with offenders, we would say that whatever stigma there is would attach to any hospital providing for the treatment of mentally disordered patients requiring special security, irrespective of the presence or absence of offenders among them.

3.5 Many hospitals find it possible to accept and treat these mentally disordered offenders, and seem to deal with some of the most difficult offenders without specially secure conditions. The reluctance of others to accept offenders is expressed mainly in relation to the mentally handicapped, the psychopathic, and those requiring some degree of security, though we have also heard of difficulties in arranging for the admission of those on the border-line of mental disorder such as epileptics, drug addicts and alcoholics. It is in respect of these often difficult and unresponsive patients that the hospitals are most likely to exercise their powers of refusal of admission.[2] Hospitals for the mentally handicapped are generally full and it is not always possible for a hospital place to be found for a case which on medical advice the court thinks should be admitted, or in which transfer may be appropriate. In these circumstances the hospital may be unwilling to give an offender, merely because he is awaiting disposal by the courts, priority over other patients who may be waiting their turn. However, it is the announced policy of the Government[3] that there should be a shift in the balance from hospital to community care and this should, in time, reduce the pressure on hospital accommodation for the mentally handicapped. The main reasons why psychopaths are generally, although not universally, unacceptable to the hospitals, are their lack of response to treatment, their often troublesome and sometimes aggressive behaviour, and in many cases the need for secure containment. An East Anglian consultant told us that experience had convinced him "that although one psychopath is acceptable in a ward, two are a menace and three completely disorganise the running of the establishment". We discuss in Chapter 5 the arrangements we propose for treating psychopaths in the future. Meanwhile, experience of the disruption caused by these patients has probably coloured the attitude of some hospital staff towards the acceptance of offenders in general.

3.6 We pointed out in paragraph 5 of our Interim Report that custodial requirements cannot be reconciled with the "open door" therapeutic policy now practiced. This problem is not confined to the treatment of offenders but arises equally with non-offender patients who need treatment in conditions of security either for their own safety or the safety of others. A patient's need for security will not always entail his being treated in secure accommodation; much can be achieved by providing an appropriate level of supervision. However, it has become clear that "open door" therapy has necessarily to be accompanied by sufficient provision of secure hospital accommodation to cater for those who simply cannot be satisfactorily dealt with, even under the closest supervision, in open conditions: this is supported by the large measure of agreement between our own Interim Report and the Report of the Department of Health and Social Security Working Party.[4] We have referred in paragraphs 1.3–1.9 above to the progress being made in implementing the proposals made in our Interim Report for secure units in each region. It is partly because of the custodial implications that many consultants are particularly reluctant to accept offender-patients if the court proposes to make a restriction order under section 65 of the Act (which would prevent the doctor from transferring the patient, granting him leave or discharging him without the concurrence of the Home Secretary). But another reason for the reluctance to accept restricted

---

[2] See paragraph 2.29.

[3] Cmnd. 4683: *Better Services for the Mentally Handicapped.*

[4] "Revised Report of the Working Party on Security in NHS Psychiatric Hospitals". London, DHSS, 1974.

patients is the administrative complication resulting from the involvement of the Home Office; we discuss this matter elsewhere (see paragraphs 7.17–7.22 and 14.22–14.23).

3.7 On the question of treating offenders and non-offenders together, our own conclusion is that while particular offenders and many classified as psychopaths may cause difficulties, no general distinction should be made between offenders and non-offenders in the question of eligibility for treatment in hospital. It is evident that many patients regarded by the hospitals as non-offenders will have had convictions at some time in the past. They have not become different people merely because they are not currently serving a sentence. Whether a man comes to be classified as an offender is a far from straightforward matter; it may depend on such contingencies as whether his anti-social activities come to light and are reported, whether the police choose to press charges, and indeed whether in making a hospital order the magistrates' court decide to convict rather than use the powers under section 60(2) of the Mental Health Act to do so without recording a conviction. Again, is a patient in a psychiatric hospital who assaults a nurse to be classified as an offender and dealt with as a different type of person because he has committed an assault, which is a criminal offence? Is he to be regarded as not an offender because in accordance with policy it has been decided not to prosecute him? Offenders are a part of that whole community for which the hospitals are provided, and the question of principle whether they should be treated with non-offenders has been pronounced upon in the recommendations of a Royal Commission and by Parliament in the legislation which gave effect to the concept of the hospital order. What is important therapeutically is that mentally disordered offenders should be put into the treatment situation, in the widest sense, which is most appropriate to their treatment needs, with proper regard for the requirements of safety.

3.8 There are various other reasons why a consultant may refuse to accept patients. Sometimes he may not feel able to offer treatment for the condition from which a particular offender is suffering, especially a psychopathic offender, while another doctor would be willing to do so. If a doctor is doubtful about a case he will take into account that if he accepts a patient under a hospital order and then finds him not amenable to treatment there is no power to transfer the patient to the penal system or to have the court's order reconsidered: the hospital may then be in the difficulty of not wishing to keep the patient but recognising that discharge into the community would be undesirable. In this situation either the patient is discharged inappropriately or, equally inappropriately, he is kept in a hospital merely for custody. (If the court has also made a section 65 order it may be difficult for the hospital to obtain the consent of the Home Secretary to the discharge of the patient after only a short period in which no effective treatment has been possible.) Some of these difficulties will, we believe, be overcome by proposals we make for improved arrangements for assessment before sentence, including interim hospital orders, and by our recommendations with regard to section 65 orders.

(3) The special hospitals

3.9 Although all the special hospitals are subject to the same legal provisions and procedures, and the same central administration by the Department of

32

Health and Social Security, it is important to bear in mind that there are significant differences among them. Broadmoor in particular is markedly different from the others, partly by reason of its history, in that it catered exclusively for offenders and was administered until 1948 by the Home Office until transferred to the Ministry of Health, but principally by reason of the differences in the patients. The proportion of psychopaths in the population is about the same in each hospital (a quarter), but as will be seen from the information given in paragraph 2.14 Broadmoor is pre-eminently a mental illness hospital, whereas about half the patients in Rampton and Moss Side are suffering from mental handicap.

3.10 The national status of the special hospitals thus allows a degree of specialisation in treating particular categories of mental disorder but it impedes the development of those close contacts with treatment and caring agencies in the patients' home areas which are desirable for the purposes of effective administration including rehabilitation in the community. In the case of Broadmoor and Rampton, an isolated situation adds to the remoteness from home which committal to a national institution entails for many patients and makes it harder for them to keep in touch with their relatives and friends and to receive visits, to say nothing of discouraging the recruitment of staff.

3.11 To the difficulties inevitably involved in treating mentally disordered people in conditions of strict security are added in the special hospitals the problems of serious overcrowding. We described this and its causes in our Interim Report. We are glad to note that certain measures have been taken which are designed to alleviate the situation to some extent,[5] but even with these measures the problem of overcrowding remains a serious one. The provision of regional secure hospital units in accordance with our proposals will also be helpful but purpose-built units will not become available for perhaps three or four years, and *ad hoc* provision is required in the meantime. It is still a fact that numbers of patients in the special hospitals no longer need the degree of security they provide, while some patients who should appropriately be placed in them cannot be accepted for lack of room.

(4) Problems of the social services

3.12 The local authority social services were completely reorganised under the recommendations in the Seebohm Report, and have subsequently, as recently as last year, been involved in the fundamental reorganisation of local government. It will be some time before they will have fully adjusted to these reforms.

---

[5] We have been informed by the Department of Health and Social Security that it is not intended to refill the places vacated by those Broadmoor patients who were transferred to the advance unit of the new Park Lane Hospital (see paragraph 2.14). The situation at Rampton Hospital has been eased by the opening in May 1974 of two new wards providing 56 places. Further relief of the situation at Rampton has come through the opening, also in May 1974, of the Eastdale Unit at Balderton Hospital. The unit's aim is to act as the first stage in the rehabilitation of those Rampton patients who no longer need treatment under secure conditions. The unit provides 20 beds and up to 30 June this year 35 patients from Rampton had been transferred to it prior to admission to a local National Health Service hospital or other accommodation. The Department have also told us that the number of admissions last year to the special hospitals was lower than the number of discharges and transfers out had been for a number of years, but it is not clear whether this is an isolated development or whether it will be repeated in future years.

3.13 Apart from the effects of these major organisational changes, the main problems which have been brought to our attention in the field of the local authority social services have been first the shortage of resources of all kinds, and secondly deficiencies of communication with the hospitals and also with the education services in relation to mentally disordered children. The Association of Directors of Social Services told us that "the concept of community care for the ex-psychiatric patient embodied in the Mental Health Act 1959 is, as yet, far from being fully realized throughout this country. Effective care and after-care of the mentally disordered can become a reality only when there is a sufficiency of facilities located in the community adequate to the task". The County Councils Association said that "public and Parliamentary expectations of improvements in the scope and quality of local authority social services tend to outstrip the resources available" and when we asked their representatives to identify the principal shortages they replied that they were of trained social workers, hostels and after-care facilities, and special provision for disturbed children and adolescents. Other evidence has supported these comments and in addition has pointed to the overloading of Child Guidance Clinics and the need for improved diagnostic services. The local authorities were required to submit 10-year development plans to the Government in February 1973. These provided for substantial expansion of residential, day and domiciliary care for the mentally disordered, but they have been cut back in consequence of economic pressures and at present there seems to be little prospect of rapid progress in these matters.

3.14 The difficulties with which the social service departments are faced make improved communications with the hospitals when patients are to be discharged to community care particularly important. The hospital should know what care can be provided and the social services department should be adequately forewarned and informed; but improved communications are desirable in any event in the interests of providing continuity of "through-care" for the patient. Improving co-operation between all services involved with the treatment of the mentally disordered offender is a subject with which we deal more fully in Chapter 20 below.

3.15 Another problem mentioned to us was that social workers with a generalist training and a heavy mixed case load, feeling unqualified to cope with mentally disordered offenders and being unable to spend time in making contact with the patient, who may be in a distant hospital, may give first priority to the other, more familiar types of case near at hand. The question has been raised of the possible need for more specialisation, and post-professional training in the handling of seriously disturbed clients. Such training is seen as being particularly important for those social workers who perform the functions of mental welfare officers (see paragraph 9.1 below). The Association of Municipal Corporations saw some merit in specialisation in mental health, "provided that the social workers concerned remain firmly attached to the main body of generic social workers". We discuss the question of specialisation further in paragraph 8.9 below.

3.16 The points made on behalf of the probation and after-care service have indicated very similar difficulties to those being experienced by the local authority social service departments. Inadequacy of resources, the need for better communications especially with the hospitals, and the problems caused when patients are discharged without consultation and without adequate time being allowed for proper preparations to be made in the community, are matters which cause no less concern to the probation service. These difficulties are discussed when we come to consider the operation of psychiatric probation orders (see Chapter 16).

3.17   In connection with the improvement of diagnostic facilities, the Chief Probation Officers have proposed that there should be "part-time psychiatric consultancy" appointments to each probation and after-care service, which would be useful both at the time of preparing social inquiry reports and subsequently during supervision. We have concluded that this proposal is not practical at present because there are too few psychiatrists with sufficient experience of dealing with offenders. The need is often not simply for advice but for access to a doctor who would take a patient for emergency observation. In the longer term the need should be met by our proposals for the development of forensic psychiatric services based on regional secure hospital units (see Chapter 20). In proposing these units in our Interim Report we specifically referred to their value as reference points for the probation and after-care service (Interim Report, paragraph 9).

II.   THE MENTALLY DISORDERED IN THE PRISONS

(1)   The provision of medical treatment in the prisons

(i)   *The difficulties*

3.18   If a mentally disordered offender awaiting disposal by the court has been recommended for hospital treatment but is not acceptable to any hospital applied to, and does not come within the narrow criteria for admission to the special hospitals,[6] the court has to decide between a non-custodial or a custodial sentence. In the event of a custodial sentence being imposed, the prison system cannot refuse the case. Many offenders sentenced to imprisonment are suffering from some form of mental disorder even though not necessarily within the scope of the compulsory detention provisions of the Mental Health Act. In any analysis of the incidence of mental disorder in the prison population much will depend on the definitions and criteria adopted but there is no doubt that a substantial minority of the prison population can properly be described, on any criteria, as mentally disordered in some degree. Sometimes the disorder is severe. Often there is a history of admission—sometimes recent—to National Health Service local psychiatric hospitals and, occasionally, to special hospitals. Witnesses pointed out to us the very wide range of types of mentally disordered offender who have to be catered for by the prisons, from a small number of mentally disordered men who have committed notorious crimes to the large number of social inadequates, many of whom are vagrants and continually in and out of prisons, hostels, reception centres and hospitals.

3.19   Probation and after-care service witnesses have expressed the view that approximately one-third of the population in the local prisons can be described as mentally disordered. The consultant forensic psychiatrists have commented that while the large majority of first offenders respond to normal penal sanctions

---

[6] Admission to the special hospitals is controlled by the DHSS (see paragraph 2.18).

and adjust their behaviour, the failure of the minority to respond and their persistence in a chaotic life style, of which offending is but one part, are indicative of mental disorder. In a study in 1966 based on a sample of some 400 prisoners and ex-prisoners in the London area Silberman and Gibbens[7] found that about 10 per cent had been in mental institutions at some time; the percentages were higher in the older age groups. A survey carried out by the Home Office Research Unit among prisoners in the 21 prisons in the South East Region in 1972, based on information in files, suggested that up to a quarter of the prisoners serving sentences of four years or less were mentally disordered or handicapped to some extent. Earlier research by West[8] indicated that a third of a sample of habitual prisoners had a history of severe mental disorder. The varying percentages are not necessarily contradictory since each sample varied in nature, ranging from men serving their first sentence to multiple recidivists.

3.20   The conditions in the prisons are by no means favourable for identifying and satisfactorily dealing with those prisoners who are mentally disordered. It is well-known that the prisons are overcrowded. There was a temporary improvement in the last two or three years, partly as a result of the successful introduction of the parole scheme, and a number of open prisons have become redundant as the numbers of the more amenable and responsive prisoners have been reduced; but it has recently been announced that the prison population is rising again, and the number of prisoners sleeping two or three to a cell in May of this year was over 14,000 compared with 12,000 a year previously. We have been given much evidence of the difficulty that may be experienced in recognising mental disorder, or incipient mental disorder, in the prison situation if it is not deliberately brought to notice by the man himself. The Prison Officers' Association informed us that the reluctance of National Health Service local hospitals to accept mentally disordered offenders has increased the number of prisoners with histories of mental disorder, of whom only a tiny proportion are transferred to hospital outside the penal system (see statistics in footnote to paragraph 3.37 below). Meanwhile, the penal system itself has in recent years introduced liberalised regimes allowing free association and movement for the prisoners, which make the identification of mental disorder by the staff more difficult; the Association stated that an inmate could reach an advanced state of mental illness before his complaint was recognised. A complicating factor was the possibility that a prisoner's unusual behaviour might often be merely "playing up". A Prison Medical Officer also referred to this difficulty, stating that numbers of prisoners for a variety of reasons feign illness or greatly exaggerate their symptoms, while others suffer considerable disabilities without complaint.

3.21   We have been told that prisoners suffering from a mental disorder which is slight can be absorbed in the rest of the prison population, which in many respects is a tolerant one, without great difficulties. But there are others, particularly among the substantial numbers of prisoners who suffer from some form of personality disorder, who present serious difficulties of control. We have been informed that more recently the increasing number of long sentence and life sentence prisoners has accentuated the problems. Prison Medical Officers informed us that they had noticed a disturbing increase in recent years

[7] Unpublished research study.

[8] West, D J *The Habitual Prisoner*. (London, MacMillan and Company, 1963.)

in violent young aggressive psychopaths and in chronic psychotics. The behaviour of these difficult prisoners, which is liable to extreme variations, is often unpredictable, and they are a source of anxiety to their fellow prisoners as well as to staff.

(ii) *Should mentally disordered offenders be treated in the prisons?*

3.22   Against this background we have considered to what extent mentally disordered offenders should be treated in the prisons.   The Royal Commission on Mental Illness and Mental Deficiency thought that in some cases normal penal measures were appropriate for mentally disordered offenders.   In discussing the compulsory admission to hospital of psychopathic patients convicted of a criminal offence they stated:

> "This does not mean that we consider it right to apply these special measures to all offenders who are psychopathic in the wide sense in which we use that term.   It would often be more appropriate to give an ordinary sentence or to use normal methods of probation.   Our recommendation is that psychopathic patients should be liable to compulsory admission to hospital or community care on conviction for a criminal offence only if the court is satisfied that normal penal measures alone are insufficient or inappropriate and that the patient requires special medical or social care which a particular hospital or local authority is able and willing to provide".[9]

They go on to say that this consideration applies to younger psychopathic patients and to severely subnormal and mentally ill patients as well as to adult psychopathic patients.[10]   This principle is embodied in Part V of the Mental Health Act.   Section 60(1)(*b*) makes provision for a hospital order to be made only when the court is of the opinion that this is the most suitable method of disposing of the case, having regard to the other available methods of dealing with the offender.   The Home Office thought it humane that mentally disordered people should be dealt with in hospitals, but recognised the problems and wondered whether more provision should be made within the prison system.   The representatives of the Prison Officers' Association thought that because of the reluctance of many local psychiatric hospitals to admit offenders, and of the overcrowding in the special hospitals, more specialised provision should be made in the prison system, on the lines already established at Parkhurst Prison (see paragraph 3.30 below); they emphasised, however, that a high staff ratio was crucial for the success of such developments.   The National Association of Chief and Principal Nursing Officers thought that treatment in prison was indicated where the patient required care but was not susceptible to curative treatment, but they recognised that susceptibility to treatment was not always easy to decide.   The British Psychological Society thought that the location of treatment was not important provided that the treatment was appropriate.   Witnesses suggesting the desirability of treatment in prison for some offender patients generally made it clear that it was an essential corollary of their remarks that the facilities and standards of treatment available in prisons should be of a high order, and indeed some postulated that prisons in their entirety should be therapeutic institutions.

---

[9] Cmnd. 169, paragraph 356.
[10] Cmnd. 169, paragraph 517.

3.23   Whilst those suffering from mental disorder should generally be treated in hospital there are certain circumstances in which exceptionally there may be good reasons for preferring a penal disposal.   In the first place there will be some mentally disordered offenders who are likely to respond better to the prison regime.   It is because we think the prison work regime, with all its facilities, will provide a more appropriate environment than a hospital regime for the development of treatment for dangerous anti-social psychopaths that we recommend that the special provision we are proposing for these psychopaths (see paragraphs 5.49–5.57) should be located within the penal rather than the hospital system.   Secondly, we have to recognise that there may be a few men for whom even the special hospitals cannot at present provide sufficient security.

(iii)   *Sexual offenders*

3.24   We have also considered the suitability of treating sexual offenders in prisons, in the light of representations made to us by members of the Law Reform Committee of the General Council of the Bar.   They felt that it might be preferable not to sentence them to imprisonment but to include them among the statutory categories of the mentally disordered, to enable the courts to make them subject to hospital orders and to receive appropriate medical treatment in a non-custodial setting.   The witnesses said that sexual offenders were often good citizens in all but this one respect, and in need of treatment rather than punishment.   We have also been told that many sexual offenders suffer victimisation from other inmates in prison.

3.25   We have much sympathy with this proposal.   However, we think it would be wrong to assume that sexual offenders are necessarily, on that count alone, mentally disordered.   It is necessary to distinguish, among the generality of those who commit sexual offences, those who do so as a result of sexual deviation, a condition recognised by the International Classification of Diseases[11] as a mental disorder, and accepted by many psychiatrists as being subsumed under "other disorder or disability of mind" within section 4(1) of the Mental Health Act 1959.   We are aware that certain forms of behaviour therapy, as well as other methods of a more medical nature, although still at the research stage, are now available to a limited extent and in a few hospitals in the National Health Service for patients with sexual deviation, in particular some types of homosexuality, transvestism, fetishism and exhibitionism.   We cannot as yet, however, assume either that such methods of treatment will prove ultimately to have efficacy, or, even if they do, that facilities throughout the National Health Service will be provided.   There is obviously a pressing need for more research into the management and specific treatment for these conditions.   We recommend that further resources should be made available for these purposes, both within the Prison Medical Service and within the National Health Service.

3.26   While we do not consider that offenders suffering from sexual deviation alone should be susceptible to section 60 hospital orders, we would draw attention to the advantage of including them within the provision of section 72 of the Act, which would enable them to be transferred from prison to hospital

---

[11] World Health Organisation, Geneva, 1968 and 1974.

for treatment as and when this becomes available within the National Health Service, should it be that such facilities do not develop or cannot be provided in prisons.

3.27 Until new treatments for sexual deviation have been developed, sexual deviation alone is unlikely to be a ground for the transfer of a prisoner to hospital. For the time being, therefore, sexual deviants will have to remain in the prison system and we are anxious about the victimisation they often suffer from the other prisoners. This may make it necessary to segregate them for their own protection, notwithstanding that segregation emphasises the stigma that attaches to them. This is essentially a matter of internal prison administration but we understand that attitudes towards sexual offenders vary widely between different institutions and that in some the problem of victimisation does not exist. The prevailing ethos within each prison presumably owes much to the attitudes of the staff and we urge the prison authorities to give as positive a lead as they can in this matter, with a view to reducing victimisation to a minimum, if indeed it cannot be eliminated.

(iv) *The need for improved facilities*

3.28 In accepting that the categories of mentally disordered offender referred to in paragraph 3.23 above should be treated in the prisons, and that the prisons must also treat the sexual deviants we have just discussed and prisoners who become mentally disturbed in the course of their sentence and have to remain in prison until a hospital place can be found, we support the representations made by witnesses as to the need for much improved treatment facilities in the penal system. While this need is general, a number of witnesses have referred particularly to inadequacies in the local prisons, and for border-line subnormals, inadequates, men with minor psychiatric disorders, alcoholics and drug addicts. The local prisons have an important role in the identification of treatment needs of recidivists at the early stages of their criminal career; but the large turnover and, in some cases, the restricted facilities militate against this work being carried out effectively.

3.29 We have received a detailed account of the medical work at Leeds Prison, the second largest of the 17 local prisons of England and Wales which accommodates up to 1,000 men. It has a medical complement of a senior medical officer, three basic-grade medical officers and a part-time medical officer, supported by a consultant forensic psychiatrist and senior registrar, whose appointments are shared with the National Health Service. The prison deals with about 9,000 new receptions a year. On first arrival in prison every prisoner is given a medical examination. This initial examination, which is necessarily brief, but not perfunctory, gives an opportunity to assess the prisoner's general state of health and possible need for more detailed investigation; it provides a basis for decisions on his accommodation, suitability for work, special dietary requirements and general management. Subsequently, apart from further investigations put in hand by the medical officer or indicated by the observation of prisoners by the staff or by other prisoners, every month some 3,500 applications are made by inmates[12] to see a medical officer, 100

[12] Not all inmates are sentenced prisoners. Some are in course of trial or on remand awaiting trial or sentence, and a small number are civil prisoners, borstallers awaiting transfer, or other categories. At any one time about 600 are sentenced adults, 200 trial and remand cases, and 160 all other categories.

are admitted to and discharged from the prison hospital, 30 inmates are sent to outside hospitals for consultation regarding their physical condition, and 60 inmates receive psychiatric treatment. While prisons differ substantially in size and functions, these statistics give some idea of what is involved in providing prisoners with medical, including psychiatric, care in a local prison.

3.30   In the contrasting situation of a training prison we were interested to see the attempts being made by the prison authorities at Parkhurst Prison's "C" Wing, which was established in 1970 and had in June of this year a complement of 34 prisoners, to develop a system of management of long-term disturbed and disruptive prisoners, but it was obvious that there were serious limitations on what could be achieved without more resources. We have been told that because of the pressures on the prison system as a whole it is not feasible to transfer accommodation or staff from other prison purposes to relieve this situation. The Director of Prison Medical Services has informed us that there is a need for more medical accommodation with suitable security in the prisons as well as in the special hospitals, and we were also informed in evidence that the Department of Health and Social Security and the Home Office were in agreement that there should be an extension of psychiatric treatment in prisons.

3.31   A number of Prison Medical Officers, as well as other witnesses, have asserted the need for improved physical facilities in the prisons, the involvement of Prison Medical Officers in forensic psychiatric work outside the prisons (on which we comment further in Chapter 20) and the need for the training of prison staff in mental nursing. One Prison Medical Officer has proposed that every prison hospital officer should be trained to the same standards and pass the same examinations as nurses do outside. The need to raise standards in prison hospitals to those of the National Health Service has been asserted by a number of witnesses. The Prison Officers' Association themselves attached importance to training in National Health Service hospitals and regretted the difficulties (in particular, problems about incompatible conditions of service) which had hitherto prevented arrangements from being negotiated.

3.32   We do not think that, as some witnesses have suggested, prisons should be equipped to deal with all forms of mental disorder. We agree with the Broadmoor Advisory Committee, the Broadmoor Branch of the Prison Officers' Association and the Royal College of Nursing who thought that while the prisons should be able to deal with short-term treatment of acute psychiatric disorders, the prison setting is not the place for the treatment of psychotic cases in the long term. Such cases should be transferred to a special hospital, a regional secure hospital unit, or a local psychiatric hospital, according to the degree of security required. However, it seems to us that the evidence of the need for a vigorous and substantial up-grading of the medical resources in the prisons, including physical facilities and staff complements and specialised psychiatric training is incontrovertible. Particular attention should be given to improving the present level of provision for those categories of mentally disturbed prisoners to whom treatment must be given within the prisons (see paragraphs 3.23–3.27 above), but all aspects of the problem require to be tackled with urgency, determination and a massive injection of money. We know full well the difficulties of finding additional finance for the penal system: it is not the most popular of causes. But somehow this must be done if the objects for which the services are provided are to have any chance of being achieved; and if they could be achieved the benefits they would bring to the community, in terms of prevention of damage and suffering, would provide a handsome return indeed on the investment.

(v) *An additional psychiatric prison*
3.33   Quite apart from the need for massive improvements in the prison medical arrangements in general, there have been many references in evidence, mostly from members of the Prison Medical Service, to the desirability of establishing a second psychiatric prison, in addition to Grendon. (The work of Grendon Prison is described in paragraphs 5.44–5.48 below.) There have, however, been divergent views about the purposes to be served by such a prison. It has been suggested that it should not be so selective as Grendon; that it should be for short-term patients, particularly simple schizophrenics, depressives and hypomanics; that it should be equivalent to Broadmoor, for dangerous and violent people; or that it should accommodate long-term occasional aggressives, and inadequates, psychopaths, or recidivists.

3.34   On the other hand a number of witnesses have opposed the provision of another specialist psychiatric prison. They have argued that special institutions tend to create special problems, diverting scarce resources, using up specialised staff and commanding better inmate/staff ratios than other establishments which may be dealing with more difficult situations. Special psychiatric prisons may also appear to be unfair to "normal" offenders, and accentuate the dichotomy between prisoners with mental disorder and prisoners without mental disorder. It has been suggested also that the treatment of a large number of unselected mentally disordered offenders in one exclusively psychiatric prison would create treatment and staffing difficulties, especially as in a prison the requirements of security must come before treatment.

3.35   We do not think that there is a sufficiently strong case at present for establishing a second psychiatric prison. The arguments of those who have advocated it have been weakened by the diversity of their opinions as to its role, and the criticism that such a project would make such demands on scarce resources as to be prejudicial to treatment in other penal establishments seems to us to have great force. We have pointed out in this chapter the pressing need to improve the general level of provision for psychiatric treatment in the prisons, and we think that priority should also be given to the establishment within the penal system of the experimental training units for psychopathic offenders which we recommend in Chapter 5 of this Report. We do not say that the time will not come when a further psychiatric prison will be justified, but before this we hope that the opportunity will have been taken to assess the functioning of the psychopathic training units, and properly to evaluate the achievements of Grendon.

(vi) *Women*
3.36   Men far outnumber women in their demands on the prison service (a ratio of about 30:1) and what we have said so far about the facilities for psychiatric treatment in prisons applies to the male offender. As regards women, the Governor and staff of Holloway in their evidence gave the following outline of the incidence of mental disorder among female prisoners:

"The ratio of disturbed against non-disturbed offenders is much higher for females than for males. There are very few 'mentally ill' women in

41

Holloway, but there are many who may be considered 'mentally abnormal' according to our definition (below) in that there is a great deviance from sociological and psychological norms. The term 'mentally abnormal' used here applies to:

(a) people with a defined psychiatric diagnosis, eg schizophrenia, which can be treated psychiatrically or medically;

(b) those people with the broad psychiatric diagnosis of 'personality disorder' or 'behavioural disorder', which might be helped with medical, psychiatric, psychological or sociological methods;

(c) those people who are classified as 'psychopaths' or 'sociopaths', whose condition cannot be treated medically or psychiatrically, but might be more appropriately treated by psychological or sociological methods.

The majority of our population would come under categories (b) and (c) described above."

Holloway is currently being rebuilt and re-developed as an establishment to provide medical, psychiatric and remedial treatment for women sentenced to imprisonment. This is a development we welcome.

(2) Transfers to National Health Service Hospitals

(i) *The statutory provisions*

3.37 If a prisoner requires psychiatric treatment which cannot be provided in prison, arrangements may be made for him to be treated in a local National Health Service hospital or a special hospital. Section 72 of the Mental Health Act enables the Secretary of State—in practice, the Home Secretary—to direct, by warrant, that a prisoner shall be removed to and detained in a specified hospital (by definition, a special hospital or other National Health Service hospital). The Home Secretary must be satisfied by reports from at least two medical practitioners, one at least being approved for the purposes of section 28 of the Act by a local authority as having special experience in the diagnosis or treatment of mental disorders, that the prisoner is suffering from mental illness, psychopathic disorder, subnormality or severe subnormality, of a nature or degree which warrants his detention in hospital for medical treatment. The Home Secretary must also be of opinion having regard to the public interest and all the circumstances that the transfer is expedient. A person when transferred is dealt with, by virtue of section 72(3), as though admitted under a hospital order, and if restrictions are not imposed under section 74 (see paragraph 3.39 below) he ceases, on transfer, to be subject to his prison sentence, and his discharge is at the doctor's discretion. As the figures given below show, few transfers are effected without restrictions: these are generally cases where the prison sentence has not long to run.[13]

---

[13] The Home Office have provided the following statistics showing the frequency of transfers: *Cases in which transfer directions were issued:*

	1972	1973	1974
Without restrictions:			
Section 72 only	15	4	4
With restrictions:			
Section 72–74	62	56	40
Section 73–74	29	19	12

3.38   Under section 73 of the Act a person who has been committed for trial or remanded in custody may similarly be removed from prison by warrant of the Home Secretary to be detained in a specified hospital if the Home Secretary is satisfied by the like reports that the person is suffering from mental illness or severe subnormality of a nature or degree which warrants his detention in hospital for medical treatment.   We have been informed by the Home Office that this procedure is adopted only where a prisoner's condition is such that immediate removal to a hospital is necessary.   Normally when he is well enough he is either produced at court from the hospital or returned to prison to await trial.

3.39   Where a transfer direction has been given under section 72 of the Act, the Home Secretary may, under section 74, also impose the restrictions provided for under section 65 (so that the patient cannot be transferred to another hospital, sent on leave or discharged without his consent); and he must, by law, impose these restrictions on untried or unsentenced persons transferred under section 73.   Under section 75(1) a transferred prisoner subject to restrictions may be returned to prison[14] if the Home Secretary is notified by the responsible medical officer before the expiration of the full term of the prisoner's sentence that he no longer requires treatment for mental disorder; or he may be released on licence if he would have been so released on return to the prison.   If he is still in hospital when the full term of his sentence expires the restrictions then cease to have effect, by virtue of section 75(2) of the Act, and by virtue of section 65(5) the patient continues to be detained as if admitted to the hospital under a hospital order made on that date.   By the operation of sections 63(3) and 43(1) this further detention under a "notional" hospital order has legal authority for one year, when the normal provisions of the Act for renewal of compulsory detention may be invoked.

(ii) *Operating the provisions*

3.40   Although there is no statutory requirement that the consent of the receiving hospital be obtained, we have been informed that the Home Office do not in practice give transfer directions without it.   This statement is at variance with the comments of some psychiatrists, but the reason for this seems to be that when the Mental Health Act came into force it was agreed between the Home Office and the then Ministry of Health that the Home Office request for a vacancy should be addressed to the Regional Hospital Board, now the Regional Health Authority, serving the area to which the prisoner belonged (or, for vacancies in special hospitals, to the Department).   Therefore the accepting psychiatrist does not himself receive an application from the Home Office for his consent, and he may be unaware of the action taken by the Home Office.   If in some cases this is so there may be perhaps a weakness in the communications between the regional authorities and the accepting doctors in this respect.

3.41   Because the arrangements described in the foregoing paragraphs may result in a transferred prisoner being detained in hospital long after the date

---

[14] In this event the period spent in hospital is treated as part of the prisoner's sentence in calculating his earliest date of release, and he is granted remission on the full period of his sentence (though any period during which he may have been absent from the hospital without leave is not treated as part of his sentence).

when he would have been released had he remained in prison, it has been put to us that transfers from prisons to hospitals should not be allowed shortly before the prisoner's earliest date of release. We have been informed that the normal practice of the Home Office is not to transfer a prisoner within a week before his earliest date of release but, if possible, to arrange for his admission to hospital on release from prison; and not to make a supplementary order under section 74 of the Act applying section 65 restrictions while the prisoner is in hospital if he is transferred within a month of his earliest date of release, but to leave his discharge at the discretion of the hospital authorities: but exceptions are made where the prisoner's condition makes this necessary. The National Council for Civil Liberties have represented that a prisoner transferred under section 72 should have his detention reviewed by a Mental Health Review Tribunal before his sentence would have expired if he had remained in prison, and that those whose sentence has expired should not remain in special hospitals unless two independent medical reports have been presented to the hospital managers stating this to be appropriate. The Medical Advisory Committee at Broadmoor Hospital have urged that there should be some recourse to the courts where the decision to transfer is made in the late stages of a sentence.

3.42 We understand the anxieties which have given rise to these representations but we think that the objections are almost entirely theoretical. Section 72 allows transfer from prison to hospital only on the basis of the medical reports specified in paragraph 3.37 above, including the certificate of the two medical practitioners that the mental disorder is of a nature or degree which warrants the detention of the patient in a hospital for medical treatment. The Home Secretary may authorise the transfer "if he is of opinion having regard to the public interest and all the circumstances that it is expedient so to do", but this discretion is given to him only when the two doctors have reported that the transfer is justified on medical grounds. Furthermore, no transfer is effected unless the patient is accepted by the hospital, and as we have explained elsewhere in our Report it is by no means the case that offenders generally have easy access to hospitals; the hospitals would be unlikely to acquiesce in the transfer of prisoners requiring not treatment but merely continued custodial detention, especially where restrictions were applied, as in most cases they are, even if the other safeguards referred to above did not exist. The figures in the footnote to paragraph 3.37 do not suggest that the transfer powers are used excessively. We do not think that any formal limitations should be placed on the timing of transfers, as transfers may become essential, despite the approach of his release date, if a prisoner's mental condition deteriorates. We have considered whether, when the sentence of a transferred prisoner eventually expires, detention in hospital should not, as now, be continued notionally under a hospital order, but should require a fresh admission to hospital under Part IV of the Act, but we do not recommend this. Like any other compulsorily detained patient, a transferred prisoner detained without restrictions will be discharged as soon as he is fit. Where the transferred patient is subject to restrictions, discharge will require, in addition to the doctor's decision, the Home Secretary's authority, until the date of expiry of the full sentence; but then the restrictions themselves expire and the patient's discharge is entirely a matter for the doctor.

(iii) *Improving the present arrangements*

3.43 Although in our opinion the powers to transfer prisoners and detain them in hospital are unlikely to be abused, we think that the following arrangements would provide reassurance. First, we suggest that every mentally disordered offender who is transferred from prison to hospital under section 72 should have the right of application to a Mental Health Review Tribunal for an early hearing when what would have been his earliest date of release is reached.[15] This right, exercisable in addition to those opportunities for application to a Tribunal for which the Act already makes provision, would provide formal protection against the patient's being needlessly detained longer than he would have been had he not been transferred. Secondly, where restrictions under section 74 have been imposed, the Home Secretary should review, at the prisoner's earliest date of release, the need for them to continue, and if possible they should be removed.

3.44 It may seem anomalous that there is (as explained above) specific provision in section 72 for the transfer to hospital of an adult psychopathic or subnormal prisoner, with the possibility of continued detention after the expiry of his prison sentence, although there is no power of compulsory admission to hospital of non-offenders suffering from these conditions. The Royal Commission on the Law Relating to Mental Illness and Mental Deficiency 1954–57, however, justified such a distinction in paragraph 356 of their Report (see paragraph 5.29 below) and we ourselves think[16] that the psychopath or subnormal person who has committed offences justifying a prison sentence may properly be subject to a greater measure of control than may be thought appropriate for non-offenders. In any event, non-offenders suffering from these conditions who were compulsorily admitted before the age of 21 can, subject to the provisions of section 44 of the Act, be detained thereafter without limit of age; and section 60 provides for the admission to hospital under hospital orders of psychopathic and subnormal patients of any age. Subject to the safeguards we have suggested, we do not propose any modification of the provisions governing the transfer and subsequent detention and discharge of these patients.

3.45 We see no reason why the power conferred by section 72 should be restricted as at present to mental illness, psychopathic disorder, subnormality and severe subnormality. The section could well be extended to all prisoners suffering from a mental disorder. This would eliminate specific reference to psychopathic disorder, and the medical recommendations for transfer could instead speak in terms of personality disorder, which, as we mention in paragraph 5.24, is the expression now preferred and which may be less stigmatic than psychopathic disorder. To the extent that sexual deviation, alcoholism and drug dependence are regarded as forms of mental disorder, if units are formed in National Health Service hospitals for the treatment of these conditions prisoners could be transferred to them. It seems clear that in such cases transfers would in practice be made only with the prisoner's consent,

---

[15] The right exists at present only when the full sentence has expired, without allowance of remission.

[16] Professor Williams dissenting.

and we see no reason why more than one medical recommendation should be required. Our proposal to widen the scope of section 72 in this way will require certain consequential amendments to be made in the Act in order to bring transfers on the ground of mental disorder within the general scheme of the Act, for example in the references in section 123 to conditions to be considered by Mental Health Review Tribunals.[17]

(iv) *Procedural delay*

3.46 Some witnesses have complained of delays in operating the procedure under sections 72 and 73 of the Act for transfers to hospital and have questioned the necessity for reference to the Home Office in every case. They explained that the papers had to be sent to the Home Office by post and although in urgent cases the Home Office, having seen the papers, would give authority by telephone, the minimum delay was likely to be two days and this was a long time in dealing with disturbed offenders. It has been suggested to us that the transfer decisions might well be made locally by the doctors in the prison and the hospital.

3.47 We have come to the conclusion that this would not be satisfactory. As we have explained, in most transfer cases restrictions equivalent to a restriction order under section 65 are imposed under section 74 of the Act and may remain in force until the expiry of the full term of the prison sentence, and in these circumstances we are satisfied that the removal of a prisoner to hospital for psychiatric treatment should be subject to the administrative approval of the Home Secretary. It is important that the conditions prescribed in section 72 should be strictly adhered to, and to avoid challenge in the courts it is necessary that the certifying documents should be checked by a Home Office legal adviser. We are informed by the Home Office that transfer directions are normally issued within a day or two of a prisoner being accepted for treatment in a psychiatric hospital, and that particularly urgent transfers can be effected by removal for treatment under the authority of section 22(2)(*b*) of the Prison Act 1952 pending the issue of a formal transfer direction under the Mental Health Act.

3.48 We have looked into complaints made of longer delays in effecting transfers to hospital, and the figures given to us for the period October 1972–September 1973 show that during that time 107 recommendations for transfer were made, 82 of which were implemented during the period, 73 of these within a month (including all 24 of the recommendations made under section 73—cases still before the courts). In nine cases action was for various reasons abandoned (four prisoners awaiting vacancies in psychiatric hospitals for from three to six months responded to treatment in prison sufficiently to make transfer to hospital no longer necessary). Sixteen cases remained pending. Of these, three had been awaiting admission to a local hospital for from one to three months. The other 13 were awaiting admission to Broadmoor. We have drawn attention in paragraph 3.11 to the difficulties caused by overcrowding

---

[17] Professor Williams takes the view that persons transferred under such wider powers should not thereby be subject to detention in hospital at the termination of their sentence.

at Broadmoor. Some prisoners during the period mentioned were waiting for admission to Broadmoor for 6 to 12 months after the reports were originally received in the Home Office.

3.49 Having made careful inquiry into these matters we find no grounds for recommending changes in the legal provisions or in the procedures as they are operated by the Home Office. It is clear that the most substantial delays that occur are the result of the congestion in the special hospitals and the difficulties of obtaining acceptance of prisoner-patients by local National Health Service hospitals. Indeed, prison service witnesses have stated that some prisons have had such experience of the reluctance of psychiatric hospitals to receive their prisoners on transfer that the possibility of obtaining the requisite treatment for them by this means is no longer considered. It will be seen from the figures in the footnote to paragraph 3.37 above that the number of transfers effected has been virtually halved in three years and is now almost negligible. We urge at a number of points in our Report that those local psychiatric hospitals which do not at present play a full part in the treatment of offender-patients as envisaged by the Mental Health Act should make a greater contribution, to provide the arrangements with the degree of flexibility which they were intended to have, and to ensure that adequate medical treatment is not denied to people who need it.

III. CONSENT TO MEDICAL TREATMENT

(1) The dilemma

3.50 In the first part of this chapter we discussed the problems of treating the mentally disordered offender in hospital and we then went on to discuss the difficulties of giving treatment in prison. Having viewed these matters primarily from the standpoint of the treaters, we now turn to consider the position of the treated. What if the offender does not wish to receive treatment? Should his consent be required? Has society the right to impose psychiatric treatment on offenders either for their own good or for its own protection? Often the offender may have been put into a treatment situation solely as a result of his offence; yet his mental disorder may be unconnected with his offending.

3.51 The Royal Commission on Mental Illness and Mental Deficiency, in formulating their proposals for compulsory powers over patients, set out (in paragraph 314 *et seq* of their Report) a number of considerations relevant to the question of compulsory treatment. They pointed out that the patient's power of judgment and appreciation of his condition may be distorted or defective as a result of his illness or disability, so that the decision ought not to be left entirely to him; and that objections may often be caused by prejudice based on ignorance. While every effort should be made to overcome objections by persuasion, "no one disputes that there are some circumstances in which society must in the last resort be able to compel some patients to receive treatment or training in their own interests or for the protection of others, and that some may need to be protected against exploitation or neglect. Indeed, we would go further and emphasise that when every effort has been made to overcome the unwillingness of the patient or his relatives by persuasion, doctors and others should not be too hesitant to use such compulsory powers as the law may provide if this seems the only method of giving the patient the treatment or training which he badly needs and which is expected to cure or relieve his illness or to enable him to live a more happy and useful life."[18]

3.52   The Royal Commission thought there was a strong case for authorising the use of compulsion to ensure training or treatment in hospital or in the community for psychopathic[19] patients in early life, when it was most likely to be successful, on much the same grounds as have been accepted as justifying compulsory education (paragraph 354).   They did not recommend its continuance beyond the age of 25 except for offenders; offenders had "laid themselves open to the imposition of control" and the question was whether or not one of a variety of possible forms of control provided a suitable way of treating the individual offender.   "We consider it right that special forms of treatment or control should be applied to some psychopathic patients who have been convicted of a criminal offence which may not be applied compulsorily to adult psychopathic patients who have not committed such an offence and which do not apply to offenders who are not mentally disordered."   (Paragraph 356.)   For some psychopaths, "conviction in the courts might be the only occasion on which it would be possible to ensure that they receive the medical treatment they need".   (Paragraph 371.)

3.53   The Royal Commission, it will be seen, placed considerable emphasis on the desirability of ensuring that patients received treatment or training expected to be beneficial, and although the patient's consent should be sought they believed that compulsion was generally justifiable to this good end.   The National Association for Mental Health have expressed to us concern about treatments such as electro-convulsive therapy or long-acting phenothiazines and forms of leucotomy, and have urged that a second psychiatric opinion from outside the hospital concerned should be obtained when a detained patient objects to a particular treatment.   The National Council for Civil Liberties felt that treatment without consent should be limited to emergency procedures, for example to curtail sudden outbursts of violence or to relieve an acute depressive state.   They felt that to confer on doctors unqualified powers of treatment without consent was unsafe insofar as doctors might, even with the best intentions, abuse this privileged position in their enthusiasm to treat a disorder.   As regards irreversible procedures, even where the patient wished to accept the treatment they thought that the freedom of his choice and his understanding of the consequences was often suspect, and that the consent of a Mental Health Review Tribunal should be obtained.   In considering an application the Tribunal should, in their view, satisfy itself on three main points: first, that the treatment was appropriate and that alternative treatments had been exhaustively tried; secondly, that the patient was giving his free and informed consent without promises of early discharge and that he fully understood both the positive and negative aspects of such treatment; and thirdly, that the suggested treatment was not "inhuman and degrading" in the terms of Article 3 of the European Convention on Human Rights.   In those cases where a person was considered incompetent to give or withhold his consent they proposed that the doctor in charge of his treatment should have to apply to a Tribunal on this point.

---

[18] Cmnd. 169, paragraph 316.

[19] It is important to bear in mind that the Royal Commission used the term "psychopath" to include the subnormal (see paragraph 5.12 of our Report).

(2) Our findings

3.54   The question of consent to treatment raises wide issues of medical ethics and of the rights of the individual as well as being relevant to parts of the Mental Health Act which are not our direct concern.   For the purposes of our remit the relevance of the question is to mentally disordered offenders who are compulsorily detained and here we have reached the following general conclusion.   Treatment (other than nursing care) should not be imposed on any patient without his consent if he is able to appreciate what is involved.   Three exceptions should be allowed: treatment may be given without such a patient's consent (*a*) where (not being of a hazardous or irreversible[20] character) it represents the minimum interference with the patient to prevent him from behaving violently or otherwise being a danger to himself or others; or (*b*) where it is necessary to save the patient's life; or (*c*) where (not being irreversible), it is necessary to prevent him from deteriorating.   Where, by reason of his disability, the patient is unable to appreciate what is involved, despite the help of an explanation in simple terms, the treatment may be given: but special considerations apply to treatment involving irreversible procedures (see paragraph 3.56 below).

3.55   We accept that it may be difficult for patients who are compulsorily detained to come to a proper decision on such a matter, particularly where the treatment in question is irreversible.[21]   Apart from possible reduction of their capacity to make a rational judgment, the incentive to accept treatment in the hope of release must be very strong, even if those in charge of the patient are careful to refrain from saying anything to connect the two decisions.   It is inherent in the situation that the protection of society may require the patient's continued detention if he does not receive treatment, and therefore he may suppose or be persuaded that his chances of early discharge from hospital, or release on licence from prison, may be improved if he agrees to certain forms of treatment, including, possibly, procedures which if he were free he would be reluctant to accept; and if he is detained in hospital the pressure upon an offender is the stronger in that he lacks the alternative possibility of release by his relatives which is provided for non-offenders.   He may also expect or hope that treatment may reduce, if not eliminate, the possibility of his re-offending. If it is a fact that his discharge or early release depends on an improvement in his medical condition, it seems not only right but essential that this should be carefully explained to him, together with the nature of the treatment required and the prospects of its success.   Even if nothing is said to him by anyone in authority, he is likely to think about the relevance of treatment to his prospects of release, and may be influenced by the comments of other patients, and friends and relatives if he has any, whether well or ill informed.   Is it not better that he should also be given the professional medical advice of those responsible for his care?

3.56   Needless to say, prospects should not be held out to the patient unless they are genuine and fully justified by the prognosis.   We recognise that in this respect, as in others, the patient is well safeguarded by the professional

---

[20] By "hazardous or irreversible" procedures we mean those entailing immediate significant physical hazard or having unfavourable irreversible physical or psychological consequences.

[21] As defined in footnote to paragraph 3.54.

ethics of the doctors responsible for his treatment.[22]   For this reason we have rejected any idea of proposing detailed rules for the guidance of doctors, with a view to the protection of patients.   Nevertheless, because of the pressures on the patient, we see force in some of the arguments for safeguards over and above the requirement for the patient himself to consent, especially in relation to irreversible procedures.[23]   We doubt whether it would be appropriate to require the consent of a Mental Health Review Tribunal, but for irreversible treatments a second medical opinion would be in the interests of the patient as well as being valuable to the treating doctor.   Our recommendation[24] is that a second psychiatric opinion, independent of the treating hospital or prison, should be obtained (in addition to the patient's consent, if he is capable of giving consent) before irreversible treatments are carried out on prisoners or patients detained under Part V of the Mental Health Act, unless delay would cause or increase a danger to life.   The nearest relative (or failing this in the case of a hospital patient, the patient's "guardian" where a "guardian" has been appointed) should also be consulted if this consultation would be possible within a reasonable time.   As we have indicated, we see no reason why the principles we have proposed should not apply in prison hospitals, except that we would not expect a prisoner who is so mentally disordered as to be incapable of giving consent to treatment to be in prison.

(3) The existing legal position and present practice

3.57   In the light of our conclusions, we have considered the existing legal position.   Certain eventualities, such as the need to restrain a patient during a violent episode by the injection of a tranquilliser, or to use medical procedures to save the life of a patient who lacks understanding, would be covered by common law, treatment being justified on the ground of presumed consent or necessity.   To what extent compulsory treatment is authorised by the Mental Health Act 1959 is not entirely clear.   The matter has not to our knowledge been considered by the courts.   We have sought the comments of the Department of Health and Social Security and the Department's legal advisers take the view that since the various sections of the Act which authorise compulsory admission (sections 26, 60 and 72) are couched in terms of the nature and degree of the patient's mental disorder being such as to warrant his detention in hospital for medical treatment, one purpose at least of the detention must be to enable the patient to receive any recognised form of treatment for the mental disorder from which he is suffering.   In their opinion, such treatment as is

---

[22] The Ethical Code of the Commonwealth Medical Association (of which the British Medical Association is a member), approved at its meeting in Jamaica in 1974, includes the following:
"1.   The doctor's primary loyalty is to his patient.
2.   His vocation and skill shall be devoted to the amelioration of symptoms, the cure of illness, and the promotion of health.
3.   He shall respect human life and studiously avoid doing it injury.
4.   He shall share all the knowledge he may have gained with his colleagues without any reserve.
5.   He shall respect the confidence of his patient as he would his own.
6.   He shall by precept and example maintain the dignity and ideals of the profession, and permit no bias based on race, creed, or socioeconomic factors to affect his professional practice."
(NB.   The word "patient" used in this Code embraces the prisoner or other persons whom a doctor might be called upon to attend at another's bidding.)

[23] As defined in footnote to paragraph 3.54.

[24] See also the footnote to paragraph 3.59.

considered necessary may be administered irrespective of the patient's wishes or those of his relatives. In addition, they refer to section 141 of the Act, which gives general protection against the possibility of either civil or criminal proceedings for acts purporting to be done in pursuance of the statute or any regulations or rules made under it, or for anything done in the discharge of statutory functions, unless the act was done in bad faith or without reasonable care. This section applies to hospital staff who, in good faith and with reasonable care, give treatment for or connected with the mental disorder in respect of which the patient has been compulsorily admitted, even if he has not consented to the treatment.[25] (We understand that a similar interpretation of the law is given by the Medical Defence Union to its members.) The Department readily acknowledged that the point was a difficult one, however, and for this reason they invariably advised that in the case of a specific form of treatment involving any risk the patient (if he is capable of understanding) or the nearest relative should be told what was proposed and the consent of both should, if possible, be obtained as a matter of policy. In practice they told us that forms of treatment involving any special risk were not administered if the patient or his nearest relative objected.

3.58 So far as offenders are concerned, the operative part of section 60(1) of the Mental Health Act (relating to hospital orders) states only that the court "may by order authorise his [the offender's] admission to and detention in such hospital as may be specified in the order"; the court does not explicitly authorise treatment, but the medical practitioners are required to have certified that "the mental disorder is of a nature or degree which warrants the detention of the patient in a hospital for medical treatment". By virtue of section 63(3) of the Act, a patient admitted to hospital in pursuance of a hospital order is to be treated as if he had been admitted "in pursuance of an application for admission for treatment made under Part IV". However, as we have just explained, the interpretation of Part IV in relation to compulsory treatment is not beyond doubt. In view of the obscurity of the law, section 141 of the Act, referred to by the Department of Health and Social Security as mentioned above, has great importance. It seems to mean that if a doctor or nurse applies any medical treatment to a patient against that patient's wishes but believing the treatment to be lawful, he is exempt from any civil or criminal proceedings, because under the section such proceedings can be brought only where "the act was done in bad faith or without reasonable care".

3.59 We recommend that when the Mental Health Act is under review, consideration should be given to making clear the intention in these matters on the lines indicated in the preceding paragraphs.[26]

---

[25] *R* v *Bracknell Justices, ex p Griffiths* [1975] 3 W.L.R. 140.

[26] Professor Williams and Mr. Hodgson concur in this recommendation with the following modifications of the proposals made in the preceding paragraphs:—

  (a) In paragraph 3.56, they would extend the requirement of a second opinion to cases where chemical treatment is proposed to be given to sexual offenders.
  (b) It seems that shock treatment, although often beneficial, arouses particular apprehensions among some patients, and they think that it should be provided that this form of treatment should never be administered to a protesting patient.
  (c) In their view, section 141 of the Act needs general reconsideration, but in any case they think that the section should be qualified by making it clear that the protection from liability does not extend to mistakes of law.

3.60   We asked the Prison Department of the Home Office what their practice was in relation to prisoners receiving treatment in penal institutions.   The Prison Rules (17(1) and 18(2)) make it clear that the medical officer of a prison shall have the care of the health, mental and physical, of the prisoners in that prison, and require that he shall pay special attention to any prisoner whose mental condition appears to require it and make any special arrangements which appear necessary for his supervision or care.   However, the Prison Department do not have the legal protection of section 141 of the Mental Health Act and the Department commented that Prison Medical Officers sometimes feel that they are on less sure ground in dealing with mentally disordered patients than are their colleagues in psychiatric hospitals who care for patients detained under compulsory powers.   Prisoners may accept or decline medical advice and treatment, and the Prison Department policy is not to give treatment without consent except in extreme situations where the life of the prisoner may be at risk.   In this the Department rely on the ruling of Lord Alvestone, Chief Justice, in *Leigh* v *Gladstone*[27] that "it is the duty of those who have in their charge a prisoner to do what they reasonably can to keep in health, and (still more clearly) to save him from death.   If, therefore, by neglect of this duty a prisoner dies, those who have neglected the duty to keep him alive, if they reasonably can, may find themselves exposed to a charge of manslaughter."

3.61   The precise extent of the obligation falling upon a Prison Medical Officer will vary from case to case, but it must normally include at the very minimum an explanation to the prisoner of the consequences for his health of his refusal of treatment.   Special difficulties have from time to time arisen in this connection over the question of artificial feeding of prisoners weakened by self-starvation, but the position with regard to the refusal of food and drink by mentally disordered prisoners is still governed by the above stated principle; the discontinuance of forcible feeding, announced by the Home Secretary in the House of Commons on 17 July 1974, did not relate to mentally disordered prisoners.

3.62   It appears that the Prison Department policy satisfies the requirements we have set out at paragraphs 3.54–3.56 above, except for any specific requirement to obtain an independent psychiatric opinion and, where possible, to consult the nearest relative, before irreversible procedures are carried out.

PROBLEMS OF THE PRESENT TREATMENT ARRANGEMENTS

SUMMARY OF CONCLUSIONS

I.   Treatment by the Health and Social Services

1.   Although, in general, the 1959 Act has been successful in relation to the treatment of mentally disordered offenders, the time has now come to build on it, in order to deal with some major deficiencies in the practical application of its principles.   The lack of co-ordination among the treatment services is fundamental to the problems we have examined.   (Paragraphs 3.1–3.2.)

---

[27] *Leigh* v *Gladstone* (1909), 26 T.L.R. 139.   Professor Williams questions the validity of the ruling in this case.

2. The treatment in local psychiatric hospitals of offenders, particularly of difficult and unresponsive patients such as the psychopathic and the subnormal and those requiring some degree of security, can give rise to problems. Custodial requirements cannot be reconciled with the "open door" therapeutic policy which has been developed in recent years, and there is a need for secure hospital accommodation (such as we advocated in our Interim Report) to cater for the difficult patient. However, no general distinction should be made between offenders and non-offenders in the question of eligibility for hospital treatment. Mentally disordered offenders should be put into the treatment situation which is best suited to their treatment needs, with proper regard for the requirements of safety. (Paragraphs 3.3–3.8.)

3. The national status of the special hospitals, whilst helping specialisation in certain forms of treatment, is not conducive to effective on-going care. A serious problem is that of overcrowding and we are glad to note that, since our Interim Report, certain measures have been taken to ease the situation. (Paragraphs 3.10–3.11.)

4. Apart from the need for time to recover from recent reorganisations, local authority social services departments are faced with problems of inadequate resources and difficulties of communication with other bodies. A particular need is for improved communication with hospitals to ensure continuity of care on the discharge of patients into the community. Social workers now receive a generalist training and the lack of specialisation during post-qualification in-service training is seen as posing difficulties in dealing with mentally disordered offenders. The probation and after-care service share these problems. The need seen by the probation and after-care service for "part-time psychiatric consultancy" appointments should be met by our proposals for the development of forensic psychiatric services. (Paragraphs 3.12–3.17.)

II. The Mentally Disordered in the Prisons

5. A substantial minority of offenders in prison are mentally disordered to some degree, but conditions in prisons are not favourable for the identification and treatment of mental disorder, and problems arise particularly with those suffering from personality disorder. Hospital is generally a preferable disposal for mentally disordered offenders but prison is appropriate for some who are likely to respond better to the prison regime and for those few offenders who require greater security than even the special hospitals can provide. (Paragraphs 3.18–3.23.)

6. We recommend that more resources should be made available for research into behaviour therapy and other forms of treatment for patients suffering from sexual deviation. Such deviants should be included within the scope of section 72 of the Mental Health Act to permit their transfer from prison to hospital in the event of effective treatments becoming available. We share the anxiety of witnesses that sexual offenders in the prisons should be safeguarded against victimisation. In this we think that the attitudes of the staff are of great importance, and the prison authorities should give as positive a lead as they can. (Paragraphs 3.24–3.27.)

7. There is need for a vigorous and substantial up-grading of the medical resources in the prisons, including physical facilities and staff complements

and specialised psychiatric training. All aspects of the problem require to be tackled with urgency, determination and a massive injection of money. (Paragraphs 3.28–3.32.)

8. We do not recommend the provision at present of a second psychiatric prison in addition to Grendon. Priority should be given to improving the general level of psychiatric provision in the prisons, and to establishing experimental training units for psychopathic offenders. (Paragraphs 3.33–3.35.)

Transfers to Hospital

9. It appears there that may have been, and there may still be, a weakness in communications between the regional authorities and the hospital consultants when the Home Office has requested the regional authorities to accept a prisoner on transfer. (Paragraph 3.40.)

10. We think that fears that transfers to hospital of prisoners when they are approaching their release date may be used improperly, merely to prolong a man's detention, are unjustified. Nonetheless we propose that, as a safeguard, prisoners transferred to hospital under section 72 should have a right of application to a Mental Health Review Tribunal for an early hearing at what would have been their earliest date of release. At this time, also, the Home Secretary should review the need for the continuation of section 74 restrictions if these have been imposed. We do not propose any modification of the provisions governing the transfer and subsequent detention and discharge of adult psychopathic or subnormal prisoners. (Paragraphs 3.41–3.44.)

11. We recommend that the scope of section 72 should be widened to enable prisoners suffering from any form of mental disorder to be transferred to hospital. Certain consequential amendments would be required in other parts of the Act. (Paragraph 3.45.)

12. The transfer of prisoners to hospital could not appropriately be arranged locally, between the prison doctors and the hospital doctors, without reference to the Home Office. In cases where there is special urgency the patient can be removed to hospital under section 22(2)(*b*) of the Prison Act 1952 pending the issue of a formal transfer direction under the Mental Health Act. (Paragraphs 3.46–3.47.)

13. We find that long delays in effecting the transfer of prisoners to hospital for treatment are attributable to the congestion in the special hospitals (causing delays in some cases of as much as 12 months) and difficulties in obtaining their acceptance by local hospitals. Some prisons have concluded that attempts to transfer prisoners to local hospitals are a waste of time, and have given up trying. We urge, in this connection, as we have in others, that the local National Health Service hospitals should accept the responsibility of playing a larger part in the treatment of mentally disordered offenders than many now do, to provide the flexibility which the treatment arrangements in the Act were intended to have, and to ensure that adequate medical treatment is not denied to people who need it. (Paragraphs 3.48–3.49.)

III. Consent to Medical Treatment

14. We have considered whether and when the consent to medical treatment of the mentally disordered offender should be required. Where a patient's condition does not prevent him from appreciating what is involved we do not think it justifiable to impose treatment (other than nursing care) without his consent. There are three exceptions to the general rule. Treatment may be given without consent (*a*) where it is not hazardous or irreversible and is the minimum necessary to prevent the patient behaving violently or being a danger to himself or others; or (*b*) where it is necessary to save his life; or (*c*) where (not being irreversible) it is necessary to prevent him from deteriorating. Where by reason of his disability the patient is unable to appreciate what is involved, despite the help of an explanation in simple terms, the treatment may be given; but special considerations apply to treatment involving irreversible procedures (see conclusion 16 below). (Paragraphs 3.50–3.54.)

15. We recognise the difficulties for the detained patient of coming to a proper decision, but these are inherent in the situation and make it essential that the nature of the treatment proposed, and the prospects of success, together with the implications in relation to his prospects of release, should be carefully explained to him. Needless to say, prospects should not be held out to the patient unless they are genuine and fully justified by the prognosis. (Paragraphs 3.55 and 3.56.)

16. The patient is well safeguarded by the professional ethics of the responsible doctors, but in view of anxieties expressed to us about irreversible procedures we propose that, where these are involved, in addition to the consent of the patient (where the patient is capable of giving it) a second psychiatric opinion independent of the treating hospital or prison should be obtained, unless delay would be likely to endanger life; and the nearest relative (or the guardian, if there is one) should also be consulted if this can be done within a reasonable time. (Paragraph 3.56.)

17. In view of the obscurity of the legal position with regard to the compulsory treatment of detained patients we recommend that consideration should be given to clarifying it when the Mental Health Act is under review, to conform to the requirements we have indicated. (Paragraphs 3.57–3.59.)

CHAPTER 4

DANGEROUS MENTALLY DISORDERED OFFENDERS

I. GENERAL MATTERS

(1) Introductory

4.1 We recognise the anxiety and concern felt by members of the public and voiced in the Press when serious offences are committed by people released from institutions to which they were sent, following earlier acts of violence, because of their mental disorder. Cases in point have been those of Graham Young and Terence Iliffe.[1] We have given long consideration to the various situations in which the problems may be posed and have taken full account of these specific cases.

4.2 As regards discharges from hospitals, the Aarvold Committee, set up in June 1972 to advise on the procedures for the discharge and supervision of hospital patients subject to special restrictions under section 65 of the Mental Health Act, recommended new procedures to identify cases requiring special care in assessment and an advisory board to assist the Home Secretary in reaching decisions in such cases. These recommendations, which we refer to in paragraphs 4.19–4.20 below, have already been put into effect, providing new safeguards. We propose in paragraphs 4.21–4.25 that the role of the advisory board should not be limited to considering only selected cases, but should be extended to advising the Home Secretary on all restricted cases in the special hospitals and advising on some restricted cases in local psychiatric hospitals. We also suggest in paragraphs 14.30 and 14.32 arrangements for facilitating the return to hospital of restricted patients whose behaviour or condition gives cause for anxiety after they have been discharged into the community, and in paragraph 14.31 we propose a new legal power for the Home Secretary to authorise the emergency admission of such a patient to "a place of safety" (a regional secure hospital unit or the hospital of a local remand prison or a remand centre) for a period of up to 72 hours if a place in hospital cannot immediately be obtained. We put forward in paragraphs 4.39–4.45 a proposal for a new form of prison sentence designed to afford society some further protection against the possibility that dangerous individuals will be released into the community prematurely. Under all these arrangements—the Aarvold procedures for restricted hospital patients as we propose they should be modified and extended, and our proposals for a new form of "reviewable" prison sentence—the final decision whether to return the offender to the community rests with the Home Secretary. We make clear in paragraph 7.16 our opinion that the maintenance of public confidence in the system should properly be a factor in his decision.

---

[1] Graham Frederick Young was convicted, on 29 June 1972, of murder and other grave offences committed by poisoning between February and November 1971, while on conditional discharge from Broadmoor Hospital. Terence John Iliffe, who also had been given a conditional discharge from Broadmoor, was convicted on 9 April 1974 of the murder of his fourth wife. Both he and Young were sentenced to imprisonment for life for these offences after medical witnesses had said in evidence that they were not suffering from any mental disorder susceptible of psychiatric treatment. A full account of the circumstances of the Young case was given by the Home Secretary to the House of Commons on 29 June 1972 (*Hansard*, Col. 1673–85) and of the Iliffe case on 9 May 1974 (*Hansard*, Col. 553–557). The Young case was considered by the Aarvold Committee (paragraph 4 of Cmnd. 5191).

4.3 The public are entitled to know that every check that can reasonably be provided is provided and used conscientiously; but there is no way which would be acceptable in a civilised society by which the public can be absolutely assured that no one released from an institution will ever commit a violent offence subsequently. In this chapter we indicate the problems that have to be faced and the limitations on what can be done. We also describe the safeguards that are in operation, and give our opinion on the possibilities of further precautions.

(2) The concept of dangerousness

4.4 Some misconceptions must first be disposed of. One concerns the relationship between criminal behaviour and mental disorder. If someone commits an offence while suffering from some degree of disorder it is likely to be assumed by the public at large that the mental condition and the offending act are connected; but this is not necessarily so. A person may have been led to commit an offence as the direct result of a mental disorder. In such a case, the cure of the disorder may be expected to dispose of the likelihood of any further offence, unless there is a relapse; but where his lawbreaking is not directly connected with his disordered mental condition, the cure of the mental disorder will have no effect on the commission of further offences. This fact reflects on the question people ask when an offender patient commits a further offence after being discharged from hospital—"Why was he let out before he was cured?". A person may be cured of his mental disorder but still disposed to commit crime.[2] But where it was established in the original court proceedings that a particular offender's violent crime was linked with his mental state it will obviously be the responsibility of those who have to decide on his release to satisfy themselves that his cure gives reasonable grounds for confidence that the propensity to commit a violent act has been adequately diminished.

4.5 In the majority of cases offenders convicted of violent offences are not again convicted of violence; any subsequent convictions tend to be for non-violent offences. On the other hand there is evidence that the more violent offences a person has committed the more chance there is that he will commit another.[3] Dangerousness depends in the majority of cases not only on the

[2] It is relevant to mention here a comparison which the Home Office Statistical Department made at our request, between 334 men discharged from mental hospitals in 1971 after being subject to a hospital order, 2,796 male prisoners sentenced to 18 months imprisonment or less and discharged in the same year, and 350 men dealt with non-custodially in the same year for standard list offences. A two-year follow-up showed the highest reconviction rate amongst the ex-prisoners (54 per cent) and the lowest amongst the non-custodial cohort (17 per cent) with the hospital order cases intermediate (32 per cent). But when only reconvictions for violent or for sexual offences were counted the rates for ex-prisoners and ex-hospital men were similar (6 per cent), and greater than that of the non-custodial men (2 per cent). The differences and similarities persisted when the samples were analysed by age and previous convictions; and the differences were statistically significant.

[3] Nigel Walker, William Hammond and David Steer analysed the convictions for violence of 264 males over 11 years as recorded in Glasgow's Criminal Record Office. They found that with each successive conviction for personal violence the probability of a further conviction for violence increased as follows:

Table: Percentages of those currently convicted of personal violence who were convicted of personal violence on a later occasion (the figures in brackets exclude convictions of men under 21):

1st such conviction	14% of 264 (12% of 195)
2nd ,, ,,	40% of 45 (35% of 31)
3rd ,, ,,	44% of 16 (40% of 10)
4th or subsequent such conviction	55% of 11 (67% of 9)

For details of the study see Walker, Hammond and Steer (1967) *Criminal Law Review*, pp. 465–472.

personality of the potentially dangerous offender but also on the circumstances in which he finds himself. The practice of referring to some individuals as "dangerous" without qualification creates the impression that the word refers to a more or less constantly exhibited disposition, like left-handedness or restlessness. It is true that there are people in whom anger, jealousy, fear or sexual desire is more easily aroused and whose reactions are more extreme than in most people, prompting them to do extremely harmful things. But these emotions are aroused and lead to harmful behaviour only in certain situations. A persistent housebreaker may go right through his criminal career without physically harming anyone; but if one day he is surprised, or cornered, he may have it in him to commit an offence of violence. For some people drugs, alcohol or the excitement of a crowd may be a precipitating factor. The situation and circumstances which are potentially dangerous can often be defined, and sometimes foreseen and avoided or prevented. The individual who spontaneously "looks for a fight" or feels a need to inflict pain or who searches for an unknown sexual victim is fortunately rare, although such people undoubtedly exist. Only this last category can justifiably be called "unconditionally dangerous".

4.6 Allowing that most offenders convicted of violent offences are not dangerous except in certain situations it must be added that this implies a heavy responsibility resting on those who advise the release of such patients; they have to take into account the prospect of their being exposed to situations likely to have a "trigger" effect. Some stimulative influences such as drink or a sexual relationship are so common in society that they are more likely than not to be encountered. Where those who have the responsibility decide on balance to release such offenders, they also have a responsibility to ensure that they are subject to reassessment and control appropriate to their needs, that is to say having regard to the particular situations in which they may find themselves, and their possible reactions to them.

4.7 The point is illustrated by the case of Iliffe[4] which has occurred since the Committee began its work and whose circumstances we have carefully considered. Iliffe was conditionally discharged because the assessments made of him gave no reason to believe that he would present any general risk to the public: we have found no evidence suggesting that this judgment was incorrect. It was appreciated however that if Iliffe were to re-marry there might be a specific risk to his wife, and it was recognised by the supervising social workers as well as by the hospital that if he indicated any such intention his prospective wife must be fully informed of his background. It was not foreseen that he would actually re-marry without the knowledge of his supervising officer. When this was discovered appropriate action was taken to inform Mrs Iliffe of the facts about her husband, but tragically to no avail. All this was stated by the Home Secretary in the House of Commons. Clearly, where specific risks are involved, the assessment of the likely effectiveness of subsequent control in the particular circumstances must be a major consideration when the decision whether or not to release is taken. In the end this is a matter of judgment, which may turn out to be mistaken.

---

[4] For details see footnote to paragraph 4.1.

4.8   Again it is sometimes argued that dangerousness is largely the product of the institutions society has created to deal with offenders who alarm it.[5]   To what extent this is true is virtually impossible to assess, and it is worth noting that even the proponents of this theory do not claim that it is true of all "dangerous offenders".   In any case it does not dispose of the problem posed by the person who has become dangerous: the problem remains whatever the explanation.

4.9   We were impressed by the general agreement amongst our witnesses that dangerousness was a necessary and valid concept, though opinions differed as to the proper extent of the term.   For example, Dr Peter Scott suggested that the criteria for recognising dangerousness should be:—

  (i) the irreversibility of the damage done;
  (ii) the quantity of the damage (including how long it has gone on); and
  (iii) the infectiousness of the behaviour (which may be connected with the general climate of opinion).

Dr Scott's criteria suggest an analogy with physical disease, which only becomes dangerous if its ravages are irreversible and severe, and if it is readily transmitted from person to person.   Society may develop safeguards against dangerous disease, by eradicating its causes, isolating its carriers, or acquiring general immunity to its effects.   Dr Scott has also stressed the importance of probable repetition of the conduct in question, since however hurtful, destructive or grave a man's behaviour, he is likely to be labelled as a dangerous man only if such behaviour is expected to continue.   The Consultant Forensic Psychiatrists defined dangerousness as covering "unwanted behaviour which is threatening or disturbing to the public and may require that the offender be placed in custody to protect the public"; what was tolerable would be for the public and the court to decide.   Dr McGrath defined as dangerous "those who would probably inflict physical harm on others"; this would exclude property offenders.

4.10   In our discussions we were not entirely satisfied with any of these definitions, and for our part have come to equate dangerousness with a propensity to cause serious physical injury or lasting psychological harm. Physical violence is, we think, what the public are most worried about, but the psychological damage which may be suffered by some victims of other crimes is not to be underrated.   The importance of being clear about the sense in which one is speaking of dangerousness is that the prospects of predicting future dangerousness and the choice of procedural safeguards will depend in part upon the nature of the danger to be guarded against.   Moreover, unless the limits of the dangerousness to be dealt with are clearly laid down any suggested safeguarding procedure may gradually be extended in the course of time to other categories of less dangerous offender for whom it was not intended.

(3) Difficulties in assessing dangerousness

4.11   In deciding what to do about dangerousness the impossibility of certain prediction is the central problem.   There has been a great deal of research

---

[5] See, for example, Professor T R Sarbin (1967) "The Dangerous Individual: an Outcome of Society Identity Transformations" *British Journal of Criminology*, 7, pages 285–295.

into the practicability of "predicting" future behaviour, and especially law-breaking behaviour, by the actuarial use of information about people's past behaviour, age, circumstances, psychological and social characteristics, as well as assessments of them by other people with relevant training or experience (such as psychiatrists or other professional staff). "Prediction" of this kind assigns individuals to "probability-groups" with differing rates of law-breaking (or whatever behaviour is in question). While some such groups have very high rates or very low rates it is never possible to predict of an individual that he will inevitably or never break the law in the future. Moreover, a review of the literature[6] strongly suggests that while actuarial prediction methods can identify high-risk and low-risk groups, they will always leave a residual majority in "middling-risk" groups, whose rates are too near "fifty-fifty" to be of much use. Secondly, very little systematic research has concerned itself with the actuarial prediction of dangerous behaviour (in our sense): most of it has been concerned with miscellaneous forms of law-breaking. On the other hand, the fact that we cannot quantify the probability of future dangerous behaviour with actuarial precision is often allowed to obscure the fact that we can point with some confidence to categories of people who are more likely than others of the same sex and age-group to act in this way. Some kinds of sexual offence seem to be very repetitive: fortunately most of them do little harm (an uncomplicated case of indecent exposure is the best-established example, although some exhibitionists commit more serious offences from time to time). Men with several convictions of violence are considerably more likely than their peers to be convicted of violence in the future. Again, it is sometimes argued that even if there are good grounds—clinical or actuarial—for assigning the individual to a high-risk group, he might be one of the minority in that group who in the event will not behave in accordance with probability. But this dilemma is inescapably involved in every decision which is based on probabilities. All that can be done is to weigh the unpleasantness of the consequences for the individual against the harm which he may do to others. If the harm is likely to be slight the decision should be in his favour: if great and highly probable—for example, if a sexual offence is accompanied by serious violence—the best we can do is to make sure that the precautions are as humane as possible.

4.12 Recognising the limitations of objective assessment, is it better to rely on a continuing process of treatment and subjective assessment in which checks and adjustments are constantly made in the light of the developing pattern of behaviour evinced by the individual concerned? Unfortunately, subjective judgment, based on however much experience, professional knowledge and available information, and exercised however conscientiously, is inescapably unreliable. Even the obvious and generally admired sense of responsibility with which the Parole Board have approached their task, and the wide spread of professional knowledge and skill they bring to bear, have not been able to prevent their judgment being belied in some—extremely rare—cases, by a parole licensee committing a serious offence while still on licence. In the Board's own words[7]: "Despite every care in the process of selection, the imposition of conditions, and the supervision of paroled offenders, serious

---

[6] See, for example, F H Simon in *Prediction methods in Criminology,* Home Office Research Studies, No 7 (HMSO, 1971).

[7] Report of the Parole Board for 1969, paragraph 99.

lapses must be expected to occur occasionally . . . Notwithstanding the greatest care and judgment, there can be no certainty in the prediction of human affairs."

4.13   The Parole Board are concerned only with offenders in the prison system. That their comments are of wider application is borne out by the fact that there have also been serious failures among persons discharged from hospitals.   But again such failures have been extremely rare.   Those who have the task of advising on the discharge of mentally disordered offenders know full well what a heavy responsibility they bear.   They also know that, however careful they are, their opinion of any case may turn out to be wrong.   If they have advised in favour of discharge, their mistake may lead to catastrophe and criticism, whereas if they have advised against release, they cannot be faulted; for normally this advice is likely to be accepted, and no one will ever know whether the assessment of the case was right or wrong, since a person who is not released is thereby prevented from demonstrating that if released he would have resettled safely in the community.   Although no doctor is likely to be unmindful of his responsibilities to his patient, neither can he evade the pressure on him to protect society.   The tendency (which many members of the public would applaud) will generally be to err on the side of caution, with the result that some people will continue to be detained who, if released, would not commit further violent offences.   In deciding whether society requires more protection, the question has to be faced: how many probably safe individuals should cautious policy continue to detain in hospital in the hope of preventing the release of one who is still potentially dangerous?

4.14   The consequences of excessive caution are often emphasised by references to the *Baxstrom* case, which occurred in New York State a few years ago. Baxstrom had been found insane while serving a criminal sentence and transferred to a State institution for insane criminals.   When his sentence expired in December 1961 he was retained in the institution under provisions of the Correction Law.   In February 1966 the Supreme Court decided that the law under which he was being detained was unconstitutional; it followed that the continued detention of all other mentally disordered offenders held under this law beyond the expiry of their sentences was unconstitutional as well.   They had therefore to be dealt with under normal civil procedures.   From March to August 1966, 969 patients were transferred under civil commitment from Correction Department hospitals to civil hospitals, 711 being moved in March and April.   The receiving hospitals it was said quickly found that the Baxstrom cases were indistinguishable from the generality of their patients.   Yet all these patients had previously been denied transfer by experienced psychiatrists from the Department of Mental Hygiene on the grounds that they were too disturbed or potentially dangerous.   By the end of February 1967, 147 had been discharged into the community and only seven had been found difficult enough to warrant a judicial commitment to special security.   Of those released there was, by the end of 1967, only one record of subsequent arrest, and that was for minor theft[8].

---

[8] Robert C Hunt and E David Wiley, "Operation Baxstrom after one year". *American Journal of Psychiatry*, 124 (1968), 134/8~ 974-976

4.15 It must be pointed out, however, that a one-year follow-up is hardly long enough for a thorough assessment of the consequences of the transfers and discharges. Research workers who followed up a 20 per cent sample of the Baxstrom men and all the Baxstrom women for four years found that 20 per cent of the men and 26 per cent of the women were recorded as having assaulted people. These percentages might well have been higher had the patients been transferred years earlier when they were younger, since there was the usual inverse relationship between age and violence. (The mean ages on transfer were 46 for men and 48 for women, and the median periods of pre-transfer detention were 13 years for men and 17 years for women.) In any case, 49 per cent of the men and 53 per cent of the women had either remained in or been returned to hospital. Ten per cent of the men and 13 per cent of the women had died by the end of the four-year period[9].

4.16 A balance must be achieved between the right of the public at large to reasonable protection and the right of mentally afflicted individuals in psychiatric hospitals or in prisons to be returned into the community when their detention is no longer justified. In the light of these general observations about the difficulties of prediction and the conflicting interests to be taken into account, we now consider separately the dangerous offenders in the hospital system and those in the penal system.

II. DANGEROUS OFFENDERS IN THE HOSPITAL SYSTEM

(1) Discharge

4.17 As we have explained elsewhere (paragraph 2.31) those mentally disordered offenders admitted to hospital under section 60 of the Mental Health Act who the courts consider present a risk to the public may be made subject to an order under section 65 which makes their discharge, transfer or eligibility for home leave subject to the approval of the Home Secretary. Section 66(2) of the Mental Health Act empowers the Home Secretary by warrant to discharge a restricted patient from hospital, either absolutely or subject to conditions; and section 66(3) enables him to recall to hospital any conditionally discharged patient during the continuance in force of the order (under section 66(1) restriction orders continue in force until the Home Secretary terminates them). Many witnesses have thought these provisions for conditional discharge, which allow the patient to be kept under supervision and to be brought back into hospital if necessary, the most valuable feature of the system of restriction orders. Certainly discharges into the community under these provisions have been largely successful. A study undertaken on behalf of the Aarvold Committee of restricted patients who were discharged in 1966 and 1967 indicated that of 180 patients conditionally discharged during this period 84 per cent were not subsequently convicted, and the convictions of a further 12 per cent were for property offences alone. Despite the fact that 43 per cent had originally been admitted to hospital after incidents involving homicidal assault, no offences of this nature were committed during the follow-up period[10]. The rarity of serious failures of the system tends to be obscured by the enormous publicity which any failure attracts.

---

[9] See A Halfon, M David and H Steadman "The Baxstrom Women: a four-year follow-up of behaviour patterns" in *Psychiatric Quarterly*, 1972 *45*, 1–10; and H Steadman and A Halfon, "The Baxstrom Patients: backgrounds and outcomes" in *Seminars in Psychiatry*, 1971, 376–85.

[10] Cmnd. 5191, paragraph 15 and Appendix B.

4.18   Other figures prepared for the Aarvold Committee indicate that the rate of re-conviction of male patients during the two years following conditional discharge was substantially lower than that of prisoners released after serving sentences of more than 18 months, even when allowance is made for the type of the original offence (including whether or not it was an offence of violence), age, and the shorter criminal records of the patients.   To what extent the comparatively successful way in which the generality of discharged section 65 patients in this country have settled down is due to cautious discharge policy, or to other factors, including the treatment and supervision given both before and after discharge, is uncertain.   The Aarvold Committee stressed how important it is for the doctor responsible for the patient's treatment to be able to avail himself of all possible information both within the hospital and outside it, throughout the course of treatment.   A number of witnesses have referred to the importance of continuing assessment, on the ground that dangerousness is not a constant feature of personality and may appear only sporadically.   We agree that the most essential safeguard is thorough assessment bringing into play the knowledge and expertise of all disciplines concerned in any way with these patients.   The need for a "team" approach was also stressed in the institutions on the Continent which some of our members visited.   In particular it is essential to bring to bear all the available information and expertise when discharge is being decided upon.   The responsible medical officer must retain his proper responsibility; he alone is in charge of the case. But he cannot adequately discharge this heavy responsibility if he is unaware of some of the available information, and this includes the expert opinions of any of his colleagues, of whatever disciplines, who have had an opportunity of observing the patient.

(2) Reference to an advisory board

4.19   The Aarvold Committeee recommended[11] that within three months after the admission to hospital of a restricted patient the Home Office should inquire of the responsible medical officer whether the patient is one who requires special care in assessment.   To assist the doctor in considering this question the criteria to be applied should be drawn up and made available to the consultants concerned: the criteria were expected to include a clearly unfavourable or an unpredictable psychiatric prognosis and an indication of risk of the patient harming other persons.   Neither the formal psychiatric diagnosis nor the legal description of a past offence would be an adequate criterion for the identification of these cases.   Once a patient has been classified as requiring special assessment the Committee recommended that the reason should be recorded and a note made in the Home Office to ensure that special attention is thereafter given to the case; and the classification should not be removed. These recommendations have been accepted by the Government and are now in operation with regard to special hospital cases.

4.20   In cases identified as needing special care in assessment the Aarvold Committee recommended[12] that on a proposal entailing substantial relaxation of control over the patient a second opinion should be obtained from an authoritative source which was independent of the hospital involved before the Home Secretary reached his decision.   The Committee also recommended[12]

---

[11] Cmnd. 5191, paragraphs 20–24.
[12] Cmnd. 5191, paragraphs 30–38.

that in all these cases the Home Secretary should be assisted in carrying out his responsibilities under section 65 of the Act by an advisory board, comprising a legal chairman, a forensic psychiatrist and a representative of the social work profession. These recommendations have also been adopted and put into effect.

4.21 We think that these arrangements will afford a valuable safeguard for the future, but we believe that they should be modified and extended. We appreciate why they were proposed to apply only to cases where psychiatric prognosis was clearly unfavourable or unpredictable and where there was an indication of a risk of the patient harming other persons, but other cases in the special hospitals may also involve risks. Furthermore, we have been made aware of difficulties experienced by the responsible medical officers in identifying cases within the three months originally prescribed, and even the extension of the period allowed to six months may not be adequate in all cases. Other objections to the system of selection have also been expressed; in particular we have had representations that the special classification is stigmatic and may impede the progress of the patient. We have rejected a proposal for a right of appeal against special classification because where the Home Secretary has been advised on expert consideration that special classification is necessary, which merely indicates the need for particularly careful consideration of the case in the future, it would not be reasonable for him, on the appeal of the offender, to decide that special care need not be exercised when his discharge is eventually in question. We have also rejected provision for "de-classification", which in our opinion would lead to additional problems.

4.22 Having regard to all these considerations and the stress we have put, elsewhere, on the desirability of bringing to bear a wide range of expertise in making decisions about cases where risks may possibly be involved, we propose that the Aarvold arrangements should be modified and extended in the following ways. First, all restricted patients in the special hospitals should come within the purview of an appropriately constituted advisory body. This would eliminate the problems faced by the responsible medical officers in the special hospitals in deciding which cases need to be referred to the board, and it would also remove any feelings among the patients of unfair discrimination. The board would be supportive to the responsible medical officer and enable him to place more emphasis on his professional relationship to his patient, being less concerned with the heavy personal responsibility which the custodial function at present imposes upon him, with presumable benefit to the patient's attitude towards his treatment. Meanwhile, the Home Secretary would have independent advice in making decisions in these difficult cases. Secondly, as regards restricted patients in local psychiatric hospitals and the regional secure units, the advisory board should be available to the Home Secretary and to the responsible medical officer in any such case when they have to make decisions about the discharge, supervision or recall of a restricted patient and would find an independent opinion helpful.

4.23 We do not think that we should be dogmatic about the composition of this body; it would be better for this to be considered by the Government, after the normal processes of consultation. The volume of work entailed would probably put the task beyond the capabilities of the Advisory Board as at present constituted, and obviously a cadre of supporting staff would be required. It might be possible to expand the existing Advisory Board arrangements; this seems to us to be the most promising approach. We have considered whether the work might be added to the burdens of the Parole Board, but it will be apparent that the role of the body we are proposing would be in principle the opposite of the Parole Board's existing role, for they would in essence be required to consider whether to refuse a doctor's recommendation that a patient should be released, the court having specifically chosen a medical disposal, whereas at present the Parole Board decides whether to relieve prisoners of penal sanctions imposed by the courts. We think it important that the advisory board for restricted cases should not be associated with the penal system. It would in our opinion be extremely valuable for the composition of the board to include a senior doctor with experience of special hospital work. The board should invariably discuss each case with the responsible medical officer before deciding what advice to tender to the Home Secretary.

4.24 The new arrangements should include reference to the advisory body of proposals to transfer restricted special hospital patients to local psychiatric hospitals (or secure units), to grant patients so transferred leave or to discharge them into the community. The board should continue to be concerned with former special hospital restricted patients throughout their period of supervision and should be involved in the recall of any such patient. We regard this as essential, as it is not satisfactory, in our view, for the recall of such cases to be decided administratively in the Home Office, in consultation with the responsible medical officer, without recourse to independent professional advice. If the recall arrangements were modelled on those for paroled prisoners immediate recall could be effected administratively in case of emergency. The advisory board should also advise the Home Secretary on proposals for the termination of supervision in special hospital cases.

4.25 It is not our intention that under the arrangements we propose discharge in the generality of restricted cases should be made more difficult by the adoption of more selective policies. It must be acknowledged, nevertheless, that the additional procedures would inevitably import some administrative complications and delays into the handling of the many restricted cases in the special hospitals which are not at present within the scope of the Aarvold arrangements, and those in the local hospitals which would be subject to the new arrangements. Discharges from the special hospitals would be to some extent slowed down, particularly if local hospitals became more reluctant to accept cases from the special hospitals on transfer because of the involvement of the board, and this would increase the pressures on their accommodation. We hope that such adverse effects will be minimised, but a major consideration in our proposing the extension and modification of the Aarvold arrangements in this way is to improve the protection given to the public, and in our opinion the unavoidable consequences of these additional safeguards must be accepted.

(3) Transfer of special hospital cases to local hospitals

4.26 The Aarvold Committee recommended[13] that a patient leaving a special hospital should not normally be discharged direct to his family or to casual lodgings but wherever practicable should go first to a local psychiatric hospital

---

[13] Cmnd. 5191, paragraph 31.

or a hostel for an initial period of rehabilitation. This recommendation was supported in evidence to us by the Chief and Principal Nursing Officers. The Aarvold Committee noted, however, that "in some parts of the country hostel accommodation is at a premium and that local psychiatric hospitals are sometimes unable to accept patients on transfer from special hospitals". We discuss the question of hostels in Chapter 8. Meanwhile we consider here the evidence given to us which has confirmed the increasing difficulties in recent years of securing transfers from the special hospitals to local psychiatric hospitals. It appears that the special hospitals often have to bring pressure to bear by insisting on a "one for one" exchange when a local psychiatric hospital seeks to transfer a dangerous patient to a special hospital.

4.27 We referred in our Interim Report to the development in local psychiatric hospitals of treatment in "open" conditions, which militates against require-ments of secure custody. One hospital consultant has referred to the unattractive prospect of accepting responsibility for special hospital patients in these circumstances, knowing that one's hospital is unable to exercise sufficient control to be sure of preventing an occurrence which might cause a public outcry. The National Association of Chief and Principal Nursing Officers have told us that the special hospitals are being asked to take more patients but local psychiatric hospitals are increasingly unwilling to receive them back after treatment. They attributed this reluctance to the lack of secure facilities, lack of staff training to cope with troublesome patients under conditions of tension, and objections to offenders as such. The Association said that the situation varied among the different regions, different hospitals and individual consultants. Among other difficulties, mention has been made of the distance between the special hospitals and the local hospital to which the patient should be transferred, which imposes considerable difficulties in effecting adequate consultation on both sides.

4.28 The evidence of the British Society for the Study of Mental Sub-normality has suggested to us that another reason for the reluctance of local hospitals to accept cases from the special hospitals may be the difficulty of getting them re-admitted to the special hospitals if the patient fails to settle down satisfactorily, or fails to respond to treatment and deteriorates. The Society have suggested that transfer to the local hospital should be for a trial period in the first instance, with ready re-admission to the special hospital, if needed. This seems to us a very helpful suggestion, and greatly to the advantage of the special hospitals in overcoming some of the difficulties of obtaining acceptance of their patients by local hospitals. Our members who visited Holland were told at the Selection Institute in Utrecht, which places offenders after they have been "placed at the disposal of the Government" by a court, that the assurance of immediate, unquestioning re-admission of patients, at any hour of the day or night, was an essential feature of the arrangements for transferring them to other hospitals or to community care and did much to overcome resistance to accepting potentially troublesome cases. We are convinced that the adoption of a similar policy here would be no less successful in facilitating transfers from the special hospitals to local hospitals.

4.29 The regional secure hospital units we have proposed in our Interim Report, equipped with adequate rehabilitation services and in close liaison with outside agencies, will have an important role in the future in accepting patients from the special hospitals. However we do not suggest that all patients in the special hospitals should be transferred to the secure units as a stage towards eventual discharge: on the contrary, this would be both undesirable and unnecessary. By no means all such patients when they are fit to leave the special hospitals will require the degree of security provided by the units; many will be suitable for transfer to local psychiatric hospitals or to hostels, and we hope, as we said in our Interim Report,[14] that the psychiatric hospitals and psychiatric units in general hospitals will play their part in the continued treatment and rehabilitation of offender-patients not requiring secure conditions. What we have just said about ready re-admission of patients transferred from the special hospitals applies equally to patients transferred from the special hospitals to the secure units.

(4) Supervision

4.30   Even if these new precautions are introduced the fact must be faced that so long as decisions to discharge patients have to be entrusted to human judgment there can be no absolute guarantee against assessments made with the utmost diligence turning out to have been wrong. A patient who is a model of conformity and good behaviour and exhibits no symptoms of mental disorder in the hospital over a period of years may behave very differently after release, given the greater opportunities and the greater stresses which freedom in the community must bring. Supervision cannot provide, and is not intended to provide, physical surveillance hour by hour and day by day, and it is evident that control over the personal relationships of a person who is subject to supervision entails particular difficulty. The Aarvold Committee emphasised the importance of continuing assessment of restricted patients following their discharge and made the point that each member of the team who takes part in this process should be fully informed about the patient's background and current situation.[15] We share their concern that all those involved in the patient's rehabilitation—the responsible medical officer at the hospital, the local consultant concerned with continuing medical care (if other than the responsible medical officer), the patient's general practitioner, the hospital social worker, the supervising officer and the Home Office—should work closely with one another so that progress or changes in the patient's social circumstances and mental condition may be made known and their implications fully appreciated. This requires the full and free exchange of information between all those who will have the responsibility for the continuing aftercare of a patient who may be a danger to others. We discuss in paragraphs 20.4–20.12 below the difficult question of the confidentiality of personal information which this poses.

4.31   The supervising officer is sometimes in a position to recognise that the discharged patient may be moving into a similar situation to that which originally precipitated an offence of violence; or to perceive other signs indicating the likelihood of a repetition of dangerous behaviour. Where this is so he can take steps to warn the patient and if necessary arrange for him to be recalled to hospital, or, in emergency, to a "place of safety" for up to 72 hours under the new power we propose in paragraph 14.31 if a hospital place cannot immediately be obtained. But the exercise of the power to recommend recall raises

---

[14] Cmnd. 5698, paragraph 19.
[15] Cmnd. 5191, paragraph 43.

formidable difficulties of judgment. The main purpose of supervision by the probation and after-care service or local authority social services departments after discharge is to assist the patient to settle down in the community and to this end to help him to cope with his problems by providing him with professional guidance, support and control while he does so. If he is recalled to the institution as soon as a difficulty or risk arises, not only is the patient not helped to deal with the situation but he suffers a positive set-back and a fresh interruption of his life, while his attitude towards his supervising officer is likely to be seriously undermined. For these reasons the supervising officer must have discretion as to the degree of possible risk which may be acceptable. To refuse him this discretion in order to eliminate such risks would in effect make the task of supervision impossible. However, where the supervising officer is of opinion that the behaviour of the patient gives sufficient cause for anxiety to justify recall, the co-operation of the hospital is necessary before recall to the hospital can be effected. While the supervising officer may be mistaken and the hospital may not be convinced of the need for recall the consequences of failure to recall in a deteriorating situation may be serious, and we have no doubt that in general the presumption on the part of the hospital should be in favour of supporting the supervising officer by readily agreeing to accept a patient on recall, even if only for a brief period of observation.

4.32 The supervising officer is also in a position to advise the Home Office when the behaviour and circumstances of the discharged patient have been satisfactory for sufficient time to justify consideration of ending the supervision, which the Home Secretary is empowered to do by section 66(2) of the Mental Health Act 1959. We understand that in practice the formal supervision of a conditionally discharged patient is normally maintained for five years if he has a history of serious violence or sexual offences and for two years where he has no such history. In general the division falls between those who have spent some time in a special hospital and those who have not. Supervision is removed when the appropriate number of years have passed only if the patient's progress has been steady and if his mental condition and behaviour have given no cause for concern. It is removed *before* the appropriate time only if progress has been exceptionally good or if special circumstances make it awkward or inappropriate for formal supervision to continue. We agree that these standards are reasonable as general guides, but we suggest that where there is a medical expectation of recurrence of the mental disorder supervision should be extended for more than the usual period related to the gravity of the offence. We understand that the Home Office intend to apply similar considerations and the "five-year norm" to the removal of supervision in cases classified under the Aarvold procedures as needing special care in assessment (see paragraphs 4.19–4.20), but there has not yet been time for any such cases to reach this stage. If our recommendations for the modification of the Aarvold arrangements are implemented, special classification will be abolished; otherwise we would have proposed that in cases classified as requiring special care in assessment the question of the removal of supervision should be referred to the Aarvold advisory board for a recommendation. Under our proposals the removal of supervision will in any event be a matter for the advisory board in relation to any case coming within its continuing purview.

4.33 The Aarvold Committee said that "the complete elimination of any risk to the public could only be achieved by continuing to detain these patients perhaps indefinitely, long after many of them had recovered from their mental disorder, and for periods in excess of any term of imprisonment they might have served as sentence for their offences. We are sure that in our society this would be seen as an inhumane avoidance of the responsibility for making a proper judgment in each case".[16] We agree, and while we are confident that the safeguards which are now in operation, when modified and supplemented in accordance with our recommendations, will offer the public all the protection that could reasonably be expected or devised, we repeat what we said in the introduction to this chapter: in the end it has to be accepted that society cannot be made entirely safe.

III. DANGEROUS OFFENDERS IN THE PRISON SYSTEM

(1) When release is inevitable

4.34 The Home Office and Department of Health and Social Security, in their joint memorandum of evidence to us, drew our attention to the problem of the legal obligation to release, at the end of determinate prison sentences, a small number of men who are probably dangerous but who are not acceptable for treatment in hospital. We were informed that although the Prison Medical Service try to ensure that follow-up care and supervision are provided in such cases, if voluntarily accepted, nevertheless this is not a safeguard on which much reliance could be placed. Some of these prisoners have spent time in Broadmoor but have been returned to prison as not treatable. All have either been refused parole or have exercised their option not to be considered, and their potential dangerousness generally precludes them from the normal "socialising" prison release schemes, such as home leave and the Pre-release Employment Scheme. Therefore, paradoxically, these, of all people, are discharged direct from prison to the community without acclimatisation beforehand or supervision and control afterwards. Where community support is arranged for them the majority of these men do not want to have anything to do with it. The Prison Medical Officers quickly lose sight of them, until such time as they are reconvicted for a subsequent offence.

(2) Possible solutions

4.35 Even allowing for the fact that the estimates of future dangerousness made by Prison Medical Officers or other prison staff in particular cases would be found, on a systematic follow-up, like all other such predictions, not to be invariably justified by subsequent events (and it is disappointing to find that no systematic follow-up has been done), nevertheless there is obviously, here, a serious defect in society's defences which ought to be made good, so far as may be possible. Not all those who are thought to be dangerous will show any sign of mental disorder, but we have felt justified in considering what steps may be taken to deal with the problem posed by those whose dangerousness does arise from mental disorder of some kind. In particular we recognise that our proposals in Chapter 5 for the exclusion of dangerous anti-social psychopaths from disposal under a hospital order with its element of indeterminacy adds to the need to provide greater safeguard than the fixed sentence alone.

---

[16] Cmnd. 5191, paragraph 57.

4.36 Among the possible approaches to this problem, the essential choices are as follows:—

(a) arrangements might be made for identifying dangerous mentally disordered prisoners in prison and for determining, towards the end of their sentence, the necessity for their further detention, under new statutory provisions, in the interests of public safety; or

(b) provision might be made to enable the court to impose an indeterminate sentence at the outset, where it is likely that the offender will pose a continuing threat to society; or

(c) there could be various arrangements based on combining determinate sentences with licensing after normal release at the end of the sentence, taking into account remission (as distinct from parole licensing before the end of the sentence).

All these approaches, which we examine below, would require legislation. Our recommendation, which we discuss further in paragraphs 4.39–4.45, is based on the second of them.

4.37 Although a number of witnesses, including several Prison Medical Officers, favoured the first solution, we do not think that it would be acceptable to set up what would in effect be a procedure for re-sentencing, whether the review was carried out by a panel of doctors, a body on the lines of the Parole Board, or one akin to the Aarvold advisory board, as witnesses have variously proposed. Re-sentencing could properly be carried out only by the courts, but the arguments which have been advanced by the Criminal Law Revision Committee[17] against allowing the judiciary to exercise such a power seem to us to be decisive; such a procedure would, as the Committee remarked, amount in effect to disguising life sentences as determinate sentences.

4.38 Nor do we favour the third possible solution mentioned in paragraph 4.36 which would combine determinacy of sentencing with licensing after normal release at the end of the sentence, allowing for remission. In the type of case we are discussing a short licence period would be ineffective. Licences would have to be for an indefinite period, if necessary for life, with the same strict enforcement of the conditions as is applied with parole licences, and ready recall to prison for any infringement. But if the licensee is liable to be recalled to prison at any time, and thereupon to be detained in prison for so long as the authorities think necessary before being again released on a life licence, the offender is virtually in the same position as if he had been sentenced to life imprisonment in the first place; the "determinate sentence" would be of a wholly artificial nature since it would carry no implication that detention would be limited, except initially, to the determinate period. The proposal has been rejected by the Criminal Law Revision Committee on the ground that it would be unacceptable for a person who had been released after serving a determinate sentence imposed by a court to be recalled to prison by administrative action and detained there perhaps for the rest of his life.[18] The Committee pointed out that there is a significant difference between recall as applied in the case of a life sentence prisoner, whose release on licence is a benefit not guaranteed by his sentence, and recall of a prisoner who has already served the determinate sentence imposed at his trial. We agree with their conclusion.

[17] Cmnd. 5184, paragraph 21.
[18] Cmnd. 5184, paragraph 21.

(3) Our solution: the reviewable sentence

4.39 We are sure that any special provisions to protect society against the premature release of dangerous mentally disordered individuals must be applied at the time of sentencing and by the sentencing court. One witness pointed out that prisoners serving life sentences can be released at the optimum time, can thereafter be under compulsory and competent supervision and can be easily recalled if necessary; but for a number of reasons we do not think that the existing form of life sentence would be wholly satisfactory in relation to potentially dangerous offenders who are mentally disordered. A special sentence is occasionally called for in cases where a life sentence either cannot or would not in practice be imposed; for example attempts at certain offences, which if carried out successfully would qualify for a life sentence.[19] Again, the aim of life sentences is ambiguous: they are sometimes imposed because they are the heaviest punishment permissible to the law, sometimes compassionately, to allow for flexibility with regard to release, which in suitable cases may be granted earlier than would be possible under the determinate sentence which would otherwise have been imposed for the offence. Consideration of the release of life sentence prisoners involves not merely the question whether their release would be safe but also the question whether they have been detained as long as the circumstances of the offence require for the purposes of punishment, whether retributive or deterrent. For this reason the procedure prescribed by statute includes consultation with the Lord Chief Justice and, where possible, with the trial judge. In our opinion there is a need for an indeterminate sentence which will not entail these considerations, release being dependent entirely on the issue of dangerousness, and not necessitating the same consultations with the judiciary. The new sentence would not be punitive in intent but designed to enable the offender to be detained only until his progress under treatment, and other factors referred to below, allow him to be released under supervision without serious risk to the public. Finally, the new sentence would be subject to mandatory review, whereas a life sentence is not, and may in practice be reviewed at rather long intervals. Unless initial examination of the case papers shows that there are special considerations, the first review takes place after seven years, and thereafter reviews are arranged at whatever intervals are deemed to be appropriate in the circumstances. These arrangements are operated by the Home Office and the Parole Board in joint consultation.[20]

4.40 The new kind of sentence which we are proposing is intended to avoid as many as possible of the disadvantages of indeterminacy as well as those of the determinate sentence. It is meant for offenders who:

    (a) must be regarded as dangerous, in the sense we have discussed; but,

    (b) while presenting a history of mental disorder, cannot be compulsorily admitted, whether under civil or criminal procedure, to a mental hospital; and

    (c) for the reason given in the previous paragraph should not receive a life sentence.

---

[19] An example is rape which is punishable with life imprisonment, while the maximum sentence for attempted rape is seven years' imprisonment.

[20] Report of the Parole Board for 1973, paragraphs 22-23.

Its essential feature is that it should be subject to obligatory review at regular intervals; and we have therefore called it "the reviewable sentence". We propose that the review should be carried out every two years. It having been recognised that the offender is mentally disordered, the review will enable account to be taken of factors such as his susceptibility to treatment, changes in the circumstances which precipitated the offence and an increased maturity with the simple passage of time, which may all contribute to an improvement in the offender's mental condition justifying his release. Its other important feature is that when a review results in the release of the offender he should be under compulsory supervision, again subject to a regular review.

4.41   It should in no circumstances be mandatory on the court to impose the sentence, and as it is likely to be thought a graver deprivation of liberty than a determinate sentence it is obviously necessary to restrict with some care the range of cases in which it can be used.   In the first place, it should be restricted to persons convicted of offences which either have caused or might well have caused grave harm to others.   Many, but by no means all, such offences already carry the possibility, though not the probability, of a life sentence; and where this is so it is clearly not an unacceptable extension of the sentencing powers of the judiciary to introduce a form of sentence which entails more safeguards for the offender against unduly prolonged detention than does the life sentence.   We do not, however, recommend that it should be available for every kind of offence which at present carries a maximum of "life"; it seems inappropriate, for example, to apply it to illegal abortion.   We have therefore drawn up in Schedule A (see Appendix 4) a list of those "life"-carrying offences which in our view should qualify for such a sentence, provided of course that our other stringent requirements are satisfied (see next paragraph).   There remains the problem of the offence which is not life-carrying but has, or might well have, caused grave harm to another person.   Our list of these will be found in Schedule B in Appendix 4.   We have considered whether a conviction of such an offence should, if our other requirements are satisfied, qualify for a reviewable sentence; and indeed it is arguable that this would be consistent with our aim.   On the other hand, it would represent an important extension of the sentencing powers of the judiciary for a range of offences which at present carry only determinate sentences.   We therefore propose that an offence of this sort—ie a Schedule B offence—should qualify for a reviewable sentence only if the offender has previously been convicted of a life-carrying offence for which he could, under our proposals, have been given a reviewable sentence.   It is consistent with our aim that not only the scheduled offences themselves but also attempts, and incitements to commit them, and threats to commit them where these are made an offence by statute, should attract a reviewable sentence.

4.42   The experience of preventive detention and extended sentences suggests that the court would tend to exercise its discretion in favour of the defendant by awarding determinate sentences in most cases, and certainly we do not intend the reviewable sentence to be used often.   It should not, in any case, be imposed unless the following further conditions are met:

 (a)   the offender is old enough to be outside the jurisdiction of a juvenile court (ie aged 17 or older);

 (b)   the offender has been convicted on indictment or committed to a Crown Court for sentence;

(c) the court is satisfied, on the evidence of two psychiatrists one of whom must report orally, that the offender shows or has shown evidence of mental disorder but that he cannot be satisfactorily dealt with under the Mental Health Act 1959, whether because his disorder is not sufficiently severe or because no suitable hospital will receive him or for other reasons, for example, that he is a psychopath with dangerous anti-social tendencies;

(d) the court has considered a social inquiry report on the offender;

(e) the court is satisfied, on its information about his previous convictions, or findings of guilt, the evidence of psychiatrists, the social inquiry report, and the police antecedents report, that there is a substantial probability of his committing a further offence involving grave harm to another person;

(f) the defence have had prior notice that the defendant appears eligible for such a sentence (so that, for example, his counsel can call psychiatrists to say that he can be satisfactorily treated in hospital, or adduce evidence that the situation leading to the offence is most unlikely to recur).

4.43 We do not think it necessary or desirable for the court to lay down or recommend a minimum period for which the offender must be detained in custody, so as to ensure that the period of detention is appropriate to the gravity of the act. As we have said above the new sentence will not be punitive in intent. If the offender is simultaneously (or subsequently, while at large) convicted of another offence for which the reviewable sentence is not appropriate it should be open to the court to impose a determinate sentence for the second offence to run concurrently, but not consecutively, with the reviewable sentence.

4.44 If in the course of the sentence it is decided that the offender can be satisfactorily dealt with in a psychiatric hospital the Home Secretary should have the power (which he now has in respect of all other sentenced prisoners) to authorise the prisoner's transfer from prison to hospital under section 72 of the Mental Health Act 1959. We would expect the Home Secretary to exercise his power under section 74 of the Act to place a restriction on the prisoner's discharge from hospital in every such case.

4.45 The mandatory two-yearly review of the continued need for detention should be carried out by the Parole Board, which already reviews the case for the release on licence of other offenders who have committed serious offences. The Board would no doubt obtain psychiatric reports on the prisoner, as is their normal practice in all appropriate cases, and would make recommendations to the Home Secretary. As with their recommendations in the case of determinate sentences, it should not be within the Home Secretary's power to release the prisoner without a favourable recommendation from the Board, but given a favourable recommendation he should nevertheless have discretion to decide against release. Prisoners released from reviewable sentences should be on licence and subject to recall for the same reasons as other licensed prisoners. As with life sentences, the duration of the licence should be unlimited, but its conditions should be reviewed every two years with a view to the possibility of their eventual removal.

DANGEROUS MENTALLY DISORDERED OFFENDERS

SUMMARY OF CONCLUSIONS

I. GENERAL MATTERS

1. The idea of dangerousness is open to a number of misconceptions. The commission of an offence by a mentally disordered person does not presuppose any connection between the offence and the disorder. Dangerousness is not a constant disposition. There are a very few "unconditionally dangerous" people who spontaneously look for trouble or search for victims, but dangerousness is generally a potential reaction which may be triggered by particular situations. In any case where it is probable that the offender-patient will encounter on return to the community situations likely to produce in him a dangerous reaction, there is a particular responsibility on those who have to decide whether to discharge the patient in relation both to the discharge decision itself and to subsequent reassessment and control. (Paragraphs 4.4–4.8.)

2. Many different definitions of dangerousness have been formulated. For the purpose of our discussion we equate it with a propensity to cause serious physical injury or lasting psychological harm. (Paragraph 4.9–4.10.)

3. In deciding what to do about dangerousness, the impossibility of certain prediction of future human behaviour is the central problem. Actuarial methods can go some way to indicate the probability of future dangerous behaviour in certain categories of people but for individuals within the defined categories the risks cannot be quantified with precision. Nor can a continuous process of treatment and subjective assessment forecast the individual's future performance with any assurance of accuracy. (Paragraphs 4.11–4.12.)

4. Doctors and others who have responsibility for violent offenders are likely to err on the side of caution in deciding on their discharge and there can be little doubt that, as a result, some people continue to be detained who, if released, would not commit further violent offences. A balance has to be struck between the need to protect society and the right of the individual to return to the community when his detention is no longer strictly justified. (Paragraphs 4.13–4.16.)

II. DANGEROUS OFFENDERS IN THE HOSPITAL SYSTEM

5. The discharge procedures for section 65 patients have been largely successful. It is essential that the responsible medical officer's decision as to the patient's suitability for discharge should be based on continuing inter-disciplinary assessment of the patient. (Paragraphs 4.17–4.18.)

6. To improve the protection given to the public we propose that the procedures instituted in 1973 for the special assessment of certain section 65 patients should be modified and extended to cover all restricted patients in the special hospitals. The advisory body should not only be involved in discharge and transfer decisions in these cases but should continue to be concerned with former special hospital restricted patients subsequently as regards the grant of leave and their eventual discharge from local hospitals or secure

units and throughout their period of supervision, including the question of recall, if it arises. It should also be open to the Home Office or the responsible medical officer to consult the advisory board in any case where an independent opinion would be helpful in making a decision about a restricted patient who has not been transferred from a special hospital. (Paragraphs 4.19–4.25.)

7. These proposals for extending the work of the advisory board will probably require its reconstitution. It will be for the Government to consider the composition of the new board, after the normal processes of consultation, but we think it would be valuable to include a senior doctor with experience of special hospital work. Supporting staff will be required. The board should discuss each case with the responsible medical officer before deciding what advice to tender to the Home Secretary. (Paragraph 4.23.)

8. The Aarvold Committee recommended that on discharge from special hospitals patients should, wherever practicable, go to a local psychiatric hospital or a hostel as a first stage in rehabilitation. As local hospitals are sometimes reluctant to take patients from the special hospitals, we recommend that these transfers should be for a trial period in the first instance with ready re-admission to the special hospitals if needed. The proposed regional secure units will have an important role to play in taking some patients from the special hospitals and special hospitals should readily re-admit patients transferred to the secure units should the need arise. We deal with the question of discharging patients to hostels in Chapter 8. (Paragraphs 4.26–4.29.)

9. Co-operation, including free exchange of information, among all those involved with the patient after discharge is necessary to ensure his successful rehabilitation. (Paragraph 4.30.)

10. With regard to the recall to hospital of a discharged restricted patient the supervising officer must have discretion as to the degree of possible risk to the public that may be acceptable. Where he thinks that recall is necessary the presumption on the part of the hospital should generally be in favour of accepting the patient, even if only for a brief period of observation. (Paragraph 4.31.)

11. The standards adopted by the Home Office as general guides for deciding when supervision should be withdrawn are reasonable, but where there is a medical expectation of recurrence of the mental disorder supervision should be extended for more than the usual period related to the gravity of the offence. If our proposals for the modification and extension of the Aarvold arrangements are implemented, the removal of supervision will be a matter for the advisory board to advise upon in those cases which come within their continuing purview; otherwise, the existing board's advice should be sought in cases classified as requiring special care in assessment. (Paragraph 4.32.)

12. We are confident that with the modifications and extensions we propose the existing safeguards in relation to discharge and supervision will offer the public all the protection that could reasonably be expected or devised. In the end it has to be accepted that society cannot be made entirely safe. (Paragraph 4.33.)

III. DANGEROUS OFFENDERS IN THE PRISON SYSTEM

13.   There is a problem of a small number of men serving determinate sentences of imprisonment who have to be released when their sentence expires although they are thought to be dangerous.   (Paragraph 4.34.)

14.   Of the possible solutions, we have rejected proposals which would involve determining, towards the end of the sentence, that the prisoner should be further detained in the interests of public safety.   We have also rejected combining determinate sentences with a system of licensing after the end of the sentence.   (Paragraphs 4.35–4.38.)

15.   We think it essential that any special provisions be applied at the time of sentencing and by the sentencing court.   We propose that a new form of indeterminate sentence should be introduced for offenders who are dangerous, who present a history of mental disorder which cannot be dealt with under the Mental Health Act, and for whom the life sentence is not appropriate.   It should be subject to statutory review at regular (two-yearly) intervals, release being dependent entirely on the issue of dangerousness.   On release the offender should be under compulsory supervision, again subject to statutory review.   (Paragraphs 4.39–4.40.)

16.   Imposition of the sentence should be restricted to conviction of those offences which caused or might have caused grave harm to others and are either "life"-carrying sentences as drawn up in Schedule "A", or non "life"-carrying sentences as drawn up in Schedule "B" provided, in the latter case, that there has already been a conviction of a Schedule "A" offence.   Threats (where these are made an offence by statute), together with attempts and incitement to commit these offences, are included.   We have set out strict conditions to be met before the reviewable sentence can be imposed. (Paragraphs 4.41–4.42.)

17.   If the offender is simultaneously (or subsequently, while at large) convicted of another offence for which the reviewable sentence is not appropriate, it should be open to the court to impose a determinate sentence for this other offence to run concurrently with the reviewable sentence.   (Paragraph 4.43.)

18.   The Home Secretary should have the power to authorise the transfer of a prisoner serving a reviewable sentence from prison to hospital under section 72 of the Mental Health Act.   In every such case a restriction under section 74 of the Act should be placed on the discharge from hospital of the prisoner. (Paragraph 4.44.)

19.   The two-yearly review should be carried out by the Parole Board who, as in other cases, should make recommendations to the Home Secretary.   The Home Secretary's powers to accept or reject the Board's recommendations should be the same as in relation to determinate sentences.   Release should be on licence of unlimited duration, but the conditions should be subject to a two-yearly review, with the possibility of their eventual removal. (Paragraph 4.45.)

CHAPTER 5

PSYCHOPATHS

I. THE NATURE AND DEFINITION OF "PSYCHOPATHIC DISORDER"

5.1 We were made aware at the outset of our inquiry that one of the most perplexing questions we were to be faced with would be "what to do about the psychopath". In the evidence we have received, it has indeed proved that many of the difficulties arising in the present arrangements are related to people so diagnosed. The problems associated with psychopathic disorder have for long been recognised and discussed, all over the world, and methods of treatment have been the subject of experiment and research. The subject was well explored in Parliament in the debates on the Mental Health Bill. Yet we soon found that while the solutions adopted in the Act have not proved entirely satisfactory there is no clear trend of expert opinion about what the preferable solutions may be, nor even any general agreement about the nature of the disorder.

(1) Historical developments

5.2 Since its introduction more than 90 years ago the term "psychopathic disorder"[1] has been subject to a variety of different practical usages: it has been taken to cover either a narrow or a broad group of mental disorders, and to indicate differences either of causation or of clinical manifestation from other mental disorders. In consequence there is now a multiplicity of opinions as to the aetiology, symptoms and treatment of "psychopathy", which is only to be understood by reference to the particular sense in which the term is being employed by the psychiatrist in question. It is relevant therefore to preface our detailed proposals on the treatment of psychopaths with a brief account of the origin and development of the concept of psychopathic disorder.

5.3 From the time of Hippocrates and Plato a distinction has been recognised between Divine Madness and Natural Madness, or in modern terms between mental disorder due to psychological causes and that due to medical disease. Ever since there has been controversy as to which is which. Since the seventeenth century the notion that there is a single kind of disorder at the root of all ailments, whether it be demoniacal possession, sin, humoral (chemical) pathology or "tension in tissues" has lost adherents. It was then that began the search for specific physical causes associated with specific clinical entities, which for psychiatry reached its zenith at the beginning of the present century, when medical science acquired the techniques to demonstrate the pathology in the brain associated with the organic psychoses. During the previous century, side by side with the effort to classify mental disorders according to a supposed physical pathology went the attempt to do so on the basis of the old "faculty psychology", ie by considering which psychological functions (emotion, intellect or volition) were defective or deviant.[2]

---

[1] For the reasons given elsewhere in this chapter we have concluded that the terms "psychopathic disorder" and "psychopath" are unsatisfactory from both the medical and legal point of view, but it has not been easy to think of short and more appropriate alternatives. We have therefore continued to use the terms as convenient "umbrella" descriptions covering a range of conditions and sufferers from them.

[2] Meninger, K, *The Vital Balance*, Appendix, pp 419–489. (New York, Viking Press, 1966.)

5.4 It is probable that philosophers and physicians had recognised the group of so-called "psychopathic disorders" as early as the seventeenth century.[3] Certainly 150 years ago French and German psychiatrists had done so. In 1801 Phillippe Pinel described "manie sans délire", of which the specific features were on the one hand absence of any appreciable alteration in the intellectual functions, perception, judgment, imagination, memory, but on the other hand pronounced disorder of the affective (emotional) functions and blind impulse to acts of violence, even murderous fury. In 1818 in Germany "moral diseases of the mind" were described, including "moral dullness", "congenital brutality" and "moral imbecility".[4] In England the notion of a defect or disease of the moral faculty (ie the emotional faculty) was popularised by J C Prichard (1835) who saw it as a "morbid perversion of the natural feelings, affections, inclinations, temper, habits, moral dispositions and natural impulses, without any remarkable disorder or defect of the intellect or knowing or reasoning faculties and particularly without any insane illusion or hallucination".[5]

5.5 Throughout this period when a defect or disease in the hypothetical moral faculty was largely accepted, European psychiatry came under the influence of French writers who believed that these disorders were the result of hereditary degeneration. It was alleged that the degenerative process (a physical disorder) showed increasing severity in successive generations, leading finally to the disappearance of affected individuals and their families. It was claimed that in its severe form the degeneration led to subnormality of intelligence, in its less severe form to moral defects, and that physical and psychological stigmata could be identified in both. Iombroso in Italy, for example, described the "born delinquent". In this way ideas about the nature of mental defectiveness (subnormality) and of moral defectiveness became entwined and in the United Kingdom they were not to be wholly disengaged until the Mental Health Act of 1959.[6] For almost a century many people in the English-speaking world associated "moral defect" with mental defectiveness and identified it as a form of subnormality. Indeed this idea influenced the recommendations of the Royal Commission on the Law relating to Mental Illness and Mental Deficiency in 1957.[7] None of these notions has stood the test of time but both moral defect and degeneration were to influence the concept of the psychopathic personality when this emerged in Germany to replace them.

5.6 The term "psychopathic inferiorities" was introduced in Germany in 1891 to describe this group of disorders, and although the pejorative "inferiority" was soon abandoned, a narrower concept of psychopathic personality, distinct from the neuroses, was introduced by Kraepelin and has remained. At the start the psychopathic inferiorities implied a physical basis for these disorders—either a degenerative process or a congenital or acquired inferiority of brain constitution. Kraepelin retained the idea of degeneration, but was uncertain. Now, 60 years later, research still continues to try to

---

[3] Nigel Walker and Sarah McCabe, *Crime and Insanity in England*, Vol 2, Chapter 9. (Edinburgh, 1973.)

[4] Gröhmann (1818) quoted by A Lewis in *Psychopathic Personality: a most elusive category*. Psychol. Med. 4, 133, 1974.

[5] J C Prichard: *A Treatise on Insanity and other Disorders affecting the Mind* (London, 1835).

[6] See paragraph 5.13.

[7] Cmnd. 169, paragraphs 185–198 (see below at paragraph 5.12).

establish the truth of this idea, but the greater emphasis is upon efforts to elucidate the psychological and sociological factors affecting personality development now believed to be more relevant.

5.7   The schools of psychiatry in Germany at the beginning of this century had a profound influence not only upon the subject but also upon the classification of mental disorders throughout the world.   Originally the "psychopathies" embraced all mental disorders which were not "psychoses" (major mental illnesses).   Since the psychoses were defined as disorders of known or suspected physical ("organic") causation, they were regarded as illnesses in the medical sense, in contrast with the psychopathies which came to be regarded as extreme variations in personality from some hypothetical norm—an abnormal deviation from normal mental life.   Psychiatrists nowadays draw attention to the fact that many biological characteristics of man, such as height and intelligence, are distributed in the population according to a standard pattern (technically a "Gaussian" curve).   There are, for example, at the extremes very short and very tall people, very dull (subnormal) and very intelligent people.   Thus the psychopathies came to be regarded, as they still are by many, as the extreme expression of normal biological variation.

5.8   The original European concept of the psychopathies included the greater proportion of the mental disorders that are known today, although Kraepelin himself had distinguished psychopathic personality from the neuroses and the subnormal.   Attempts were made to define special categories within the psychopathic group and different authorities produced different lists.   These were all based on the most outstanding anomalies of psychological functioning rather than on the overt behaviour which the patient showed.   For example, the categories of one famous classification included amongst others the depressive, the self-insecure, the fanatical, the emotionally labile, the attention-seeking, the explosive, the feelingless and the weak-willed.   Unfortunately, the categories were not mutually exclusive.

5.9   This simple body of theory did not remain unchallenged for long.   Some psychoanalysts and sociologists objected that these deviations of personality, and particularly the neuroses, were of acquired origin, that either internal psychological or external social causes were the most important factors, and that in many cases it was possible to detect the origins of these conditions and to treat their manifestations, regardless of any "natural" biological variation between individuals.   As a result new terms were evolved to describe some of these categories: psychoanalysts spoke of the character neuroses, while American sociology developed the notion of sociopathy to convey a propensity for behaviour which is regarded as criminal or anti-social. Prominent psychiatrists throughout the world developed their own definitions and classifications based upon their own theories and explanatory hypotheses, and in some cases they were accepted by the various national bodies for official purposes.   Some classifications implied the existence of fairly specific clinical entities, particularly in relation to psychopathic patients showing serious anti-social tendencies.   It is the failure to substantiate these claims of specificity which has been one of the causes of the present confusion surrounding the concept of psychopathy.

5.10 An important impetus to the development in this country of the idea of psychopathy as a clinical entity was provided during the middle decades of the present century by the work and teaching of Sir David Henderson. He drew attention to what he regarded as the essential elements of psychopathic disorder, particularly its anti-social aspects, using the definition in a restricted and rather specific sense:

> "The term psychopathic state is the name we apply to those individuals who conform to a certain intellectual standard, sometimes high, sometimes approaching the realm of defect but not amounting to it, who, throughout their lives or from a comparatively early age, have exhibited disorders of conduct of an anti-social or asocial nature, usually of a recurrent or episodic type which in many instances have proved difficult to influence by methods of social, penal and medical care and treatment or for whom we have no adequate provision of a preventive or curative nature. The inadequacy or deviation or failure to adjust to ordinary social life is not mere wilfulness or badness which can be threatened or thrashed out of the individual so involved but constitutes a true illness for which we have no specific explanation".[8]

But Henderson's three sub-divisions of the disorder—predominantly aggressive, predominantly inadequate and predominantly creative—were brought together in one category by a highly complex psychological theory and were not based on descriptions of observed behaviour. Each sub-division embraced a wide variety of different types of behaviour. For example the first group (predominantly aggressive) included "(a) those who attempt to injure themselves, (b) those who attempt to injure others, (c) the alcoholic and drug addict, (d) the epileptoid, (e) the sex variants, who form a kind of bridge between the more aggressive and the more passive or inadequate group".

5.11 Henderson's psychological concepts have not been adopted in any official medical classification but his work has encouraged the popular belief that the psychopathic personality may be categorised as either aggressive or inadequate. Such terms refer to overt observable behaviour rather than behaviour interpreted by inference from psychological theory, and their use is therefore largely at variance with Henderson's own formulations. Nevertheless Henderson's ideas have done much to influence clinical practice and research and have made their mark on legislation.

(2) The Royal Commission and the Mental Health Act 1959

5.12 The Royal Commission on the Law Relating to Mental Illness and Mental Deficiency 1954–57 proposed that for broad administrative purposes three main groups of patients should be recognised. The higher grade feeble-minded and moral defectives "and other psychopathic patients" should be recognised as together constituting one main group of mentally disordered patients; the other two groups were the mentally ill and the severely subnormal.[9] The first of these groups would comprise patients suffering from a personality disorder which did not make them severely subnormal but was recognised medically as a form of mental disorder resulting in abnormally aggressive or

---

[8] D K Henderson, *Psychopathic States* (London, 1939).
[9] Cmnd. 169, paragraph 187.

inadequate social behaviour. For this group the Royal Commission recommended that the terms "psychopathic patient" and "psychopathic personality" should be used. They recognised that this use of the term "psychopathic" would be wider than the sense in which it was usually then used. The psychopathic group would include those patients who would be classified under the then existing law as feeble-minded persons or moral defectives and who were not severely subnormal; and those inadequate or aggressive psychopaths who were not considered certifiable as mentally defective or as "of unsound mind". The psychopathic group would include, therefore, a sub-group in which one sign of the patient's personality disorder would be that the intelligence was well below average, and a second sub-group in which the intelligence was near or above average. The first group might be described as "feeble-minded psychopaths". The differentiation between the two sub-groups was proposed only in connection with the provision of suitable forms of care; the same compulsory powers should apply to both and no distinction need appear in the law.[10]

5.13 The recommendations of the Royal Commission were largely implemented in the Mental Health Act 1959, but in relation to psychopaths an important departure was made. Instead of the three main groups defined by the Royal Commission, section 4 of the Act refers to four main groups of mental disorder, namely, mental illness, severe subnormality, subnormality and psychopathic disorder. In other words, the group comprised in the Royal Commission's definition of psychopathic disorder has been sub-divided in the Act into "subnormality" and "psychopathic disorder". Any causal association between subnormality and psychopathic disorder has been finally broken (cf paragraph 5.5 above). "Subnormality" is defined in section 4(3) as "a state of arrested or incomplete development of mind (not amounting to severe subnormality) which includes subnormality of intelligence and is of a nature or degree which requires or is susceptible to medical treatment or other special care or training of the patient". "Psychopathic disorder" is defined in section 4(4) as "a persistent disorder or disability of mind (whether or not including subnormality of intelligence) which results in abnormally aggressive or seriously irresponsible[11] conduct on the part of the patient, and requires or is susceptible to medical treatment". This definition carries no implication that psychopathic disorder is a single entity, any more than does the definition of subnormality in section 4(3) of the Act. Neither "psychopathic disorder" nor "subnormality" is a specific diagnosis; they are generic terms adopted for the purpose of legal categorisation and capable of covering a number of specific diagnoses, although in the case of the psychopathic disorders reliable specific diagnoses have still to be developed.

5.14 The Parliamentary history of the present statutory definition of psychopathic disorder is of some interest. When the Bill which became the Act of 1959 was introduced the definition stood as follows: "a persistent disorder of personality (whether or not accompanied by subnormality of intelligence) which results in abnormally aggressive or seriously irresponsible conduct on

---

[10] Cmnd. 169, paragraphs 190, 194.

[11] It is important to note that the statutory definition of "psychopathic disorder" includes not only the abnormally aggressive person but also, under the criterion of serious irresponsibility, such a person as the compulsive gambler.

the part of the patient, and requires or is susceptible to medical treatment". At the Committee Stage in the House of Lords Lady Wootton moved to substitute "a mental abnormality (whether or not accompanied by sub-normality of intelligence) which results in dangerously and persistently aggressive or persistently irresponsible conduct and is susceptible to medical treatment", arguing that persons who were to be labelled as "psychopaths" should manifest some abnormality of mind other than their persistently anti-social behaviour, that the criterion of dangerousness should be included, and that the clause should be limited to cases really likely to benefit from medical treatment, not extended to those who might "require" it but not be responsive to it.[12] The Lord Chancellor thought that the criterion of dangerousness was already included in the words "abnormally aggressive" and that the word "requires" should be retained for cases where the doctor might hope that the patient would respond[13] but in the light of the Committee Stage discussion the Government, on Report,[14] substituted a revised clause of their own which met Lady Wootton's first point by substituting reference to persistent disorder or disability of *mind* for persistent disorder of *personality*. The resulting definition is that which now appears in section 4(4) of the Act.

5.15 From both the medical and legal points of view the historical development of the concept of psychopathy has given rise to serious confusion. In essence it was originally a causal theory about hypothetical brain disorder to explain and to bring into one category all those persons who were not "insane" yet not mentally normal. This theory is no longer held. Later the term was used to describe clinical types but the definitions themselves and the types included in them varied from author to author. The late Sir Aubrey Lewis summed up the historical use of the word when he said:

> "Psychopathic personality is one of a cluster of terms which have been used, interchangeably or successively, in the last 150 years to denote a life-long propensity to behaviour which falls midway between normality and psychosis. Mania *sine delirio*, moral insanity, moral imbecility, psychopathy, degenerate constitution, congenital delinquency, constitutional inferiority—these and other semantic variations on a dubious theme have been bandied about by psychiatrists and lawyers in a prodigious output of repetitious articles".[15]

(3) The International Statistical Classification of Disease (ICD)

5.16 It is evident that it was necessary to divorce as far as possible from any definition or classification any reference to alleged causes, to psychological theories and to hypothetical psychological mechanisms. This task has been undertaken by the World Health Organisation which started its work in this area in 1947. Since then there have been eight revisions of the International Statistical Classification of Disease (ICD), Section V of which refers to Mental Disorders. The latest revision appeared in 1968. A number of countries, including the United Kingdom, have accepted it for official administrative purposes, and national and personal classifications are being abandoned.

---

[12] House of Lords Official Report 23 June 1959, Cols 91–93.

[13] ,, ,, ,, ,, ,, 23 June 1959, Cols 97–98.

[14] ,, ,, ,, ,, ,, 9 July 1959, Cols 951, 954.

[15] A Lewis: *Psychopathic Personality: A most elusive category.* Psychol. Med. 4, 133, 1974.

5.17 The ICD (1968 Revision) recognises three major groups of mental disorders: the psychoses (the major mental illnesses); mental retardation (severe subnormality and subnormality); and the neuroses (personality disorders and other non-psychotic mental disorders) of which there are nine sub-categories. Among these are personality disorders, sexual deviation, alcoholism and drug dependence. Each category has a number of recognised sub-categories, which are to some extent arbitrary, since they do not rest upon any objective clinical, psychological or other differences. The terms "psychopath", "psychopathic disorder" and "psychopathic personality" are not used. However, in the British Glossary to the classification prepared by a sub-committee of the Registrar-General's Advisory Committee on Medical Nomenclature and Statistics, under the main category of Personality Disorders (301)[16] it is stated that this category "includes what is sometimes called 'psychopathic personality'." More specifically the Glossary states that the sub-category "Anti-social" (301.7) includes those individuals who are classified in the Mental Health Act 1959 as suffering from "psychopathic disorder". The British Committee refer to those suffering from personality disorder of the anti-social type as follows:

> "This term should be confined to those individuals who offend against society, who show a lack of sympathetic feeling, and whose behaviour is not readily modifiable by experience including punishment. They are affectively cold and callous. They may tend to abnormally aggressive and seriously irresponsible conduct".

It is evident however that some other sub-categories of personality disorder describe patients who for reasons connected with their particular disability may well come within the definition of psychopathic disorder in the Mental Health Act. The "explosive" (301.3)[17] for example shows "marked instability of mood with particular liability to outbursts of irritability, anger, aggression and impulsive behaviour", but "are not otherwise prone to anti-social behaviour".

5.18 A further revision of the International Classification is currently being prepared. In 1974 the World Health Organisation published a glossary for international usage.[18] Hitherto only the glossaries prepared by individual national Committees had been available, and these were naturally subject to some variation on points of detail. The section on personality disorders[19] in the international glossary includes a reference to "what is sometimes called psychopathic personality" in its description of the main category, but it is still not possible to identify "psychopathic disorder", as defined in the Mental Health Act, with a particular sub-category, several of which may include patients who show "abnormally aggressive or seriously irresponsible" tendencies.

II. PSYCHOPATHIC DISORDER IN THE MENTAL HEALTH ACT 1959

(1) The arguments for removing "psychopathic disorder" from the Act

5.19 We have received much evidence suggesting that the references to psychopathic disorder in section 4 of the Mental Health Act should be deleted.

---

[16] See Appendix 5(1).
[17] See Appendix 5(1).
[18] *Glossary of Mental Disorders and Guide to their Classification* (W.H.O. Geneva 1974).
[19] See Appendix 5(2).

It is not within the competence conferred on us by our terms of reference to recommend the deletion of the term altogether from the Act because of its effect on Part IV and civilly committed patients, but we feel justified in making one or two observations about this possibility. We note that the Government have announced[20] their intention to review the working of the Mental Health Act in the light of our Report and of the views of other interested bodies and individuals and to issue a consultative document, possibly later this year. We think that in this review the references in Part IV of the Act to psychopaths should be considered in detail. The weight of evidence we have received on the subject and our lengthy discussions on psychopathic offenders have led us to certain views about psychopaths in general which it may be helpful to this purpose for us to record.

5.20   Among the arguments advanced by various witnesses in favour of deletion of the term are the following:

(a) Psychiatrists disagree about the meaning of the term "psychopathic disorder" and about its diagnosis in particular cases. While some would limit it to a narrow group of dangerously anti-social individuals, others seek to extend the concept to cover inadequates of all descriptions, "those with alcoholism and drug addiction, those with sexual and marital disorders and those with employment disorders".[21] One witness expressed the view that the definition of "psychopathic disorder" in the Mental Health Act was so wide as to be meaningless. Many others agreed that it is undesirable in principle, inconvenient in practice, and potentially open to abuse that a statutory provision on which a person's liberty may depend should be so uncertain.

(b) It was suggested that the concept of psychopathy is logically defective insofar as it infers mental disorder from anti-social behaviour, while purporting to explain the anti-social behaviour by mental disorder.

(c) One witness said it may commonly be supposed of anyone described as a psychopath that he will persistently act as if under stress, that all his conduct will be pervaded by anti-social attitudes; but this is not necessarily so. Some psychopaths act normally for some of the time and there may be no clear distinction between their behaviour and that of offenders not diagnosed as psychopaths. The witness saw the concept of psychopathic disorder as part of the general attempt of a secular society to replace moral explanations of behaviour by medico-scientific explanations. Other witnesses expressed similar opinions.

(d) In the same vein it has been argued that labelling people as psychopaths has proved stigmatic, harmful and indelible, and in practice makes those so labelled more difficult to handle both in institutions and in the community, since it carries the popular implication that they are both dangerous and incurable.

(e) The definition of mental disorder in section 4(1) without the reference to psychopathic disorder would still cover all cases of psychopathy (since they would then fall within the residual group of other disorders

---

[20] House of Commons Official Report, 24 January 1975, Cols 2172–2173.

[21] T C N Gibbens, "Treatment of Psychopaths", *Journal of Mental Science*, 107 (1961), 181.

or disabilities of mind) and, to the extent that they were considered treatable, would enable them to be admitted to hospital. (But this is not correct: see the following paragraph.)

(f) Witnesses also drew attention to the fact that in Scotland and in Northern Ireland it has not been found necessary to make use of this term in legislation.

5.21   But what would be the situation if, as suggested, "psychopathic disorder" were deleted from section 4 of the Act? Hospitals could still admit psychopaths for up to 28 days for observation, under section 25 of the Act (or in emergency for up to 72 hours under section 29), or for treatment informally: they would continue to be covered by the remainder of the comprehensive definition of "mental disorder" in section 4(1). But compulsory admission of young non-offender psychopaths for treatment under section 26 would no longer be possible since this section extends only to the four named conditions, and not to the residual group of "other disorders or disabilities of mind" mentioned in section 4(1). Nor could offender psychopaths be made subject to a hospital order under section 60, since this power also extends only to the four named conditions. Psychopaths denied admission to hospital would often, as now, find their way into penal system. (We say more about this occurrence later.) Further, differences of opinion among psychiatrists as to the diagnosis of a mental disorder in psychopaths, and as to susceptibility to treatment, would not be prevented by the deletion of "psychopathic disorder". This has been the experience in Scotland, where the law makes no mention of psychopathic disorder but where people who in England and Wales might be classified as suffering from that disorder are often admitted to hospital because of the indications they have given of mental illness or subnormality. It can be maintained that the problems arise from the nature of psychopathic characteristics and the uncertainties about treatment, rather than from the statutory definitions, and that it would be regrettable if, without gaining substantial countervailing advantages, revision of the definitions gave any discouragement to those doctors and hospitals at present willing to accept psychopaths for treatment. In this connection, perhaps, it is not sufficiently recognised, or always remembered, that the Act defines medical treatment as including not only nursing but also care and training under medical supervision (section 147(1)). Subnormality is often not treatable except in this limited sense, but no one would suggest that it should on that account be excluded from the Act or from the hospitals.

5.22   On the other hand, we have no doubt that it is highly undesirable to label people as psychopaths. This is especially true of juveniles, and psychiatrists are understandably reluctant to use the term psychopath of adolescents or to place them into recognised categories of mental disorder. Once applied the label sticks, and may serve to discourage a thorough investigation of a kind which might unmask a specific condition. On both counts research is impeded. To avoid the element of stigma, therefore, there is much to be said for urging Parliament formally to disown the term, in the way that stigmatic terms such as "lunatic", "idiot" and "imbecile" have already been disowned.

5.23   A further argument in favour of abandonment of the term is that the statutory classification should not only be understood by medical and legal

85

practitioners but should also be in line with their current domestic and international usage. As we have indicated in the first section of this chapter, psychopathic disorder is no longer a useful or meaningful concept; it is not associated with any of the sub-categories of mental disorder contained in the International Statistical Classification of Disease; and it is not used for statistical purposes in the National Health Service. The class of persons to whom the term "psychopathic disorder" relates is not a single category identifiable by any medical, biological or psychological criteria.

(2) A possible solution

5.24   If it were decided that the term psychopathic disorder should no longer be used in the Act it seems to us that it would not suffice simply to delete references to "psychopathic disorder" despite the apparently satisfactory experience in Scotland of its omission from the corresponding statute: it is one thing to have an Act of Parliament which has never included the term, but another to withdraw it after it has been in a statute for 16 years. As we have pointed out in paragraph 5.21, deletion of "psychopathic disorder" would technically exclude everyone with this diagnosis from compulsory admission to hospital for treatment. This would inevitably be construed as the intention of the amendment, but it is not a result we would wish to bring about. The solution might be to substitute in section 4(1) the recognised classification of personality disorder, which subsumes the category now known as "psychopathic disorder". This section would then read: "In this Act 'mental disorder' means mental illness, arrested or incomplete development of mind, personality disorder and any other disorder or disability of mind; and 'mentally disordered' shall be construed accordingly". This would embrace those cases where compulsory admission to hospital is indicated in the interest of the public and of the patient. Section 4(4), in which the definition of "psychopathic disorder" is given, could be deleted. It would not be possible to provide a usable definition in the Act for "personality disorder" which, as we have indicated, is a group of disorders. No definition of the term "mental illness" was attempted by or possible for the writers of the Act, since again mental illness is a large group of dissimilar disorders and no comprehensive short definition is possible. We consider that the same applies to personality disorder which is defined in the International Classification of Diseases (1968) as shown at Appendix 5(1).

5.25   Section 4 is the base on which the Mental Health Act rests, and changes in that section would be reflected in all other parts of the Act including section 60 relating to hospital orders. But we would have reservations about the unqualified inclusion in section 60 of "personality disorder" in view of its potentially wide interpretation. In our view if the term were adopted in section 60 it would be necessary to tie it closely to the conditions at present defined by section 4(4). Were other counsels to prevail, and should the term be included in section 60 without qualification, we are agreed that the offender's consent should be required to a hospital order on ground of personality disorder. The proviso which we propose in paragraph 5.40 should be added to section 60 would be appropriate whatever the substitution.

5.26   When considering the possibility of amending section 4 it must be borne in mind that there may be some groups suffering from personality disorders or allied conditions such as sexual deviation and drug or alcohol dependance for whom it would be undesirable or unreasonable, *by reason of their deviance alone*, to provide for compulsory detention in hospital under civil powers. If the term personality disorder were to be substituted for psychopathic disorder in the Act, section 4(5) should be amended to include the statement that sexual deviation *alone*, or alcohol or drug addiction *alone*, does not imply that a non-offender patient may be dealt with under the compulsory powers of Part IV of the Act. Nevertheless we would agree with those who have suggested that some offenders with these characteristics may be able to benefit from treatment in hospital, particularly the sexual deviants (see paragraphs 3.24–3.27), as we are aware that forms of psychological treatment which can offer the expectation of therapeutic help to those unfortunate people are now being developed in the National Health Service. We should not wish section 60 to apply to these groups; as indicated in the foregoing paragraph, we see difficulties in the widening of section 60. But our proposals in paragraph 3.45 for the transfer of prisoners on grounds of *any* mental disorder would allow the transfer of prisoners suffering from sexual deviation or alcohol or drug addiction to receive treatment in hospital if they are willing.

III. THE TREATMENT OF PSYCHOPATHS

(1) The findings of the Royal Commission

5.27 When they came to consider what provisions they should recommend for the treatment of psychopaths, the Royal Commission recognised that they were confronted with one of the great dilemmas in forensic psychiatry: is a psychopath diagnosed only by being a recidivist; are all recidivists by definition psychopaths? They noted differences of opinion on whether special compulsory powers were justified at all in relation to "psychopaths" within their definition (see paragraph 5.12 above), and the difficulty of making certain forms of behaviour in themselves grounds for segregation from society, which almost amounted to the creation of new criminal offences. "The treatment and the use of compulsion must be based on a medical diagnosis of the individual patient's mental condition, not merely on evidence of his behaviour. The difficulty is that with patients in the psychopathic group it is their behaviour which provides the main evidence of their mental condition" (paragraph 339).[22]

5.28 The Royal Commission observed that considerably more experience had been gained in treating "feeble-minded psychopaths" than those of higher intelligence because a much larger number of the feeble-minded had been dealt with under the Mental Deficiency Acts. Various methods of treatment in hospital had been provided for psychopaths, ranging from training under conditions of strict security to physical treatment, psychotherapy and group therapy as practised in mental or neurosis hospitals, including Belmont Hospital where patients were given the maximum possible freedom of expression and of action. Some psychopathic patients responded to each of these methods and some did not. Some responded to the punitive and deterrent effect of normal penal processes in much the same way as more normal people, but

---

[22] This and subsequent paragraph references in paragraphs 5.27–5.30 are to the Report of the Royal Commission, Cmnd. 169.

others did not. "A fine or a period of imprisonment or of probation or supervision may be a more appropriate and effective way of treating some psychopaths who have broken the law than treatment or training in hospital" (paragraph 344). Even in cases where it was not possible, in the present state of knowledge, to cure the underlying mental condition giving rise to inadequate or aggressive tendencies, treatment or training might enable the patient to regulate his general behaviour so that he could live a normal social life in spite of the underlying disorder.

5.29 It was generally considered, the Royal Commission said, that the prospects of success were greatest when the patient's disorder was recognised early in life and when he received treatment or training before his inadequate or aggressive behaviour had become ingrained (paragraph 345). For this reason the Royal Commission considered that there was a strong case for authorising the use of compulsion to ensure training or treatment in hospital or in the community for psychopathic patients in adolescence and early adult life (paragraph 354). But they did not consider that there was sufficient justification for special compulsory powers in relation to adult psychopathic patients except when their conduct was anti-social to the extent of constituting an offence against the criminal law. When a person had broken the criminal law he had laid himself open to the imposition of control because of behaviour which had been judged by standards which applied to all citizens. It was no longer in question whether or not he should be considered liable to control at all; the question had become whether or not one of a variety of possible forms of control provided a suitable way of treating the individual offender. The Royal Commission considered it right "that special forms of treatment or control should be applied to some psychopathic patients who have been convicted of a criminal offence which may not be applied compulsorily to adult psychopathic patients who have not committed such an offence and which do not apply to offenders who are not mentally disordered", but this did not mean that they considered it right to apply these special measures to all offenders who were psychopathic in the wide sense in which they used that term. It would often be more appropriate to give an ordinary sentence or to use normal methods of probation (paragraph 356) and the Royal Commission stressed the need to ensure that the power to apply special forms of treatment or control after the commission of an offence would be used only in cases for which normal penal measures alone were clearly inappropriate (paragraph 517). Under their proposed compulsory powers there was a danger that psychopathic patients might be kept in hospital when their detention could no longer be justified by the prospects of benefit from further treatment (paragraph 345). On the other hand, for the protection of the public there should be special safeguards, under the control of the Home Secretary, relating to the discharge of psychopathic patients who were recognised as dangerous to other people (paragraphs 518–519).

5.30 The Royal Commission thought it possible "that for some time to come the application of any special compulsory powers to psychopaths of higher intelligence would in practice be limited by the extent to which hospital facilities for treating them can be developed" but they noted that some hospitals already specialised in the treatment of such patients and saw no reason why the new compulsory powers should not be used immediately for the admission of psychopathic patients to any hospital prepared to provide suitable treatment for the individual patient (paragraph 352). Residential homes or hostels should be provided by the local authorities for severely subnormal and psychopathic patients (paragraph 618). With the general expansion of community mental health services it was foreseen that it might be found possible in future to do more for psychopaths of normal intelligence living in the community (paragraph 679). With special reference to young psychopathic patients, local authorities and hospitals should be prepared to develop their services and when necessary to use their powers of compulsion to ensure that the services were used for the patients who could benefit from them most (paragraph 680).

5.31 These recommendations, in so far as they required legislation, were put into effect in the Mental Health Act 1959: in particular, in the exclusion from compulsory admission for treatment of psychopathic or subnormal non-offenders aged 21 or over (section 24(2)), and the provision for control 26 by the Home Secretary over the discharge of dangerous patients (section 65).

(2) The Working Party on the Special Hospitals

5.32 The Report of a Working Party on the Special Hospitals published in February 1961, while remarking that so soon after the coming into effect of the new statutory classification they could have no clear idea of the numbers of people who would be requiring compulsory treatment for "psychopathic disorder" because they did not know how the new provisions would be used and interpreted either by doctors generally or by the courts, and noting that medical knowledge of psychopathic disorder was still at an early stage and that there was little agreement as to what medical treatment was appropriate or possible (paragraph 31), stated that nevertheless a considerable number of patients, a main constituent in whose condition was psychopathic disorder, were already being treated in the special hospitals, and that the same was true at a number of local psychiatric hospitals. The Working Party did not wish in any way to discourage the treatment of such patients by psychiatric hospitals generally and commented that, indeed, the more avenues of approach that were tried, the better; they hoped that hospitals would play an active part in research on problems connected with psychopathic behaviour, as to the urgent need for which they found themselves in agreement with a sub-committee on psychopathic personality set up by the Clinical Psychiatry Committee of the Medical Research Council (paragraph 32). The Report recommended the establishment of diagnostic and treatment centres with three main functions: to provide an investigatory and diagnostic service for the patients referred to them and to give advice on subsequent disposal and treatment; to provide treatment, where necessary on a long-term basis; and to provide facilities for research (paragraph 36). These recommendations were based on evidence from, among others, the British Medical Association and the Royal Medico-Psychological Association. The functions that might be served by such centres, the sources from which they might receive their patients, and their location and organisation were described in the Report in some detail. Their object was summarised as "to provide services for patients who present special difficulty because of their aggressive, anti-social or criminal tendencies, and who also present special problems of diagnosis, treatment and management".

Besides investigatory and diagnostic services the centres should provide treatment, where necessary on a long-term basis, and facilities for research. There should be the closest possible liaison between the centres and the remand and observation centres in the penal system. One or two centres should be established initially when the necessary finance was available, and later developments made in the light of experience. Centres should be provided by Hospital Boards but the Minister should take the initiative, be closely associated with the planning, and make a special financial allocation to meet capital expenditure.

5.33 The recommendations of the Working Party were commended by the then Ministry of Health to Regional Hospital Boards, Hospital Management Committees and Boards of Governors in a Circular dated 13 July 1961 (HM(61)69); projected diagnostic and treatment centres were included in the Hospital Plan of 1962.[23] But six years later, in February 1968, when the Parliamentary Estimates Committee questioned representatives of the Department,[24] it appeared that virtually no progress had been made either in establishing diagnostic and treatment centres or in setting up secure units in the regions, which the Working Party had also recommended. As the Departmental witnesses said, it was not clear whether the centres and the secure units were intended by the Working Party to be separate. The one diagnostic centre which the witnesses stated had been planned has not, in the event, been put to the purposes originally intended. The recommended provision for the diagnosis and treatment in suitably secure accommodation of the "difficult psychiatric cases" identified by the Working Party (paragraph 35)—cases not exclusively but largely represented by psychopaths—has not come about.

(3) The evidence before us

5.34 This lack of material progress in provision for the diagnosis and treatment of psychopathic conditions, with associated research, within the National Health Service is apparently matched by continuing uncertainty as to the treatability of the various conditions. The great weight of evidence presented to us tends to support the conclusion that psychopaths are not, in general, treatable, at least in medical terms. The Home Office and the Department of Health and Social Security stated in a joint memorandum that understanding of causes and of response to treatment is still very slight. The views expressed to us by individual consultant psychiatrists and senior medical officers of the Prison Medical Service have been almost uniformly pessimistic: "There are no agreed criteria for assessing treatability in psychopaths and indeed no agreed combination or sequence of therapeutic procedures for their treatment"; "There is no known treatment for the great majority of psychopaths and control is all that medicine has to offer"; "The possibility of treatment of aggressive psychopaths is extremely debatable—the aim has to be day to day management and support, concentrating on helping the individual through his crises with the minimum damage to himself and others"; "The belief that the psychopath is responsive to medical treatment has not been substantiated in the period since the Mental Health Act came into force"; "Court orders directing the admission of psychopathic personalities to hospital for treatment are in the

---

[23] Cmnd. 1604.

[24] Second Report from the Estimates Committee, Session 1967–68, Minutes of Evidence, Questions 1844–1863.

most part unsuitable, since there is no recognised effective treatment at present for such personality defects"; and the British Psychological Society have pointed out that there is "No solid evidence of the effectiveness of treatment for psychopaths in this country".

5.35 A number of witnesses mentioned to us the reputed success achieved in the specialist psychiatric treatment institution for psychopaths at Hersted-vester in Denmark, where we were told that pressures were put upon psychopathic patients to respond to treatment by the imposition of indeterminate sentences. Our members who visited the Continent therefore made their way to Denmark with some expectation of discovering answers to our problems—only to find that the use of indeterminate sentences had been severely reduced by statute. This change had come about chiefly as a result of objections to the principle of indeterminacy, but also in the light of research comparing relapses of psychopaths discharged from Herstedvester Treatment Centre with relapses of prisoners released from the special prison at Horsens and ordinary State prisons. This research, relating to inmates released between 1 January 1959 and 31 December 1964, showed no significant difference in the reconviction rates except that offenders released from Herstedvester had on average been reconvicted after a longer interval than those released from Horsens and the other prisons. Since 1 July 1973, when the statutory changes mentioned above became effective, the use of indeterminate sentences has been limited to people convicted of crimes dangerous to the life, body, health or freedom of other people (mainly murder, robbery or rape), and we under-stand that out of more than 200 admissions a year less than 10 are on indeterminate sentences.

5.36 In Sweden and Holland also our members received the impression that there was diminishing confidence in the possibilities of psychiatric treat-ment for psychopathic offenders, although different methods of treatment are being applied by a number of psychiatrists in each country, who generously made their time, experience and ideas available to our delegation.

(4) Treating the dangerous psychopathic offender

5.37 In this country there are at present broadly two main methods of treatment for psychopaths. On the one hand there are the various types of therapeutic community treatment, practised, for example, at Grendon Prison and Garth Angharad Hospital; on the other hand there are the various methods of behaviour modification (eg social skills training and aversion or operant conditioning) practised by clinical psychologists in certain hospitals. Although successful results are claimed by some hospitals and by Grendon Prison in the treatment of selected patients, these methods are not suitable for many of the more aggressive offenders who are often not willing or not able to co-operate in the treatment offered. Their behaviour is often disruptive, liable to extreme variations and unpredictable. They require secure contain-ment. In prison or hospital they are a source of anxiety to their fellow prisoners or patients, as well as to staff. If they are located with the rest of the prison or hospital population they represent an unsettling element and the risk of unexpected violence has to be accepted and lived with. If on the other hand they are located separately, they make a further demand on scarce accommoda-tion and staff, and may present special problems of control. On any of these counts, they are not usually suitably placed in local psychiatric hospitals. Apart from the reluctance of the hospitals to accommodate people who will not co-operate, or for whom no treatment is available, the local psychiatric hospitals do not contain facilities to cope over long periods of time with dangerous patients in whom the dangerousness[25] may be the outstanding clinical problem, and it would be unreasonable to expect them to do so. These dangerous psychopaths have therefore usually been sent to prison.

5.38 We think that the penal system should continue to receive them and that, if certain attitudes and policies, which we describe later, were adopted it could become capable of offering the prospect of important advances in the understanding and treatment, in the broadest sense, of the dangerous psychopath. We have been told by a number of witnesses that the passage of time modifies the behaviour of psychopaths and that there is nothing to be done but to wait for the change to take place; but the British Psychological Society remarked in their memorandum of evidence that "any placement of an offender that is against his will is liable to produce, if not overt behavioural changes, at least modifications of attitude and probably also of emotional reactions"; there was no such thing as "neutral" detention, and custodial detention should be regarded as "inevitably a behavioural treatment" and the opportunity should be used "to effect whatever beneficial change is suggested from principles of group treatment and contingency management". Modification of social behaviour is the essential object of the treatment of the dangerous psychopath, and whatever the difficulties confronting the penal system it is among the aims of any penal establishment to re-socialise the offender and equip him to lead a constructive life in the community after discharge. The penal system is provided with industrial workshops and educational activities of a high standard, often, indeed, superior to those available in many hospitals; these are facilities particularly relevant to the social training requirements of many psychopaths. Properly used, the prison environment can possibly provide the situation within which dangerous psychopaths can most readily be helped to develop more acceptable social attitudes.

5.39 There is need of a controlled programme of experiment and research to establish what conditions and regime produce the most encouraging results. At present the dangerous anti-social psychopath is likely to be placed among the general prison population, with little prospect of any special regime being devised for him, and with the consequent difficulties of control to which we alluded in paragraph 3.21. We think it may be found that a treatment regime based on a combination of long term medical, psychological and social management, in the hope of encouraging the natural processes of maturation, would have some success, and we describe in paragraph 5.49 the regime of work and social activity we suggest should be tried for these most difficult people. We recognise that the prison service is a generalist service which has difficulty in providing special forms of treatment to meet special needs, but for the purpose of the form of treatment we are suggesting and for the purposes of systematic research segregation from the general prison population in a special unit or units within the penal system would be essential. The units

[25] As defined in paragraph 4.10—"a propensity to cause physical injury or lasting psychological harm".

should not be labelled as units for psychopaths; like Grendon, they should have a non-committal name. We shall refer to them in this Report as "training units". In paragraphs 5.49–5.57 we describe them in more detail.

(5) Amendment of the statute

5.40   Consistently with these recommendations it appears to us that it would be advantageous to remove any ambiguity about the responsibility of the prisons to cater for offenders with dangerous anti-social tendencies which may arise from the power in section 60(1) of the Mental Health Act to base hospital orders on a diagnosis of psychopathic disorder.   To bring the statutory provision into conformity with the proposed policy, we suggest that a proviso on the following lines should be added to section 60(1) of the Mental Health Act:

> "Save that no order shall be made under this section in the case of an offender suffering from psychopathic disorder with dangerous anti-social tendencies unless the court is satisfied:
>
> (a)   that a previous mental or organic illness, or an identifiable psychological or physical defect, relevant to the disorder is known or suspected; and
>
> (b)   there is an expectation of therapeutic benefit from hospital admission".

This proviso should not apply to juveniles under the age of 17 for whom prison is not a suitable disposal and who should preferably be dealt with in hospital or in the community.   (We discuss provision for mentally disordered juveniles and young adult offenders in Chapter 17).

5.41   The evidence has not persuaded us that the option of a hospital order should be withdrawn from all psychopathic offenders.   Where the offender is not dangerous and a hospital is prepared to accept him, we consider that this disposal should remain available to the court as should a guardianship order; and even where dangerous anti-social tendencies are present, placement in hospital should not be debarred where there is an associated condition pointing to the need for medical care.

5.42   The power under section 72 of the Act to transfer psychopaths from prison to hospital should continue in force.   It may be found that a psychopath who has been sentenced to imprisonment is after all suitable for medical treatment in a local psychiatric hospital or special hospital and that a place can be provided for him.   The retention of the power of transfer combined with the proviso proposed for section 60(1) would mean that dangerous anti-social psychopaths would be "screened" by the prison system before they were admitted to any psychiatric hospital; and as they would invariably be transferred subject to restrictions under section 74 of the Act, they could be returned to prison if their behaviour in hospital was disruptive or attempts to treat them proved unavailing.   The possibility of this sanction might in itself be beneficial.   (We have proposed in paragraph 3.45 that the power to transfer prisoners to hospital should be extended to all categories of mental disorder, and we have discussed in paragraphs 3.42–3.44 the question of the continuance or termination of compulsory detention in hospital of transferred prisoners when their prison sentence expires, which is of particular interest with regard to adult psychopaths since they cannot be admitted compulsorily to hospital by reason of this condition alone).

IV. TRAINING UNITS

(1) Psychiatric treatment in the penal system

5.43 We have indicated that in our view dangerous anti-social psychopaths should be dealt with in special institutions in the penal system. As we have said the needs of this particular class of offender will often include social training and psychological treatment which can, for these people, most satisfactorily be provided in this way. In the following paragraphs we consider how these new institutions, which need not necessarily entail new building, will fit into the penal system; and we go on to express some necessarily tentative views as to the aims and methods of such units and the types of regime which we think may be found most appropriate. Some of the prisoners to be catered for may well be subject to the new "reviewable" sentence we have proposed in the previous chapter for men with violence in their record who commit fresh offences of serious violence and who cannot be dealt with under the Mental Health Act. The majority, however, will be subject to determinate prison sentences. We have in mind that if the trial judge considers that allocation to a training unit is desirable he should write privately to the Home Secretary to inform him of his opinion. (This would involve no threat from the point of view of civil liberties since we propose in paragraph 5.50 that admission to the units should be entirely voluntary.) Where a reviewable sentence is imposed, this in itself would indicate the possible need for training in a special unit. As we have explained, we think that a prison work regime and the prison situation may in itself be helpful and therapeutic, and we believe that there are specific forms of treatment, psychotherapeutic and behavioural, which probably have a measure of efficacy; but these theories (and others) require validation by scientific research, which ought to be a major function of the concentration of these prisoners in the special units.

(2) Grendon Prison

5.44 We first describe the methods adopted at Grendon Prison, as it is necessary to make clear the distinction between the new units we propose and the one prison which already specialises in the treatment of psychopaths. At present there are 43 penal establishments in England and Wales with psychiatric units, the largest and most important of which is Grendon psychiatric prison. Opened in 1962, Grendon has throughout been under the direction of a psychiatrist as medical superintendent. As a secure prison it is an integral part of the prison service, but although not a hospital it complements the special and psychiatric hospitals of the National Health Service, providing psychiatric treatment for men and youths (adult and young prisoners and borstal trainees), who are not eligible to be dealt with under the provisions of the Mental Health Act 1959. We have looked carefully at the work done at Grendon to see whether it offers any pointers to the type of institutional treatment which may be appropriate to the group of offenders with whom we are here concerned.

5.45   The objectives of Grendon are (*a*) to investigate and to treat offenders suffering from disorders which call for a psychiatric approach; (*b*) to investigate the mental condition of offenders the nature of whose offences suggests mental disorder; and (*c*) to explore the problem of the psychopath and to provide treatment or management to which he might respond.   Grendon does not accept inmates direct from the courts but receives them from prisons and borstals on the direction of the Prison Department after selection and preliminary investigation by medical officers at those establishments.   The inmates must be willing to undergo psychiatric investigation and treatment since the Grendon concept aims at securing and maintaining the co-operation of the patient in a liberal or permissive regime.   Drug addicts and alcoholics who satisfy these requirements may be accepted.   Not regarded as suitable for treatment at Grendon are prisoners suffering from mental disorder to such an extent that they may be dealt with under section 72 of the Mental Health Act, or from permanent organic cerebral change who are unable to respond to treatment, or those who are unable to participate in a community life.

5.46   The treatment at Grendon takes a variety of forms: psychotherapy, electro-convulsive therapy, insulin treatment, narcosis and other drug treatment, aversion treatment, occupational therapy, physiotherapy and relaxation and speech therapy.   Each new arrival receives an electro-encephalography examination and the clinical interpretations made by a consultant neurophysiologist are passed to the appropriate therapists.   The new arrival also undergoes psychometric tests and in special cases individual assessments of intelligence and personality are made.   The prison is essentially a therapeutic community, and the treatment depends for its success on good staff/inmate relationships and inmate participation.   These are achieved by frequent meetings of small counselling groups, work groups and psychotherapeutic groups of inmates and staff of entire wings of the prison and inmate committees for various activities, for example entertainments, inmates' suggestions and communications to the staff on general administrative matters.   Violent, bullying or unco-operative inmates are quickly transferred away from Grendon.

5.47   Although research is being conducted under the auspices of the Home Office Research Unit into a number of aspects of the Grendon regime, it is still too early to assess the results.   A two-year follow-up of Grendon discharges, conducted in 1971, produced some evidence of a correlation between the length of time spent at Grendon and avoidance of subsequent reconviction, and suggested that a minimum period of between 12 and 18 months was required for successful treatment[26] but this finding was not subject to controlled comparisons with other institutions.   As regards borstal trainees at Grendon, it was found that for releases from borstal during the period 1966–1970 Grendon had the lowest reconviction rate of any closed borstal, despite the fact that it accepts mentally disturbed borstal inmates; but follow-up studies of releases between 1964 and 1966 produced no significant evidence that adults did significantly better after release than other groups of prisoners who had not received treatment at Grendon, even when allowance was made for length of stay.[27]   Reconviction rates are not the only or even necessarily

[26] W J Gray "The Therapeutic Community and Evaluation of Results", *International Journal of Criminology and Penology*, 1 (1973), 327–334.

[27] Margaret Newton. *Reconviction after Treatment at Grendon* (Home Office, CP Report, Series B, No. 1, 1971).

the most valuable yardstick for evaluating the success of an institution such as Grendon, and other research has concluded that the therapeutic community model is particularly successful in the management of disturbed prisoners, by lessening their general opposition to authority, breaking down the traditional prison sub-culture and improving the inmates' own self-esteem.

5.48   Some of the limitations of the Grendon regime may be inferred from what has been said already.   Its intake, though composed predominantly of men with personality disorders, is a highly selected group.   Only men of average intelligence or above are admitted, and it is freely acknowledged that the pattern of life at Grendon is unsuitable for offenders who, because of immaturity or low intelligence, require a more structured and disciplined regime with closer supervision.   Those found unsuitable for any reason are readily transferred back to the general prisons.

(3) The new units
5.49   For offenders suffering from personality disorders who may not display any strong or continuing motivation for treatment, and who may on occasions prove violent and disruptive, we see a need for a treatment institution founded on principles different from those of Grendon and employing different methods, based essentially on the idea of training.   The Grendon approach towards resocialisation is based in considerable part on promoting insight through self-analysis and self-questioning on the part of the offender in the hope of enabling him to come to terms with the problems which lie behind his law-breaking.   But not all offenders suffering from personality disorders which manifest themselves in seriously anti-social behaviour are amenable to such an approach.   In many cases the need appears to be to develop in the offender patterns of social behaviour which are normally acquired during childhood and adolescence but have never been satisfactorily learned by the psychopath. In the present state of knowledge it is believed that this may come about either in a psychotherapeutic setting or in a behaviour therapy setting and for this type of offender such treatments could be developed only in a structured environment providing a degree of control and security.   In our view it would be appropriate for the new units to set out to establish a realistic regime on these lines, based on roughly equal periods of work and social activity but adjusted to the particular needs of individual inmates.   We accept that some would argue that it is inappropriate in a treatment situation to impose a particular regime based on certain arbitrary assumptions about normality, and we agree that the training programme must be matched to the individual. But we are not impressed by the results which have been achieved by the approach which some of us saw adopted in certain Continental institutions, whereby patients were allowed to do nothing.   Work and activity have always been the cornerstones of education and rehabilitation and it is difficult to see what effective alternative regime could be offered to an offender suffering from a psychopathic disorder to enable him to find his place in the community on release.

5.50   We should make it clear that we do not not intend that the proposed units should cater for those cases in which psychopathic behaviour is a function of some underlying mental or organic illness where medical treatment might well be helpful.   Nor do we think that the regime will, in general, be suitable for the younger inadequate prisoner, who requires intensive long-term support but presents little physical risk to the community, although he is likely to be an annoyance and a nuisance. It is our intention that training units should cater for psychopaths with dangerous anti-social tendencies aged between 17 or 18 and 35, for whom special psychiatric treatment is not available, who are willing to undertake the training offered and are likely to be able to benefit from it and will have a chance of employment on release, but who in the meantime require secure containment. The offender's consent should be obtained before admission to a unit. We would emphasise that the age limits we have mentioned are to be regarded as illustrative rather than precise. The lower age limits we have proposed are linked with the minimum ages at which an offender is normally dealt with in an adult court and a sentence of imprisonment imposed, as well as representing the lowest ages at which most doctors would be willing to attach any diagnostic label to an offender. The upper limit is intended to exclude the older inadequate personality.

5.51 While any estimate is difficult, we can foresee a probable ultimate need for about 750 places in units of the sort we are proposing, although we would not suggest that it would be desirable for them all to be brought into being at once, even if it were practicable to do so. Although it is for the Government of the day, not for us, to decide on the allocation of resources, we are very conscious of the severity of the present economic climate which makes this an unpropitious time to put forward proposals with any substantial financial implications, and that our recommendations as a whole embody a number of competing demands upon the public purse, in particular, the establishment as a matter of urgency of regional secure hospital units and forensic psychiatric centres and an expansion of community facilities for mentally disordered persons, whether offenders or not. We are aware that Grendon is criticised by some members of the Prison Medical Service for taking more than its fair share of doctors, nurses and other staff and money to be used on a comparatively small number of specially privileged inmates, and we are also aware that there is little justification, based upon scientific evidence, for new optimism in this field. For these reasons we think it would be desirable to start new units at first on a limited scale and on a research basis. To provide for comparative research we propose that two units should be established at the outset; variations in selection of the intake, the regime, and other factors can then be systematically assessed in relation to the results achieved. Two units will also be better than one to permit transfers between the units, which may be an important safety valve if tensions develop, and so that inmates may not be too far distant from their homes and families, making possible a more effective process of after-care following release. We stress the importance of associating these units with research, from the earliest stages of planning, so that full advantage can be taken of the opportunities they will offer for increasing our understanding of personality disorder and its treatment, and pointing the way to the most promising lines of development in the future. Then it may be easier than it is now to decide how large a share of the resources of the penal system should be concentrated on these difficult, unco-operative and dangerous offenders. We suggest that since the success of our proposals will depend upon the setting up of a scientifically valid pilot research study, the assistance of the Medical Research Council should be requested. Initially such a pilot study might well be carried out without the building of a unit by occupying an existing part of a prison.

5.52   The ideal size of a unit must in part be determined in the light of experience.   We think it would be right in the first instance to be guided by the outcome of the pilot study, bearing in mind on the one hand the advantages in
terms of management and control which go with small units and on the other
the economic pressures which operate strongly in favour of large institutions.
On the merits of providing specialised units for groups of difficult prisoners
there is room for more than one view.   It may be objected that to collect
together in one institution numbers of psychopaths some of whom may be of
high intelligence will produce a potentially dangerous situation, but our own
view is that by placing such men together under peer pressure they may well be
less of a risk than where they have the opportunity of manipulating other
prisoners.   Nonetheless, it will be important to provide a regime which leaves
little time for inmates to foment trouble, and while, as we have made clear,
we do not think the units should be selective, as Grendon is, and indeed it
would defeat their purpose if they were, in the last resort it must be open to the
prison authorities to arrange transfer to another unit or, if necessary, back to
the general prisons.

5.53   Work programmes in the units must, as we have said, be adjusted for
different needs.   An offender just entering the institution may require only
part-time work in his first few months, either because of the need to make a
thorough medical and psychiatric assessment of him during this period or
because he may never previously have had to discipline himself to the demands
of a full-time job.   Workshops must therefore be able to provide employment
ranging from minimum part-time to full-time.   The industrial processes carried
out in the units should be realistic and demanding and should be clearly related
to a useful end product.   Work experience will be an integral part of the regime
of the unit and the work must not be seen simply as something to give the
inmates to pass the time.   We hope that it may be possible for programmes of
work to be fitted into the local industry of the area where the unit is situated,
and to equip the offender for future employment in the community after release;
vocational training will be required with specialist help towards gaining qualifi-
tions.   Workshops must be run on factory lines, geared to a production line,
starting and finishing at set times and with provision for refreshment breaks.
We would hope that the wages which are paid could be calculated from a basic
rate with provision for incentive bonus schemes.   We recognise however that
on the question of pay regard must be had to ensuring consistency with the
policy prevailing in other areas of prison industry.

5.54   A full programme of social activities should also be developed ranging
from educational to purely recreational.   They should be both participatory
and non-participatory, and should draw fully on the many different facets of
community leisure activity.

5.55   Medical treatment will be interwoven in the total activities of the units
but there should be a full initial assessment of inmates from both a medical
and psychiatric standpoint, including complete psychological investigation.

5.56   The units must be able to provide a level of security equivalent to that
found in high security prisons but they could be so built as to provide a series
of different levels within one complex: total security in an inner core with areas
of lesser security surrounding it, with an outer unit which, if necessary, could be

a hostel area. In the top security area inmates will best be accommodated in single rooms, but in other areas small dormitories may be thought more suitable.

5.57 Although we have expressed the opinion that medical treatment as such has not been successful in treating psychopaths, nevertheless, because of the long association of the medical profession with the treatment of personality disorders it will probably be appropriate, at least initially, for a psychiatrist to head each unit. In the light of experience, it may be found suitable to appoint from other professional disciplines. The staff will be drawn from the fields of psychiatry, psychology, the social sciences and industry as well as from members of the Prison Service serving in the various governor and prison officer grades. Clinical psychologists with specialist knowledge and experience of behaviour therapy will have a particularly important to play. Staff will need to be of high quality and will require constant support from all disciplines outside the institution. They should therefore be associated with the appropriate academic departments in the universities, a link which we hope will also serve to encourage research in the field of treatment of personality disorder.

PSYCHOPATHS
SUMMARY OF CONCLUSIONS

I. The nature and definition of psychopathic disorder

1. We have given some account of the historical development of the concept of psychopathic disorder and of the continuing diversity of opinion as to its nature. (Paragraphs 5.1–5.18.)

II. Psychopathic disorder in the Mental Health Act 1959

2. Dissatisfaction with the concept has led many witnesses to suggest that "psychopathic disorder" should be removed from the definitions of mental disorder in section 4 of the Mental Health Act. This is outside our remit because of the effect on Part IV, but in view of the evidence we have received and the consideration we have given to the whole subject we have made what we hope may be some helpful observations on the implications of this course. (Paragraphs 5.19–5.26.)

III. Treatment of psychopaths

3. The Royal Commission on Mental Illness and Mental Deficiency 1954–57 recommended that only where penal measures alone were clearly inappropriate should offender psychopaths be treated by other means. For those thought suitable for medical treatment diagnostic and treatment centres, with associated research, were recommended by the Working Party on the Special Hospitals in 1961 but have not been provided, and there is continuing uncertainty as to the treatability, in a medical sense, of the various conditions covered by the term "psychopathic disorder" or of the methods to be used. The Continental experience of specialist psychiatric treatment institutions for psychopaths is discouraging. Some treatment methods practised in this country which are claimed to have some success are not suitable for the more aggressive psychopathic offender when they can be provided only in the open conditions of local

99

psychiatric hospitals. These offenders are generally sent to prison. Modification of their social behaviour is the object of treatment of these cases and the penal system should continue to receive them. (Paragraphs 5.27–5.38.)

4. Controlled research and experiment are necessary to determine what conditions and treatment regime produce the most encouraging results, but our view is that a long-term training regime designed to encourage the natural process of maturation would be likely to have success. We envisage this training programme being carried out in special units within the prison system. (See further at conclusion 6 below.) (Paragraphs 5.38–5.39.)

5. We propose an amendment of section 60(1) of the Mental Health Act to make clear the responsibility of the prison system to deal with dangerous anti-social psychopathic offenders where there are no indications of justification for admission to hospital. The amendment should not apply to juveniles under the age of 17; they should not be sent to prison. It should continue to be possible to transfer psychopaths from prison to hospital under section 72. (Paragraphs 5.40–5.42.)

IV. Training units

6. We put forward proposals for the training and treatment of dangerous anti-social psychopaths on a voluntary basis in special units within the penal system and have suggested the type of regime we think may prove successful. A start should be made on an experimental basis and research should be "built-in" from the outset. A scientifically valid pilot research study should be set up with the help of the Medical Research Council; initially this might be carried out in existing prison accommodation. (Paragraphs 5.43–5.57.)

CHAPTER 6

PROVISION FOR INADEQUATES

(1) Characteristics of the "inadequate"

6.1 In recent years there has been an increasing public awareness of the considerable numbers of rootless and often homeless persons in London and other large conurbations who are incapable of living in the community without continuous supervision and support and who are loosely labelled "inadequates".[1] Among this group are to be found individuals suffering from distinct psychiatric disorders, often personality disorder, chronic schizophrenia or organic psychosis, a number who are subnormal and many others on the borderline of mental disorder or dependent to some degree upon drugs or alcohol. Most have some experience of institutional treatment whether in prison or hospital, voluntary hostel or government reception centre, and while some may by temperament be natural "loners", others are completely institutionalised and quite unable to cope with life on their own.

6.2 It should not be supposed that they are therefore always receptive to help. On the contrary, help offered is often rejected. When offered sheltered accommodation to go to on their release from prison, for example, they may well refuse it, or accept it but not turn up, or leave within a matter of hours. The help of voluntary organisations is often more acceptable than that of the local authority social services or other statutory bodies with their hint of officialdom. Another factor is that the accommodation provided, modest though it may appear to the rest of us, may yet be too well furnished and equipped to be familiar and comfortable for those who have been used to living without even basic amenities. Many "inadequates" prefer to sleep rough, in the open or in derelict property, where it is likely that nobody will question who they are or what they are doing. Few are employed or even employable, and those who are seldom hold down a job for more than a few days. They often come to the notice of the police as a result of petty acts of lawbreaking or because their behaviour is offensive or frightening to passers-by or local residents. Sometimes they commit apparently pointless offences in order to secure their return to the familiar surroundings of a prison cell.

6.3 No reliable statistics are available. The Working Party on Vagrancy and Street Offences have referred in a working paper issued in 1974 to an estimate by the former National Assistance Board in 1965 that over the country there were probably between 13,000 and 14,000 people who sometimes slept rough, and have referred also to a physical count made on one night in December 1965, when 275 people were found actually sleeping rough in London and 965 in the whole country. A count made by voluntary organisations on 20 October 1972 is said to have found some 1,400 people sleeping out in London. One estimate of the total number of people in the country either sleeping rough or staying in lodging houses, night shelters or reception centres, referred to by the Working Party, has put the figure at over 40,000. The average number of beds occupied each night in reception centres in London has risen from 590 in 1970 to 871

---

[1] Not to be confused with the now outdated concept of the "inadequate psychopath". We recognise that the word "inadequate" may be regarded as pejorative; however, we use the term with compassion. Interpreted in the same spirit its meaning in the present context will be generally understood, and we have preferred to avoid recourse to obscure circumlocutions.

in 1973. Of course, not everyone who sleeps rough or uses reception centres or similar accommodation is necessarily "inadequate" or a vagrant: for example, some people with only temporary problems do so. But the great majority are permanently socially handicapped, and many circulate round the psychiatric hospitals, the prisons, and the various types of accommodation provided by the official and the voluntary agencies. About one in five of those using the Camberwell Reception Centre have or have had some form of mental disorder. Women and some young people of both sexes are among the ranks of the homeless "inadequates", and their needs must be kept in mind when provision is being made.

(2) Reduction in accommodation

6.4 Although the problem of the socially inadequate is by no means new, various factors have combined to make it increasingly acute. Historically, the first was the closure by the National Assistance Board in the 1950s of many of the reception centres which had taken over the function of the pre-war casual wards. Next, with the passing of the Mental Health Act 1959 considerable numbers of patients who had hitherto been compulsorily detained, often for long periods, under the provisions of the Mental Deficiency and Lunacy and Mental Treatment Acts could no longer be legally held and were discharged into the community or discharged themselves, although facilities for their continuing care in the community were lacking. Subsequently, the shelter of the large mental hospitals was withdrawn from others as a result of developments in the treatment of mental disorder. The policy embodied in the Hospital Plan of 1962[2] of providing for the treatment of short-stay mental illness patients in small units as near as possible to their homes, and of subnormal patients in units of up to about 200 beds in areas where after training employment would be available, was expected to mean that in course of time a large number of the existing mental hospitals would be abandoned, their functions being shared between community agencies and psychiatric units in general hospitals. These developments, as we have remarked elsewhere, have been accompanied by a move away from the concept of the closed hospital and the locked ward in favour of therapeutic policies based on the open-door principle. As a result the hospitals are unwilling to accept custodial responsibilities for their patients, and find it increasingly hard to contain patients who are disruptive or unco-operative. Many hospitals have shed their former role as a sanctuary for patients unable to profit from specific short-term medical treatment but merely requiring care and control in an institutional setting. A general effect of these policies and developments has been to reduce the possibilities for the socially inadequate of finding places of refuge in the old mental hospitals.[3]

6.5 Other relevant factors include the widespread closure of common lodging houses, which provide simple accommodation and an undemanding environment for many social inadequates; and a reduction in the number of beds provided by voluntary organisations for homeless "inadequates". A report by a Home Office Working Group on Residential Provision for Offenders in

---

[2] Cmnd. 1604, paragraphs 27 and 28.

[3] We have been informed by the Department of Health and Social Security that the number of available hospital beds for mentally ill and mentally handicapped patients in England and Wales dropped from 212,700 in 1960 to 174,800 in 1973.

the Community ascribes the general and substantial reduction of this accommodation to modernisation (including the replacement of dormitories by single rooms), financial problems and social trends.

(3) Solutions

(i) *The role of the National Health Service*

6.6   We regret the loss of the provision of a modest protected environment in local psychiatric hospitals for this type of offender.   Many such hospitals would still be in an excellent position to supply sheltered lodging and working conditions well within the patient's restricted capabilities, and would certainly be appropriate in many cases even on an informal basis. Where an "inadequate" offender displays a recognisable psychiatric disorder it should be the responsibility of the hospitals to provide appropriate treatment.   Hospitals also have a role in the continuing care of those who cannot be discharged into the community without a serious risk of relapse through self-neglect.   Although we accept that hospitals may be unable to prevent "inadequate" patients discharging themselves we think that they should in general be prepared to re-admit such cases where, for example, they are subsequently detained by the police under the provisions of section 136 of the Mental Health Act or otherwise come to the attention of the authorities.   Notwithstanding the difficulties that may sometimes be involved for individual hospitals, the National Health Service should in our view consider whether it could not play a greater part in the provision of shelter for these people, bearing in mind that medical treatment "includes nursing, and also includes care and training under medical supervision" (section 147(1) of the Act), and the important contribution that might be made by the social workers in the hospitals.   The reintroduction to some extent of a sanctuary role would particularly serve those people who are already so damaged that they are unable to take advantage of the rehabilitation measures which hospitals normally pursue.   We hope that the projected White Paper (see paragraph 2.12 above) will deal with this point.

(ii) *Facilities for alcoholics and drug takers*

6.7   Some of the people we are discussing will be in need of special services and treatment as alcoholics or drug takers.   Implementation of the recommendations made by the Working Party on Habitual Drunken Offenders in 1971 (which have been accepted by the Government) would be helpful in meeting the needs of alcoholics.   The recommendations included a considerable increase of hostel beds for homeless alcoholics; the development, in the light of experience of experimental detoxification centres, of facilities where drunken offenders could sober up and be helped to withdraw from alcohol; and the provision of treatment, supportive accommodation and other assistance. Under a scheme introduced in 1973 the Department of Health and Social Security offer capital and revenue grants to voluntary bodies providing hostels and other accommodation for alcoholics (for details see paragraph 8.16). Section 34 of the Criminal Justice Act 1972 gave the police power to take a person found drunk in a public place direct to an approved medical treatment centre for alcoholics, the general intention being that constructive efforts to help the alcoholic should be preferred to prosecution, but unfortunately progress in providing the treatment facilities recommended by the Working Party has been slow.   We understand that since the former Regional Hospital

Boards were asked in 1971 to consider setting up a number of experimental detoxification centres with the help of central funds, only in Manchester, where a detoxification service is expected to open in 1976, has a scheme been agreed. In Birmingham, the one other region to show interest in establishing a hospital-based detoxification centre, local difficulties which held up progress for a time have now been resolved and planning discussions are proceeding. In London it has not been possible to obtain proposals for a hospital-based centre and efforts are being made to establish a community-based centre run by a voluntary body in co-operation with hospitals, the police and local authorities. A proposal to establish a community-based experimental detoxification centre in Leeds is also known to the Department of Health and Social Security and the possibility of supporting it financially is being considered. This slow progress is most disappointing. We understand that the position will now be for consideration by the newly appointed Advisory Committee on Alcoholism and that a sub-group of the Committee has been charged specifically to study the needs of the homeless alcoholic and to promote the relevant services. For drug takers treatment services, though overloaded in some areas, exist under the National Health Service and detoxification may be carried out as a part of treatment, usually by means of short periods of in-patient hospital care. Community services for rehabilitation or support are mainly provided through voluntary bodies.

(iii) *Resettlement in the community*

6.8   Effective resettlement in the community, with whatever support may be necessary, is the ideal to be aimed at.[4]   We have been interested to see that the Working Group referred to in paragraph 6.5, although technically concerned only with accommodation for offenders, has thought it right to observe that the need is to provide for the "inadequate" homeless in general: " . . . we believe strongly that inadequate offenders and discharged offenders should not be regarded as a race apart from other inadequate people.   On the contrary, their needs are often identical or very similar and it is often only a matter of chance whether a homeless inadequate person is, at any particular point of time, strictly to be regarded as an offender or a discharged offender or neither." At present the requisite resources are not generally available, and we agree that there is a great need for the provision by local authorities and voluntary bodies of more long-term caring or supportive accommodation for single homeless people, amongst whom many "inadequates" are to be found.   But with the pressures on local authorities and the financial problems already arising it is evident that progress in expanding this provision will be slow. A circular (37/72) issued by the Department of Health and Social Security in 1972 invited local authorities to consider the needs of adults with personality disorders in their areas and what action might be taken either by the local authority itself or by mobilising or co-operating with voluntary effort.   It was suggested that what was required was practical experiment by means of a range of small scale projects to find ways of helping these unsettled people towards a more stable, less self-destructive life.   We are informed by the Department that the circular has encouraged greater interest in the problem, and that a number of schemes have been started (for example, a day shelter in Leeds)

---

[4] We deal with question of the general provision of hostel accommodation in paragraphs 8.11–8.19.

with the help of an initial grant from the Department; but in view of the increasing financial difficulties of the local authorities it would not be realistic to expect many new major projects to be launched in the near future. The lack of local authority accommodation and supporting resources generally means that the needs of mentally disordered "inadequate" people are not met, despite the obligations on local authorities to provide for them. In this connection we welcome the provisions of the Housing Act 1974 under which hostels become eligible for housing association grant and other financial support. While we recognise that financial assistance to hostels will be available only to those whose primary purpose is to provide housing and that those whose primary purpose is to provide a substantial degree of residential care will not qualify for housing association grant, we hope that the new provisions will, perhaps indirectly, help to ease the problem of accommodating single homeless inadequate people.

6.9   We refer in paragraph 8.15 to the financial help given by the Home Office in connection with the rehabilitation of offenders to voluntary organisations prepared to set up and run "after-care" hostels (as they are called, although they are not limited to taking offenders from prisons or hospitals); and in paragraph 8.18 we describe the powers conferred on probation and after-care committees by section 53(1) of the Criminal Justice Act 1972, now consolidated in paragraph 11 of Schedule 3 of the Powers of Criminal Courts Act 1973, to provide after-care hostels, among other types of establishment, though none has yet done so. The existing after-care hostels do not accept many of the mentally disordered, and we point out in paragraphs 8.17 and 8.19 the need for much more accommodation to be provided with these people specifically in mind. Supportive accommodation, if possible offering sheltered employment, is particularly important for the inadequate, and we hope that every encouragement (especially, for the voluntary bodies, generous grants-in-aid) will be given by the Government to secure its sufficient provision. In this connection, Government reception centres have a substantial contribution to make. So also have day training centres, which the statutory provisions mentioned above enabled the probation and after-care service to set up, to provide, as a condition of a probation order, full-time non-residential training for offenders. We refer to these centres again in paragraph 8.20.

(iv) *Custodial control*

6.10   The Departmental Working Group referred to in paragraph 6.5 proposed that probation homes, hitherto provided only for juveniles, should be established for adults, and in particular for the older institutionalised or "inadequate" men who are unable to hold employment in the community. There they would stay under the control of a probation order, with suitable sheltered employment. We have been informed that four of these homes, including one for women, are now being established, the first of which should be open by the end of 1975, and we believe that developments on these lines offer considerable hope. Research into the operation of these homes and the results achieved should be established at the outset and plans should be made for quick expansion of the provision if it proves successful.

6.11   The courts already have power to direct offenders to probation hostels and homes, after-care hostels and other similar establishments available for use in connection with the rehabilitation of offenders, by making a probation order with an appropriate condition of residence attached: this, however, requires the consent and subsequent co-operation of the offender. The offences the "inadequate" mentally disordered offender commits are usually trivial, but in practice prison is often the only disposal at present available to the court which will ensure a period of care and containment. This will in many cases benefit the man himself, who may be in need of nourishment and medical care, in addition to shelter; moreover, the formal structure and regular routine of prison life provide an environment which "inadequate" people tend to find reassuring and acceptable. We think that the Home Office should examine the possible need for special arrangements to cater for this class of offender.

6.12 Although prison is likely to continue to be the most common disposal for "inadequate" offenders, and it does, as we have said, at least provide the structured and disciplined environment which many of them require, we accept that there are substantial objections of principle to subjecting to incarceration in penal institutions those whose primary need is for long term support rather than punishment. The suggestion was made to us in evidence by HM Judges that there was a need for some form of institution midway between the psychiatric hospital and the prison where custodial as opposed to penal control could be exercised. Such an institution would deal with cases where the court was satisfied that there was evidence of some mental disorder and that some form of appropriate custodial care was required, but the medical authorities were unwilling or unable to provide it in hospitals. Although the aims of the institution would not primarily be therapeutic, it was envisaged that it would have adequate medical provision so that any indication that psychiatric treatment was required could be followed up. Entry to the institution would be by order of the court and it was for consideration whether a maximum term should be specified or whether an indefinite period was to be preferred.

6.13 While we fully appreciate, and share, the Judges' concern at the lack of suitable provision for this group of offenders we do not think the answer lies in the establishment of an institution on the lines proposed, which might prove to be open to many of the same objections as the prisons without their corresponding advantages. In particular there would be the difficulty of deciding on an appropriate sentence. It is unacceptable on general penal principles to commit a person to any form of indefinite detention except for a grave offence; and, whereas indeterminacy in the hospital context may be justifiable on medical grounds where there is the prospect of treatment or cure of the psychiatric condition, we note that the aim of the proposed institution is not primarily therapeutic. But if offenders would be sent to such an institution only for a determinate period the period fixed by the court would inevitably be fairly short. We believe that the need seen by the Judges would be substantially met by the provision of more of the institutions (general hostels and more particularly probation homes) to which we have already referred (see paragraphs 6.9 and 6.10 above).

(4) Conclusion

6.14 In discussing appropriate treatment and facilities for "inadequates" it is difficult to draw a line between those measures that may properly be imposed by a court when sentencing a person found to have committed a particular offence, and those which, although they may appear desirable in the interests of the long-term rehabilitation and support of that person, or the protection of society against his possible future law-breaking, can scarcely be justified in terms of the offence which has brought him to notice. It is obviously right that a person suffering from mental disorder should be given the opportunity to receive appropriate treatment and access to such after-care facilities as may be available; and that society should take steps to protect itself against those who otherwise may commit offences which may do serious and irreparable harm. But in cases where treatment and facilities are offered but repeatedly rejected and where any future law-breaking is likely to be minor or solely of nuisance value, we think that it may be right to accept, in the end, that the particular offender is not susceptible to rehabilitation by the efforts of the official agencies and that, apart from the courts imposing any penalties appropriate to the offences he may go on to commit, the official services can fulfil no useful purpose by continuing attempts to induce him to accept their help.

PROVISION FOR INADEQUATES
SUMMARY OF CONCLUSIONS

1. The large numbers of socially "inadequate" persons who are largely dependent for their survival on assistance by institutions, social services and voluntary organisations include many who are suffering from some form of mental disorder. The reduction over the years in the accommodation which has traditionally catered for these people has led to the problem becoming particularly acute. (Paragraphs 6.1–6.5.)

2. The Committee regret the loss of the protected environment role in local psychiatric hospitals and think consideration should be given to the possibility of the National Health Service playing a greater part in the provision of shelter for "inadequates". (Paragraph 6.6.)

3. Hospitals and other specialised institutions should provide for the medical treatment of "inadequates", including alcoholics and drug takers, where this is required. We note the disappointing lack of progress in providing detoxification centres, as recommended by the Working Party on Habitual Drunken Offenders in 1971, and hope that the new Advisory Committee on Alcoholism will be able to suggest ways of overcoming the difficulties. (Paragraph 6.7.)

4. There is a great need for local authorities to provide more long-term supportive accommodation for single homeless people, many of whom are "inadequates", regardless of whether they are offenders. The resources to support their effective resettlement in the community do not generally exist at present. But we recognise the financial problems with which the local authorities are currently faced. (Paragraph 6.8.)

5. The provision of "after-care" hostels by voluntary organisations under the Home Office scheme for rehabilitation of offenders and, in future, by the probation and after-care service, is of particular importance for the support of the inadequate mentally disordered offender. We urge the provision of more of this accommodation particularly hostels providing sheltered employment, with "inadequate" mentally disordered offenders specifically in mind.

Government reception centres also have an important contribution to make. The new probation homes for adults seem a hopeful development and plans should be made for a quick expansion of this provision if they prove successful. (Paragraphs 6.9–6.10.)

6. In practice prison offers the only disposal available to the court for many "inadequate" mentally disordered offenders who require care and containment for a while. Although there are objections of principle to placing in penal institutions men for whom the courts do not consider a penal sanction is appropriate, prison provides them with in some respects a suitable (and, in many cases, familiar) environment. It may be that special arrangements could be devised for them. The Home Office should consider this. (Paragraphs 6.11–6.12.)

7. We do not think that the needs of the "inadequate" mentally disordered offender can be suitably met by the establishment of a new form of institution offering facilities half-way between those of the psychiatric hospital and the prison. (Paragraphs 6.12 and 6.13.)

8. Where a man's offences, although persistent, are trivial and make him merely a nuisance, and he rejects all attempts to help him, it may be right in the end to accept that the official services cannot usefully do anything more. (Paragraph 6.14.)

CHAPTER 7

DISCHARGE

I. DISCHARGE OF PATIENTS DETAINED UNDER HOSPITAL ORDERS[1]

(1) Role of the responsible medical officer

7.1   Except in cases dealt with by Mental Health Review Tribunals, which we discuss later in this chapter, the decision to discharge a patient who is detained in hospital under an order made under section 60 of the Mental Health Act, without any accompanying restriction order, is a matter for the clinical judgment of the responsible medical officer. The information he will require will vary from case to case, according to the circumstances. In its strictly medical aspects, the decision to be made for an offender-patient is essentially no different from the decision to be made for a non-offender patient. As we explained in paragraphs 4.11–4.16 above we are in no doubt of the difficulty of forecasting future behaviour. A patient who behaves perfectly well in hospital may behave very differently outside. The fallibility of psychiatric judgment has been mentioned by various witnesses; and the Aarvold Committee said that the judgment of the responsible medical officer might, in some circumstances, be affected by influences of which he was unaware and in spite of his search for objectivity. A doctor who was formerly at Rampton Hospital has told us his opinion that the responsibility of deciding on discharge (and on transfers to other hospitals) is often too heavy for one man. We have considered whether there should be a statutory requirement that before deciding on the discharge of a mentally disordered offender detained under a hospital order without restrictions the doctor should always obtain the opinion of another doctor. We do not make such a recommendation because circumstances vary widely and there are many cases in which a second opinion would not be justified. The normal procedure should not be made unduly cumbersome. A doctor who is in any doubt about the decision he should make can readily obtain the opinions of colleagues. He should in any event always take into account the views of staff of other disciplines, as we remark in paragraph 7.12 below. We think that as regards patients subject to hospital orders without restrictions the matter should be left on this discretionary basis.

7.2   The decision to discharge any patient should not be taken without considering the situation awaiting him outside the hospital, and for offenders the problems of return to the community are generally particularly acute. It is not the doctor's job to make the requisite inquiries and arrangements, but we think it is for him to satisfy himself that proper inquiries and arrangements have been made before he exercises his very responsible function of deciding that the patient is to be returned into the world at large. We refer in paragraph 8.3 to the evidence obtained from research as to the value of any form of contact by the hospital or after-care agencies with offender-patients after their discharge from hospital in reducing the likelihood of reconviction and fostering the patient's stability in employment. This is, in our view, so important that

---

[1] The situation that sometimes occurs where a patient subject to a hospital order is discharged very soon after admission because it is found that he does not need in-patient treatment, or has no intention of co-operating, is discussed in paragraphs 14.8–14.12 below.

while we have rejected the imposition on the responsible medical officer of a statutory requirement to certify that he has satisfied himself that so far as is practicable in the circumstances suitable after-care arrangements have been made before the patient's discharge becomes effective, we think that good practice requires that he invariably should so satisfy himself. Where, exceptionally, he regards after-care as unnecessary or impracticable we hope that he will officially record his reasons. This information may be important if the patient offends again.

7.3 Some of the present difficulties surrounding the discharge of patients subject to section 60 orders might, we think, be avoided if discharge were conditional in the first instance. Section 39 of the Mental Health Act provides that patients compulsorily detained in hospital under Part IV of the Act may be given leave of absence by the responsible medical officer either for a specified period or indefinitely. The patient is subject to recall to hospital at any time but the power to revoke leave of absence lapses after six months. These provisions apply also to section 60 hospital patients. It is the practice of some doctors to grant patients long home leave under these provisions before deciding on their final discharge, and this enables them to bring their patients back to hospital if this seems desirable. The value of this system was recognised by the Royal Commission on the Law relating to Mental Illness and Mental Deficiency.[2] They contemplated that well before the end of the six months' period of leave during which, should it prove necessary, the patient may be recalled, his day-to-day care might be taken over by the local authority social service department. Arrangements on these lines seem to us to be very sensible and we hope that in future home leave will be more widely utilised as a prelude to discharge, or as a stage in the process of discharge. We have noted that the six months' limit provided for under section 39 is sometimes avoided by recalling the patient to hospital for a few days, near the end of the six months, and then sending him out on a fresh period of leave. While this practice can be defended on the ground that the patient's progress ought to be assessed by the doctors before he is finally discharged, and that he will be discharged as soon as the doctors are satisfied, we think that the renewal of the hospital's hold over a patient is difficult to justify where the patient has been living satisfactorily in the community for nearly six months.

(2) Role of the Mental Health Review Tribunal

7.4 As a safeguard for psychiatric patients in general against unjustified detention in hospital or control under guardianship the Royal Commission on the Law Relating to Mental Illness and Mental Deficiency recommended[3] that cases should be subject to review from both medical and non-medical points of view by some local body. They proposed that patients should have an opportunity to apply to a Tribunal which would consist of medical and non-medical members selected from a panel of suitable persons appointed for each hospital region. These recommendations were carried into effect in the Mental Health Act, section 3 of which provided for the setting up of Mental Health Review Tribunals; the procedures to be followed were laid down in the Mental Health Review Tribunal Rules, 1960.[4] The powers and proceedings

[2] Cmnd. 169, paragraphs 469–477.
[3] Cmnd. 169, paragraph 442.
[4] SI 1139, 1960.

of the Tribunals are dealt with in sections 122–124 of the Act. The circumstances in which offender-patients may apply to the Tribunal for a review of their case are prescribed in a number of provisions in the Act which are summarised in Appendix 6 to this Report. Broadly the position is that patients subject to hospital orders may apply to the Tribunal once within the six months from the date of the order[5] (or, if under age 16, when admitted, from the 16th birthday); and (for patients aged 16 or over) after any renewal of the authority for detention (which may take place after the end of the first and second years in hospital and thereafter at two-year intervals). The patient's nearest relative has the right to apply to the Tribunal once in the first 12 months after the making of the order and once a year thereafter.

7.5   Section 123(1) of the Act empowers a Tribunal in any case where application has been made by or in respect of a patient to direct that the patient be discharged; and the Tribunal must so direct if they are satisfied:

"(a) that he is not then suffering from mental illness, psychopathic disorder, subnormality or severe subnormality; or

(b) that it is not necessary in the interests of the patient's health or safety or for the protection of other persons that the patient should continue to be liable to be detained; or

(c) in the case of an application under subsection (3) of section 44 or subsection (3) of section 48 of this Act, that the patient, if released, would not be likely to act in a manner dangerous to other persons or to himself".

Under subsection (2) the Tribunal have a similar discretionary power in respect of a patient subject to guardianship, and are required to direct that he be discharged if they are satisfied:

"(a) that he is not then suffering from mental illness, psychopathic disorder, subnormality or severe subnormality; or

(b) that it is not necessary in the interests of the patient, or for the protection of other persons, that the patient should remain under such guardianship".

7.6   We have explained in the introductory chapter the reasons why we have concluded that we would not be justified, under our terms of reference, in reviewing povisions and arrangements which apply not merely to mentally disordered offenders but to offenders in general or to the mentally disordered in general. On this basis we have found ourselves in some difficulty about Mental Health Review Tribunals, which are provided as a safeguard for all psychiatric patients compulsorily detained or subject to guardianship. We have received various proposals for changes in the composition of the Tribunals, but we do not think that we could properly make general recommendations on this matter, on which we have no evidence with regard to non-offender cases. We may perhaps be allowed to express the hope, however, that forensic psychiatrists, as they increase in numbers, may have the opportunity of serving on the Tribunals.

7.7   But because of the particular importance of adequate after-care arrangements for mentally disordered offenders, which we shall enlarge upon in

---

[5] For patients transferred to hospital from prison or guardianship the relevant date is the date of the transfer direction.

Chapter 8, we feel entitled to comment on one of the main criticisms of the operation of Mental Health Review Tribunals, put to us by a number of witnesses, namely their failure, or at any rate the failure of some of them, to ensure that appropriate arrangements have been made before they order the discharge of a patient. The explanation seems to lie in the interpretation of the Tribunal's functions as prescribed in section 123 of the Act (see paragraph 7.5 above), and in the Rules (see next paragraph). The view taken is that as soon as the criteria for discharge have been established it is improper for the patient to be further detained even briefly. No doubt the patient himself often adds to the sense of urgency by insisting on being released and denying that any arrangements need be made for his after-care. Some witnesses have suggested that Tribunals should have power to delay release pending the completion of after-care arrangements.

7.8 Rule 27(3) of the Mental Health Tribunal Rules 1960 provides that the decision of the Tribunal shall be communicated in writing within seven days to the responsible authority, the applicant, and the patient if he is not the applicant. Once the letter is received the patient may leave hospital immediately he wishes. We have been informed that in local psychiatric hospitals patients may remain informally whilst after-care arrangements are made but this is not possible in the special hospitals because of the terms of section 40 of the National Health Service Reorganisation Act 1973, which permit detained patients only to be accommodated (see paragraph 2.14). In practice most patients in the special hospitals are prepared to remain for a few days as "guests", but they can insist on leaving at once. A patient who is discharged by the Tribunal is discharged unconditionally and cannot be compelled to comply with any after-care arrangements made for him, although it is obviously to his advantage to do so.

7.9 The Department of Health and Social Security have informed us that inquiries made of the special hospital medical superintendents in 1970 as to whether it would be helpful for an amendment to be made to the Rules to allow the Tribunal to postpone discharge for 14 days to allow arrangements for after-care to be made showed that there had been very few cases in which this would have been of any advantage. It was considered that a patient who was not willing to spend a few extra days in a special hospital as a guest while arrangements were made was unlikely to take full advantage of any arrangements eventually made for him.

7.10 It is always open to a Tribunal to adjourn a hearing if they consider that any further inquiries ought to be made before a decision is reached. We think that this is the appropriate solution to the problem, and we recommend that Tribunals should not reach a formal decision that any mentally disordered offender patient should be discharged until they have established that whatever needs to be done to return him to as satisfactory a situation as possible in the community has, so far as may be practicable, been done.

II. DISCHARGE OF RESTRICTED PATIENTS

(1) Introductory comments

7.11 We have described in Chapter 2 (paragraphs 2.31–2.32) and Chapter 4 (paragraphs 4.17–4.33) the existing provisions and arrangements relating to restriction orders made under section 65 of the Mental Health Act, and our recommendations for their modification and extension. The changes we have proposed relate almost entirely to special hospital cases, including those transferred to local psychiatric hospitals or the regional secure units or discharged into the community; under our proposals all section 65 patients in or transferred from the special hospitals would have their cases referred to an advisory body before the decision to discharge them into the community was taken. The final decision would continue to be for the Home Secretary. The present system will continue without substantial alteration in respect of other section 65 (non-special hospital) cases treated in the local psychiatric hospitals. It is not necessary for us to repeat here the account we have already given of the applicable legal provisions, but we now discuss some of the criticisms put to us of the operation of the section 65 system which will still apply to these local hospital cases.

7.12 Apart from the intervention of the Home Secretary the problems involved in the decision to discharge these restricted patients are essentially the same as those in unrestricted hospital order cases, which we have outlined in paragraphs 7.1–7.3. The difficulties of prediction of future behaviour are likely to be more significant in cases where risk to the public has previously been suggested, and, as the Aarvold Committee recommended,[6] in considering the question of discharge the responsible medical officer should take account of information and opinions from as many sources as possible, covering not only the patient's past behaviour but his probable future situation. We ourselves attach great value to inter-disciplinary case conferences, not only for decisions about restricted patients. We also agree with the Committee[7] that wherever possible the recommendation of a responsible medical officer for the discharge of any restricted patient from hospital should be supported by the recorded views of other professional personnel with knowledge of and responsibility for the patient, including his rehabilitation.

7.13 Arrangements for after-care are of even greater importance for restricted patients than for other hospital order patients. The Home Secretary is particularly concerned to ensure that satisfactory arrangements have been made before he authorises the discharge of a restricted patient, and difficulties sometimes arise between the hospital and the Home Office when the arrangements made are considered by him to be unsatisfactory and delays in discharge result. We deal with this point further in paragraph 7.18 below.

(2) Questions arising

(i) Criticisms of the Home Secretary's powers

7.14 A number of witnesses have argued that the Home Secretary's powers should be reduced. Some have objected to the intervention of a political Minister in what they see as primarily a question of the release of a hospital patient on the grounds that he may be open to pressure of general public opinion or even of his constituency interests. Others have referred to the complications and delays, which may be detrimental to the patient, resulting from the need to inform, consult and satisfy the Home Office before clinical decisions to give a patient leave of absence, or to transfer or discharge him, can be carried out.

---

[6] Cmnd. 5191, paragraph 18.

[7] Cmnd. 5191, paragraph 32(i).

It has been proposed that discharge of restricted patients in local psychiatric hospitals should be decided by the hospital managers or by a Mental Health Review Tribunal. Another suggestion has been that the final decision might rest with an enlarged Mental Health Review Tribunal or with a Committee of the Appeals Court, but that whatever tribunal or body might be given the power of final decision in these cases it should conduct its proceedings in public and the patient should be legally represented. The British Medical Association, stressing the encroachment on the doctor's time of communicating with the Home Office, have recommended that discharge should be settled at the regional level.

7.15 Other evidence has supported continuance of the exercise of responsibility by the Home Secretary in section 65 cases, particularly having regard to the need to ensure the protection of the public. A variant has been the suggestion of the Confederation of Health Service Employees that the discharge of all mentally disordered offenders convicted of offences not triable summarily should rest with the Home Secretary advised by a panel of medical, social and legal experts; while the discharge of mentally disordered offenders convicted of less serious offences should require the authority of the Secretary of State for Social Services, advised by similar regional panels.

7.16 It seems to us that the question whether it is safe to release a section 65 patient, who by definition has been identified by the court as possibly representing a future risk to the public, necessarily involves considerations of public safety and the maintenance of law and order which cannot appropriately be withdrawn from the Home Secretary's responsibilities. Similar questions are involved in deciding whether prisoners (who may also have some mental disorder) can be paroled, or released on licence from life sentences, and in these cases also the final responsibility rests with the Home Secretary, advised by the Parole Board. We do not think that it would be acceptable to public opinion that the discharge from hospital of offender patients identified by the court as potentially dangerous should be decided locally by the hospital managers or a Mental Health Review Tribunal, who are not primarily concerned with public safety, or publicly accountable for their decisions. If the decision is to remain Ministerial it seems essentially one for the Home Secretary, along with his functions in relation to the release on licence of prisoners, rather than for the Secretary of State for Social Services. It seems to us proper that in discharging his constitutional responsibility for the protection of the public the Minister should have regard to, among other things, the maintenance of public confidence in the system.

(ii) *Criticisms of the Home Office*

7.17 We have looked into the question of the difficulties which arise between some hospital consultants and the Home Office. Home Office representatives giving oral evidence readily acknowledged that the Home Office, like other institutions, suffers from limitations of staff and pressure of work which sometimes lead to unjustifiable delays; but they made the point that some of the difficulties complained of by doctors in their dealings with the Department arise where the doctor is not familiar, from past experience, with the procedure required to enable the Department to carry out its responsibility for balancing the clinical interests of the patient, which are the primary concern of the doctor, against the protection of society. Some problems arise from lack of communication: for example, one complaint made to us was that restricted patients could not participate in outside activities, and a normal programme of rehabilitation was therefore impossible for them, because they could not leave the hospital, even if accompanied, without the prior permission of the Home Secretary; but the Department have told us that they are usually able to give the doctor a general covering authority in all suitable cases, and repeated applications to the Home Office for the same patient are not necessary. The Department's remarks have been largely borne out by the discussions we have had with doctors and other hospital staff on our visits, and the British Medical Association have said that much depends on the relationship between the individual psychiatrist and the Home Office.

7.18 If the Department is to exercise responsibly its statutory function in connection with the discharge of restricted patients, it can do so only on the basis of adequate information, including knowledge of the arrangements for subsequent supervision, and an assessment of the risks involved. Some doctors do not provide adequate information when they seek the Department's agreement to the patient's discharge, which perhaps they regard as merely a tiresome formality. It is then necessary for the Department to request the information. Another reason for delays is that sometimes arrangements made by the hospital for after-care and supervision are not satisfactory from the point of view of the Department's responsibilities and the papers have to wait while further inquiries and alternative arrangements are made. It has to be recognised that in restricted cases the Home Secretary himself may have to defend his decision in Parliament and it is the duty of his Department to ensure that all proper steps have been taken. But the officials are acutely aware that a doctor who has a section 65 patient and finds difficulty in coping with the formalities involved will be reluctant to accept further restricted cases, and we have no reason to doubt that they wish to be as helpful as they can in these matters.

(iii) *Home Office delays in Mental Health Review Tribunal cases*
7.19 Concern has been expressed to us by a number of witnesses about the time it takes in some cases for the Home Secretary to decide whether to accept recommendations of the Mental Health Review Tribunals in restricted cases. Unfavourable recommendations are generally accepted and notified quickly, but the complaint is mainly of delay in notifying decisions on recommendations for discharge. In some cases the delay was said to have amounted to seven months, nine months, and over 12 months. Such delays obviously cause the patient and his family considerable anxiety and may involve substantial injustices. The Chairman of a Mental Health Review Tribunal regretted the rejection "too often" of recommendations to which time and care have been given by Tribunal members but other witnesses in oral evidence said they knew of no resentment, or reluctance to serve on the Tribunals, on this account. The National Council for Civil Liberties said that on 57 occasions since the introduction of the Mental Health Act the Home Secretary had overridden a Tribunal, and in their view this implied that political considerations were brought to bear. One witness recommended that a time limit should be introduced within which the Home Secretary should give his decision; failure to do so within this specified period should be deemed to authorise the patient's release.

7.20 Complaints that recommendations carefully and conscientiously worked out by the Tribunals have been rejected by the Home Secretary seem to us to be based on the misapprehension that the function of the Tribunals and of the Home Secretary in this matter are the same. On the contrary, as has been explained above (see paragraph 7.4) the Tribunals exist as a safeguard for the patient against unjustified detention, whereas the primary function of the Home Secretary in considering these cases is the protection of the public. This is not to say that the Tribunals do not have some regard to the safety of the public, nor that the Home Secretary has no concern with the interests of the patient; but their main responsibility is different and their roles are complementary.

7.21 The criticisms of delays in deciding cases are more substantial, and we have investigated the facts. In June 1973 the Home Office provided us with details of the 686 restricted patients in all the hospitals in England and Wales in respect of whom advice was received from Tribunals in the period of two years ending on 30 April 1973. 613 of these patients were under treatment at the three special hospitals and the remaining 73 were in local hospitals. In June 1973 decisions had been reached in 647 of the 686 cases, leaving 39 still under consideration. The times taken to arrive at decisions were as follows:—

	No of Cases	%
Less than one month	474	73
More than one month, less than three months ...	52	8
More than three months, less than six months ...	77	12
More than six months	44	7
	647	

Of the 39 cases still undecided, 21 were more than three months old. The Home Office agreed with the evidence given that cases in which the Tribunal does not recommend any change in the patient's position are quickly disposed of. Where, however, the Tribunal advises a change such as discharge from hospital, or transfer from a secure special hospital to an open local one, this advice sets in train the processes of consideration by the Department which have to be applied to all such proposals, whether or not they originate with Tribunals. In many cases further inquiries are necessary, for example into the social setting to which the patient may be discharged, and decisions in cases of this kind cannot be reached quickly. In 65 of the 121 cases in which it took longer than three months to reach a decision it was eventually necessary to reject the advice of the Tribunal. The Home Office pointed out that this is a step which is never taken without very careful consideration, further inquiries where necessary and eventual reference to a Minister for final decision. In the remaining 56 cases there were features of difficulty to be investigated and overcome before it was felt right to accept the Tribunal's advice. The Department informed us that in the later half of the period covered by our review of the arrangements, the aftermath of the Graham Young case tended to cause additional delays because of the uncertainties to which the case gave rise, and the introduction of new procedures in decision taking and in making arrangements for the conditional discharge of restricted patients. But the Department stated that a regular watch was kept on the situation to ensure that decisions were reached as quickly as the circumstances of each case permitted.

7.22 The Committee recognise the importance of making adequate inquiries and ensuring that arrangements are as satisfactory as possible before authorising the discharge of section 65 patients. Delays which are strictly attributable to this cause must, in our view, be regarded as justified. We also think that it would be regrettable if negative decisions were made because of pressures to provide a quick answer, when allowing more time for inquiries and for arrangements to be worked our might enable a favourable answer to be given. However, to be fair to the patients and to spare them and their relatives unnecessary suspense and anxiety it is obviously of the greatest importance that any necessary consultations be dealt with under the greatest sense of urgency both within the Home Office and by the outside agencies concerned. Thought might also be given to sending some form of interim communication to the patient to inform him at least that his case is being pursued, and if possible to inform him of the nature of the difficulty to be resolved, but it may be that where there is unavoidably a long delay the receipt of a succession of merely interim messages may be scarcely more satisfactory than complete lack of news.

(iv) *Safeguards for the restricted patient*

7.23 An enlightened society will be concerned not only about its own protection but also about the protection of the mentally disordered person who, as a result of committing an offence, has been committed to hospital under a restriction order of indefinite duration. The overwhelming majority of section 65 orders are made without limit of time. Of 2,059 patients (male and female) in hospital under restriction orders at the end of 1974, 422 (one in five) had been detained for more than ten years. A few cases remain in detention for life. A count made of the restricted patients who were discharged from all hospitals in 1974 showed a total of 160, with an average period of detention of four years seven months. Half of this total had spent more than three years ten months in detention.

7.24 There are two main elements to be satisfied before a restricted patient is discharged: from a medical point of view he must have sufficiently recovered his health; and from the point of view of society there must be, so far as can be assessed, little risk of further serious offending. We have referred in a previous chapter (paragraph 4.13) to the pressures on the doctors to err on the side of caution. What safeguards should be provided for the patient, to protect him from being detained longer than is strictly necessary? Obviously a long-term psychiatric patient, especially if he has no interested relatives or friends, is not well able to safeguard his own interests.

7.25 The Consultant Forensic Psychiatrists and the Royal College of Psychiatrists suggested to us that regular reports should be submitted to the Home Secretary on patients under restriction orders, as a safeguard against abuses. We understand that it is the practice, although not a statutory requirement, for the responsible medical officer to submit formal reports to the hospital managers on the suitability of restricted patients for discharge, or the need for their further detention, at intervals not less frequent than those stipulated in section 43 of the Act for the renewal of the authority for detention of unrestricted patients. In the case of patients detained for long periods such reports need only be made at two-yearly intervals. While the Home Office may receive copies of these reports by courtesy of the hospital managers we do not think that such an arrangement is a satisfactory substitute for the submission of regular reports on the patient's condition direct to the Home Office, in recognition of the Home Secretary's responsibility for restricted patients. Regular reports—say, at annual intervals—might dispose of some of the problems which arise between the Home Office and the hospital psychiatrists through inadequacy of communication. We have considered whether psychiatrists who are now willing to accept section 65 patients might object to this obligation; but we think this unlikely and are encouraged in this opinion by the fact that the psychiatrists have themselves suggested the procedure. If there are any doctors who might object they are probably those who are already unwilling to accept restricted patients.

7.26 Another safeguard suggested to us is that a guardian or patients' friend should be appointed, to whom the patient could turn for help and support. One witness saw the need for a legal guardian, whose responsibility would be to visit the patient, and his family and friends if any, to watch over his interests and if necessary to provide legal representation, for example before the Mental Health Review Tribunal. The National Society for Mentally Handicapped Children similarly recommended that someone, such as a solicitor or relative, be appointed with a statutory duty to be concerned with the patients' interests and well-being, and especially to ensure that subnormal patients do not remain in hospital unnecessarily.

7.27 Such proposals may be considered as following the precedent set by section 24(5) of the Children and Young Persons Act 1969, under which persons may be appointed by local authorities to visit, advise and befriend children in community homes who have little or no contact with their parents or guardians. The position of mentally disordered offenders in institutions is, no doubt, similar in some respects to that of these children, and there might well be value in a similar safeguard for offenders who have no family contacts or whose families, as sometimes happens, are concerned only to keep them under detention so as to be spared responsibility for accommodating and supporting them.

7.28 A difficulty in the way of these proposals is that it may not in practice be possible to find enough suitable guardians. We understand that local authorities often encounter difficulty in finding suitable people for appointment under the Children and Young Persons Act. In many cases it may be possible to implement the proposals only by appointing the local authority or some other official body to discharge the responsibility, and this would not satisfy the intended object of appointing someone independent of official agencies. However, the proposals have obvious merits, and we feel that where suitable people who are willing to help mentally disordered offenders in this way can be found they should be given every encouragement. Statutory provision for their appointment as "guardians" should be made and section 24(5) of the Children and Young Persons Act 1969 might be taken as a guide in determining their duties. In view of the difficulties mentioned above appointment of a "guardian" should not be mandatory in all cases, but dependent on the availability and willingness so to act of a suitable "independent" person.

7.29 Finally, we think it right to add that if the Mental Health Review Tribunals carry out in the spirit as well as the letter the primary function for which they were established, they will take every precaution to ensure that the patient's natural rights are safeguarded, and that he receives whatever help he needs in putting his case.

DISCHARGE

SUMMARY OF CONCLUSIONS[8]

1. The decision whether to discharge a patient subject to a section 60 order is a heavy responsibility for the doctor, but he can readily consult colleagues if he wishes and should invariably take into account the views of staff of other disciplines. We are not in favour of a formal requirement that he should do so. (Paragraph 7.1.)

2. It is desirable, and we believe essential, practice for the responsible medical officer to satisfy himself that the best after-care arrangements possible in the circumstances have been made before a patient is discharged. Where, exceptionally, he regards after-care as unnecessary or impracticable we hope that he will officially record his reasons. (Paragraph 7.2.)

3. We agree with the Royal Commission on the Law Relating to Mental Illness and Mental Deficiency (paragraph 476 of their Report) that it is often helpful if discharge is preceded by home leave for a period long enough to ascertain whether discharge is likely to prove successful and whether the after-care arrangements are adequate. The provisions of the Act relating to home leave should not be used to maintain control over patients indefinitely. (Paragraph 7.3.)

4. The criticism has been made of Mental Health Review Tribunals that they do not always ensure that adequate after-care arrangements have been made before they order the discharge of a section 60 patient. We see no advantage in altering the Mental Health Review Tribunal Rules to permit the postponement of discharge, following notification of the Tribunal's decision, pending completion of adequate after-care arrangements. Tribunals should, as they may, adjourn hearings until they are satisfied that, so far as is practicable, suitable arrangements have been made. (Paragraphs 7.4–7.10.)

5. We agree with the recommendations of the Aarvold Committee on the need for the responsible medical officer in deciding whether to recommend the discharge or transfer of patients subject to a restriction order under section 65 to take account of all the available information and opinions, including the views of staff of other disciplines. (Paragraph 7.12.)

6. Public safety is an essential consideration in deciding the discharge of potentially dangerous people, and responsibility for this decision in respect of patients subject to a restriction order should remain with the Home Secretary, who is publicly accountable. (Paragraphs 7.14–7.16.)

7. Difficulties can arise, through defects of communication and lack of mutual understanding, between hospital consultants and the Home Office in dealing

---

[8] See also, as regards special hospital cases, Chapter 4, conclusions 5–8.

with restricted cases, but much depends on the relationship between the individual psychiatrist and the Department, which should rest on appreciation that each has a role quite different from the other. (Paragraphs 7.17–7.18.)

8. Criticisms have been made of the delay that is sometimes involved in making known the decision of the Home Secretary on a recommendation by Mental Health Review Tribunals for the discharge of section 65 patients and of the too frequent rejection of the Tribunal's recommendations. The latter criticism fails to recognise the difference in the responsibilities of the Tribunals, which exist primarily to safeguard the patients' interests, and of the Home Secretary, whose primary concern is the protection of the public. We have inquired into the complaints of delay and it is evident that in general the delays are occasioned by the need for the Department to be satisfied about aspects of public safety, including the circumstances into which the patient is to be discharged. We recognise this need for care in all restricted cases, but we stress that all consultations should be carried out with the greatest sense of urgency. (Paragraphs 7.19–7.22.)

9. To ensure that section 65 patients, most of whom are subject to an order made without limit of time, are not detained longer than necessary, we recommend that regular annual reports on such patients should be submitted to the Home Secretary by the responsible medical officer. We support proposals for the appointment of a guardian or patient's friend to watch over the interests of individual patients, and propose that statutory provision should be made for this. It is a proper function of the Mental Health Review Tribunals to be vigilant to safeguard patients' natural rights and to ensure that they receive any necessary help in putting their case. (Paragraphs 7.23–7.29.)

CHAPTER 8

AFTER-CARE

(1) General

8.1 The practice of "after-care" covers a wide variety of arrangements, from a single appointment for the patient to be seen a few weeks after discharge, to a continuing and close concern which may entail a social worker whether of the local authority social services department or the probation and after-care service, seeing the patient frequently and helping him with his problems, including perhaps problems of employment and accommodation and family relationships. Many offender-patients discharged from psychiatric hospitals and released from prisons have to return to unstable and unsatisfactory situations in the community. Besides the difficulties faced by all psychiatric patients when they are discharged, as offenders they have a particular handicap: the stigma of having offended is a cause of rejection by relatives, friends, landladies and the community in general, including employers, and thus destructive of self-confidence. Everything possible should be done to ensure that these people take full advantage of the general after-care facilities that are open to them. It is particularly important that after discharge they should have somewhere to live, and someone to turn to. Hospital staff who participate in discharge decisions and arrangements should themselves be on their guard against giving these people less help than others simply because they are offenders: on an objective assessment they often need more help, not less. Ideally, as we suggest later, arrangements should be taken in hand well before return to the community becomes an immediate issue: a sense of continuity between the patient's life "inside" and his future life "outside" should be actively fostered both in patients and in staff of all disciplines.

(2) After-care for discharged hospital patients

(i) *Should after-care be compulsory in all cases?*

8.2 In hospital order cases without restrictions after-care is available on a voluntary basis, but where the patient, having been detained under a section 65 order, is subject on discharge to the conditions of a licence he is required to co-operate, and the sanction of recall may be exercised if the licence conditions are infringed. (Difficulties in exercising the recall sanction where the hospital is unwilling to re-admit the patient are discussed in paragraphs 14.28–14.32). In these cases after-care involves a supervisory element. With variations of detail, a substantial volume of evidence has suggested that after-care should be compulsory for all offender-patients subject to hospital orders. The Magistrates' Association, for example, thought it desirable that the discharge arrangements should be similar to the system of parole which applies to people released from prison on licence before the expiry of their sentences, imposing a requirement to continue psychiatric oversight for a period, and that there should be comparable provision for recall, to hospital instead of to prison, in the event of breach of the conditions of licence. The County Councils Association also favoured provision for conditions to be imposed, to include continuing supervision and an approved place of residence, with the sanction of recall, and thought that this might make it possible to discharge offender-patients earlier than at present, thereby reducing the pressure under which the psychiatric hospitals have to work and freeing places for other patients.

121

Evidence in the same sense has come from the Central Council of Probation and After-Care Committees, the Royal College of Nursing, the Justices' Clerks' Society, and numerous other witnesses. The Consultant Forensic Psychiatrists pointed out the anomaly that supervision by the probation and after-care service after in-patient psychiatric treatment is a normal feature of psychiatric probation orders, which, as a rule, are less serious cases than those in which hospital orders are made. The Medical Advisory Committee at Broadmoor recommended that a compulsory supervision order, on the lines of a probation order with a condition of psychiatric treatment under section 3 of the Powers of Criminal Courts Act 1973, should be added to a hospital order in some cases where the full machinery of restricted release under section 65 of the Mental Health Act was not necessary.

8.3   Research has shown that there is some evidence that any form of contact by the hospital or the social services with offender-patients after their discharge from hospital is associated with a lower probability of reconviction, and a more stable employment record,[1] and we have no doubt that it is highly desirable they they should receive after-care.   Current trends in psychiatric practice are in the direction of community care.   Many hospitals take considerable trouble to ensure not only contact but some degree of supervision following discharge. We were glad to be informed by representatives of the Department of Health and Social Security that it is hoped to increase the provision of after-care for all categories of psychiatric patients, and not just offenders.   Meanwhile, the staffing situation varies from one area to another, but there are at present too few social workers, and community services are not adequately equipped to fulfil after-care requirements.   Some offenders, once released from institutions, are reluctant to co-operate in after-care, whether voluntary or compulsory, and the sanction of recall, even if it were thought intrinsically desirable, might in practice be too extreme, and therefore ineffective.   To provide for the possibility of compulsory after-care in all hospital order cases would amount to imposing on all these patients the supervision arrangements provided in restriction order hospital cases and on life sentence prisoners.   Release would be delayed while the formal arrangements were made.   The parallel sought to be drawn with the parole scheme is mistaken because the parole licensee is still serving his prison sentence while on licence and cannot validly complain of being supervised and liable to be recalled.

8.4   Our view is that it should be normal practice on the discharge of all hospital order cases for the hospital to arrange psychiatric follow-up (for example at an out-patient clinic), together with after-care by the probation and after-care service or local authority social services department, where the patient accepts this voluntarily.   We believe, however, that it would be wrong in principle to impose any statutory requirement for after-care in these cases. We have described, in paragraph 7.3, the existing provisions of section 39 of the Mental Health Act, under which patients may be given a trial leave of absence and have commended its use in appropriate cases.   We do not think that any further legal provision can be justified.   It will be particularly important to give attention to arrangements for voluntary after-care for patients who

---

[1] Nigel Walker and Sarah McCabe, *Crime and Insanity in England*, Vol 2 (Edinburgh 1973), pages 186–193.   See also the later analysis of their data in "Predicting offender-patient's reconvictions" by C Payne, S McCabe and N Walker in *British Journal of Psychiatry*, 1974 *125*, 60ff.

have been transferred from prison subject to restrictions under section 74 where, under our proposals in paragraph 3.43, the Home Secretary has decided to remove the restrictions at the "earliest date of release", allowing for remission on the prison sentence.

8.5   In the absence of compulsory after-care we do not regard a power of recall on its own as either appropriate or desirable.   While it might avoid the reappearance, perhaps at frequent intervals, of some offenders in court if they could instead by returned direct to hospital, we think that the existence of the power might present difficulty for a hospital which could do nothing for a particular case, and that recall could operate only in a very random way if it were not linked to continuing supervision.

(ii)   Co-operation in after-care

8.6   We would emphasise the importance of close co-operation between the hospitals and outside agencies.   If satisfactory after-care is to be arranged, especially for homeless and friendless patients, there must be consultation with whichever social service will be responsible (see paragraph 8.7 below), so that the patient can be found somewhere suitable to live and can be put in touch with the people he will be dealing with.   The social worker in the home area will be able to advise on home conditions, the support available in the community, hostel accommodation and employment prospects.   Whenever possible this liaison should be established well before the patient is ready to be discharged: is this is done, it may sometimes expedite discharge when the medical treatment has been completed.   But if this has not happened earlier, the social services should at least be given reasonable notice of the patient's impending discharge, so that something can be done.   We have been told by probation and after-care service and social service department representatives of discharged patients arriving at their offices with no previous arrangements made or notification given.   As one witness put it, "Decisions are made by the medical profession, and the social services are expected to accommodate these decisions." Such occurrences are unfair to the social workers and detrimental to the interests of the patient.   Sometimes they result from the immediate operation of decisions by Mental Health Review Tribunals: we deal with this problem at paragraphs 7.7–7.10 above.   Failure to inform the social worker in good time is especially regrettable where the discharged patient is subject to a probation order.   On this point, we offer a recommendation in paragraph 16.14.

(iii)   Responsibility for after-care of hospital patients

8.7   We have received various opinions on the question whether it is preferable for the local authority social service departments or the probation and after-care service to be responsible for the after-care of discharged section 65 patients.[2] In discussions with representatives of the two services we were reassured to find them thinking in terms of co-operation rather than rivalry.   There may be something in the point made to us that the probation and after-care service

[2] In the five years to 31 December 1974 the numbers of section 65 patients discharged to the supervision of each of the services were: probation officer supervision, 158; social worker supervision, 492.   In general the probation and after-care service tend to have responsibility for those patients for whom a more lengthy period of supervision is desirable.   In addition, besides their supervision of psychiatric probation order cases (for figures see paragraph 16.1) probation officers have responsibility for supervising parole licensees who are receiving psychiatric treatment as in- or out-patients.

has more experience in dealing with offenders and is therefore better able realistically to appraise their capabilities and may more probably have previous knowledge of the offender and his family. Be this as it may, we do not think that it would be useful for firm dividing lines to be laid down, but rather we agreed with the recommendation of the Aarvold Committee[3] that supervision should be undertaken by the person who can bring most to the case in the way of knowledge, expertise and resources in the particular circumstances of the case. The arrangements may need to take particular account of the needs of public safety.

(3) After-care for released prisoners

8.8 The importance of continuity in the treatment of the offender within the institution and his resettlement in the community has been increasingly recognised in the penal system. Responsibility for the after-care of released prisoners, including supervision of those released on parole licences, rests with the probation and after-care service. On 1 January 1966 the probation and after-care service assumed responsibility for social work in prisons and arrangements were introduced for seconding probation officers for this work with a view to securing closer co-operation between the institution and the probation officers in the prisoner's home area who would be in touch with him after his release. Attention to satisfactory after-care arrangements before a prisoner is released on parole has been a cardinal principle with the Parole Board since the parole scheme started on 1 April 1968. The representative probation and after-care service organisations informed us in their memoranda of evidence that arrangements for release of prisoners, particularly under the parole system, had been more successful than those for release on supervision from local hospitals and the special hospitals. Apart from the statutory obligation of the probation and after-care service to provide after-care, they identified the following factors as significant in the success of the arrangements under the parole system:—

(a) "through-care" — a continuity of contact and support given to a man and his family from the time of sentence, throughout his prison sentence, into the period of licence;

(b) a sharing and flow of information between the outside probation officer and the probation officers working in the prison as welfare officers;

(c) participation by the probation and after-care service in the decisions to do with parole at all levels;

(d) pre-discharge planning;

(e) the centralised operation of the Parole Board and the Parole Unit, with coherent procedures that are well understood by all involved.

(4) Specialisation in after-care of mentally disordered offenders

8.9 We have recognised, in paragraph 3.15, the reservations felt by some social workers, having received a generalist training, about their ability to cope with the special problems of mentally disordered offenders. This question is related to that of specialisation by social workers in the care of mentally

---

[3] Cmnd. 5191, paragraph 48.

124

disordered people in general. In our view social workers and probation officers should be given opportunities by in-service training to acquire the specialist knowledge and expertise necessary to enable them to approach the particularly difficult cases of mentally disordered offenders with confidence. We are not in favour of intensive specialisation by a few selected people in each area, which would result in the emergence of a new class of "psychiatric" social workers and probation officers. Specialisation is desirable not in the sense of an exclusive commitment to the problems of the mentally disordered but rather as the special development of one branch of the generalist's knowledge, and the "specialist's" case load should reflect this. The opportunity of specialising in mental health should be given after initial training and when a broad general knowledge has been acquired through experience. The object of the special in-service training should be to provide a comprehensive knowledge of the problems peculiar to mentally disordered offenders and of the ways of dealing with them seen in the wider context of supervision and after-care in general. The special training will be particularly important for those local authority social workers who are appointed to work with the mentally disordered under the Health Services and Public Health Act 1968 (see paragraph 9.1 below).

8.10 An important part in after-care will be played by the forensic psychiatric services, including the provision of practical placements for social workers during initial generic training, and contributions towards in-training and post-qualification specialist training, all of which we discuss in more detail in Chapter 20.

(5) Hostels

(i) The "half-way house"

8.11 The first requirement of a discharged patient or released prisoner is somewhere to live. Not all are fortunate enough to have a home to go to, or a welcoming family, and many need not only the accommodation but also the support which can be provided by a hostel with an understanding warden and links with the social and medical services. The other residents in a hostel will mostly be people contending with similar personal problems, and against such a background the newcomer feels less conspicuous. We were told at Grendon Prison of the problems faced by prisoners when they are released and suddenly find themselves without the close supervision and support the prison has provided. Their biggest problem was that of loneliness. At the request of some of them a meeting place had been provided in London, and this had developed into a residential unit for three or four at a time, to help them over the bridge between Grendon and freedom in society. Similarly we were informed when we visited Feltham Borstal of a project known as the Thursday Cellar Club which is run under the joint auspices of the Inner London Probation and After-Care Service and the Borstal. It is staffed by the Borstal Medical Officer (a psychiatrist) and Senior Psychologist, probation officers and voluntary probation associates and has been in existence since 1968. Its members are mostly homeless ex-Feltham Borstal trainees, and it meets weekly in central London. Many of these homeless young men gravitate to the West End on discharge, where they are particularly vulnerable to bad influences. The aim of the Club is to help them to establish themselves and sort out their problems with the assistance of the staff and other members. It provides a valuable bridge between the institution and the outside world, and by reason of the fact that members of the Borstal staff go out to the Club and London probation officers go into the Borstal continuity of care and understanding of the trainees is achieved, which is of great importance to these homeless adolescents. We were informed at Grendon that the prison feels the need of its own half-way house, which should preferably be within 40 miles of the prison, and near to work and transport, but local objections have so far prevented this development in areas where suitable premises have been found. It was thought that it would be advantageous if such a post-release hostel could be staffed by Grendon officers, in order to continue the personal relationships formed during the period of treatment.

8.12 In their evidence to us the Broadmoor Branch of the Prison Officers' Association advocated the use of the open prisons as half-way houses for discharged Broadmoor patients, as they thought that a hostel established especially for patients from Broadmoor would be strongly opposed by local public opinion wherever it was proposed to locate it. In his evidence before the Select Committee inquiring into the Special Hospitals in 1967 Dr McGrath gave as his view that a special half-way house for Broadmoor patients was not a good idea. It would present difficulties from the point of view of staffing, administration and public opinion. He did not favour the grouping together of offenders discharged from the special hospital but thought that they should be diluted into the community. The Select Committee concurred.[4]

8.13 We do not think that, in any event, the open prisons could suitably be used for a stage in the release of special hospital patients. There are often restrictions on the categories of offender who may be accepted in them; they would not generally be well situated as staging posts between the special hospitals and the patient's home area; nor would their regime and facilities be entirely suitable. Finally, there are objections of principle to the transfer to a prison by the executive of a patient who has been committed by the court to the care of a hospital.

8.14 The concept of hostels linked to particular secure institutions also seems to us to be open to conclusive objections, some of which have been mentioned in paragraph 8.12. A hostel near the special hospital or psychiatric penal establishment would generally not be helpful in re-establishing the patient in the community, especially as it would seldom be in the area where the patient would eventually reside. A more distant location might still not be particularly helpful to many patients, while it would inevitably pose difficulties of administration, and draw away trained staff from the parent establishment. Further, a hostel which catered only for those discharged from a particular special hospital or prison establishment would inevitably retain something of the closed atmosphere of the parent institution, even coming to be regarded by the patients as an extension of it. While we appreciate the concern for the patients that stimulates such proposals, we think that the preferable answer lies in the provision of more general hostel accommodation, catering not only for discharged mentally disordered offenders, whether from the prison, the special hospitals, the regional secure units or psychiatric hospitals, but for all those in need of the support and facilities that hostels can offer. It is important that

---

[4] Second Report from the Estimates Committee, Session 1967–68 (HMSO, 31–vii) Minutes of Evidence, page 58, Question 231; and paragraph 104 of the Report.

discharged offender-patients should be associated with non-offenders, and in the environment of a general-purpose hostel the necessary support would be available but the discharged offender would be on his way to seeing himself as a member of a wider community. We understand that some Regional Health Authorities provide hostels and houses for patients discharged from hospital in their area. Assuming that these are available to informal and detained patients alike, and to offenders and non-offenders, the reservations we have expressed about undesirable segregation will evidently not apply to them.

(ii) General hostel accommodation

8.15 A great weight of evidence has impressed upon us the serious lack of hostel provision. By far the majority of hostels for all the different kinds of people needing them have always been provided by voluntary organisations relying mainly on charitable funds. Grants in aid of expenditure by voluntary organisations in providing hostel places for convicted offenders with a view to their rehabilitation are payable by the Home Office under section 51(3)(f) of the Powers of Criminal Courts Act 1973, as they were under the previous legislation which the 1973 Act consolidated.[5] The current rates of grant from 1 April 1975 are up to £215 a year for places for ordinary offenders and up to £350 a year for places offered to specially difficult residents such as those with drink or drugs problems. Many residents in these hostels are on probation; others are well known to the probation and after-care service. There are invariably close links between the Home Office supported hostels and the probation and after-care service. The Home Office also provides financial support to the Bridgehead Housing Association which was established in 1967 to assist with the acquisition of premises to be run by voluntary bodies as after-care hostels. On 1 April 1975 190 after-care hostels were receiving Home Office grants and providing 1,875 places for offenders.

8.16 Similar arrangements are operated by the Department of Health and Social Security for the payment of grants to support, in particular, hostels for alcoholics. Under section 64 of the Health Service and Public Health Act 1968 funds are made available to the Department for grants to national voluntary organisations. The Department uses some of these funds to supplement the support which individual voluntary hostel projects receive from other sources. Since May 1973 capital grants have been paid in relation to 13 hostels providing 183 new places for alcoholics, and deficit revenue grants have also been authorised for these hostels. In addition, on 1 April 1973 the Department of Health and Social Security took over responsibility from the Home Office for deficit revenue grants to 20 hostels providing 247 places for alcoholics.

8.17 Much remains to be done. A Home Office Working Group have recently reported[6]:—

> "It has been represented to us that a particular problem is presented by discharged offenders suffering from mental disorders of a degree which does not justify admission to hospital, or of a kind which is not susceptible

---

[5] Section 77(3)(e) of the Criminal Justice Act 1948 as amended by section 96(1) of the Criminal Justice Act 1967.

[6] Report of the Working Group on Residential Provision for Offenders within the Community, paragraph 60.

to treatment. Such men are not accepted in many after-care hostels or lodgings and tend to drift into very poor accommodation, or to sleep rough, and in the absence of support the risk of their committing further offences is high. We understand that local authorities have power to provide, or finance the provision of, hostels for ex-patients of mental hospitals and persons who are mentally sub-normal. We welcome the encouragement recently given to local authorities by the Department of Health and Social Security to increase the amount of accommodation available for single homeless persons of all kinds. But, while it may be possible for some discharged offenders to obtain accommodation in local authority sponsored hostels, it is likely to be some time before local authorities make adequate provision. We accordingly recommend that voluntary organisations should be encouraged to provide hostels specifically for discharged offenders suffering from mental disorders, and that such hostels should attract the higher rate of Home Office grant".

8.18 Section 53(1) of the Criminal Justice Act 1972 made provision for probation and after-care committees with the Home Secretary's approval to provide and carry on "day training centres, bail hostels, probation hostels, probation homes and other establishments for use in connection with the rehabilitation of offenders"; and under this provision, now consolidated in paragraph 11 of Schedule 3 to the Powers of Criminal Courts Act 1973, it is open to probation and after-care committees to provide hostels suitably organised and supported for the accommodation of mentally disordered offenders living in the community. We understand, however, that up to June 1975 no committee had submitted proposals to provide an after-care hostel for any category of offender.

8.19 The Working Group referred to in paragraph 8.17, while recognising the value of variety in the types of accommodation provided, in one way or another, for offenders, who are so various in their characteristics and needs, have been critical of the lack of co-ordination among the various agencies, official and unofficial, providing and administering hostels. They have recommended that in every area of a suitable size there should be developed "a constellation system" which should provide in the area a wide variety of accommodation for offenders and discharged offenders; and that the local authorities should be involved in setting up and operating constellation systems, with liaison at a senior level between the constellation system and the social services departments operating in the same area. The Working Group also suggested that an experimental scheme might be set up in a selected area. We have been informed that experimental schemes have since been set up in Hampshire, Lancashire and South Yorkshire and that progress is being made in these areas towards the development of "constellation systems" on the lines envisaged by the Working Group. Other areas of the country have also expressed interest in these schemes. We welcome these developments, in which we see great value from the point of view of mentally disordered offenders and "inadequate" offenders, and we express our support of those who have already urged and striven to bring about much increased provision of accommodation for these needy people. This provision should be accepted as a continuing commitment, requiring regular review, by the Departments of State concerned, the local authorities and the social services, including probation and after-care committees, as well as by the voluntary organisations who were the pioneers in this field.

(6) Day training centres and day treatment units

8.20   An element in the movement away from treatment in institutions is the provision of new or additional facilities in the community for day treatment. These are of two clearly distinguishable kinds, and care must be taken to avoid the confusion which may arise from the use, without sufficient discrimination, of the terms "day centre" and "day unit". As mentioned above, section 53(1) of the Criminal Justice Act 1972, now replaced by paragraph 11 of Schedule 3 to the Powers of Criminal Courts Act 1973, enabled probation and after-care committees, with the approval of the Home Secretary, to provide and carry on day training centres; section 20(1) of the 1972 Act, now replaced by section 4(1) of the 1973 Act, enabled a court to include in a probation order, subject to the provisions of the section, a requirement that an offender should during the probation period attend at a specified day training centre. The Home Secretary is empowered, now by section 48(3) of the 1973 Act, to make rules for regulating the training given at day training centres and the provision and carrying on of such centres under the provisions of the Act. The Central Council of Probation and After-Care Committees stated in their memorandum of evidence that they would like to see the day training scheme enlarged and expanded as soon as possible. They informed us that these centres should ideally fulfil a dual role: (*a*) to train the inadequate disordered offender on a short-term basis to manage his day to day life with more competence; and (*b*) to provide sheltered workshops for those who cannot cope with competitive working conditions, so that they may be permanently and usefully employed. Pilot schemes have been set up in a number of areas, and one of our members visited the centres in London and Liverpool. Each area running a pilot scheme has been given a free hand in establishing the regime. We recognise that the use of facilities of this kind for people with mental disorders will depend upon the careful experimental development of the centres and the provision of adequate psychiatric support, both for the clients and for the staff. It would seem desirable for centres of this type to be associated with regional forensic psychiatric services.

8.21   The need for day treatment units, on the other hand, has been put to us by medical witnesses, and the British Psychological Society have referred in their memorandum of evidence to their importance in providing continuity of treatment as part of the process of discharge from hospital, enabling follow-up consultations and support to be provided. We discuss these units, which would form part of comprehensive forensic psychiatric services, in Chapter 20.

AFTER-CARE

SUMMARY OF CONCLUSIONS

1.   The problems of discharged mentally disordered offenders on their return to the community are acute, and all assistance should be given to them in overcoming the difficulties of transition. There is a need for continuity in the treatment of the offender within the institution and on his return to the community. (Paragraph 8.1.)

2. We do not consider it necessary to make after-care compulsory in all hospital order cases, but research has shown the value of contact with patients after their discharge and it should be normal practice for hospitals to arrange for after-care with psychiatric follow-up on a voluntary basis. This will be particularly important for patients transferred from prison under section 74 restrictions where, under our recommendation in paragraph 3.43, the restrictions have been reviewed by the Home Secretary and removed at the "earliest date of release". In the absence of compulsory after-care the power of recall to hospital for all hospital order patients is neither appropriate nor desirable, but doctors should use trial leave to test a patient's ability to live in the community. (Paragraphs 8.2–8.5.)

3. If satisfactory after-care arrangements for hospital cases are to be made it is important that there should be close co-operation between hospitals and outside agencies. (Paragraph 8.6.)

4. Responsibility for the after-care of discharged offender hospital patients should be given to the person who can bring most to the case in the particular circumstances, including considerations of public safety, regardless of whether he or she belongs to the local authority social service department or the probation and after-care service. (Paragraph 8.7.)

5. The importance of continuity of treatment in the institution and afterwards in the community has been increasingly recognised in the penal system, and has been developed by the secondment of probation officers for social work in prisons, by the attention given by the Parole Board to after-care arrangements for prisoners released on licence, and by the administrative arrangements set up for the purposes of the parole scheme. (Paragraph 8.8.)

6. Special in-service training within the existing services would be valuable to enable supervising officers, who receive a generalist training, to cope with the special problems of mentally disordered offenders; but we do not favour intensive specialisation in mental health cases by a few selected people in each area. An important part in the provision of training will be played by forensic psychiatric centres. (Paragraphs 8.9–8.10.)

7. Hostel accommodation is appropriate to the needs of many newly discharged mentally disordered offenders. We do not support the proposal that open prisons should be used for a stage in the release of special hospital patients, and we are not in favour of the establishment of special hostels to cater for those discharged from the special hospitals or from psychiatric penal establishments. We urge a substantial increase in the provision of general hostel accommodation to provide for all social inadequates, and greater co-ordination between the various bodies, both statutory and voluntary, who provide and administer hostels for discharged offenders. (Paragraphs 8.11–8.19.)

8. We recognise that the use of day training centres for people with mental disorders will depend upon their experimental development and the provision of adequate psychiatric support. The centres should be associated with regional forensic psychiatric services. (Paragraph 8.20.)

CHAPTER 9

PRE-TRIAL ACTION

I. SECTION 136 ARRANGEMENTS

(1) Existing provisions

9.1 We have referred in paragraph 1.15 to the importance of the exercise of discretion by the police from the moment when they begin to have responsibility. One situation in which this applies is where the police have to deal with a person who is causing some disturbance or concern in a public place by behaviour which may possibly be attributable to mental disorder: for example, he may be undressing in the street, or shouting or lunging at passers-by. Sometimes it may not be easy for the policeman to know whether the man is mentally affected or is under the influence of drink or drugs. Section 136(1) of the Mental Health Act 1959 empowers a constable to remove to a place of safety a person found in a place to which the public have access, who appears to the constable to be suffering from mental disorder and to be in immediate need of care or control, if he thinks it necessary to do so in the interests of that person or for the protection of other persons. A "place of safety" as defined in section 135(6), includes a hospital, police station, mental nursing home, or any other suitable place the occupier of which is willing temporarily to receive the person. By section 136(2) a person thus removed may be detained for a period not exceeding 72 hours for the purpose of enabling him to be examined by a medical practitioner and to be interviewed by a mental welfare officer[1] and of making any necessary arrangements for his treatment or care, which may be entered into voluntarily if the circumstances allow. The role of the mental welfare officer includes contacting the detained person's relatives, and ascertaining whether there is a history of psychiatric treatment. Should admission to hospital prove necessary this information may indicate which hospital would be most suitable; but he should always consider whether any course other than admission to hospital is appropriate. Knowing the range of resources available, he is in a position to assess all the circumstances and is responsible for making sure whether treatment in hospital is the only solution. We have stressed at paragraph 8.9 above the importance of ensuring that social workers, and particularly those who are appointed to perform the functions of mental welfare officers, receive adequate specialist training in dealing with mentally disordered people.

9.2 Although section 136(1) of the Act refers specifically to the powers of the constable, we have no doubt that its authority extends to persons acting under his direction, such as the ambulance staff who are taking the disordered person to hospital. It will be seen that the powers of detention given by section 136(2) are not conferred expressly on the police, but are given to any person who is a party to the detention of the disordered person once he has been brought to a place of safety. Under the above-mentioned definition of "place of

---

[1] Section 12(1)(d) of the Health Services and Public Health Act 1968 which replaced section 6(2) of the Mental Health Act, requires local social services authorities to appoint "officers to act as mental welfare officers under the Act". The social workers so appointed are not now always known as mental welfare officers but it is convenient in discussing section 136 to use this description to refer to the officers appointed to carry out these functions.

safety" these powers provide protection not only to the medical staff of a hospital which has received such a person but also, for example, to any householder who may have given him temporary shelter while arrangements were being made.

9.3 Provisions of one sort or another for enabling potential offenders to be taken to a "place of safety" can be traced back to the Criminal Lunatics Act of 1800 and section 136 of the 1959 Act is a modification of the powers of relieving officers, parish overseers and constables under the Lunacy Acts Amendment Act of 1885.[2] In operating these arrangements nowadays the police are advised by the Home Office Consolidated Circular to the Police on Crime and Kindred Matters, the relevant paragraphs of which are reproduced at Appendix 7, that a person who is removed under section 136 should normally be taken direct to a hospital, or, if this is not practicable, that the assistance of the mental welfare officer should immediately be sought. The statutory provision does not stipulate that an offence must have been committed before the police can use the powers, but it will no doubt often be the case that the behaviour of the person removed would justify his being charged with an offence against public order, for example conduct likely to lead to a breach of the peace.[3]

9.4 Care is needed in the interpretation of the statistics about the extent of use of the section 136 powers. These appear to show that the powers are used frequently by the Metropolitan Police but very little outside London, and much of the evidence we have received has been based on this understanding. It may well be true, as is often maintained, that the proportion of mentally disordered people in London is higher than elsewhere, but we do not consider this to be the full explanation, and we suggest below some qualifications which must be kept in mind when considering the statistical data. Regional variations in the published statistics of the use of section 136 may be seriously misleading. Figures provided for us by the Department of Health and Social Security show that of 1,555 admissions to hospital under section 136 in 1973, no less than 1,376 were to hospitals in the area covered by the four Metropolitan Regional Hospital Boards. According to the figures, Wales accounted for only 10 admissions, and the Mersey Region for only one. The first point to be recognised is that section 136 is recorded as coming into play *only when the police themselves take the person somewhere*. If the policeman or a bystander simply telephones for an ambulance the admission to hospital will be recorded as a normal admission under Part IV of the Mental Health Act—probably under section 29 ("admission for observation in case of emergency"). We were informed for example, that in the Liverpool and Bootle Constabulary the standing instruction is that a mentally disordered person wandering at large

---

[2] Nigel Walker and Sarah McCabe, *Crime and Insanity in England*, Vol. 2, Appendix A. (Edinburgh, 1973.)

[3] The Department of Health and Social Security, so far as they are concerned, have expressed the opinion that the power of removal conferred upon a police officer by section 136(1) is not exhausted until the person removed is accepted by the occupier of a place of safety (eg, a hospital officer or officer in charge of a police station) for detention under section 136(2), so that he may there be examined by a doctor and interviewed by a mental welfare officer and have his future care or treatment arranged for, as provided by that subsection. If, for example, the police officer has previously called at a hospital which finds itself unable to accept the person concerned for the purposes of section 136(2), or if the police officer has taken the person concerned to a police station in order to telephone for a police car, his powers of removal under section 136(1) would not in these circumstances have terminated.

is taken by ambulance to hospital, and that many more such persons are dealt with in this way than are indicated in the statistics above. In London it has been normal practice for the Metropolitan Police to provide the transport and take people to the hospital and on arrival at the hospital they have been clearly identifiable as section 136 cases. In other areas, when the police take people to the police station under the authority of section 136 to be examined there by a doctor and interviewed by a mental welfare officer, emergency admission to hospital, if this results, will be arranged under Part IV (section 29) procedure, and not under section 136. The hospital admission figures therefore reveal only part of the picture.

9.5 The fact that section 136 is invoked whenever the police remove an apparently disordered person from a public place to the police station as a place of safety is not generally recognised. It seems to be widely supposed that the section applies only when they take the person to hospital. This misapprehension is sometimes shared by the police themselves: we were surprised that in reply to our enquiries a number of chief constables stated that the section was not used because it was the practice in their force area to take such disordered persons to the police station and not direct to hospital.[4]

9.6 It may be thought that we are concerning ourselves here with mere technicalities. There are two reasons why we have thought it important to devote time and space to these points. The first is that research workers and others concerned in this field may be considerably misled because of the wide-spread misunderstanding of what is involved in section 136, and public discussion may be conducted on false premises. As we have shown above, not only may the statistics deceive but statements by the police themselves about their use of section 136 may be based on misconceptions. But secondly, and more importantly, the points we are making have a direct bearing on the initial question in our enquiry, namely whether the police really need the powers provided by section 136. If we had established that, as the statistics seemed to show, the police forces in the large provincial cities made virtually no use of section 136 powers, their necessity in London would have required to be specially demonstrated. As it is, we find that the powers are widely in use.

9.7 The Association of Chief Police Officers in evidence to us were strongly opposed to the repeal of section 136 which they thought would leave the police in a difficult position with no power to act. We see that without such a power the police might be in danger of accusations of wrongful arrest. Where some action has to be taken to deal with a disordered individual in a public place it is better for the police to cope rather than a doctor or social worker, whose authority may not be so readily recognised and who may not be quickly on the scene in an emergency. No power of arrest is conferred by section 29. There are certain common-law powers of arrest of mentally disordered offenders, but the powers are obscure and the police should not be forced to rely on them.[5] We are satisfied that the section 136 powers of removal to a place of safety are both necessary and generally beneficial.

---

[4] This practice does not conform to the guidance in the Home Office Consolidated Circular, referred to in paragraph 9.3 above, but some of the problems involved are discussed in paragraph 9.8 below.

[5] We do not recommend any amendment of the law on this point because the questions raised are not specific to mentally disordered offenders and so are regarded as outside our terms of reference.

(2) Problems and criticisms

9.8 We believe that the procedure adopted by the police is normally laid down in the standing orders in each force. Evidence we have received has tended to confirm that outside London direct admission to hospital by the police is something of a rarity, despite the official policy indicated in the Home Office Consolidated Circular (see paragraph 9.3 above) and this evidence has also illustrated some of the difficulties which may explain why this is so. Local psychiatric hospitals are sometimes unwilling to admit cases brought to them by the police: some consultant psychiatrists have frankly stated that they are opposed to the treatment of offenders in local National Health Service psychiatric hospitals; and we have also been told in evidence that some psychiatrists argue that as a police station is a place of safety for the purpose of section 136 there is no need for the police to trouble the hospital. These cases tend to occur late at night, often on a Saturday or public holiday, when a consultant may not be readily available. Another difficulty is that the casualty officer in a general hospital is usually a surgical officer and to get the patient examined by a psychiatrist the police may have to take him to a distant psychiatric hospital. This problem may in some places be produced administratively, the boundaries of a hospital catchment area cutting the police off from the nearest hospital. If the initial examination takes place at the police station a hospital must still be found that is willing to receive the patient, and similar difficulties may arise. The problem of obtaining a hospital bed may be the more acute in the case of those on the border-line of mental disorder—alcoholics, drug addicts or epileptics.

9.9 Even in London difficulties of this sort have been encountered and the Metropolitan Police have in the past drawn the attention of the Home Office and the Department of Health and Social Security to the reluctance, and at times refusal, of many hospitals to accept patients whose home addresses were not within their catchment area. It has been put to us in evidence by a group of consultant forensic psychiatrists that there is a need in London for a separate psychiatric unit for the emergency reception of section 136 cases. We are not convinced that this would be desirable, particularly in the light of experience of the working of the former observation units in the London area in the years before the 1959 Act. Separate units present problems of control and, lacking ready access to the full range of hospital facilities, would be unable to provide adequate immediate investigation or treatment. It is a difficulty that London's catchment area psychiatric hospitals are some distance away from the central area, but we think that the eventual solution lies rather in developing psychiatric facilities in district general hospitals so that they are able to deal with emergency admissions. Meanwhile, the Department of Health and Social Security have recently issued to all London Health Authorities and the Metropolitan Police a code of practice for the operation of section 136 in the Greater London Area. This code, which has been agreed with the Home Office, the Police, the Regional Health Authorities and the London Boroughs Association Directors of Social Services, lays down a strict procedure for the admission to hospital of section 136 cases and should overcome the previous problems. We welcome this development in co-operation among the various authorities and services.

9.10 It is interesting to note that Dr Rollin, the consultant psychiatrist at Horton Hospital, Epsom, where many of the London cases are directly

134

admitted, has remarked in the course of a study based on his experience of section 136 admissions[6] that in the vast majority of cases the action of the police in taking the person to the hospital was fully justified. In two-thirds of the cases studied there was a long history of mental illness, and most of these patients had been admitted to psychiatric hospitals on numerous previous occasions. Many were suffering from chronic schizophrenia, and a quarter of the cases had been discharged from a psychiatric hospital less than a week before their referral by the police. Some 40 per cent had previous criminal records.

9.11 Some further information about section 136 admissions has been submitted to us in a memorandum by Professor Gibbens, Professor of Forensic Psychiatry at the Institute of Psychiatry. He cites a research study carried out by Dr H R George, now Consultant Psychiatrist at St Francis Hospital, Haywards Heath, which suggests that those dealt with under this section tend to have come to police attention by threatening or bizarre behaviour, including wandering, self-neglect, suicidal threats or attempts, verbal and physical aggression, expression of gross delusions, sexual misbehaviour and traffic disturbances. Among a sample of 856 admissions studied, 45·4 per cent reverted after 72 hours to become informal patients,[7] and in 54·6 per cent of the cases a section 25 order[8] was made. Three-quarters of the patients ultimately left hospital in the normal way, but 11·2 per cent absconded and a further 11·2 per cent were transferred to other hospitals. 27 per cent of the sample had no fixed address, and only 14 per cent were married and living with their wives. Like Dr Rollin, Pofessor Gibbens concludes that the police almost never act wrongly or unnecessarily in bringing cases under section 136 to hospital; indeed, he points out that the figures for previous admissions suggest that in many cases patients may be well known to the police.

9.12 The evidence we have received has indicated a general desire that maximum use should be made of section 136 arrangements to ensure that as many as possible of the mentally disordered offenders within the scope of the provision are referred at the outset to the treatment agencies. We agree. The procedure may usually avert the need to bring these people before the courts and thereby possibly into the penal system. The Institution of Professional Civil Servants, representing members of the Prison Medical Service, have pointed out that a considerable part of the work of penal institutions dealing with remand cases consists of reporting on very minor offenders, often of no fixed abode, who have committed offences as a consequence of mental disorder and have been charged by the police. Their treatment needs could often be met by the National Health Service, and many of them could suitably be admitted directly into psychiatric hospitals, or into other psychiatric units, by the machinery of section 136.

9.13 The only proposal put to us in favour of specific changes in the section 136 procedure was that of the National Council for Civil Liberties who expressed concern that the provision might be used to secure three days' detention in

---

[6] H R Rollin, *The Mentally Abnormal Offender and the Law*, Chapter 5. (London, Pergamon Press, 1969.)

[7] See paragraph 2.19.

[8] See paragraph 2.21.

hospital, rather than merely to obtain emergency medical examination. This might occur particularly at weekends, when consultants were not readily available. They suggested that the time for which someone could be kept under observation should be reduced from 72 to 24 hours, and that the definition of a place of safety should be limited to a police station. We invited the National Council to furnish us with specific evidence of abuses of the provisions, but we have not been given any specific examples. Another of our witnesses, himself a former mental welfare officer, pointed out that the choice between police station and hospital may be largely a matter of geography; circumstances vary widely and in some country areas it might be quicker to take somebody to a nearby psychiatric hospital than to arrange for examination at a police station. He doubted whether it was the usual practice to detain disordered persons in a police station for more than a few hours while they were seen by a doctor and mental welfare officer, but insofar as there were occasional delays he thought the remedy should be administrative rather than legislative. Certainly the purpose of the power of detention provided by section 136 is only to allow a person to be kept, whether at the police station or in hospital or elsewhere, long enough for appropriate examination to be carried out, and, where necessary, for the mechanics of admission to be performed, whether admission be voluntary or compulsory. We think besides that the law must make some allowance for exceptional difficulties, such as might arise, for example, in remote areas or at holiday periods. In the absence of any specific evidence of abuse by unnecessarily long detention in a police station or arbitrary admission to hospital we think it would be difficult to justify amending the law in the way proposed by the National Council for Civil Liberties. An important safeguard against a person being detained in hospital against his wish and without clear need is the involvement of the mental welfare officer in emergency admissions to hospital under section 29 and in the procedure for detention in a place of safety under section 136(2). Applications for admission under section 29 can be made only by the mental welfare officer or by a relative of the patient; and section 136 expressly states that detention is for the purpose, *inter alia*, of interview by a mental welfare officer, whose safeguarding role we have described in paragraph 9.1.

9.14 The evidence shows that difficulties sometimes arise which prevent the section 136 procedure being used as effectively as it might. No doubt what happens in practice is determined to a large extent by the interplay of personalities in the local situation, and it must in the last resort be for individual police and hospital authorities to discuss with one another their common problems and to work out the detailed administrative arrangements needed to operate the statutory provision effectively. (As we point out in paragraph 9.9 above, this has already been done in the Greater London Area.) Some of the problems we have heard of point to a need for greater local consultation and mutual understanding rather than to the desirability of any change in the law itself. We would hope that Area Health Authorities might operate their hospital catchment area policies with a measure of flexibility so that disordered people might be taken by the police to the hospital for the area in which they were found or to the nearest hospital (after all, police time is valuable) rather than necessarily to the hospital for their home area. There may also be room for a fuller interchange of information between the police and hospital staff in individual cases. We have heard that the police sometimes take people to a hospital under section 136 but fail to mention to the doctor the circumstances in which the patient has been found and the reasons for bringing him. More could be done in some parts of the country to see that procedures for handling these cases are agreed locally and known to all those involved.

(3) Prosecution in section 136 cases

9.15 The question whether the police should eventually prosecute people dealt with under section 136 is referred to in the Home Office Consolidated Circular[9] which advises the police to consider whether, in the light of all the circumstances, including the medical reports from the hospital, it would be appropriate to take further action with regard to the offence. Where the offence is not punishable by imprisonment the circular suggests that it should generally be unnecessary for the offender to be charged. The Association of Police Surgeons of Great Britain told us in their memorandum of evidence that while in their experience the police took the advice of the police surgeon or other experienced doctor in allowing offenders to be admitted to psychiatric hospitals without at that stage preferring a charge, they had little information as to whether charges were later preferred. They thought that the police surgeon originally concerned, who may often be able to obtain relevant confidential medical information from other sources about the mental health of an offender, could give the police valuable advice on the exercise of their discretion as to prosecution; but they accepted that this would require caution, and generally they thought it best to leave it to the good sense of the police to withhold charges in the case of minor offences. Our impression is that in general where section 136 is used prosecution is avoided, although in some cases it may subsequently be found necessary to bring the offender to court and the result may be that a section 60 order is ultimately made. If a serious offence has been committed the police will arrest the offender in the normal way and if necessary arrange for admission to hospital at a later stage. We think that the police must retain their discretion in these matters, but we suggest in the following paragraphs the considerations which should be taken into account when deciding whether to prosecute, and we emphasise in particular that the prosecution of a mentally disordered person should not be pursued unless it would serve some useful public purpose. It appears to us that this criterion could seldom be satisfied in section 136 cases.

II. RELIEF FROM PROSECUTION

(1) General considerations

9.16 A number of witnesses have expressed to us their concern that seriously disturbed people should not unnecessarily be subjected to the ordeal of appearance in court. Such appearances may impede treatment and delay recovery, besides providing a pathetic and unseemly public spectacle. If the outcome is likely to be a finding that the defendant is under disability in relation to the trial, or not legally responsible for what he did, followed by commitment to hospital or, under proposals advanced in this Report, perhaps to community care, is any over-riding public interest served by bringing these cases into court?

---

[9] Reproduced at Appendix 7.

9.17   We have considered whether magistrates' courts and examining justices in committal proceedings should be enabled, having regard to social inquiry reports and medical reports, to put an end to a prosecution.   For the protection of the public, such a power should be exercisable only with the consent of the prosecution, who might have information not available to the court showing the defendant to be dangerous.   The defence should have a right to be consulted.   To ensure reasonable consistency throughout the country magistrates' courts would need to be given clear guidance about the use of this power, but suitable criteria, which would admit the cases for which the procedure was designed but exclude all others, would be difficult, if not impossible, to devise. Even if feasible, we have concluded that such elaborate arrangements would not be justified.   We are satisfied that the desired object can be achieved more simply as explained below.

9.18   Although not all prosecutions in England and Wales are undertaken by public authorities, as they are in Scotland, proceedings in the type of cases we are concerned with here would almost certainly be in the hands of the Director of Public Prosecutions or the police.   The Director and the police have discretion whether to initiate, and whether to continue, a prosecution. There are arrangements for the police to consult the Director in certain cases, and for the Director to take over responsibility for the prosecution in appropriate circumstances; it is not necessary here to describe this machinery in detail.   The Director has informed us of the considerations which contribute to a decision whether to proceed with a prosecution.   Where cases are referred to him he looks at them on their merits and considers all the circumstances as a whole; he has listed as follows some of the factors he takes into account in arriving at a decision where the proposed defendant is mentally disordered:—

"(a) The nature of the alleged offence or offences.   Clearly, the graver the offence the greater is the requirement in the public interest that proceedings should be brought.   If the offence is comparatively venial other circumstances may more readily be accepted as weighing against prosecution.

(b) The period for which the accused has been under treatment since the alleged offence.   If this has been very prolonged and the offence has in consequence become stale, this would tend to weigh against proceedings.

(c) The accused's mental condition at the time of the alleged offence. Here, great care must be taken against trespassing on the province of the court which, save in very exceptional circumstances, must be left to decide this question; but where it is clear on the evidence that the result of proceedings would almost certainly be a special verdict that the accused was not guilty by reason of insanity, there would, except in cases such as murder or attempted murder, or grave bodily harm, be little purpose in bringing him to trial if the other factors tend to weigh against prosecution.

(d) The accused's present mental state and what would be the likely effect on it of proceedings being instituted.   A medical opinion that the institution of proceedings would have anything less than a seriously detrimental effect on the accused's mental condition should not, I think, be afforded any very great weight against proceedings, at any rate where the offence is other than venial. Where, however, the likely result of proceedings would be that the accused will be rendered unfit to plead, or his mental condition would be seriously and irrevocably harmed or if he is likely to have a complete collapse on his appearance before the court, these would be factors against a prosecution".

The Director has no doubt that chief officers of police have regard to similar considerations with cases within their own discretion.

9.19   Clearly the prosecuting authorities have a difficult task.   They must balance the circumstances of the alleged offender and the gravity of the offence against the importance of not pre-empting the functions of the court, which might result in alienating public confidence, on which the administration of justice ultimately depends.   It should be recognised, however, that the public interest may sometimes be best served by dispensing with needless, expensive and harmful formalities, where the apparent offender is clearly in urgent need of psychiatric treatment and where there is no question of risk to members of the public.   Indeed, the public's understanding of mental disorder has become increasingly enlightened and sympathetic in recent years, and we think that there would be wide acceptance that, especially where there has been no previous criminal behaviour, the mental condition of an alleged offender, whether at the time of the act charged or at the time when proceedings are being considered, may justify dispensing with proceedings entirely, even where very grave offences are involved, in order to allow medical treatment to begin at the earliest possible moment, and with the best prospects of success.   It appears, from (c) in the Director's list of factors, that the public interest has hitherto been thought to require prosecution in cases of homicide or attempted homicide, or grave bodily harm.   While it goes without saying that these offences cannot be regarded as other than extremely serious, and we agree that usually the public interest will require that they be prosecuted and adjudicated by a court, we do not think that the gravity should of necessity, whatever the circumstances, be regarded as decisive.   We think that in these cases, as in others less serious, the question should always be asked whether any useful public purpose would be served by prosecution, and in coming to a decision the medical report should be taken into account, together with, where possible, a report on the circumstances by a social worker.

9.20   We hope that the prosecuting authorities may feel encouraged by these observations to attach considerable weight to the desirability of not proceeding in the type of cases we have been discussing.   We think that chief officers of police should review their policy and practice in the cases for which they have responsibility and that the Director of Public Prosecutions should give them guidance in this review.

9.21   One undesirable consequence of non-prosecution may be that the medical authorities do not receive full information about the act committed by the disordered person, and about the social circumstances, as they would if the case came before the court and a hospital order was made.   It is obviously important that those undertaking medical treatment should be in possession of all available facts about the previous behaviour of their patient, and the home situation. Where it is decided not to prosecute a disordered person, we urge the prosecuting authorities to arrange for any medical and social inquiry reports that may have been obtained to be passed on to the responsible doctor, whether in hospital or general practice. They should also communicate a statement of the facts of the charge, provided that the person charged admits that he did the act in question. If he denies it, this would be a strong reason for taking the case to court, in order to have the facts established in the usual way. Otherwise, there may be a danger that the doctor may assume that the charge has been made out, and this may influence his decision in relation to the compulsory commitment of the patient.

(2) Prosecution of hospital patients

9.22 One situation in which it is sometimes particularly appropriate to refrain from bringing proceedings is where a patient admitted to a psychiatric hospital under the provisions of the Mental Health Act commits an offence within the hospital. We were informed by the Justices' Clerks' Society that when psychiatric hospitals were "closed" institutions such matters as thefts by patients of other patients' belongings or assaults by a patient on staff or other patients could be contained without reference to the police, but that such incidents now appeared increasingly to be reported to the police and to result in criminal proceedings. The court was left with a difficulty of disposal: there might be no suitable alternative to returning the offender to the hospital, yet the hospital might be reluctant to accept him back.

9.23 We recognise that there are circumstances in which prosecution of patients is desirable. Some offences are in themselves so serious that the public interest is not served by refraining from prosecution simply because the defendant is a hospital patient. Prosecution may be necessary if there is evidence that a patient has committed an offence which is more than a mere nuisance before entering hospital, while temporarily absent from it (whether with permission or not), or even while inside it. One justification for prosecution will sometimes be that unless an offence is proved in court, and the details recorded in the patient's papers, insufficient account may be taken of it when the ultimate decision is reached on the patient's suitability for discharge into the community. In the case of a patient admitted informally or under the compulsory provisions of Part IV of the Act, it may also be desirable to bring proceedings in some circumstances where there is a possibility of seriously harmful behaviour in the future so that a hospital order with restrictions under section 65, ensuring appropriate control over discharge and subsequent supervision, may be made.

9.24 But in general we think that the presumption should be against bringing charges which may result in the ordeal of court appearances and the stigma of conviction, with no compensating advantage. Anti-social and troublesome conduct in a patient may often be merely symptomatic of his mental disorder and underline his need of treatment. Psychiatric hospitals expect and accept much undesirable behaviour which would not be tolerated in most other types of institution. Prosecution should be seen as a last resort which should not be embarked upon where it is not clearly in the interests of the patient or the community. Transfer to another hospital, if necessary a special hospital, may often be a more appropriate course. We appreciate that the discretion whether to institute proceedings does not always lie with the hospital authorities, even in cases which occur within the hospital precincts, and hope that the prosecuting authorities themselves in reaching a decision on any case will take due account of the considerations mentioned in this paragraph as well as of any representations which may be made to them by those responsible for the treatment of the offending patient.

9.25 When implemented, our proposals for regional secure hospital units should go far to meet this problem. Since places in the units will not be confined to those sent by the courts it will be open to hospitals to transfer patients who require conditions of stricter security to the units, by agreement, without the necessity of court proceedings. Where it is thought desirable to institute proceedings, for example in the circumstances mentioned in paragraph 9.23 above, it will be possible for the patient to be remanded to a unit while awaiting trial, so being kept out of the penal system, and, where appropriate, to remain there afterwards under a substantive hospital order with or without restrictions on discharge.

PRE-TRIAL ACTION

SUMMARY OF CONCLUSIONS

I. Section 136 Arrangements

1. Under section 136 of the Mental Health Act 1959 the police have the power to remove to a place of safety any person found in a place to which the public have access who appears to be suffering from mental disorder and to be in immediate need of care and control, in the interests of himself or for the protection of others. The statistics understate the frequency with which the police act under the authority of this provision. It is evident that it is now widely used, and we are satisfied that the police have a clear need for the power which it affords. (Paragraphs 9.1–9.7.)

2. We think that these arrangements should continue to be used to the maximum to ensure that as many as possible of the mentally disordered offenders within the scope of the provision are referred at the outset to the treatment agencies, without the need to bring them before the courts. (Paragraph 9.12.)

3. The difficulties that arise in the use of section 136 require administrative rather than legislative remedies. In the absence of special evidence of abuse we do not think any case for amendment of the existing provision has been established, particularly since it already embodies certain safeguards against arbitrary practice. There is a need in some areas for closer co-operation between the police and health authorities to ensure that the statutory provision is operated effectively. (Paragraphs 9.8, 9.13 and 9.14.)

4. We do not think it desirable, as some witnesses have proposed, that there should be a separate psychiatric unit in London for the emergency reception of section 136 cases. We look forward to the development of adequate psychiatric facilities within district general hospitals and in teaching hospitals in Central London which should then be responsible for the admission of patients within their catchment area. Meanwhile, we welcome the formulation of an agreed code of practice for the Greater London Area. (Paragraph 9.9.)

141

5. We think that the police must continue to have ultimate discretion whether to prosecute persons detained under section 136, but that the power should generally not be used unless a useful public purpose will be served by prosecution, and that this criterion could seldom be satisfied in section 136 cases. (Paragraph 9.15.)

II. Relief from prosecution

6. Where any apparent offender is clearly in urgent need of psychiatric treatment and there is no question of risk to members of the public the question should always be asked whether any useful public purpose would be served by prosecution. The medical report should be taken into account, together with, where possible, a report on the circumstances by a social worker. These remarks apply in cases of homicide or attempted homicide or grave bodily harm as in less serious cases. Chief officers of police should review their policy and practice in the cases for which they have responsibility and the Director of Public Prosecutions should give them guidance in this review. (Paragraphs 9.19–9.20.)

7. Those undertaking medical treatment should be as fully informed as possible and the prosecuting authorities should arrange for any medical and social inquiry reports that may have been obtained to be passed on to the responsible doctor together with a statement of the facts of the charge, provided that the person charged admits that he did the act in question. (Paragraph 9.21.)

8. Although there are circumstances in which prosecution of patients in hospital for offences committed before entering hospital, while temporarily absent from it, or while inside, may be desirable, in general the presumption should be against bringing charges which may result in the ordeal of court appearances and the stigma of conviction, with no compensating advantage. Prosecution should be seen as a last resort, and should not be embarked upon where it is not clearly in the interests of the patient or the community. (Paragraphs 9.23–9.24.)

CHAPTER 10

DISABILITY IN RELATION TO THE TRIAL

I. PRELIMINARY MATTERS

10.1 Despite what we have said in the foregoing chapter about the protection of mentally disordered people from the distress of court appearances, there will continue to be cases in which on a balance of considerations it is necessary for them to be brought into court. There will also be people coming before the courts whose mental disorder has not previously manifested itself or has not previously been observed. What procedure should the courts adopt in these situations? Before answering this question, we must deal with a number of preliminary matters.

(1) Terminology

10.2 Where the defendant's mental condition is such that he is not fit to be tried, he is generally said to be "unfit to plead". This is not a statutory expression, but it appears in the marginal note to section 4 of the Criminal Procedure (Insanity) Act 1964, and is commonly used by those who write about or are involved in the criminal law and the business of the criminal courts. Although familiar to these practitioners, the term is inaccurate and misleading. It may be defended on the ground of its long established general acceptance, but we think it desirable that, if possible, it should be supplanted by something more apt. A person who is "unfit to plead" is usually suffering from substantial mental incapacity (although occasionally he may be a deaf-mute) and we think that the position would be more clearly conveyed by the phrase "under disability in relation to the trial", which could be shortened, colloquially, to "under disability". This form of words is, indeed, used in the substantive text of the 1964 Act. We realise that the use of the term "unfit to plead" will not be forsworn immediately by all those for whom its use is habitual; but we think its eventual supersession is desirable and should be officially encouraged.

(2) Criteria

10.3 The existing criteria for determining whether a defendant is under disability are whether he is able to understand the course of proceedings at the trial, so as to make a proper defence, to challenge a juror to whom he might wish to object, and to understand the substance of the evidence. A number of witnesses have represented that these criteria work well: one or two have suggested minor changes. HM Judges have recommended to us that the present tests should be modified by omission of the reference to challenging a juror, and the addition of two more criteria; namely, whether the defendant can give adequate instructions to his legal advisers, and plead, with understanding, to the indictment. The criteria so modified seem to us to be an improvement, and we recommend their adoption.

(3) Amnesia

10.4 We have given very full consideration to the question whether amnesia which prevents a defendant from remembering events at the time of the alleged offence should be regarded as rendering him unfit for trial. This is a situation which occurs frequently, especially in the context of traffic accidents.

143

10.5   At present amnesia does not in itself raise an issue of fitness to stand trial.   There is an argument against this, since a person who has no recollection of the events charged against him, for example as a result of brain damage, perhaps from concussion, or of a hysterical reaction, is seriously handicapped in instructing counsel and making his defence.   On the other hand, it is clear that there are many difficulties which may handicap the defence but which should not operate to bar trial.   The defendant may have failed to trace essential witnesses through no fault of his own, or he may have lost his diary and so be unable to recollect where he was on the day of the crime, or he may never have kept a diary and simply have forgotten.   Obviously, such difficulties cannot be allowed to bar the trial.   The question is whether amnesia should be regarded as equivalent to a mental disability of the kind traditionally accepted as a reason for barring trial, or whether it should be regarded as equivalent to other adventitious difficulties affecting the defence.

10.6   The majority of the Committee favour the continuation of the present rule.   In their view, the law of unfitness to stand trial is a concession to notions of justice in certain extreme cases, but it cannot be extended too far.   Those extreme cases have been cases where the "unfitness" has been on grounds of mental disorder or deaf mutism and not on other grounds.   A defendant who is unable to remember the events comprising the alleged offence is really saying that there is another witness, namely himself, who would be able to give an account of what happened but who cannot be put in the witness box because he cannot remember.   The lack of memory may be caused by forgetfulness, by hysterical dissociation, or by concusssion (whether or not connected with the circumstances of the offence).   This has not hitherto been within the concept underlying the tests of unfitness to stand trial, and ought not to be brought within it by giving too literal a meaning to the criteria suggested by HM Judges, who, incidentally, were not in favour of extending their tests to amnesia.   There are two other relevant distinctions in respect of mental disorder.

   (a)   The defendant for whom the issue can at present be raised is severely affected in mind, so that in many cases he must in any event be subjected to control for a considerable period.   Even if he did the act, the public interest will be protected by the fact that he can, if necessary, be confined.   In contrast, the amnesic defendant is normally able to maintain himself in the community; he does not need to be a hospital patient, so that keeping him in hospital cannot be represented as a benefit to him.

   (b)   The defendant for whom the issue can at present be raised not only is severely affected at the time of trial but probably was so affected at the time of the act charged, so that, if he did the act, he is probably not responsible on the ground of insanity or, even if he is convicted, is a fit case for a hospital order.   In contrast, retrograde amnesia arising by reason of an event after the act charged is in no way inconsistent with full responsibility for the act.   If it were allowed to bar the trial, this would mean, for example, that a murderer could avoid conviction merely because after the crime he tumbled off his motor cycle and suffered concussion with retrograde amnesia.   In

144

default of a conviction there would not in practice be anything that could be done with such a person other than to set him free. This would be an unacceptable outcome,

10.7 Another objection to recognising amnesia as operating to bar trial is that it can readily be feigned, and neither doctors nor psychologists can always state positively whether or not it is genuine. It is true that in some cases there is medical evidence to support the patient's claim to amnesia. But even if the amnesia results from some incontestable medical condition, the view of the majority is that it should not operate to bar trial, for the reasons already given.

10.8 A minority of the Committee[1] argue that it is inconsistent to concede, on the one hand, that conditions such as severe subnormality, deaf mutism, psychosis, or depression may render a person unable to conduct a proper defence, and on the other to maintain that complete loss of memory can *never* render anyone unable to conduct a proper defence. If it were not for the loss of memory the defendant might be able to give important evidence on the facts in issue[2] or on the issue of *mens rea*. Moreover, there are cases in which both retrograde and anterograde amnesia may be caused by an event prior to the act charged, such as an epileptic fit or head injury which can produce an anterograde amnesia.

10.9 The minority are not arguing that mere forgetfulness should entitle someone to be regarded as "under disability"; they point out that it can readily be distinguished from amnesia caused by physical illness or injury or severe mental disorder[3] and it is only the latter which, in their view, should be accepted by the court. Moreover, they would limit the concession to cases in which the court was satisfied[4] not only that the amnesia was so caused but also that the circumstances were such that it was likely to prevent the defendant from giving adequate instructions for his defence. The argument that he is in the same position as the defendant who cannot trace a witness or his diary fails to recognise that the latter knows what his defence is and merely cannot produce evidence, whereas the amnesic defendant does not know what his defence might be.

10.10 The suggestion that HM Judges' new criterion—inability to give adequate instructions to one's legal advisers—is not to be "given too literal a meaning" (paragraph 10.6) seems to the minority to amount to a concession that if this test were to be logically applied the amnesic defendant would have

[1] Professor Sir Denis Hill and Professor Walker.

[2] For example, B picks a fight with A, who defends himself. A is concussed by B's friends who tell the police that A assaulted B. When tried A cannot recall (because of the concussion) what happened, and so cannot put up his valid defence.

[3] This excludes hysterical dissociation where it is the only evidence of mental disorder.

[4] It has been argued that there might well be circumstances in which the court would have to be informed about the alleged facts on which the charge was based before it could decide whether the amnesia of the defendant rendered him unable to give adequate instructions for his defence. To this the minority reply first that such a possibility is not confined to amnesia, but could arise where the defendant had suffered, after the alleged act, a head injury which made it impossible for him to discuss the charge coherently with his legal representatives; second that the objection points to the need for a procedure which will allow the court to hear the alleged facts rather than to the rejection of amnesia as a form of disability.

to be regarded as being under disability. As for the argument in paragraph 10.6(*a*), this appears to the minority to be an irrelevancy. What is at issue is not disposal but conviction: and both majority and minority are agreed that not all of those who will be found under disability, for whatever reason, will require admission to hospital (see paragraphs 10.27–10.30 below).

10.11   To sum up, while we are all concerned to ensure that any defendant who is under a mental disability should be treated with due consideration for his difficulties, the majority of the Committee think that this requirement is adequately safeguarded by the court itself under the present arrangements and that in any event the objections to including amnesia within the scope of the criteria for exemption from trial outweigh the arguments for making such a change.

(4) Importance of establishing the facts

10.12   If a person is mentally unfit to be tried there are obviously strong arguments for establishing this at the earliest possible moment.   The sooner the defendant can be relieved of the stress of appearance in court, and can begin uninterrupted treatment, the better for him, the better for the dignity of the legal process, and the greater the saving of public time and money.   However, there are arguments in the other direction.   There must be safeguards against the possibility that it might become too easy for people to be put away, perhaps for long periods, without proper justification.   We have the example of what happens elsewhere to warn us against instituting any system which might be open to the suspicion that arbitrary committals to hospital might take place, perhaps to suit the convenience of the authorities.   Members of the public may equally look for reassurance that criminal offences are not being glossed over on a pretext that the defendant is not fit to stand trial.

10.13   The Criminal Law Revision Committee have noted the dilemma that a person may be entitled to an acquittal on the facts and yet it may be impossible to try him properly because of his disability[5].   Clearly there are powerful arguments in favour of trying to establish the facts in such cases, before accepting that a defendant should be committed to indefinite detention.   There will often be no justification for putting him in hospital if he did not commit the offence charged against him.   He may, for example, be a mentally handicapped person living peaceably with his mother, and a grievous wrong would be done to him if he were committed to hospital on a charge that could not be substantiated.   If he is so committed the hospital doctor and the advisers of the Home Secretary must naturally act on the assumption that the patient committed the offence charged against him, and this may affect the estimation of when he is safe to be released.

10.14   We have been informed in evidence that some people who have been committed to indefinite detention in a psychiatric hospital, having been found unfit to be tried, feel it to be an injustice that they have not been tried.   The grievance may be felt notwithstanding that their mental condition required detention for treatment in hospital in any event and the sense of grievance may itself make treatment difficult.

---

[5] Criminal Law Revision Committee: Third Report.   Cmnd. 2149, paragraph 18.

10.15 What is needed is a system which will, on the one hand, provide the genuinely disordered person with speedy medical attention, but, on the other hand, will ensure that the facts of the case are publicly inquired into without undue delay. How far do the existing arrangements correspond to these requirements?

II. THE CROWN COURT

(1) The existing procedure

10.16 The statutory provisions relating to the Crown Court are contained in the Criminal Procedure (Insanity) Act 1964, which was based upon the Third Report of the Criminal Law Revision Committee (Cmnd. 2149). The question whether the defendant is under disability may be raised by the defence or the prosecution or the court itself, and section 4 of the Act enables the court, if of the opinion "that it is expedient so to do and in the interests of the accused", to postpone consideration of the question until any time up to the opening of the case for the defence. This means that the court may require the prosecution to deploy its case, and it is possible for the defendant to be acquitted by decision of the judge if the prosecution case is insufficient to be left to the jury. Subject to this power for the court to defer consideration of the question, the Act provides that the question of fitness to be tried shall be determined as soon as it arises, and it is to be determined by a jury subject to appeal[6]. If it is decided that the defendant is under disability, the trial proceeds no further. Under section 5 of the Act the court then has no option but to make an order that the accused be admitted to such hospital as may be specified by the Home Secretary.

10.17 If subsequently the patient's mental condition improves, the Home Secretary is empowered by section 5(4) of the Act to remit him for trial. The use of this power was explained to us in the memorandum of Departmental evidence in the following terms:

"Home Office policy in this respect has regard to the general principle that a person who has been accused of an offence ought to be brought to trial so that the issue of guilt or innocence may be properly determined. There may, however, be practical difficulties in proceeding with the prosecution of a person who has been detained in hospital for a long time, and if he were returned to hospital after trial either in consequence of a finding of not guilty by reason of insanity, or in pursuance of a hospital order with restrictions made on conviction, his status in the hospital would be effectively unchanged. In practice, the Home Secretary's power to remit the accused person for trial is sparingly used, generally in cases in which his mental condition improves rapidly (or perhaps is found to have been feigned), and in which the desirability of reaching a formal decision as to guilt is not counterbalanced by other considerations. Where necessary, the prosecuting authority would be consulted before reaching a decision whether to remit the accused for trial. Where the accused is

---

[6] The requirements of medical evidence are dealt with in paragraphs 10.41–10.42 below. We note, in passing, that the court has no power to remand a defendant on bail with a condition of submitting to a medical examination before the finding of guilt (see also paragraph 10.33), and that there is no power at present to remand any defendant to hospital (see paragraph 12.2).

not remitted for trial, proposals which the responsible doctor may wish to put forward for the grant of leave or discharge from the hospital can be considered on their merits at any time".

(2) Shortcomings of present arrangements

10.18   It will be seen that, measured against the provisions we suggested as desirable, these statutory arrangements are defective.   The disability of the defendant must wait to be determined at the Crown Court, as the magistrates cannot deal with it.   Once it has been determined that the defendant is under disability there is no provision for the facts to be investigated by the court: even where the prosecution evidence has been given, there is no provision for any evidence by the defence, and unless an acquittal is returned on the evidence of the prosecution alone the person under disability must be committed to hospital under an indefinite order.   Finally, a person so committed to hospital must remain there, untried, until the Home Secretary decides otherwise, and this may mean a very long period of detention, even detention for life.   As things stand at present it is not in the interests of the defendant to seek the protection of a disability plea unless the charge is very serious.   If the trial went ahead he might be acquitted altogether, but even if convicted he could hope to receive from the court a more acceptable sentence than committal to hospital for an indeterminate period.   The Criminal Law Revision Committee gave considerable thought to these problems,[7] and the provision which was embodied in the Criminal Procedure (Insanity) Act 1964, allowing the decision about disability to be postponed up to the opening of the case for the defence, was favoured by the majority of that Committee.

(3) Our proposals

(i) *Determination of disability*

10.19   In order to reduce the number of occasions on which disability has to be found, we recommend the following procedure at the trial.   When the question is raised whether the defendant is under disability it should be decided at the outset of the trial, or otherwise as soon as it is raised.   If disability is found but the medical advice indicates the possibility of recovery within a few months, the judge may adjourn the proceedings for a maximum of six months,[8] and at the adjourned proceedings the question of disability will be re-opened.   It may be found at that time that the defendant has become fit to stand trial.   If he is found to be still under disability, a trial of the facts will take place in the way described below (paragraphs 10.24–10.26).   (In the event of the defendant recovering from his disability within the six months period, the trial should immediately proceed; similarly, where the defendant proves to be unresponsive to treatment even before the six months have elapsed, trial of the facts should take place without further delay.)   Under these arrangements the trial of the facts in the case of a severely subnormal person would take place without adjournment since the medical advice would not indicate any prospect of early recovery.

---

[7] Criminal Law Revision Committee: Third Report.   Cmnd. 2149, paragraphs 17–18.

[8] See paragraph 12.8.   The adjournment should be for up to three months in the first place, with renewal for a month at a time up to six months altogether.

10.20 We also recommend that the trial judge should have a limited power to decide the question of disability. He should decide the question if the medical evidence is unanimous. He should also decide the question in the event of disputed medical evidence unless the defence desire that it should be decided by a jury, in which case it must be so decided.

10.21 In concluding that the question of disability should be determined by the judge alone, except where, in the event of disputed medical evidence, the defendant asks for the matter to go to the jury, we have taken account of a number of considerations. The Criminal Law Revision Committee considered the question[9] and decided that "owing to the great importance of the issue from the point of view of the accused and of the public . . . it would be in accordance with the established principles as to the respective functions of the judge and jury in criminal cases that it should continue to be determined in all cases by a jury". At that time capital punishment had not yet been abolished and this was no doubt a factor in the Committee's reluctance to propose withdrawing the issue from the jury.

10.22 It is arguable that the jury are not a suitable body to decide a medico-legal issue and that the judge is better able to form a view on the basis of the medical reports, if necessary in the absence of the defendant. This is the practice in the United States of America. The involvement of the jury in the process of determining disability is a historical survival from the days when prisoners were subjected to "peine forte et dure"; for this purpose, if they refused to testify, the jury had to decide whether they were mute of malice or mute by visitation of God. Insofar as the question is whether the trial should proceed, juries are not normally involved in a decision of this sort. Insofar as the question relates to the commitment of an untried defendant to hospital, this again is not a matter that is entrusted to a jury where a trial is not proceeding. A decision of the issue by the judge would be more expeditious than trial by jury, and this is of some importance where the decision has to be made in the middle of the trial.

10.23 No doubt in many cases the issue of who should decide whether a defendant is under disability is largely a theoretical one; there is often little difference of opinion as to his mental state, and after a short direction from the judge the jury quickly return an appropriate finding. In such circumstances it does not greatly matter whether the issue is decided by the judge or the jury, since in effect the judge decides and the jury will normally follow his direction. On the other hand it is highly desirable that in the occasional cases where the defendant's fitness to stand trial is disputed, there should be no grounds for any suspicion that the judges and psychiatrists are committing people to hospital in an arbitrary fashion, and we feel that the option of a jury decision should be available to the defence on request. In so recommending we have taken note of the position in Scotland where the law allows the judge or the jury to decide the issue. We understand that in practice the judge invariably makes the decision, even in cases where the psychiatrists disagree, and, if our proposal is accepted, we are confident it would be rare for a jury in England or Wales to be asked to form a view on this matter. A jury which did decide such an issue should not proceed to find on the facts of the case; a separate jury would need to be empanelled for this purpose.

[9] Criminal Law Revision Committee: Third Report. Cmnd. 2149, paragraph 15.

(ii) *Trial of the facts*

10.24 If the defendant is found to be under disability, there should neverthe-less be a trial of the facts to the fullest extent possible having regard to the medical condition of the defendant. The object of this proposal is primarily to enable the jury to return a verdict of not guilty where the evidence is not sufficient for a conviction. If a normal verdict of not guilty is to be possible, the normal rules of evidence and burden of proof must apply. It follows that on the trial of the facts the judge should direct the jury that if they are not satisfied that the defendant did the act with the necessary mental state they must return a verdict of not guilty. We have found some difficulty in formulat-ing the opposite verdict, namely one of guilty in all but name. This would be apt, for example, in a case where the mental condition of the defendant was normal at the time of the offence but had so deteriorated by the time of trial that he was then under disability. If it were not for the accused's present disability the verdict would be a conviction, but we do not think that in the circumstances it should carry either the name or the effect of a conviction; and we have chosen the formula that "the defendant should be dealt with as a person under disability". This new formula is for use in cases where the prosecution's case has been established, but where the verdict of guilty is not appropriate by reason of the defendant's disability. It might be misleading for the jury simply to be directed to report that the facts have been proved, because the word "facts" might be understood to refer only to the external facts, the act done or omission made, whereas the issues to be established by the prosecution include the defendant's state of mind. If this were not so, the defendant would not obtain his verdict of not guilty even though there was insufficient evidence that he had the requisite intention or other mental state for the crime—indeed, he would not obtain it even though it was clear that the affair was an accident. This would clearly be unsatisfactory.

10.25 It may be asked how the prosecution can establish their case if the defendant is unable to make a proper defence and in particular how they can prove intention in these circumstances. The answer is that intention is proved as it almost always is in court: by inference from the evidence of what the defendant did. There is, of course, always the possibility that some explana-tion could have been given if the defendant had been able to defend himself—an explanation that does not appear from the evidence that is available; so there is a possibility of a wrong verdict. It is because of this possibility that we are not proposing that the verdict should count as a conviction, nor that it should be followed by punishment.

10.26 We have considered whether the defendant should have the right to waive trial of the facts. We do not think he should, for the reason given in paragraph 10.46 below.

(iii) *Disposal*

10.27 In the event of a verdict that the defendant should be dealt with as a person under disability, we propose that the present law should be changed to give the court a discretion as to disposal. At present, as we have mentioned in paragraph 10.16 above, section 5 of the Criminal Procedure (Insanity) Act 1964 provides that in every case where a defendant is found under disability in relation to trial the court must make an order for his admission to such hospital as may be specified by the Home Secretary. The Criminal Law Revision Committee recommended[10] the continuation of the system of mandatory commitment to a hospital on the grounds that this system worked satisfactorily in practice, that the Home Office was in a better position than the courts to investigate the questions relevant to the defendant's treatment and that uniformity of practice in dealing with these cases was highly desirable and much more likely to be achieved if handled by a single experienced authority than by a great many different courts. The Committee recommended one exception to the rule of mandatory commitment, namely, that if the court was satisfied that the detention of the defendant in hospital was unnecessary it should be given power to order his immediate release, but before exercising this power the court should be required to be satisfied by medical evidence that it would be safe for the public as well as the defendant himself to do so. This recommendation was not carried into effect since it was felt that there were objections to dividing the responsibility for release between the Home Secretary and the courts—a view shared by the Lord Chief Justice and HM Judges at that time.

10.28 We think that there has been a change in opinion on this subject, and that it would generally be thought acceptable that the court should have a discretion. Almost all the evidence we have received has recommended against mandatory disposal on a finding of disability. In their evidence to us the Judges were in favour of the court having discretion to decide the appropriate disposal in each case.

10.29 We cannot envisage any circumstances in which an overtly penal disposal—prison, borstal or fine—would be suitable for a defendant found under disability and we think it would be wrong in principle for the court to be empowered to pass such sentences. Our recommendation is that after the trial of the facts, on a finding that the accused should be dealt with as a person under disability, the court should have power to make any of the following social or medical orders:—

(a) an order for in-patient treatment in hospital with or without a restriction order;

(b) an order for hospital out-patient treatment;

(c) an order for forfeiture of any firearm, motor vehicle, etc., used in crime;

(d) a guardianship order;

(e) any disqualification (eg from driving) normally open to the court to make on conviction;

(f) discharge without any order.

The usual criteria for the making of orders under (a), (b) and (d) should be observed.

10.30 We considered whether it would be appropriate for the court to have power to make a supervision order, perhaps on the lines of a juvenile care order, under which the defendant would be placed under the care of the local authority

---

[10] Criminal Law Revision Committee: Third Report. Cmnd. 2149, paragraphs 30–34.

social services department who would then consider what arrangements should be made for his effective supervision and support. One objection to such an order, although not in our view decisive, is that it would not be possible in relation to the disordered offender to establish sanctions which would effectively operate in the event of breach of the conditions of the order. Even without sanctions, a supervision order would alert the social services department to the needs of the defendant and provide an opportunity for social work to be carried out where appropriate. But we doubt the justification for proposing new machinery to deal with such a tiny category of cases, particularly since guardianship orders, which give the social worker certain relevant powers to be exercised in the interests of the patient, are already available to the courts and may often be appropriate in cases of disability. Probation and community service orders and conditional discharge have not been included among our recommended disposals since they render the defendant in the event of default liable to be returned to court to be sentenced for his original offence.

(iv) *Appeal*

10.31 The defendant should be entitled to appeal against a finding of disability, as now, and a finding that he should be dealt with as a person under disability would count as a conviction for the purposes of appeal, though not for other purposes. There is a precedent for this in section 2 of the Criminal Procedure (Insanity) Act 1964.

10.32 In the event of the defendant's recovery after a return of the disability verdict following the trial of the facts it should be open to the defendant to apply to the Court of Appeal for a normal trial. In deciding whether to grant such an application the Court would no doubt wish to take account of the lapse of time since the events took place and whether witnesses were still available. It should be open to the Court to refuse a normal trial, and there should in any event be a bar to further prosecution after the trial of the facts, otherwise than at the instigation of the defendant.

III. THE MAGISTRATES' COURTS

(1) Shortcomings of present arrangements

10.33 There are certain difficulties in relation to the determination of fitness to stand trial in magistrates' courts. First, there is no explicit power for magistrates to remand a case for medical examination before a finding of guilt. The powers provided by section 14[11] and section 26 of the Magistrates' Courts Act 1952 for the court to obtain a medical report are available only after conviction or after a finding of guilt respectively. The Criminal Justice Act 1967, section 21, enables special conditions to be attached to a grant of bail, and we see no reason of policy why attendance for medical examination should not be made such a condition where the question of disability is raised; but few cases involving the question of disability in relation to the trial are likely to be suitable for the grant of bail and it is unfortunate that the Magistrates' Courts Act does not clearly provide powers to enable a medical report to be obtained

---

[11] In *Boaks* v *Reece* [1957] 1 Q.B. 219 it was held that the general power provided by section 14 included power for the court to remand in custody or on bail for a medical report after conviction even though the offence was not punishable with imprisonment so that the case did not fall within section 26.

in disability cases by remand in custody, in hospital or on bail as may be most appropriate. Moreover there is no statutory authority enabling the magistrates to hear evidence on the issue of fitness to stand trial.

10.34   Again, if the court is of opinion that the defendant is unfit to stand trial and that he ought to be admitted to hospital the court has no authority to detain the defendant for this purpose; though, since the court room is a place to which the public have access, a police officer in court may exercise the power under section 136 of the Mental Health Act, if all the elements of the section are satisfied, to remove the defendant to a "place of safety" with a view to having him admitted to hospital.   The provisions in section 60(2) of the Mental Health Act, which enable magistrates to deal with people suffering from mental illness or severe subnormality without proceeding to conviction, apply only where the court is satisfied that the defendant did the act or made the omission charged, and are therefore not apt for the defendant who is under disability, although we were told that in practice they are sometimes used in such cases.[12] In trivial cases the magistrates may properly have recourse to the expedient of adjourning the proceedings *sine die* or of simply not proceeding.   Where the defendant is allowed to consent to the summary trial of an indictable offence, his disability may prevent him from consenting, and the case may, therefore, have to go to the Crown Court for disposal, although the nature of that disposal, having regard to the mental state of the defendant, may be a foregone conclusion.   This obviously involves the accused person in stress, and the authorities in expenditure of time and money, which might often be avoided if the magistrates had wider powers under which to proceed.

(2) Our proposals

(i) *Determination of disability*

10.35   In our view jurisdiction to determine the issue of disability in relation to the trial should be given to magistrates' courts.   Also, where there is doubt about a defendant's ability to consent to the summary trial of an indictable offence, his representative (see paragraph 10.47) should be empowered to consent on his behalf, but in the event of his recovery and trial the defendant should be asked personally whether he elects to be tried summarily (see paragraph 10.37) below.   This would enable the magistrates to proceed to investigate the question of his disability.   We also think it essential that magistrates should have the power to call for reports on the mental condition of the defendant at any stage in proceedings where it is thought that he may be under disability, or unable to give, with understanding, his consent to summary trial. Such reports should be in the form required for orders under section 60 of the Mental Health Act.

10.36   We have considered whether the same magistrates' court that hears evidence on the question of disability and decides the question should subsequently proceed to the trial (whether the full trial or the trial of the facts as the case may be).   We think it desirable that the trial should take place before a differently constituted court; this is consistent with our recommendation in paragraph 10.23 that a second jury be empanelled for the trial if a jury determination of disability is made.

---

[12] In connection with our proposals for new provisions relating to the special verdict we are recommending the repeal of section 60(2) of the Mental Health Act (see paragraph 18.19).

(ii) *Procedure in cases of disability*

10.37 In parallel with the arrangements we have proposed for the Crown Courts, where the medical evidence of two doctors indicates that the defendant is under disability and there is no prospect of his recovery within six months the trial of the facts should proceed immediately: but magistrates' courts, like the Crown Courts (see paragraph 10.19), should have power to remand to hospital on medical evidence for a period of treatment not exceeding six months, at the end of which, if the defendant is still under disability there should be a trial of the facts, without proceeding to conviction. The magistrates' court should have power to make any of the orders open to the Crown Court in similar circumstances, and should therefore be able to make a hospital order except that they should not be able to impose an order restricting discharge under section 65 of the Mental Health Act. If the defendant is found to be unresponsive to treatment before the expiration of the six months, trial of the facts should thereupon proceed without further delay. If on the other hand he recovers before the end of the six months, the normal trial proceedings should at once be resumed. In such a case, if the defendant's legal representative has previously consented, on his behalf, to summary trial the defendant should now be asked personally whether he elects to be tried summarily; he should have a right to elect trial by jury in any case where the law allows it.

10.38 We have proposed in paragraph 10.32 above, arrangements for application to the Court of Appeal for a normal trial by a defendant who recovers after a trial of the facts by a Crown Court. Where the trial of facts has been conducted by a magistrates' court application should be to the Queen's Bench for leave to appeal.

10.39 We are conscious that a defendant who, if found guilty, would have been liable at most to a sentence of three months imprisonment may, under our proposals, be remanded to hospital for up to six months on a finding of disability and then, having recovered, be tried for the offence and sentenced to three months imprisonment. The time allowed for treatment in hospital is for the patient's own benefit, and it would clearly be wrong to specify a shorter maximum period for remands by magistrates' courts than for remands by the Crown Court, since the treatment required depends on medical, not legal, considerations. We would hope that in such a case as we have envisaged where the defendant has recovered, the court subsequently trying him, knowing his history, will pay due regard to the fact that he has spent time in hospital. In suitable cases the prosecution could be asked to drop the case and the justification for this will increase with the length of time the defendant has remained on remand for treatment.

10.40 We recognise that many cases coming before magistrates are trivial, and we would not suggest that all should be dealt with under the powers we have proposed. We have already referred (paragraph 10.34) to the expedients at present used by the justices in trivial cases where the defendant is plainly disordered of persuading the police to drop the charge or adjourning the proceedings *sine die* on being assured that arrangements are made to admit the defendant to hospital under Part IV of the Act. We think that these methods of disposing of the charge in minor cases are good and sensible and their continued use should be encouraged. (See, in this connection, our remarks on relief from prosecution in the foregoing chapter.)

IV. ALL COURTS

(1) Medical evidence as to disability

10.41 A number of those who have submitted evidence to us have argued that a decision that may result in a defendant being deprived of his liberty for a substantial period should be based on the evidence of more than one doctor. The practice of requiring evidence from two doctors was recommended by the Atkin Committee, the Royal Commission on Capital Punishment and the Criminal Law Revision Committee. The latter body said[13] that they refrained from recommending legislation to this effect only because they understood that it was the invariable practice. There is, however, evidence that the practice is not invariably followed, although the exceptions are rare; and we take the view that there should be a statutory requirement for the supporting evidence of two doctors before the defendant can be found to be under disability in relation to the trial. It may seem unnecessary to insist on a second opinion where there is one clear medical recommendation, accepted by the defence, but we hold that the defendant should not be put in jeopardy of loss of his liberty unless there is an agreed opinion by two doctors, as indeed is already the requirement for orders made under section 60 of the Mental Health Act.

10.42 We have considered whether, to avoid the risk that undesirable pressures might be brought to bear on general practitioners, it might be desirable for both doctors who give evidence to be approved by Area Health Authorities under section 28 of the Mental Health Act. It seems to us preferable, however, not to exclude the evidence of the defendant's own doctor who would already have knowledge of his history and, therefore, might well be the most suitable witness as to the defendants ability to comprehend the proceedings. We also think that it would be inappropriate to have different requirements for medical evidence in disability cases and in those where orders are made under section 60 of the Mental Health Act.

(2) Determination in absence of the defendant

10.43 An obviously mentally deranged person sitting in the dock while the issue of his unfitness for trial is decided presents a pathetic spectacle, and we have given thought to the possibility of avoiding it. We were glad to have the opportunity of consulting HM Judges about this problem, when they gave us oral evidence. While they were fully sympathetic to the object, they pointed out that the argument was not all one way. In the first place, the defendant himself, being the most concerned party, should be consulted. A case was cited in which the prosecution and defence doctors had been in agreement that the defendant was unfit to plead, but on the day of the trial the defendant himself, who was suffering from a type of episodic insanity, had been capable of arguing his case. Arrangements which prevented him from doing so would have been an infringement of liberty. It was put to us that there are also some cases where it might be beneficial to the defendant to allow him to appear in court and to feel that he had taken part in the proceedings even though he might be manifestly unfit to be tried. There was also the most important consideration of the public interest: decisions to commit defendants to psychiatric institutions should be arrived at in public, on the basis of evidence

---

[13] Criminal Law Revision Committee: Third Report. Cmnd. 2149, paragraph 16.

publicly presented, and defendants should be seen in court, so far as possible. The judges expressed the opinion that in a case where it seems desirable to excuse the defendant from appearing in court he should certainly be represented by counsel, or if he has repudiated counsel the court should arrange for someone to act as *amicus curiae*. We endorse this proposal and moreover recommend that if counsel is repudiated this procedure should operate whether or not the defendant is present in court. The Director of Public Prosecutions, who in written evidence acknowledged that in some cases it might be undesirable for the defendant to appear in court, also stressed the need for limitations and safeguards.

10.44 We attach importance to the physical presence of the defendant in court at the outset of a summary trial or upon arraignment in the Crown Court for two main reasons. First, we regard it as essential that the court should have the opportunity to satisfy itself that the defendant is indeed the person named in the summons or indictment, and we doubt whether this can satisfactorily be done unless the defendant is present in court either to identify himself or to be identified by his relatives or friends. (Identification of the defendant as the offender does not arise at this stage.) Secondly, a criminal trial is essentially a public proceeding and we think it would be open to criticism if there were no requirement for the defendant to be present at any stage.

10.45 On the trial of the facts the defendant should normally be present for two reasons. First, it is just conceivable, and on rare occasions has happened, that an important witness for the prosecution on seeing the defendant in court says for the first time that it is not the person his evidence relates to. Secondly, having the defendant present avoids the possibility that later he may consider himself aggrieved at having been tried and disposed of in his absence. On the other hand, it might sometimes be positively harmful to insist on the presence in court of the defendant and be prejudicial to any subsequent psychiatric treatment: an example might be where a mother has killed her baby while suffering from severe depression; no good purpose would in our view be served by compelling her to listen in court to detailed pathological evidence of the offence, but it might easily exacerbate her condition. The court already has a discretion to dispense with the presence of the defendant after plea, and we think it would be proper for this discretion to be exercised provided certain conditions are met. The defence and prosecution doctors must be in agreement that the defendant is under disability and that attendance in court is likely to prove deleterious to his health and inimical to the chances of any future recovery; the defendant must be legally represented; it must be established that the defendant has, so far as possible, been consulted and has not expressed the wish to be present in court; and the court must be satisfied that the interests of justice or of the public do not require his attendance. Where these conditions obtained it would be possible for the defendant to receive continuous hospital treatment throughout his trial, without having to undergo more than one brief court appearance. In such circumstances the defendant's legal representative should be empowered to enter any plea on his client's behalf other than a plea of guilty. The court could not then proceed to make any order—other than on a technical plea such as *autrefois acquit*—without investigating the facts.

156

10.46 As indicated in paragraph 10.26 we do not think that the defendant should have the right to waive the trial of the facts. By definition the defendant under disability cannot exercise judgment to save himself from a possible miscarriage of justice. To allow him to exercise a waiver in this regard would open the way to criticisms that improper pressure had been applied. Justice must be seen to be done.

(3) Legal representation

10.47 A difficulty which arises at present in respect of the legal representation of a person who is under disability is that of validating the appointment of a legal representative. We think it should be expressly provided that where relatives of a defendant who seems to be under disability have appointed a solicitor to represent him, or counsel has been instructed, the court should be able to accept this representative. If there is none the court may appoint one. Where the defendant is legally aided, and we say more about this below, the solicitor, and if appropriate, counsel retained by relatives should normally be assigned under the legal aid order.

10.48 Although the court may dispense with formal application by a mentally disordered defendant for legal aid, the Justices' Clerks' Society have drawn our attention to the requirement under section 29(4) of the Legal Aid Act 1974 that the defendant furnish a written statement of means before legal aid can be granted. There is no provision under the Legal Aid Act for safeguarding the position of a defendant who is so disordered that the issue of disability has been raised and who by definition would be unable to complete such a statement of means. We are aware of the provision of section 29(6) of the Act that, where a doubt arises whether legal aid should be given to any person the doubt should be resolved in that person's favour. Nevertheless, in our view the law should recognise the special position of such defendants and provision should be made, where disability has been raised, for courts to grant legal aid on the basis that a statement of means be furnished subsequently on behalf of the defendant and the legal aid then be confirmed if appropriate. These arrangements will ensure that the defendant who may be under disability is legally represented from the outset, and thereafter the legal representative will be enabled to decide whether to consent to summary trial, to participate in the process of deciding whether the defendant is under disability and to conduct the case for the defendant on the trial of the facts.

10.49 The National Association for Mental Health suggested to us that the Official Solicitor should be appointed in cases of disability in relation to the trial to act as *guardian ad litem*, as the defendant might be unable to instruct a legal adviser and the Official Solicitor would accumulate expertise in dealing with these cases which lawyers in ordinary practice do not have. We have carefully considered this proposal, but we do not think that this would be a suitable function for the Official Solicitor. Our proposals for trial of the facts within six months, and for discretionary disposal instead of mandatory commitment to hospital should, we think, go far to meet the anxieties felt by the National Association for Mental Health in this connection. We have moreover recommended in paragraph 10.43 the appointment of an *amicus curiae* where the defendant has repudiated counsel.

(4) Disposition of the untried defendant

10.50 While we think that the court should have the power to expedite the admission to hospital of the untried defendant where this is necessary, we wish to make it clear that we do not regard the exercise of the power as following inevitably upon a finding of disability in relation to the trial. If the court is satisfied that some other arrangement can be made for the defendant (such as his admission to a hostel on a voluntary basis, or his return home), and that this disposition is likely to be as satisfactory as admission to hospital, it is obviously preferable for this to be done. To this end we think it important that the court should normally obtain a report on the defendant from either the local authority social services department or the probation and after-care service as appropriate, with a view to considering all possible alternatives to hospital admission.

DISABILITY IN RELATION TO TRIAL

SUMMARY OF CONCLUSIONS

I. Preliminary matters

1. The expression "unfit to plead" is unsatisfactory, and should be replaced by the phrase "under disability in relation to the trial", shortened colloquially to "under disability". (Paragraph 10.2.)

2. The criteria for determining whether a defendant is under disability should be whether he can:

> (i) understand the course of the proceedings at the trial so as to make a proper defence;
>
> (ii) understand the substance of the evidence;
>
> (iii) give adequate instructions to his legal advisers;
>
> (iv) plead with understanding to the indictment. (Paragraph 10.3.)

3. We do not favour any change in the present rule under which amnesia does not of itself constitute disability. (Paragraphs 10.4–10.11.)

4. There is a need to ensure speedy medical attention for the disordered person, whilst establishing the facts of the case without delay. (Paragraphs 10.12–10.15.)

II. Crown Court

5. The question of disability should be decided at the outset of the trial or as soon as it is raised. Where disability has been found and where there is (on medical evidence) a prospect of early recovery the judge may adjourn the trial for up to three months in the first place with renewal for a month at a time up to a maximum of six months. If the defendant recovers within the six-month period the normal trial should proceed immediately. A trial of the facts should take place as soon as disability has been found if there is no prospect of the defendant recovering or as soon during the six-month period as he may prove to be unresponsive to treatment, or recovers. (Paragraph 10.19.)

6.   The issue of disability should be decided by the judge except if the medical evidence is not unanimous and the defence wish a jury to determine the issue. (Paragraphs 10.20–10.23.)

7.   If the defendant is found to be under disability there should nonetheless, at the appropriate time, be a trial of the facts.   If a finding of not guilty cannot be returned the jury should be directed to find "that the defendant should be dealt with as a person under disability".   This new verdict should not count as a conviction nor should it be followed by punishment. (Paragraphs 10.24–10.25.)

8.   The court should have a discretion as to disposal in the event of the new verdict being returned, but an overtly penal disposal should be excluded. (Paragraphs 10.27–10.29.)

9.   The defendant should be entitled to appeal against the finding of disability, and against the return of the new verdict.   In the event of his recovery after the new verdict being found he should also be entitled to apply for a normal trial. Except in these circumstances, after the trial of the facts there should be a bar to further prosecution.   (Paragraphs 10.31–10.32.)

III.   Magistrates' courts

10.   Magistrates' courts should have the power to determine the issue of disability and, where it is found, to order a period in hospital in the same way as the Crown Court.   Where there is doubt about the defendant's ability to consent to the summary trial of an indictable offence his representative should be empowered to do so on his behalf (but this should not be binding on the defendant in the event of his recovery and normal trial—see paragraph 10.37). Where it is thought that the defendant may be under disability or unable to give, with understanding, his consent to summary trial magistrates should have the power to call for reports on his mental condition at any stage in the proceedings.   (Paragraph 10.35.)

11.   The full trial or trial of the facts should take place before a differently constituted court from that which decided on the disability issue. (Paragraph 10.36)

12.   Similar arrangements to those for the Crown Court should apply to the timing and conduct of the trial of the facts, with any appropriate disposal within the competence of the magistrates' courts except a penal disposal. Provision should be made for appeal.   In sentencing a defendant who has been found to be under disability and who has subsequently recovered courts should take into account any time he may already have spent in hospital prior to the normal trial.   (Paragraphs 10.37–10.39.)

13.   In trivial cases the present practice of adjourning the proceedings *sine die* or of not proceeding, where the defendant is plainly disordered and arrangements have been made for his admission to hospital under Part IV of the Act, should continue.   (Paragraph 10.40.)

IV.   All Courts

14.   There should be a statutory requirement for two doctors to give supporting evidence before disability in relation to the trial may be found.   In line with the requirements for section 60 orders, at least one of the doctors should be a

practitioner approved for the purposes of section 28 of the Act by an Area Health Authority as having special experience in the diagnosis or treatment of mental disorders. (Paragraphs 10.41 and 10.42.)

15. If counsel is repudiated, the court should appoint an *amicus curiae* whether or not the defendant is present in court. (Paragraph 10.43.)

16. It is important that the defendant should always be present in court at the outset of the proceedings. He should also normally be in court for the trial of the facts, but the court should be free to exercise its existing power to dispense with his presence after plea, provided that certain conditions are met. (Paragraphs 10.44–10.45.)

17. The defendant should not have the right to waive trial of the facts. (Paragraph 10.46.)

18. Provision should be made for a defendant who seems to be under disability to be represented by any solicitor or counsel who is instructed to appear on his behalf, and if there is none, for the court to appoint one. Solicitor and counsel retained by relatives should be assigned under any legal aid order. (Paragraph 10.47.)

19. The law should be amended to enable courts to grant legal aid to a defendant immediately the question of disability in relation to the trial is raised without first requiring a submission of statement of means. Such a statement should be furnished subsequently for the purpose of confirming the legal aid order. (Paragraph 10.48.)

20. We do not favour the appointment of the Official Solicitor as *guardian ad litem* to represent a defendant under disability. Our proposals for ensuring legal representation and for the appointment of an *amicus curiae* where counsel is repudiated will safeguard the defendant's interests. (Paragraph 10.49.)

21. If disability is found initially, a social inquiry report on the defendant should normally be obtained to enable the court to consider all possible alternatives to hospital admission. (Paragraph 10.50.)

CHAPTER 11

MEDICAL AND SOCIAL INQUIRY REPORTS TO THE COURTS

(1) When should reports be provided?

11.1   In pursuance of the general principles underlying the recommendations in this Report as stated in paragraph 1.21 we are concerned that in every case the court should, so far as possible, be in possession of all relevant information about the present mental state of the accused and any previous psychiatric history.   At present this is not always the case.   The Association of Directors of Social Services have stated that the majority of mentally disordered offenders, other than those who are permanently mentally handicapped or suffering from a periodic episode of mental illness, pass through the courts unrecognised as disordered unless the issue of criminal responsibility is raised, with consequent inappropriate disposal, subsequent care and after-care.   The Bar Council have expressed their concern at failures to recognise even frank mental illness in the pre-trial stages.   The Howard League have told us of a recent case in which throughout the legal processes there had been no recognition of the fact that the man had been depressed for many months; and they stressed the need for those involved at all stages of dealing with offenders, from the police initially to the court itself, to be on the lookout for signs of mental disorder.   We have also heard of cases where offenders subject to a hospital order who have been discharged from hospital have subsequently been re-convicted without any consideration of their mental condition or even awareness of the previous medical history.[1]

11.2   It would be impracticable to suggest that medical reports should be provided in all cases coming before the courts, which in 1974 totalled more than 800,000 (excluding motoring offences), of which a little under half were indictable offences.   Even if compulsory reports were restricted to the major crimes the number of potential reports would still be formidable.   The criminal statistics for 1974 show some 33,000 convictions of violence, 7,000 for sexual offences, 307,000 for offences against property, and 12,000 for minor assaults. The existing medical and psychiatric services would be inadequate to cope with such a large number of reports and one result would be greatly to increase the delay in cases coming to trial.   The reports would often serve no useful purpose: the defendant might be acquitted, or in the event of conviction there might be nothing in the medical report to affect disposal.   It seems clear that if medical reports are to be available to the court in all cases where they may be helpful, without placing intolerable burdens on available resources, some kind of screening process will be necessary.   Again, any such comprehensive proposals would be likely to give rise to widespread objections on grounds of personal liberty, since the reports would frequently need to be obtained by way of a custodial remand, either to prison, even though it might not be open to the court on conviction to pass a sentence of imprisonment, or, under new powers, to hospital.

---

[1] S McCabe and G Boehringer, *Hospital Orders in London Magistrates' Courts.*   (Oxford, Blackwell, 1974.)

11.3   One suggestion which has been made to us in evidence by Mrs Joyce Williams JP[2] is that magistrates' courts should be advised by general practitioners about the need for psychiatric reports in individual cases. Mrs Williams considers that at present medical reports are requested too frequently and without adequate justification. In some cases this may be because magistrates are undecided how to deal with the case and hope that a medical report, by revealing some mental disorder that might otherwise be overlooked, may provide them with a positive recommendation. In others a conscientious bench may be inclined to call for a report in order to demonstrate its concern for an individual in trouble. Indiscriminate requesting of medical reports involves a misuse of scarce specialist medical manpower and of other scarce resources in already overcrowded prisons. The reports themselves often disclose little that is of assistance to the courts owing in part to the pressures of work, the inadequacy of the reasons for asking for a report and the lack of background information including previous history. While we appreciate the reasons which underlie Mrs Williams' proposal we doubt whether general practitioners are well suited to perform such a role. They would be placed in a difficult situation, and we suspect that in practice they might feel unable to say that a psychiatric examination was not required and would therefore usually endorse the court's suggestion that a report be obtained.

11.4   We think that the answer to the problem lies in the use of social inquiry reports, within the structure of the Streatfeild Report[3] arrangements, as a screening process for mental disorder. A good social inquiry report will normally indicate if there is a need for medical examination (in this connection we stress the importance of social workers being watchful for signs of mental disorder or any previous history of psychiatric disorder), and magistrates' courts will thus be alerted to the need to call for a medical report. Social inquiry reports should, we propose, be mandatory in serious offences against the person. This should include all cases of grave non-sexual offences against the person, all sexual offences involving children below the age of 13 or involving violence to persons of any age, and property offences which involve risk to life (for example, arson). The court will, of course, continue to have a discretion to call for a social inquiry report in other cases, and we look forward to the time when the development of forensic psychiatric services and the expansion of other resources will enable medical reports to be provided more often. We think that magistrates' courts should be empowered to seek a medical report on the defendant before conviction only when a defence of mental disorder is raised, or when the question of disability in relation to the trial is at issue, or when the defence seek a remand to hospital. If a medical report is required solely in relation to disposal, magistrates' courts should be able to call for one after conviction or finding of guilt in any case where they think it right to do so. At present, as we have mentioned in paragraph 10.33 in connection with disability in relation to the trial, the law is in need of some clarification as to the power of magistrates' courts to remand for medical reports before conviction.

11.5   The Governor and staff of Holloway Prison have drawn our attention to the fact that the ratio of disturbed to non-disturbed offenders is much

---

[2] See also her article, "Medical Reports: What are the Needs and the Rights of Magistrates' Courts?" *Justice of the Peace and Local Government Review*, 137 (1973), pp. 404–6.

[3] Report of the Interdepartmental Committee on the Business of the Criminal Courts 1961, Cmnd. 1289.

higher for women than for men, and have suggested that social inquiry reports should be obtained in relation to all women appearing before the courts, as a means both of discovering any signs of psychiatric disorder and of avoiding unnecessary custodial remands which may have a seriously damaging effect on the women themselves and on their families. They thought that such reports should provide information about the woman's social situation, her family, whether she was pregnant, her general problem areas and whether there was a possibility of psychiatric or psychological disorder. While we agree with the principle of this proposal, we are bound to point out that the implications in terms of work-load would be considerable: in 1974, some 186,000 women appeared before the courts charged with offences. Subject to the proposal in the previous paragraph for social inquiry reports to be mandatory in certain cases, we think that it should be for the court to decide whether to obtain a report on a woman defendant: at present reports are invariably obtained where a sentence of imprisonment is contemplated. We have already stressed the importance of the court keeping a watchful eye throughout the proceedings for any sign of mental disorder and they should no doubt be specially vigilant in the case of a woman defendant.

(2) Arrangements for obtaining reports

11.6 We have received a number of criticisms of the quality of the assessments supplied to the courts on mentally disordered offenders. Some evidence has referred to the need for an expansion of the numbers of well-qualified psychiatrists, and for the training of psychiatrists in court work. We set out in Chapter 20 our proposals for the development of forensic psychiatric services; as we observed in our Interim Report (paragraph 10), the provision of assessments for the courts will be one of their most important functions. Other witnesses have referred to the need for better opportunities for psychiatric examination of accused persons, and for the availability of verified information about their histories. The importance for assessment purposes of close liaison between the various services in touch with the offender has also been stressed; this, too, is a subject that we deal with in Chapter 20.

11.7 We recommend in the next chapter that courts should be given a general power to remand mentally disordered offenders to hospital (including the special hospitals and regional secure units) for various purposes, one being (after conviction) to obtain a medical report on the defendant. We agree with those witnesses who have emphasised how important it is that doctors who are asked to assess defendants for possible mental disorder should be given adequate information about them. When medical reports are requested on a defendant remanded by a magistrates' court under section 26 of the Magistrates' Courts Act 1952, the court is already required[4] to send to the institution to which the defendant is committed, or at which he will be examined if on bail, a statement of the reasons why the court thinks an inquiry ought to be made into his physical or mental condition and of any relevant information before the court. We are not, however, satisfied at present that the examining doctor is fully

[4] By Rule 23 of the Magistrates' Courts Rules 1968. In Home Office Circulars Nos. 265 of 1968, 107 of 1971 and 113 of 1973 advice was given to magistrates on the arrangements for supplying information to doctors. The last of these circulars is reproduced at Appendix 8(1).

informed in every case of the reasons which have led the court to request the report, notwithstanding that it is in the interest of both the doctor and the court for this to be done.

11.8 We note that in their Report on Young Adult Offenders the Advisory Council on the Penal System pointed out that when magistrates' courts seek a psychiatric report on a defendant, although they are required by rules to send the psychiatrist their reasons for requesting a report, courts sometimes give only such reasons as "nature of offence" or "demeanour in court". We agree with the recommendation made in the Report that whenever magistrates' courts call for a psychiatric report full written reasons for the request should be given to the psychiatrist. Due explanation of these reasons will enable the doctor to relate his report to the points in which the court is interested. It is also important for the doctor that the court should always provide adequate particulars of the circumstances of the offence, especially where its nature suggests that the offender may be dangerous or violent. It would be helpful if the courts could make available to reporting doctors copies of any medical, probation or other reports in their possession. Besides assisting diagnosis the information contained in such reports may have an important bearing on the recommendation a doctor may make if he considers that the offender needs treatment for mental disorder. Further we think that doctors undertaking assessment of defendants in the Crown Court should always see the depositions or statements of witnesses, and after conviction a short transcript of the proceedings should be supplied (as in Appeal proceedings) if this can be obtained in good time. We appreciate that courts may not always be in possession of the full facts of a case, particularly where the defendant may have pleaded guilty and there has been no occasion for cross-examination of witnesses, but we hope they will feel able to pass on to the examining doctor such relevant information as is available to them. If doctors should require more detailed information as to the circumstances of the offence it is open to them to seek the assistance of the police officer concerned in the case. The Home Office have drawn to our attention circulars which were issued in June 1973 to Clerks to Justices and Chief Officers of Police giving general advice on the arrangements for supplying information to doctors who are asked to provide medical reports to courts. These are reproduced at Appendix 8. We hope that the recommendations they contain will be carried out by all concerned.

(3) Panels of psychiatrists

11.9 The proposal has often been made, and has been put to us by a number of witnesses, that to improve the quality of medical evidence on the psychiatric condition of defendants appearing before the courts there should be an independent panel of psychiatrists with responsibility for preparing reports on defendants with suspected mental disorder. Advocates of such a scheme generally envisage that members of the panel who have examined defendants should be open to cross-examination by both prosecution and defence, and that either side should have the right to call their own expert witnesses. The assumption is that the authority of the members of the panel would in general be sufficient in itself to discourage the parties from exercising such a right. The proposal springs from what is thought to be the questionable practice of regarding psychiatric evidence in court as susceptible to the same adversary procedures as other evidence (whether as to opinion or fact) and of leaving the jury to resolve any conflicts which may arise where opposing psychiatrists give contradictory evidence. Instead it offers the prospect of reliable and impartial evidence as to the mental condition of the defendant, without prejudice to the legitimate interests of the two parties. Such provisions exist in a number of countries on the Continent and in some American States.

11.10 Suggestions of this sort have been traced back as far as 1838 when the American doctor Isaac Ray published his influential Treatise on the Medical Jurisprudence of Insanity, which drew attention to the French procedure whereby the court could appoint experts to enquire into the mental state of the defendant and report on oath to the court.[5] Other doctors and psychiatrists have followed this lead, and similar proposals were put to the Capital Punishment Commission (1864–66), the Atkin Committee on Insanity and Crime (1923) and to the Royal Commission on Capital Punishment (1949–53), but none of those bodies felt able to recommend their adoption. Among those who have urged us to consider the question afresh have been the British Medical Association, despite their earlier opposition to the proposal at the time of the Royal Commission.[6] The Association now feel that psychiatric evidence is sometimes not well handled under the adversary system and that it would be better to have an impartial panel of psychiatrists to advise the court. Other medical witnesses in support of the proposal have referred to the undesirable practice of the defence "shopping around" for a favourable psychiatric opinion and suppressing those that are unfavourable.

11.11 As we have indicated already we think there is a clear need for some improvement in the arrangements for supplying psychiatric reports to the courts. On the other hand we would not wish to exaggerate the shortcomings of the present situation, and our impression is that the practices complained of by some witnesses are becoming much rarer. HM Judges expressed to us their general satisfaction with the quality of psychiatric evidence given in court, and pointed out that, while the motive for "shopping around" for favourable psychiatric evidence was very strong in the days of the death penalty for murder, it was much weaker now that the sentence imposed after a finding of diminished responsibility might be the same as that which followed a straightforward conviction for murder. The present practice of hearing psychiatric evidence after conviction to assist the court in disposal means that the former "battle of the experts" has largely been replaced by agreed medical reports. We are confident that if forensic psychiatric services can be developed on the lines we propose the occasions when there will be disagreements between psychiatrists will become even rarer. But in making this forecast we must not be taken to suggest any change in the present structure which permits a defendant to call as a witness his own psychiatrist if he wishes. It is our firm view that the arrangements we have described for in-patient and out-patient assessments by local forensic psychiatric centres of accused persons remanded by courts will better meet the need described by our witnesses than the alternative solution of independent panels of psychiatrists. The service which could be provided by psychiatrists from the regional centres, who will have access to a range of resources and shared experience, will offer advantages as good as those which

---

[5] Nigel Walker, *Crime and Insanity in England*, Vol. 1, pages 120–121. (Edinburgh, 1973.)
[6] Cmnd. 8932, paragraph 441.

might derive from an *ad hoc* panel while the provision of assessments for the courts will afford the centres a practical way to develop their contribution to training and research and the advancement of forensic psychiatry.

(4) Recording of medical information

11.12 In order so far as possible to ensure that a previous history of psychiatric disorder which comes to light in the course of court proceedings, will always be made available to a court on any future occasions, we propose that a note of the fact should be made by the police in their records. The information recorded should relate only to occasions when psychiatric treatment was required, and should include the name of the hospital and the dates when treatment was carried out, if known. Apart from alerting the court on subsequent occasions to the existence of a psychiatric history, if the court then requests a medical report this information will enable the examining doctor to obtain detailed case notes from the hospital concerned if necessary. Other psychiatric information which may have been brought out in evidence should not be recorded. It should not normally be necessary for the medical information contained in the record to be read out in open court as part of the antecedents. In making these recommendations we are very conscious of the considerable, and in our view, justifiable, public sensitivity about the holding of personal records and the disclosure of information kept on them, and we accept that there may be objection to the public use of such information which may in the event prove to be only marginally relevant to a case; but these considerations have to be weighed against the possible consequences if the psychiatric and the police records of a dangerous person do not come together when a court is deciding upon disposal. The study by McCabe and Boehringer, to which reference was made in paragraph 11.1 above, showed a large number of people going through the London magistrates' courts unrecognised as having had psychiatric treatment. At present if a defendant fails to disclose that he has a previous history of mental illness there is normally no way in which this will be discovered. In general, we have no doubt that it is in the interests of the public as well as, usually, the offender himself that the court should know as much as possible about his medical background since this may be essential to the appropriate disposal.

MEDICAL AND SOCIAL INQUIRY REPORTS TO COURTS
SUMMARY OF CONCLUSIONS

1. In order that courts should be in possession of all relevant information about the mental state of defendants we propose that greater use should be made of social inquiry reports as a screening process for mental disorder and to indicate the need for a full psychiatric report. Social inquiry reports should be mandatory in cases involving serious violence or danger to the person. This should include all cases of grave non-sexual offences against the person, all sexual offences on children below the age of 13 or involving violence to persons of any age, and property offences which involve risk to life (for example, arson). (Paragraph 11.4.)

2. Magistrates' courts should in all cases be empowered to seek a medical report on a defendant in relation to disposal following conviction. In other cases a medical report should be sought only when a defence of mental disorder

has been raised or where there is a possibility that the defendant may be under disability or when the defence seek a remand to hospital. The same rules should apply to reports on women defendants, but the courts should be particularly vigilant to notice signs of mental disorder in women defendants. (Paragraphs 11.4–11.5.)

3.   Doctors who are asked to prepare for the courts psychiatric reports on defendants must be given adequate information both on the reasons why the court has requested the report and on the circumstances of the offence.   For cases in the Crown Court they should always see the depositions or statements of witnesses, and where the report is requested after conviction a short transcript of the proceedings should be made available if this can be obtained in good time.   Any other reports on the defendant that are in the court's possession should also be shown to the doctors.   (Paragraphs 11.7–11.8.)

4.   We do not favour the establishment of panels of psychiatrists with responsibility for preparing reports on defendants.   (Paragraphs 11.9–11.11.)

5.   Where it comes to light in the course of court proceedings that a defendant has received psychiatric treatment a note should be made in the police records of the name of the hospital concerned and the dates when treatment was carried out, if known.   No other psychiatric information should be recorded: nor should any information from the police record normally be read out in open court.   (Paragraph 11.12.)

CHAPTER 12

REMANDS TO HOSPITAL

12.1 There are several purposes for which it seems to us that there would be advantage in giving the courts a general power to remand a mentally disordered defendant to hospital[1] for a short period before having to decide on his ultimate disposal.

(1) Remands for medical report

12.2 In the first place the court may simply require a medical report on the defendant. (See, in this connection, the foregoing chapter and in particular paragraph 11.4, where we recommend that magistrates' courts should have only a limited power to call for a medical report before conviction.) At present, where the preparation of a report on an out-patient basis is inappropriate, a medical report can be obtained only by granting bail with a condition of hospital residence (which gives the hospital no power to detain the defendant should he break this condition by discharging himself) or by remanding to prison. Remand to prison may often be unhelpful, in view of the limited facilities of certain prisons for dealing with the generality of psychiatric cases, and even undesirable, for example where the offence in question is not itself punishable by imprisonment on conviction, or a prison sentence is unlikely to be imposed. There is power under section 73 of the Mental Health Act 1959 for the Home Secretary to transfer to hospital a defendant committed or remanded in custody awaiting trial or sentence, but only if he is diagnosed by two medical practitioners as suffering from mental illness or severe subnormality. This section, which in any event gives no power to the court, could not be used to arrange for observation with a view to diagnoses. It would theoretically be possible for a court, in remanding a person on bail with a view to psychiatric observation as an in-patient, to arrange simultaneously for his compulsory admission under section 25 of the 1959 Act.[2] But, as with the section 73 procedure, this again would entail two medical practitioners certifying at the outset that the defendant was suffering from a mental disorder of the nature or degree specified in that section, so anticipating the diagnosis which it is the object of the remand to obtain. These various difficulties in the existing arrangements lead us to think that better provision for medical examination should be made.

12.3 A number of those who have submitted evidence to us have drawn attention to the Scottish procedure, contained in section 54 of the Mental Health (Scotland) Act 1960, under which a court, rather than remanding in custody a defendant apparently suffering from mental disorder, may instead commit him to a hospital "available for his admission and suitable for his detention" for the period for which he is remanded. It is argued that this procedure avoids some of the difficulties which at present arise in remands on bail with a condition of psychiatric examination where the defendant thinks he has got off with something of a "soft option" and makes little or no effort to co-operate. This is said to be one reason why some consultants are reluctant to accept defendants as a condition of bail. However, the Scottish procedure

---

[1] Including special hospital, regional secure unit and local psychiatric hospital—see paragraph 12.8 below.
[2] See paragraphs 2.21 and 2.23.

is directed, not primarily to medical examination (though use is made of the opportunity for observation and assessment), but rather to the care of the defendant suspected of mental disorder during the period of remand. The Act does not enable the court to remand to hospital specifically for a medical report, but it does provide for the court to be informed of the result of medical examination at the hospital, and if the defendant is found by the hospital not to be suffering from mental disorder warranting his compulsory detention under Part IV of the Act (compulsory detention of ordinary patients) he may be disposed of by the court to prison or otherwise, according to the law, for the balance of the remand period. While we recognise that the hospital must be able to refuse to keep a case, this provision involves the possibility of the remanded defendant being shuttled between the court, the hospital and the prison. This is something which it is desirable to avoid. In any event this provision is not apt for all the cases we have in mind where remand for medical examination may be desirable.

(2) Remands for care

12.4 The Scottish procedure affords a precedent for a second type of medical remand which we consider desirable, namely remand to hospital for care. Where a defendant known to be suffering from mental disorder has to be kept in custody on remand, perhaps for a substantial period of time while the prosecution is preparing its case, it may be preferable for him to be in hospital rather than prison. At present, as we pointed out in paragraph 12.2, persons committed in custody awaiting trial or sentence and suffering from mental illness or severe subnormality may be transferred to hospital by order of the Home Secretary under section 73 of the Mental Health Act. Our proposal would offer a simpler procedure, based on an order of the court, which need not be limited to the stipulated medical conditions and which would avoid the necessity for initial committal to prison. This procedure may be associated with our proposal for remand to hospital for medical examination, so that where a defendant so remanded is found to be suffering from mental disorder the court may, with the agreement of the hospital, order that he shall remain in the care of the hospital until such time as his case is ready to be heard.

(3) Interim hospital orders

12.5 The third situation in which a remand to hospital may be desirable is where the court may be minded to dispose of the defendant by making a hospital order but there may be some doubt whether such an order is appropriate. In our discussions with medical witnesses we gained the impression that many doctors found it difficult to decide whether to recommend that a hospital order should be made where they have been able to examine the patient only briefly in a prison hospital under the pressure of impending court proceedings, since it was often impossible to know how he would react subsequently to the psychiatric hospital regime. At present a hospital order may be made on medical recommendation but it may subsequently become clear that no treatment is possible; the patient may be unresponsive or disruptive, or he may even be found through continuous observation in hospital to have been feigning mental disorder at the time he was first examined. As the order cannot subsequently be replaced by a punitive sentence the hospital has no alternative in such a case but to discharge the patient, and he is then beyond the reach of the court. This difficulty could in part be solved if the courts had power to make what might be termed an "interim hospital order", committing the defendant to a specified hospital for a limited period of compulsory detention for diagnosis and assessment. At the latest at the expiry of the interim period, the court would again consider the case and would have discretion to confirm the order if the medical report so recommended, or, if the report indicated that a hospital order was inappropriate, to reconsider the matter and impose any other available disposal, including where appropriate a custodial sentence. (Where the interim order was made by a magistrates' court, if, at the reconsideration stage, it were considered necessary to impose restrictions on the patient's discharge, the case would have to be committed to the Crown Court in the normal way. But see paragraph 14.24 as to the need to limit the use of restriction orders.) The attendance of the patient at court would not be required at the further proceedings if he were legally represented and the court were to be advised to confirm the order: but his presence would be necessary if the court were to be advised that a hospital order was inappropriate and had to consider making a different order. The interim order would enable consideration to be given not only to the need for, and amenability to, treatment, but also to other questions such as whether a particular hospital was appropriate to deal with the case.

12.6 Since the object of the interim order will be to demonstrate whether the defendant is likely to benefit from a final order we do not think that it should be open to him during the currency of the interim order to secure his freedom from liability to detention by absconding. Under section 40 of the Mental Health Act a compulsorily detained patient who remains at large for a stipulated period of time—six months in the case of a psychopathic or subnormal patient, or 28 days in other cases—is no longer liable to be returned to the hospital. We have considered the question of the provisions on absconders in general at paragraphs 14.13–14.16, and have recommended that the present statutory provisions should be repealed and the question whether to take steps to secure the return of an absconder left to the doctor's discretion. But a patient subject to an interim order may in our view properly be regarded as still within the jurisdiction of the court, and if he breaks a condition of the order, for example by absconding, he should be liable to be returned to the court for a fresh order to be substituted.

(4) Disability in relation to the trial

12.7 The final case where a temporary remand to hospital appears to be necessary is that of the defendant found under disability in relation to the trial (see paragraphs 10.19 and 10.37–10.40). We are proposing that where disability is found but the medical advice indicates the possibility of recovery within a few months (at least to the point at which the accused would be fit to stand trial) the court should be able to adjourn the proceedings for a maximum of six months. In some cases it will no doubt be possible for psychiatric treatment to be arranged on an informal basis, or as a condition of bail, during this period, but it seems to us desirable to make provision for a formal order of the court to remand to hospital to cater for those cases where a greater measure of compulsion is required, fo example in the case of dangerous offenders.

(5) The remand order

12.8   We think that there would be considerable merit in adopting one form of order for all these situations, even though the detailed requirements for each will, to some extent, differ.   The basic need in each case is for an order of the court remanding the defendant to a particular hospital for compulsory detention over a specified period of time not exceeding a statutory maximum, for care, observation, assessment, treatment and report.   The order should not be associated with any single type of hospital but should be available equally at the special hospitals, the regional secure units, and the local psychiatric hospitals. We believe that remands to hospital for medical reports or for care should be limited to three months' duration.   But three months may not always be long enough to judge whether a defendant is a suitable subject for a substantive hospital order; nor may it be sufficient in relation to a possible finding of disability in relation to the trial, where the purpose of the remand is not merely to assess the defendant's condition and likely response to treatment, but to provide the opportunity for at least partial recovery so that he may have the benefit of a proper trial.   In these cases we consider that the remand should initially be for a maximum of three months but that it should be open to the court, on application, to extend this period for one month at a time up to an overall maximum of six months.

12.9   It should be emphasised that the periods mentioned in the previous paragraph represent the maximum time during which it will be possible for a defendant to be remanded to hospital.   It will be open to the responsible medical officer in every case to inform the court if the object of the remand is achieved before the expiry of the stipulated time, so that the adjourned hearing may be brought forward accordingly or if necessary an alternative form of remand, either in custody or on bail, may be substituted.   In some cases, for example where a hospital order is the likely outcome of the proceedings, it will be appropriate for a defendant to remain in hospital for treatment and care until his case can be heard.   The hospitals must not come to be regarded as remand centres in any general sense, since we have no doubt that it would be both unacceptable to the hospitals and unfair to the defendants were hospitals obliged to accommodate offenders awaiting trial for any length of time after their recovery or the completion of reports on their psychiatric condition, particularly where such reports were negative or continuing hospital care was not indicated.   The initiative in ensuring that such a situation does not arise must lie with the individual hospital in co-operation with the court.   The hospital must ensure that information which will enable the court to deal with the case is provided as soon as it becomes available.   From the point of view of the defendant too there is every advantage in proceeding to trial as quickly as possible, and, particularly where his employment is at risk or his family circumstances are difficult, we hope that the process of assessment will be carried out without delay and the court informed as soon as it is completed.

12.10   The proposed powers of the courts to remand to hospital should not be exercised where a custodial remand is not necessary.   Where it is possible so to do we would expect the first choice of the courts always to be to give bail. We think it should be provided, following the pattern of the requirements for hospital orders under section 60 of the Mental Health Act, that the power to remand to hospital can be exercised only on medical evidence to the effect

171

first that there is reason to suspect mental disorder and secondly that there is a hospital place available for the defendant. At present after conviction or a finding of guilt the courts can remand to custody within the penal system for psychiatric reports without the support of any medical recommendation, and such reports are freely required on persons detained in prison. Most of them prove negative, but we see no reason to limit the exercise of this power, and indeed we propose elsewhere in our Report that psychiatric examination should be called for as a precautionary measure in a greater number of cases than now. We have considered whether in the same way courts should have power to remand to hospital for reports without hearing medical evidence, where for example the defendant's demeanour in the dock gives rise to some anxiety but no question has been raised of mental disorder and no medical witnesses have been called. Bearing in mind the other pressures on the hospitals and the need to safeguard mentally normal defendants who may strongly resent the stigma of being sent to a psychiatric hospital for a medical report, our conclusion is that medical evidence should be necessary before a defendant can be remanded to hospital.

12.11 The number and nature of the medical recommendations to be required will depend on the type of remand contemplated. A distinction may be drawn between those circumstances where a defendant stands at risk of loss of liberty for an indefinite period and those where detention is temporary. In relation to remands for medical reports and for care, and remands in disability proceedings, where the defendant must normally be returned to court at the expiry of the order, we think that, in addition to the hospital's assurance that there is a bed available, it will be a sufficient safeguard to require the oral evidence of only one medical practitioner as to the mental state of the defendant. We envisage that, at least in the case of remands for medical reports and for care, it will be possible for the requisite medical evidence to be given by a general practitioner or police surgeon, and that the hospital consultant will not be put to the trouble of attending court unless he wishes. Where on the other hand the purpose of the remand is to find out whether the defendant is suitable for a substantive hospital order, the resumed court proceedings may be merely formal, although resulting in the patient's indefinite detention, unless the medical report recommends against confirmation (see paragraph 12.5 above). We therefore consider that interim hospital orders should require at the outset, as in the case of section 60 orders at present, the written or oral evidence of two medical practitioners, one of whom should be on the list maintained by Area Health Authorities under section 28 of the Mental Health Act, so that confirmation of the order need involve only one further signature. One of the medical recommendations should normally be that of the receiving doctor; the other might be the Prison Medical Officer, or a general practitioner, or a second doctor from the receiving hospital (see paragraphs 14.2–14.4 and, as regards subnormality cases, paragraph 14.5). If in addition to confirming the interim hospital order it is proposed to make a restriction order the requirement in section 65(2) of the Act that at least one doctor should give oral evidence will apply.

(6) Security and leave of absence

12.12 Remands to hospital may sometimes entail a requirement of secure custody. It will be for the court to decide whether the defendant should be sent on remand to a local psychiatric hospital or whether there is need for the greater security afforded by the regional secure units. Exceptionally the security of a special hospital might be required. If a suitable hospital place is not available there may be no alternative to remanding the defendant to prison, but we are in no doubt that a penal remand in such circumstances is generally, often highly, undesirable, and this is one of the reasons why we have thought it necessary to advocate in our Interim Report the provision of some 2,000 beds in regional secure units. In all hospital remands it is important that the receiving doctors should appreciate and accept that these patients are still within the jurisdiction of the court and are not free to come and go as they please. We considered whether doctors should have a discretion to grant home leave to patients on remand in certain circumstances, but we do not think this necessary. The question would arise only with the longer remands, particularly with patients under disability in relation to the trial, but in our view if such a patient has recovered sufficiently during his remand period for home leave to be considered he is well enough to be brought back to court for the resumed hearing of his case, and this should be the first priority. As we have pointed out in paragraph 12.9 above, doctors should bring to the court's attention without delay any case in which early recovery has been achieved, for it is in the interests of all concerned that the proceedings should be resumed as early as the patient's condition permits.

(7) Resumption of proceedings

12.13 At the expiry of the order, if not before, the defendant will usually be returned to court for the proceedings to be resumed. There are two circumstances where this will not be necessary. Where the court is to be advised to confirm an interim order there will be no point in interrupting the continuing hospital treatment by insisting on the defendant's presence in court, provided that the safeguards mentioned in paragraph 12.5 are met. Similarly, in a case of disability where it is considered undesirable in the interests of the defendant for him to be present in court (see paragraphs 10.43–10.45) and when a hospital order is to be recommended to the court, it should be possible for the court to dispense with the defendant's further attendance so that he may remain in hospital. There is a precedent for dispensing with the presence of the defendant in court in section 76(2) of the Mental Health Act. Under that section a defendant transferred to hospital under section 73 of the Act while committed or remanded in custody awaiting trial or sentence may, subject to certain conditions, be made the subject of a hospital order (with or without the special restrictions of section 65) without his being brought before the court, if it appears to the court that it is impracticable or inappropriate for him to attend.

12.14 The resumed proceedings should take place no later than the date on which the remand period expires. It may be desirable for the defendant to remain at the hospital during the period of the trial (and this will always be the case where he is not required to attend court in person) and in these circumstances some authority will be needed to detain him there. The court will have power to grant bail during the period of the trial on condition that the defendant reside in the hospital.

REMANDS TO HOSPITAL
SUMMARY OF CONCLUSIONS

1. There are four situations in which the courts should have the power to remand a mentally disordered person to hospital before deciding his ultimate disposal:

    (i) where a medical report is required on a convicted defendant; (Paragraphs 12.2–12.3)

    (ii) where the defendant requires medical care during a custodial remand; (Paragraph 12.4)

    (iii) where a period in hospital is required to determine whether a hospital order is appropriate; (Paragraphs 12.5–12.6)

    (iv) where a defendant is found under disability in relation to the trial; (Paragraph 12.7).

2. One form of court order should be adopted to cover all these situations. It should be available at all National Health Service hospitals (including the special hospitals and the proposed regional secure units), and should provide for the remand of a defendant to a particular hospital for compulsory treatment for a specified period of time. Duration should be of three months maximum where remand is for medical report or care, and of three months initially. extendable by one month at a time to a maximum of six months, in other cases. Time spent in hospital on remand should be kept to the minimum required by the circumstances of the case. (Paragraphs 12.8–12.9.)

3. Bail should always be the first choice of the courts, and remand to hospital should be considered only if remand on bail is not feasible. The power to remand to hospital should be exercised only where there is medical evidence that there is reason to suspect mental disorder and there is a hospital place available. Where remand is for a medical report or for care, or in cases of disability, the oral evidence of one medical practitioner will suffice. Where an "interim hospital order" is made two medical practitioners, one of whom should be on the list maintained by Area Health Authorities, should give written or oral evidence. One of the recommendations should normally be that of the receiving doctor. In uncontested confirmation proceedings where the patient is legally represented the signature of one doctor will suffice. If a restriction order is to be made, the oral evidence of at least one doctor will be required in accordance with section 65(2) of the Act. (Paragraphs 12.10–12.11.)

4. There will sometimes be a need for the secure custody of a mentally disordered defendant. It will be for the courts to decide whether this need will be met by remand to a local psychiatric hospital or a regional secure unit; exceptionally, the security of a special hospital might be required. If no suitable hospital place is available, remand to prison, though generally undesirable, may be unavoidable. All defendants remanded to hospital remain within the jurisdiction of the court. (Paragraph 12.12.)

5. On the resumption of court proceedings following a period of remand the defendant's presence in court will be necessary except where the court is to be

advised to confirm an "interim hospital order" and the defendant is legally represented, or in a case of disability where it is considered undesirable for the defendant to be present in court. Proceedings should resume no later than the date of expiry of the remand period. (Paragraphs 12.13–12.14.)

CHAPTER 13

THE DECISION OF THE COURT

(1) Existing powers

13.1 In cases that come to trial, the mentally disordered offender, under existing provisions, may be disposed of by the court, in the light of medical advice and subject to legal and practical limitations, in any of the ways described in the following paragraphs (in ascending order of degree of control).

13.2 Absolutely discharged or discharged subject to the condition that he commits no offence during a specified period not exceeding three years, under the Powers of Criminal Courts Act 1973, section 7, if the court is of opinion that it is inexpedient to inflict punishment and that a probation order is not appropriate.

These powers might appropriately be used, for example, where the offender does not require care or treatment; or otherwise if he agrees to receive community care from the local authority personal social services or to receive treatment voluntarily under his general practitioner or at a hospital informally as an in-patient or an out-patient; or if arrangements have been made for his admission to hospital compulsorily under Part IV of the Mental Health Act (see paragraphs 2.21 to 2.28 above). Except when he is admitted under Part IV this method leaves it to the offender whether he does in fact undergo treatment.

13.3 Required as a condition of probation to undergo treatment by or under the direction of a "duly qualified" medical practitioner[1] with a view to the improvement of the offender's mental condition, either as an in-patient or out-patient for a period of up to three years under section 3 of the Powers of Criminal Courts Act 1973.

The court must be satisfied on the medical evidence presented to it that the offender's mental condition is such as requires and may be susceptible to treatment but is not such as to warrant detention in hospital; must explain to the offender the effect of the order, including the proposed requirement as to medical treatment and that if he fails to comply with it or commits another offence he will be liable to be sentenced for the original offence (and the order may be made only if the offender consents); and must be satisfied that treatment will be available. Responsibility for seeing that the offender carries out his undertaking to receive treatment is shared by the offender, the doctor and the supervising probation officer. The court may vary or discontinue the requirement of treatment on the application of the supervising probation officer acting on a report by the doctor responsible for treatment. (We discuss "psychiatric probation orders" in Chapter 16.)

13.4 Compulsorily admitted to hospital under section 60 of the Mental Health Act 1959[2] or admitted to local authority guardianship.

---

[1] ie, a registered medical practitioner approved for the purposes of section 28 of the Mental Health Act 1959 as having special experience in the diagnosis or treatment of mental disorder.

[2] If a person is found by a jury to be "under disability" (see Chapter 10) or "not guilty by reason of insanity" (the "special verdict"—see Chapter 18), the court *must*, in accordance with section 5(1) of the Criminal Procedure (Insanity) Act 1964, order his admission to hospital. Under paragraph 2(1) of Schedule 1 to the Act this order is equivalent to a hospital order under section 60 of the Mental Health Act together with a restriction order under section 65.

The mentally disordered offender may be dealt with in this way only if his mental condition is, in the opinion of two reporting doctors, such as to warrant his detention in hospital for treatment, or reception into guardianship, as the case may be, and the hospital or local authority is prepared to receive him. The court must be of the opinion, having regard to all the circumstances and to the other available methods of dealing with the offender, that this is the most suitable method of disposing of the case. Guardianship orders return the offender to the community under some degree of supervision. Where admission to a hospital is authorised under section 60 by a superior court the court may superimpose an order under section 65—a "restriction order"— either for a specified period or without limitation of time, if the court considers this necessary for the protection of the public. (A magistrates' court has no power to make a section 65 order, but may commit the offender to a superior court if it considers such an order desirable.) Where a restriction order is imposed the patient cannot be discharged, given leave of absence or transferred to another hospital without the Home Secretary's consent while the order remains in force; he can be recovered if he absconds; and when discharged he is subject to compulsory supervision, with the sanction of recall to hospital. The restrictions may be terminated by the Home Secretary at his discretion. (Hospital orders and restriction orders are dealt with in Chapter 14 and guardianship orders in Chapter 15.)

13.5 Made subject to a normal penal sentence such as imprisonment or fine.

In some cases this may be all that is needed. If given a custodial sentence he will come within the care of the Prison Medical Service, and there is provision in the Mental Health Act 1959 under which he may be transferred to hospital if while undergoing imprisonment he is found, on reports by at least two doctors, at least one of whom has special experience in the diagnosis or treatment of mental disorders, to be suffering from mental illness or psychopathic disorder, subnormality or severe subnormality of a nature or degree which warrants detention in a hospital for medical treatment. (We have discussed in paragraphs 3.18–3.49 the treatment of the mentally disordered in the prisons, and transfers to hospital are dealt with in paragraphs 3.37–3.49.)

(2) Application to juveniles

13.6 Paragraphs 13.2, 13.4 and 13.5 above apply to offenders who have not attained the age of 17 years, except that they cannot be sentenced to imprisonment. In addition, the courts have power under the Children and Young Persons Act 1969 to make care orders committing young offenders to the care of a local authority, and supervision orders placing the offender under the supervision of the local authority or a probation officer. Supervision orders may contain a requirement, not extending beyond the person's eighteenth birthday, to submit to treatment for a mental condition. It is also possible for a juvenile found to be in need of care and control to be made subject to a hospital or guardianship order.

13.7 Section 53 of the Children and Young Persons Act 1933 applies to juveniles convicted of certain grave crimes. The effect is that:

    (a) a person convicted of murder who appears to the court to have been under 18 at the time of the offence is sentenced not, as in the case of a person over 18, to imprisonment for life but to detention during Her Majesty's pleasure in such place and under such conditions as the Home Secretary may direct;

(b) a person under 17 who is convicted on indictment of an offence punishable in the case of an adult with imprisonment for 14 years or more may, if the court considers that none of the other methods by which he may be dealt with is suitable, sentence him to be detained in such place and under such conditions as the Home Secretary may direct. The period of detention must be specified in the sentence and must not exceed the maximum term of imprisonment which could be imposed on an adult for the offence.

On rare occasions an offender sentenced under this section has been so young that detention in an approved school has been directed. Corresponding facilities remain available now that the approved schools have been absorbed in the community homes system (see paragraph 2.35). The provisions for mentally disordered juveniles and young adult offenders are discussed in Chapter 17.

(3) Recommended modifications of courts' powers of disposal

13.8   Our recommendations involve few changes in the powers of the courts in relation to disposal. We have proposed that hospital orders under section 60 of the Mental Health Act should no longer be made in respect of adult dangerous anti-social psychopaths except where there are special medical considerations (see paragraphs 5.37–5.42). And we have proposed a new form of indeterminate sentence, which we have called a "reviewable" sentence, for dangerous offenders who have a history of mental disorder but cannot, for any reason, be compulsorily admitted to a mental hospital (see paragraphs 4.39–4.45). We recommend powers for the courts to remand cases to hospital, and to make "interim" hospital orders, subject to confirmation, where it is desirable to test an offender's suitability for hospital treatment (see paragraphs 12.5–12.6). With regard to restriction orders we propose that section 65 of the Act should be amended in two respects, first to remove the power to make restriction orders of limited duration (see paragraph 14.25), and secondly to make clear the true purpose of the provision, namely to protect the public from serious harm (see paragraph 14.24).

13.9   We have also proposed that in place of mandatory commitment to hospital (see footnote to paragraph 13.4) in cases of disability in relation to the trial and cases eligible for the new, extended special verdict the Crown Courts should have discretionary powers of disposal, excluding penal disposal; and that magistrates' courts should have the same powers. Consequentially, section 60(2) of the Mental Health Act, which enables magistrates to make a hospital order without proceeding to conviction where the defendant is suffering from mental illness or severe subnormality and the court is satisfied that he did the act or made the omission charged, would be repealed (see paragraphs 10.35–10.40, 18.19 and 18.42–18.45).

(4) Sentencing considerations

13.10   We have set out in paragraphs 3.22–3.27 our views on the circumstances in which mentally disordered offenders should be committed to the penal

178

system. The guiding principle should be that the offender should be sent wherever he can best be given the treatment he needs. In general the treatment of mental disorder is most appropriately provided by the health services. We have been assured that judges and magistrates now almost invariably make a hospital order when there is medical evidence in support of one. Only in a small number of cases do they refrain from doing so—for example because they are not satisfied that the hospital in question is secure enough for a particularly dangerous offender, or because the doctor offering treatment holds out no solid hope of the treatment succeeding, or of retaining the offender if it does not (the offender having shown himself to be a considerable menace to the community), or because the defendant challenges the medical evidence and asks for a prison sentence. The general readiness of judges and magistrates to make hospital orders has been testified to us by members of the Bar Council and The Law Society and by medical witnesses.

13.11 The theory behind the present practice, which has our full support, may perhaps be stated as follows. *Prima facie* a person who has committed a serious crime may be sent to prison, even though he has some mental disorder. The aim may be general deterrence (of potential offenders), individual deterrence (of the sentenced offender), the protection of the public in general or of particular people against the offender (by incapacitating him for a time), the reformation of the offender or in some cases the declaration of society's disapproval of what he has done. But if there is medical evidence of one of the more serious forms of mental disorder, and if a psychiatrist will admit the offender to a local psychiatric hospital because he has hopes of improving his condition, or if, failing that, a special hospital will admit the offender for reasons of public security (as well as giving him such treatment as his mental state demands), then a hospital order will almost always be made. If, although the offender has one of the prescribed forms of mental disorder, a sentence of imprisonment is imposed, it is almost always because the National Health Service doctor thinks he can do nothing for him, or believes that he cannot be safely contained within an open hospital (or because the judge or bench believes this), and the special hospitals do not regard him as suitable or have no bed available. When our proposal for new secure units is fully implemented, more offenders suffering from mental disorder will be able to go to hospital for treatment instead of to prison.

13.12 When a court sentences an offender to imprisonment the prison cannot refuse the man, but the court has no control over his treatment within the penal system, nor any say in where he is placed to receive it. Occasionally when an offender is being given a prison sentence something is said to the effect that he will receive medical treatment. Such remarks are now made more rarely than in the past, but we were told that there is still a tendency for some courts to assume that the prisons are able to ensure that every prisoner is given any treatment he may be in need of, and that sentences are imposed in this expectation. This expectation may not, and indeed often cannot, be fulfilled, and it is undesirable to convey to the offender the impression that medical treatment will certainly be given to him in prison. This may lead to the erroneous assumption on his part that the sentence is being imposed for the express purpose of enabling him to receive medical treatment that will "cure" his criminal behaviour, and that this "cure" will be achieved through the treatment alone without any particular effort on his part. If, as frequently happens, it turns out that he does not receive medical treatment (perhaps, for example, because his condition is not medically treatable, or because his sentence is too short for treatment to be effective) or if he considers that the treatment has been ineffective the offender may feel that he has a grievance against the authorities and that if he offends again it is not his fault.

(5) Proposals for committal to prison hospitals

13.13 At present, prison hospitals cannot be used for the treatment of patients placed under hospital orders by the courts. Section 60 of the Mental Health Act 1959 provides that a court may make an order authorising the detention of a mentally disordered offender in "such hospital as may be specified in the order". For the purposes of the Act, by virtue of the definition of "hospital" in section 147(1), this means that all local National Health Service hospitals and the special hospitals but not prison hospitals are available to the courts for the disposal of hospital order cases.

13.14 A number of witnesses have advocated that prison hospitals, or certain designated prison hospitals, should be available for the reception of hospital order cases from the courts. They have pointed to the desirability of extending the facilities open to the courts and the need to provide hospital accommodation for those disordered offenders who require a high degree of security. At present, when faced with the absence of suitable accommodation in local psychiatric hospitals or the reluctance of hospitals to take certain offenders courts often have no alternative to imposing a prison sentence although the defendant may be in need of medical treatment.

13.15 It was common ground among advocates of the use of prison hospitals as hospitals for the reception of hospital order cases that their medical facilities and the qualifications of the staff would need to be equal to those of National Health Service hospitals; indeed, some witnesses thought that one of the merits of the proposal would be to secure the "up-grading" of the prison medical arrangements, and to encourage a more therapeutic atmosphere in the prisons generally (though this last expectation seemed somewhat at odds with the emphasis laid on the "separateness" of the designated prison hospital from the prison itself, even to the extent indicated in the extreme view that its facilities might be open to non-offenders). Clearly, equivalence of facilities and professional expertise between prison hospitals and other hospitals would make possible increased flexibility in the treatment arrangements. Transfers from local psychiatric hospitals and the special hospitals to prison hospitals would become possible. The hospital order would, in effect, be a "treatment order", the court deciding the point of entry into the treatment facilities but the patient's subsequent movement being determined solely by medical decisions, without the risk of his being consigned to the general prison population. Reciprocally this might be expected to facilitate transfers from the prisons, although some witnesses said that if prison hospitals were equivalent to National Health Service hospitals for the purpose of treatment under hospital orders the need for transfers from prison for the purposes of treatment would be reduced, and consequent difficulties avoided. Equivalence would contribute to ease of transfers not only of patients but also of staff, and thereby encourage reciprocal training arrangements and closer co-operation among the prisons, the special hospitals and the local psychiatric hospitals, to which we attach considerable importance.

13.16 Another advantage would be that prison hospitals could receive without delay a patient discharged from detention in a National Health Service hospital under a restriction order whose behaviour subsequently gives rise to anxiety, but whose re-admission to the National Health Service hospital is not acceptable to the consultant. We refer to this problem in paragraphs 14.28–14.32.

13.17 Against this, some arguments advanced in support of the proposal seem to indicate a need for special caution in considering it. One such argument was that it would be more readily possible to continue to detain as hospital patients prisoners who, at the end of their sentence, were adjudged still to be dangerous and in need of continuing psychiatric care. While this would be a valuable facility for use in fully justified cases, it would obviously be open to the possibility of abuse, and safeguards would be required. Again, it was suggested that National Health Service hospital status would give Prison Medical Officers the right to impose treatment: our comments on giving treatment against the wishes of the patient are set out in paragraphs 3.50–3.62. Thirdly, it was thought that in prison hospitals dangerous psychopaths having completed a determinate sentence could be indefinitely detained until they were judged to be safe. It seems likely that if the facility were available for psychopaths it would largely be used for them. We recognise the problems of dealing with psychopaths, but we do not think the solution is to be found in indefinite detention in prison hospitals; our own proposals are set out in Chapter 5.

13.18 We fully support the need to improve the facilities for psychiatric treatment in the prisons, and recognise the advantages of flexibility in the treatment arrangements, but we are not in favour of the use of prison hospitals for the purposes of section 60 orders. Apart from the points made above, this innovation would conflict with the general principles we have set out in paragraphs 3.7, 3.23 and 13.10–13.11 favouring the treatment of mentally disordered offenders outside the penal system. We do not think that even with improved facilities persons with overt mental illness should be treated in the prisons; almost all the evidence given to us has been opposed to this possibility.

13.19 There are other considerations. If the prison hospital had no power to refuse cases from the courts there would be a strong disincentive to consultants in National Health Service hospitals to accept section 60 cases, for they would know that the court had a "guaranteed" alternative method of securing hospital treatment. The pressures on the designated prison hospitals would be intolerable. For the same reasons as we have recommended that hospital consultants should continue to be able to refuse cases from the courts, the right of refusal would have to be allowed to the Prison Medical Officer. Even so, the Prison Medical Officer would be at a disadvantage, for if he refused a case he would know that the court might be left with no option but to commit the man to prison, and the prison has no right of refusal.

13.20 Another objection is that mixing hospital order cases with sentenced prisoners in the prison hospital would create problems of differentiation of régime—for example, as to liability to work, and in disciplinary matters.

13.21 Whilst we see the force of the arguments supporting the proposal, we believe that the recommendation we made in our Interim Report for the establishment of secure hospital units in each Regional Health Authority area will go a long way to solving the present problems and remove any need for the re-designation of the functions of prison hospitals. The units will offer the courts a new alternative means of disposal which is designed to meet the particular needs of the offender-patient by providing suitable treatment in conditions of security. In addition we hope that solutions of the particular problems presented by dangerous anti-social psychopathic offenders whom the local psychiatric hospitals are unwilling to accept will be found in the experimental units we have proposed in Chapter 5 of this Report. We have considered whether an interim scheme for the designation of prison hospitals pending the establishment of the alternative institutions might be desirable but we do not favour this. The changes involved would be considerable, and we do not think it realistic to suppose that they could be limited to a temporary expedient. Like so many temporary expedients we think such a scheme would probably become permanent, and in our view it should be rejected on long-term considerations.

(6) Appeals and the doctrine of "no greater severity"

13.22 Certain problems arise in relation to appeals. On an appeal against sentence, the Court of Appeal cannot vary the sentence to one of greater severity (Criminal Appeal Act 1968, section 11(3)). The reason is that other- wise the appellant may be discouraged from pursuing the appeal even though he appears to have good grounds for it. Although the rule is right on principle, it creates problems, particularly in the cases with which we are concerned where the appellant is mentally disordered, which we now discuss under three heads: imprisonment—hospital order; hospital order—imprisonment; imprisonment for fixed term—reviewable sentence.

(i) Imprisonment—hospital order

13.23 It has been held that on an appeal against a sentence of three years' imprisonment the court may substitute a hospital order with a restriction order of unlimited duration, because this is an individualised sentence in the defendant's interest.[3] While we appreciate that such an outcome may be for the benefit of the defendant as well as for the protection of the public, it is inconsistent with the spirit of the Criminal Appeal Act, because an offender who wishes to appeal against a sentence of three years' imprisonment, on the grounds that it is too long or because he thinks he ought to have probation, may be deterred from appealing by the possibility of being committed indefinitely to a special hospital. We recommend that on an appeal against sentence the Court of Appeal should not have power to substitute a hospital order except with the consent of the appellant. (Generally the appellant will be appealing from a sentence of imprisonment and will apply for a hospital order, but occasionally the initiative in offering a hospital order may come from the Court of Appeal, and for this reason we speak of the consent of the appellant rather than of his application). If the appellant withholds his consent he can still be transferred from prison to hospital if his mental condition warrants

---

[3] R v Bennett [1968] 1 W.L.R. 988.

it (Mental Health Act, section 72). The present procedure and our proposals with regard to transfers from prison to hospital are set out in paragraphs 3.37–3.49.

(ii) *Hospital order—imprisonment*

13.24 An appellant may object to a hospital order that has been made in respect of him and ask the Court of Appeal to substitute a sentence of imprisonment. It would be rare for the court to wish to accede to such a request, but occasionally there may be grounds for doing so, and we see no reason why the court should not possess the power for use in an appropriate case, provided that the appellant consents.

(iii) *Imprisonment for fixed term—reviewable sentence*

13.25 There may be cases where it is felt that the proposed new, reviewable sentence (despite its indeterminacy) is preferable to a long fixed-term sentence when such a sentence has been imposed on a mentally disordered offender. Similar cases occur now in respect of the life sentence, which may be preferable to a fixed-term sentence for, for example, an inadequate or unstable person who is convicted of rape after previous similar offences,[4] but the Court of Appeal cannot substitute the life sentence because this is theoretically more severe than the longest fixed-term sentence. We recommend that, provided the appellant consents, the court should have the power to substitute the reviewable sentence for a fixed-term sentence. We feel that a similar power may also be appropriate in respect of the life sentence.

13.26 If the above recommendations are accepted, it will still be impossible for the Court of Appeal to substitute a sentence of greater severity without the offender's consent. Cases have occurred in which a hospital order has been made but upon further consideration the doctors decide that it is inappropriate, the patient not being mentally disordered or otherwise not being suitable for hospital treatment. We do not feel able to make any recommendation for this case, but we hope that our other proposals will eliminate or greatly reduce the risk of the situation occurring.

THE DECISION OF THE COURT
SUMMARY OF CONCLUSIONS

1. The guiding principle in disposal of mentally disordered offenders by the courts is that they should be sent wherever they can best be given the treatment they need: generally treatment by the health services is appropriate. If it is necessary to impose a prison sentence on a mentally disordered offender the court should not hold out to him the prospect that he will receive medical treatment in prison. (Paragraphs 13.10–13.12.)

2. We are not in favour of the use of prison hospitals for the purposes of hospital orders. (Paragraphs 13.13–13.21.)

3. The doctrine of "no greater severity" can give rise to problems in connection with appeals against the form of disposal imposed by the courts. We

---

[4] A recent illustration is *R* v *O'Dwyer* [1975] Crim. L.R. 247.

recommend that the Court of Appeal should be able to make the following substitutions only if the appellant gives his consent: a hospital order for a sentence of imprisonment; a sentence of imprisonment for a hospital order; a reviewable sentence (or possibly a life sentence) for a fixed-term sentence. (Paragraphs 13.22–13.26.)

CHAPTER 14

HOSPITAL ORDERS

I. GENERAL MATTERS

(1) Statutory requirements

14.1   Before a court can make an order under section 60 of the Mental Health Act 1959 authorising the admission to and detention in hospital of a mentally disordered offender a number of conditions must be satisfied.   First, he must have been convicted of an offence: in the Crown Court, of an offence other than an offence for which the sentence is fixed by law; in a magistrates' court, of an offence punishable on summary conviction with imprisonment.   Secondly, the court must be satisfied, on the written or oral evidence of two medical practitioners, at least one of whom must be a practitioner approved by an Area Health Authority for the purposes of section 28 of the Act (namely signing recommendations for applications for admission to hospital under Part IV of the Act) as having special experience in the diagnosis or treatment of mental disorders, that the offender is suffering from mental illness, psychopathic disorder, subnormality or severe subnormality (*not* any other form of mental disorder)—the last three conditions being defined in section 4 of the Act. Thirdly, the court must also be satisfied by the evidence of these practitioners that the mental disorder is of a nature or degree which warrants the detention of the patient in a hospital for medical treatment.   Fourthly, the court must be of opinion, having regard to all the circumstances including the nature of the offence and the character and antecedents of the offender, and to the other available methods of dealing with him, that the most suitable method of disposing of the case is by means of a section 60 hospital order.   Finally, in practice, section 60(3) of the Act means that it is also necessary for the court to be satisfied that the hospital specified in the order of the court is willing to accept the offender.

(2) Medical evidence

(i) *The second signature*

14.2   On occasions, although rarely, the required recommendations by two medical practitioners as to the nature and degree of the offender's mental disorder are made by a consultant psychiatrist and his registrar, and it has been put to us that this largely defeats the object of requiring two doctors to give evidence, since it will in practice be difficult for the registrar, as a student of the consultant, to disagree with his assessment.

14.3   The Royal Commission on the Law Relating to Mental Illness and Mental Deficiency made the point in connection with admissions to hospital under compulsory powers of civil commitment that it should not be permissible for more than one of the two medical recommendations to be given by members of the receiving hospital.[1]   They proposed that one of the medical recommendations should be given by a doctor specially experienced in the diagnosis or treatment of mental disorders and the other, if possible, by the patient's general practitioner or another doctor who already knew the patient.   So far

---

[1] Cmnd. 169, paragraph 414.

as admissions by court order were concerned the Royal Commission recommended that the medical reports should be obtained from doctors with experience or knowledge similar to that which would qualify them to give medical recommendations under the civil procedures for compulsory admission.[2] However, while section 28(3) of the Mental Health Act provides that in relation to civil commitment one (but not more than one) of the medical recommendations may be given by a practitioner on the staff of the receiving hospital, section 62, dealing with admissions under hospital orders, makes no corresponding limitation. We have made inquiries into the origins of these provisions but we have been unable to discover any conclusive reason for this apparent anomaly.

14.4 We do not think that the case for insisting on an independent recommendation is sufficiently strong to outweigh the difficulties to which in some cases this might give rise. If our proposals for remands to hospitals and to forensic psychiatric centres are adopted it will not always be possible to obtain a second medical recommendation from someone independent of the hospital or psychiatric centre, the consultants of which might belong to the hospital. In cases where the hospital order is unopposed by the defendant the question of the independence of the two signatories is of no practical importance, but it may be otherwise where the defendant objects to the order being made, and in these cases we think it must be left to those concerned to see either that one of the recommendations is made by a doctor who is not connected with the receiving hospital, or, where this is not possible, that the two doctors concerned have no especially close relationship with one another. There are various circumstances in which two opinions from closely associated doctors, not necessarily working in the same hospital, ought not be accepted; for example doctors who are husband and wife. Section 28(4) of the Mental Health Act contains various specific limitations covering these contingencies and we think it desirable that the doctors who have responsibility for recommending the making of hospital orders should pay due regard to these provisions and to the principle which underlies them.

(ii) *Evidence of the receiving doctor*
14.5 We think that one of the medical recommendations should normally be that of the doctor who will receive the patient, and we understand that this is indeed the practice in most cases. The Royal College of Psychiatrists have recommended to us that before a hospital order is made there should be a requirement for the receiving doctor to give evidence to the court, but we are not convinced that such a provision would be helpful. There may be some circumstances in which it would be unnecessary or inconvenient to insist on such a practice, for example where a doctor in a distant hospital was prepared to receive the patient without having seen him personally; it would not always be reasonable for the receiving doctor to travel a long way to see the patient, and the patient might not be fit to be taken long distances for examination. Moreover, under our proposal in paragraphs 12.5–12.6 for a power of remand to hospital the doctor who would receive the patient in the event of a substantive hospital order being made would already have had a close opportunity to examine him during the assessment period and it may be an unnecessary formality for him to attend court in a case where such an order is clearly indicated.

---

[2] Cmnd. 169, paragraph 522(f).

(iii) *Subnormal offenders*

14.6 A number of those giving evidence to us pointed out that when a hospital order is made for persons suffering from subnormality there is a possibility that they may be detained in hospital for a long time, even if their offence is trivial. Improvement in their condition, if feasible, requires long-term treatment; meanwhile they tend to become institutionalised and therefore increasingly difficult to re-establish in the community. Yet, until their offence brought them before the court they may have been subsisting in the community reasonably satisfactorily and unless they had offended they could not have been compulsorily admitted to hospital under the Mental Health Act if they were over 21. In general, the right place for the care of the subnormal is in the community, and as a safeguard for the subnormal offender we propose that in all cases where it is proposed to make a hospital order on the grounds that the defendant is suffering from subnormality one of the doctors giving medical evidence to the court should be a specialist in subnormality. Usually, this will be ensured by the recommendation in the preceding paragraph.

(3) Consent of the receiving hospital

14.7 Whether or not the receiving doctor gives evidence we regard it as essential that his consent to receive the patient should be obtained before any order is made. We do not think it would be desirable, as one or two witnesses suggested to us, for local psychiatric hospitals to be required to accept mentally disordered offenders, provided only that they had a bed available. It is not unreasonable that consultants should establish criteria for selecting patients for treatment, and we have had no evidence that in the exercise of their discretion over admission policies consultants in practice act other than in the interests of their staff and other patients. We note that, within the prison system, Grendon Psychiatric Prison (the regime of which is discussed more fully in paragraphs 5.44–5.48) is allowed control over the selection of cases for admission and quickly arranges for the transfer of unco-operative inmates. Psychiatric hospitals would find it impossible to do their work if they were forced to accommodate all such cases as the courts thought right to send them, regardless of their ability to provide suitable treatment.

(4) Effect of hospital orders

14.8 By virtue of section 63(3) of the Act, the effect of a hospital order is to place the patient in the care of the hospital on exactly the same basis as patients admitted for treatment under the "non-offender" provisions of section 26 of the Act, except that the age-limits for admission and detention of psychopathic and subnormal patients do not apply, and the nearest relative has no power to discharge the patient, but only a right to apply, at stated intervals, to a Mental Health Review Tribunal. In making a hospital order, the court is placing the patient in the hands of the doctors, foregoing any question of punishment, and relinquishing from then onwards its own control over him. When the doctor, or the Mental Health Review Tribunal, thinks it right, the patient will be discharged.

14.9 If it quickly appears that the patient does not need in-patient treatment, or that he has no intention of co-operating, he may be discharged very soon. We were informed at the outset of our inquiry of the dissatisfaction felt by some courts at the almost immediate discharge from hospital into the community of offenders who would have received a punitive custodial sentence for their offences had the court not accepted medical recommendations in favour of sending them to hospital under a section 60 order. In such cases the impression may be given that the gravity of the defendant's condition was overstated at the trial, or that an unacceptable risk has been taken in discharging the patient so soon.

14.10 A number of witnesses proposed a variety of solutions to this problem. It was suggested that the executive authorities should be enabled to transfer to prison at their own discretion a person whom a court has deliberately decided, on medical advice, to send to hospital in lieu of imposing a penal sentence. This solution is unacceptable in principle. Another suggestion was that the court when making a section 60 order might simultaneously impose a prison sentence as an alternative, to be served if the offender proved unresponsive to treatment or not to need treatment. A variant of this is the idea of a "treatment order", made by the court, expressly enabling treatment to be carried out wherever might be most convenient and suitable. While the fact that transferability from hospital to prison would under these arrangements be authorised at the outset by the court makes the proposal more acceptable than that of a general discretionary power of transfer vested entirely in the executive, it seems to us undesirable that the court should not clearly decide, in so important a matter as the loss of a man's liberty, between a punitive sentence and an order for medical treatment. If the need for medical treatment continued beyond the end of the alternative prison sentence, the patient might with some justification feel aggrieved at still being detained in hospital after the date when he would have been released from prison. On the other hand, if treatment was successful before the end of the custodial sentence, it would seem illogical and inappropriate, having cured the patient, to remit him to prison: such a prospect would be unlikely to encourage the patient to co-operate in his treatment.

14.11 The alternative of reference to the Court of Appeal to consider substituting a different order has some attraction, but there might be too many cases to be handled conveniently. Some witnesses have proposed that perhaps within a specified time limit it should be possible for the patient to be referred back to the sentencing court, which should be enabled to substitute another sentence. This proposal is closely similar to our own recommendation, explained in paragraphs 12.5–12.6, that in addition to much improved arrangements for assessment before sentence, including power for the court to remand to hospital for report, there should be a new "interim hospital order" which will enable an offender to be sent to hospital for treatment for a limited period in the first place, to test his suitability for treatment under a substantive hospital order. The interim order would be subject to confirmation by the court, which could be merely formal if no problems had arisen. With these arrangements we are confident that cases in which hospital orders subsequently prove to have been mistaken should become much rarer.

14.12 We think that some of the criticisms of the early discharge of patients under hospital orders have arisen solely from a lack of understanding of the implications of the court's making a hospital order. It should be more clearly understood and accepted that the court in making such an order (without a restriction order) is deciding that henceforward the offender is to be dealt with on the basis of the same medical considerations as would govern the treatment and discharge of any other patient. He is being removed from the penal process; it is being decided not to punish him. The possibility of his early discharge must be taken into account by the court. If necessary for the protection of the public a restriction order should also be imposed (but never without the receiving hospital's consent; and we emphasise in paragraph 14.24 the importance of keeping the use of restriction orders to a carefully selected minimum of cases); or a prison sentence may be indicated.

(5) Absconders

14.13 A variation on the theme of premature discharge of patients under hospital orders is the problem of the absconder. Under section 40 of the Mental Health Act limits are placed on the periods within which patients who have absented themselves from hospital, or from their permitted place of residence while on leave from hospital, may be apprehended and returned to the hospital. The effect of these provisions is that a psychopathic or subnormal patient over the age of 21 who remains absent for more than six months cannot thereafter be compulsorily returned to the hospital, and that all other patients detained under the Act legally regain their freedom if they are absent for 28 days. The provisions of section 40 do not apply to those cases where a court has made a restriction order as well as a hospital order, but only to offenders committed to hospital under a hospital order alone. A number of witnesses have represented to us that it is indefensible that an offender who has been sent to hospital (in preference perhaps to being committed to prison) with a view to receiving medical treatment which has been said by two doctors to be necessary, should be able just to walk out and evade completely the court's order merely by remaining at large, in some cases for as short a time as 28 days.

14.14 The present provision is not entirely without justification. So far as frustrating the order of the court is concerned, any patient can do this quite easily by simply not co-operating with the hospital staff. It is doubtful whether any useful medical or social purpose will be served by the forcible return to hospital of a patient who has absconded and who is unlikely to co-operate. The provisions for ensuring the return of restricted cases are primarily for the protection of the patient. If the patient is unwilling and treatment is impracticable the hospital staff do not want to assume the role of mere custodians. Absconding often results either from mistaken diagnosis leading to inappropriate disposal to the hospital system or from the patient's inability to accept and co-operate in treatment (and some psychiatric treatment can be extremely demanding). Our proposals for improved arrangements for assessment, and for interim hospital orders in doubtful cases, should go some way to eliminate absconding, by ensuring that hospital orders are not made in unsuitable cases.

14.15 The expedient of "discharge by operation of the law" originates from a time in the nineteenth century when it was believed—probably with some justification—that it was too easy for relatives who wished to secure control of someone's property to have him committed to an asylum with little hope of release. As a precaution it was provided by the Lunacy Act of 1890 that an absconding patient could not be retaken after succeeding in remaining at large for 14 days, this being assumed to indicate that he was not sufficiently incompetent to justify compulsory detention. This assumption may have been to some extent justifiable when asylums took considerable precautions against escape, and energetic steps to recapture escapers; but it is much less justifiable in the era of the open door, when hospitals take no trouble to recapture most absconders. A patient's ability to remain "at large" for a few weeks might well be due to the kindness of friends rather than to his capacity for independent living.[3] Moreover, now that compulsory patients have the protection of Mental Health Review Tribunals this crude safeguard seems superfluous.

14.16 It seems to us that the advisable course is to replace the automatic operation of the law in the case of offenders by the discretion of the responsible medical officer. Our proposal is that when a patient who is subject to a hospital order absconds it should be for the responsible medical officer, during the currency of the order, to decide whether to seek to have him returned to hospital. In other words the doctor should have the power, but not the obligation, at any time within the operation of the order to recall an absconder. We believe that this proposal comes closer than the existing provisions to meeting the practical needs of the present-day hospital situation without giving rise to serious risk to the public. In these cases there is presumably no great risk to the public if the patient goes free; otherwise the court should not have imposed a hospital order alone but should have added restrictions under section 65. Ordinarily it is the doctor who is best able to judge the prospective risk if the patient remains at large and to what extent the patient might be willing or able to respond to medical treatment should he be returned. It is the doctor, too, who knows what further treatment can be provided. Our proposal also goes some way to satisfying those critics who feel that the present provisions allow the authority of the court to be obstructed by the patient who absconds after only a brief stay in hospital and who succeeds in remaining at large for a sufficient time. If these proposals are accepted it will be necessary to amend section 40 of the Mental Health Act 1959.

(6) Duration of hospital orders without restrictions

14.17 Among the provisions of Part IV of the Act to which patients admitted to hospital under section 60 orders are subject are those in section 43 governing the duration of detention under the orders (the special age limits laid down in section 44 for psychopathic and subnormal patients do not apply to offenders). Unless previously discharged by the responsible medical officer or by a Mental Health Review Tribunal, a patient may be detained in pursuance of a hospital order for a period not exceeding a year, in the first instance; the authority for detention may then be renewed for a further year, and thereafter for two years at a time. Renewal is effected by the responsible medical officer furnishing to the managers of the hospital a report in accordance with the provisions of section 43(3) of the Act. He must examine the patient within the last two months of the validity of the existing order, and "if it appears to him that it is necessary in the interests of the patient's health or safety or for the protection

---

[3] There is some research evidence that offenders who are discharged by operation of the law are more likely to be reconvicted than those who are otherwise discharged.

of other persons that the patient should continue to be liable to be detained"
he so reports to the managers, and under section 43(5) this has the effect of
renewing the authority for detention.[4]

14.18 The provisions in Part IV of the Act are not within our terms of
reference, inasmuch as they refer primarily to non-offenders; but we draw
attention to the apparent anomaly between the criteria for further detention,
laid down in section 43(3) as quoted above, and the grounds on which, under
section 123(1), a Mental Health Review Tribunal *must* direct that the patient
be discharged. In section 123(1) the following are set out as alternatives.
If the Tribunal are satisfied as to any of them they are to direct that the patient
be discharged:

(a) that he is not then suffering from mental illness, psychopathic disorder,
subnormality or severe subnormality; or

(b) that it is not necessary in the interests of the patient's health or safety
or for the protection of other persons that the patient should continue
to be liable to be detained; or

(c) in the case of an application under subsection (3) of section 44 or
subsection (3) of section 48 of this Act, that the patient, if released,
would not be likely to act in a manner dangerous to other persons
or to himself.

It will be observed that (b) corresponds in negative terms to the *only* ground
which, stated positively, justifies the renewal of detention under the provisions
of section 43(3).

14.19 We think it odd that renewal of detention does not require that the
patient should be suffering from one of the conditions specified at (a) above,
and yet if the Tribunal find that he is not suffering from any of these conditions
he must be immediately discharged. We recognise that admission to hospital
for treatment depends in the first place, as prescribed in section 26 of the Act,
on establishing two elements in the patient's condition, which correspond
to (a) and (b) above; and it seems to follow that as soon as either of these two
pre-requisite conditions ceases to apply the patient should be discharged, as
indeed section 123(1) provides. If this is so section 43(3) seems defective in
requiring that only one of them needs to be established for the renewal of the
detention authority. As it has been announced that the Act is to be reviewed,
we think it right to mention this matter, which affects offenders under hospital
orders to the same extent as it affects non-offenders detained under section 26.

II. HOSPITAL ORDERS WITH RESTRICTIONS

14.20 The provisions of section 65 of the Act are summarised in paragraphs
2.31–2.32, and questions arising from the discharge and after-care of restriction
order cases are discussed in paragraphs 4.17–4.33. We deal here with points
arising in connection with the imposition of restriction orders at the time
when the court is deciding upon the disposal of the case.

---

[4] A research study of a sample of hospital order cases showed that almost half left hospital,
with or without the doctor's agreement, within a year of admission and another one-fifth in
the second year. At the end of the sixth year, one-tenth of the sample remained in hospital:
(see Nigel Walker and Sarah McCabe, *Crime and Insanity in England* (Edinburgh 1973),
Vol. 2, p. 171).

(1) Effects of restriction orders

14.21 There is much misunderstanding of the requirements imposed on hospitals by restriction orders. The Act imposes no explicit duty of safe custody. It merely makes the patient subject to the control of the Home Secretary in questions of discharge, transfer and leave, enables the patient to be returned to the hospital if he absconds, and imposes post-discharge supervision, with a power of recall to hospital (section 66(3)). The references in section 65 to "the risk of his committing further offences if set at large", and to the protection of the public, no doubt strongly imply that a degree of vigilance appropriate to the case should be exercised; but not all cases where it may be appropriate to impose a section 65 order necessarily require secure accommodation (for example, the persistent molester of small children may need the continuing supervision after discharge which a restriction order allows, and should not be permitted simply to walk out of the hospital whenever he wishes, but is unlikely to need the secure containment of bolts and bars).

(2) Consent of the receiving hospital

14.22 Nevertheless, it is strongly felt by many in the medical profession that courts should not be able to impose section 65 orders without the consent of the receiving doctor. Cases have occurred, although they appear to be rare, in which a doctor has recommended the court to impose a hospital order, and has expressed his willingness to accept the patient, only to find that a restriction order has been added. If he had known in advance of the possibility of a restriction order being added this would have made him unwilling to accept the patient. There are various reasons why doctors may be unwilling to accept a section 65 patient. Some doctors object to the control exercised by the Home Office, either because of their experience, or expectation, of delays and difficulties in obtaining decisions (we discuss these problems in Chapter 7 and explain why we think they often need not arise), or because of the loss of some flexibility in the treatment of the patient, and adverse effect on the doctor/patient relationship, from the mere fact of having to refer to the Home Office. (On the other hand, some doctors have stated that they find that having the Home Office in the background helps them in their professional relationship with the patient.) Another reason for objection may be lack of suitable accommodation or adequate staff to deal with the particular case. While we would deprecate the refusal, as a matter of principle, ever to receive any restricted patient (for the treatment system set up by the Act clearly contemplates that such patients will be dealt with in local psychiatric hospitals, as well as in the special hospitals), we recognise that there may be reasonable grounds for refusal of particular cases on particular occasions. We have no doubt that as a matter of good practice courts should invariably consult the receiving doctor before making a section 65 order, and we think that it should be a statutory provision that the consent of the doctor to accept the patient on these conditions should be required.[5] We expect that doctors

---

[5] It might seem that section 65(2) of the Mental Health Act already makes provision for ensuring that the consent of the receiving doctor is obtained before a restriction order is made. The subsection requires that one of the two doctors reporting to the court on the defendant's mental condition should give his evidence orally. However, the doctor giving oral evidence need not be the receiving doctor but could be, for instance, the Prison Medical Officer. Although the provisions of the subsection would allow the testifying doctor the opportunity to comment on the acceptability of a patient under restriction, there is no specific requirement that this consent must be forthcoming.

would recommend hospital orders in more cases than they do at present, if the possibility of a restriction order being imposed in addition, without their agreement, were removed. On the other hand we hope that, recognising that the court may be left with no other option but imprisonment, they would not use a right of refusal of restricted cases indiscriminately.

14.23 Under section 40 of the National Health Service Reorganisation Act 1973 responsibility for admissions to the special hospitals rests with the Secretary of State for Social Services. Evidently the Minister in exercising this responsibility takes into account the advice of the special hospital doctors. It sometimes happens that their opinion does not agree with medical evidence given in court which has persuaded the court that the right course would be to make a hospital order with a view to the detention of the patient in a secure hospital. The court may remand the defendant to prison while application is made for a place in a special hospital, but if this is not forthcoming there may eventually be no alternative but to sentence the man to imprisonment. It has been proposed to us that there should be a procedure for reviewing such a situation when it arises, and that possibly this might be most conveniently done by the Court of Appeal. We do not favour this procedure, which might be harmful to the mental condition of the man concerned, and would be rather cumbersome for the purpose; nor does it seem that the Court of Appeal would have more information, or more available options, than the trial court would have after the inquiries made during the remand period. We think that our proposals for courts to be enabled to remand cases to hospital (including special hospitals and regional secure units) for assessment, and to make interim hospital orders to which restrictions would apply, should largely overcome these problems.

(3) Excessive use of restriction orders

14.24 The making of a restriction order has potentially serious consequences for the defendant because of the special procedural steps, involving the Home Secretary, taken to establish that he is fit to be discharged, and that adequate after-care arrangements have been made, and because of his liability to remain subject to supervisory conditions. (Figures supplied by the Home Office based on a count of the restricted patients discharged from all hospitals in 1974 give the average period of detention under a section 65 order as about $4\frac{1}{2}$ years—see paragraph 7.23. Detention could continue for life.) For this reason and, less importantly, because of the administrative difficulties they involve, restriction orders should not be made unless they are fully justified. Evidence given to us by the Home Office has indicated the probability that these orders are imposed in numbers of cases where their severity is not appropriate. In the words of the section the court may impose restrictions where ". . . it appears to the court, having regard to the nature of the offence, the antecedents of the offender, and the risk of his committing further offences if set at large, that it is necessary for the protection of the public so to do . . .". There is no indication of the seriousness of the offences from which the public is intended to be protected by the restriction order provisions and some courts have evidently imposed restrictions on, for example, the petty recidivist because of the virtual certainty that he will persist in similar offences in the future. In our view this is not the sort of case in which a section 65 order should be imposed. The restriction order provisions derive from recommendations made by the Royal Commission on the Law relating to Mental Illness and Mental Deficiency and paragraph 519 of their Report recommends these arrangements where "there is a real danger of the commission of further *serious* offences . . ." (our italics). Figures supplied by the Home Office indicate that there has been a decline over recent years in the number of cases in which restriction orders have been imposed for the "less serious offences" (that is to say, offences other than homicide, attempted homicide, sexual offences, other offences against the person, and criminal damage). This is a welcome trend, but nevertheless we think that the wording of section 65(1) should be more tightly drawn to indicate its true intention, namely to protect the public from serious harm. A more restrictive wording of the section would help the courts in making the difficult decision whether it is appropriate to impose this severe form of control. Contributory factors to the inappropriate use of restriction orders by the courts are shortage of time and scarcity of resources which often mean that they lack complete information when assessing a defendant's suitability for restriction: we hope that our proposals for remands to hospital (paragraphs 12.2–12.3) and interim hospital orders (paragraphs 12.5–12.6) will help overcome these other difficulties.

(4) Duration of restriction orders

14.25 The statute enables section 65 orders to be imposed with or without a limit of time. It is a widely held view that a restriction order without a time limit is preferable to an order whose duration is prescribed. In *R* v *Gardiner* the then Lord Chief Justice (Lord Parker) said:

> ". . . since in most cases the prognosis cannot be certain, the safer course is to make any restriction order unlimited in point of time. The only exception is where the doctors are able to assert confidently that recovery will take place within a fixed period when the restriction order can properly be limited to that period".[6]

In their Report the Aarvold Committee[7] stressed the value of restriction orders without limit as to time, and observed with approval that of 232 hospital orders with restrictions made by the courts in 1971 only 13 were with a time limit. Many of those giving evidence before us on this point were of the opinion that all restriction orders should be made without limit of time. The argument that it is generally not possible at the time of the making of the order to determine how long it will be before the patient recovers is a strong one, and we support the view that the facility for making a restriction order of limited duration should be removed from the statute. As a safeguard against abuse, since an indeterminate power to detain carries with it the danger that the period of detention may be longer than is strictly necessary, we propose that regular reports on patients under restriction orders should be made to the Home Office by the treating doctor. Such a system of reports would also go some way to relieving the problems which sometimes arise between hospital psychiatrists and the Home Office through inadequate communication.

---

[6] [1967] 1 W.L.R. 464.

[7] Cmnd. 5191, paragraph 7.

(5) Subnormal patients

14.26 In their evidence the British Medical Association suggested that restriction orders were not appropriate for subnormal patients admitted to local psychiatric hospitals.[8] They felt that the restrictions placed on the patients' freedom of movement would conflict with the hospitals' open regime and therapeutic role, and would make difficult the patients' eventual rehabilitation. Whilst we understand the British Medical Association's reservations, in our view the restrictions imposed by a section 65 order need not be a serious impediment to rehabilitation. Where the case justifies it and where suitable arrangements have been made the Home Office will agree to a measure of discretion in the exercise of the restriction. We accept that patients subject to restriction orders will often be patients who require to be detained in conditions of physical security, such as is at present provided in the special hospitals and will in future be available in the proposed regional secure units, but, as we have already pointed out (paragraph 14.21 above) not all patients under section 65 orders require secure containment, and accommodation in local psychiatric hospitals will often be appropriate. We do not consider it desirable that subnormal patients should be expressly excluded from what may well be the most suitable place of disposal for them.

(6) Powers of magistrates' courts

14.27 Another suggestion to which we gave consideration was that power to make a restriction order under section 65 should be extended to magistrates' courts, possibly with a short limit of time. The proposal would have enabled the court to ensure that the offender would remain in hospital for a specified minimum period, within a limit prescribed by statute, both to receive the benefit of treatment and for the protection of the public. We have discussed in paragraphs 14.8–14.12 the questions involved in the early discharge of patients subject to hospital orders and we think that our proposals for interim hospital orders (see paragraphs 12.5–12.6) will reduce the possibility of problems resulting from orders being made in unsuitable cases. We have also explained in paragraph 14.24 above why we think that section 65 should be more sparingly used in future and limited to protection of the public from *serious* harm. Therefore, we do not recommend extending the provision to apply to cases ordinarily tried by magistrates.

(7) Recall of restricted patients

14.28 A problem may arise when a restricted patient has been discharged and his behaviour gives grounds for anxiety that his continued liberty may entail a risk to the public. Section 66(3) of the Mental Health Act 1959 enables the Home Secretary at any time during the continuance in force of a restriction order to recall the patient by warrant "to such hospital as may be specified in

---

[8] The following figures, supplied by the Home Office, are of patients under section 65 orders in hospitals in England and Wales other than the three special hospitals at the beginning of March 1975:

Patients suffering from:		
(a) subnormality alone		117
(b) severe subnormality alone		21
(c) subnormality with other mental disorder		5
		143

the warrant". In practice recall to hospital requires the agreement of the consultant, and difficulties arise where recall is not justified for any medical reason. The Aarvold Committee, referring to this matter in paragraph 53 of their Report,[9] noted that the issues involved were outside their terms of reference but that they might be considered by ourselves. Meanwhile they remarked that: "In cases identified as needing special care in assessment, preliminary consideration will have been given by the Home Office before discharge, in consultation with the responsible medical officer, to the circumstances in which the patient might be recalled to hospital, and any conclusions reached will be made known to the supervising officer", and they concluded: "For the present, we think we must accept the possibility that a situation might arise in which no action could be taken but to leave the conditionally discharged patient to the normal sanctions of the criminal law—after serious warning of the probable consequences of his behaviour".

14.29 Technically the Home Secretary has adequate legal powers to recall such a patient to any named hospital, and there is no statutory requirement for the hospital doctors to agree to accept him. However, we have made clear in paragraphs 14.22 above that we think the consent of the doctor to receive a restricted patient in the first place should invariably be obtained, and we have recommended that this should be a statutory provision. It would be inconsistent, and in our view unacceptable, to propose that the doctor's consent to the admission of a restricted patient recalled to hospital by the Home Secretary after discharge should not be required. Apart from any other consideration, such a provision would powerfully discourage doctors from accepting restricted cases in the first place.

14.30 It is, on the face of it, anomalous that the Home Secretary can without difficulty recall to prison a dangerous offender who has been released on licence, but may be unable to recall to hospital an equally dangerous offender conditionally discharged from hospital. We think that a partial solution may be found in adopting more generally the Aarvold Committee's recommendations in relation to "special assessment" cases. An outline agreement should be reached between the consultant and the Home Office in all section 65 cases before the patient's discharge as to the circumstances in which the responsible consultant would be prepared to recommend recall to hospital. In the event of transfer of the patient from a special hospital to a local psychiatric hospital, or on his discharge to supervision in the community, the conditions on which he would be accepted back would be agreed in advance and known to the local hospital or the supervising officer. In general, the patient himself should also be told of the conditions and should know who was being informed, and he should understand that he could be released only on acceptance of these conditions; this should be the normal practice, but we recognise that there may be circumstances in which certain of the agreed conditions should not be disclosed to the patient.

14.31 There will remain those cases of discharged restricted patients whose behaviour gives rise to anxiety on the part of the supervising officer, but whose re-admission to hospital cannot immediately be arranged either because the hospital doctor refuses on the ground that there is no medical justification for such a course or for some other reason. It seems desirable that it should be

---

[9] Cmnd. 5191.

possible to ensure the immediate safe custody of such people for a period sufficient to permit a second medical opinion to be obtained and, if necessary, for arrangements to be made for admission to hospital. Our proposal is that the Home Secretary should be enabled if he thinks fit to authorise the emergency admission for a period of up to 72 hours to a "place of safety" of discharged restricted patients where he is advised that in the opinion of the supervising officer such a course is justified by the behaviour of his client and where a place in hospital cannot be immediately obtained. We would expect the "place of safety" normally to be a regional secure unit, when the recommendations in our Interim Report have been implemented, but pending the establishment of these units detention should be in the hospital of a local remand prison or a remand centre. If in the opinion of the assessing doctor no medical treatment is required, the patient must be immediately discharged.

14.32 While we uphold the control of the hospital over admissions we underline, in respect of the recall situation where there is cause for anxiety, the remarks we have made in paragraph 14.22 above in which we have expressed the hope that in the interests of enabling the treatment arrangements set up by the Act to function as intended, for the sake both of the patient and of the public, agreement to accept a restricted case will not lightly be withheld.

HOSPITAL ORDERS
SUMMARY OF CONCLUSIONS

I. General matters

1. We do not recommend a formal requirement that the two doctors recommending the court to make a hospital order should be independent of each other, but regard should be paid to the provisions in section 28(4) of the Act (relating to recommendations for the admission to hospital of non-offenders) and to the principle which underlies them. The matter may be important where the defendant objects to an order being made, and in such cases particular care should be exercised in this connection. (Paragraphs 14.2–14.4.)

2. One of the medical recommendations should normally be that of the doctor who will receive the patient, but there may be circumstances in which it would be unnecessary or inconvenient to insist on such a practice. (Paragraph 14.5.)

3. In all cases where it is proposed to make a hospital order on the ground that the defendant is suffering from subnormality one of the medical recommendations should be that of a specialist in subnormality. (Paragraph 14.6.)

4. It is essential that the consent of the receiving doctor should be obtained before a hospital order is made. (Paragraph 14.7.)

5. In making a hospital order the court is relinquishing its control over the offender, foregoing any question of punishment, preferring (on medical advice) to place him in the care of the doctors for treatment. It is important that courts realise this, and the consequences that the offender will be discharged as soon as the doctors so decide. If the court does not think this would be appropriate, in all the circumstances, the question arises whether a hospital order without restrictions is the most suitable disposal. (Paragraphs 14.8 and 14.12.)

6. Our proposal in paragraphs 12.5–12.6 for "interim hospital orders", to enable offenders to be sent to hospital for treatment for a limited period in the first place, to test their suitability, should avert many of the problems that now present themselves because in some cases treatment intended under a hospital order cannot be successfully implemented. (Paragraphs 14.9–14.12.)

7. We propose that section 40 of the Mental Health Act 1959 should be amended to allow the responsible medical officer full discretion to decide, at any time during the operation of a hospital order, whether to seek the recall to hospital of a patient who has absconded. (Paragraphs 14.13–14.16.)

8. We draw attention to certain anomalies in the criteria referred to in section 43(3) of the Act and section 123(1) of the Act governing respectively the renewal of authority for a patient's detention and his discharge by a Mental Health Review Tribunal. (Paragraphs 14.17–14.19.)

II. Restriction orders

9. While the Act imposes no explicit duty on the hospital of ensuring the safe custody of a restricted patient, a degree of vigilance appropriate to the case is strongly implied. For this and other reasons we think there should be a statutory requirement that the consent of the doctor to receive a restricted patient should be obtained before a restriction order is made (cf. conclusion 16 below). We hope that such a statutory right of refusal would not be used by doctors indiscriminately. (Paragraphs 14.21–14.22.)

10. We do not recommend a proposal put to us for the reference to the Court of Appeal of cases where the trial court is minded, on medical advice, to make a hospital order with a view to detention in a special hospital but the Secretary of State for Social Services, who controls special hospital admissions, has declined to make a place available. We think that our proposals for the court to be able to remand to hospital (including special hospitals and regional secure units) for assessment, and to make interim hospital orders, to which restrictions would apply, should largely overcome these problems. (Paragraph 14.23.)

11. There is some reason to think that restriction orders are sometimes made when they are not strictly necessary. We propose that section 65(1) should be revised to make it clear that its intention is to protect the public from serious harm. We recognise the difficulties of the courts who often have to decide without sufficient information whether to impose a restriction order, and we hope that our proposals for remands to hospital and for interim hospital orders will help them. (Paragraph 14.24.)

12. We think that restriction orders should invariably be made without limit of time and that the power to make orders of limited duration should be removed from the statute book. (Paragraph 14.25.)

13. To safeguard the patient who is under indeterminate detention, regular reports should be made to the Home Office by the treating doctor on all patients under restriction orders. (Paragraph 14.25.)

14. We do not accept the suggestion that it is not appropriate for subnormal patients to be admitted to open psychiatric hospitals under restriction orders. (Paragraph 14.26.)

15. We are not in favour of magistrates' courts having power to make restriction orders. (Paragraph 14.27.)

16. Although technically the Home Secretary has power to recall to any named hospital a restricted patient whose behaviour after discharge gives rise to anxiety but whose recall is not justified on purely medical grounds, we do not think he should do so without the consent of the hospital consultant (cf. conclusion 9 above). Before the discharge of any restricted patient agreement should be reached between the consultant and the Home Office as to the circumstances in which the consultant would be prepared to recommend recall to hospital. The terms of the agreement should be communicated to all concerned, including the supervising officer and the patient himself (except that there may be some circumstances in which certain of the agreed conditions should not be made known to the patient). To deal with the problem of the discharged restricted patient whose behaviour gives cause for alarm but who is refused urgent re-admission to hospital, we propose that there should be provision for his emergency admission for up to 72 hours to a "place of safety", which would normally be a regional secure unit, when these are available, but meanwhile should be the hospital of a local remand prison or remand centre, on the direction of the Home Secretary. While upholding the control of National Health Service hospitals over admissions, we hope that in a recall situation where there is cause for anxiety agreement to receive a restricted case will not lightly be withheld. (Paragraphs 14.28–14.31.)

CHAPTER 15

GUARDIANSHIP ORDERS

15.1 In paragraphs 2.41–2.44 we set out the provisions of the Mental Health Act which enable non-offenders (section 33) as well as offenders (section 60) to be placed under the guardianship of the local authority or of any other person who the local authority is satisfied is able and willing to undertake the duties involved. In accordance with the terms of our remit, the following remarks are directed to the consideration of guardianship orders made under section 60.

15.2 In some circumstances a guardianship order is more effective than a probation order. Unlike a probation order it can be used in cases where the offender does not consent, although for carrying out the order it is obviously necessary to obtain some degree of co-operation. Section 34(1) and section 63(2) of the Act confer on the guardian, in relation to the offender-patient, all the powers exercisable by a father over a child of less than 14 years of age. The limitations so placed on the person who is subject to the order are far more restrictive than those entailed in a probation order; for example, a person under guardianship cannot make a valid legal contract. The use of his earnings can be controlled, as can his place of residence and employment, and the guardian can ensure that he is provided with training or occupation or other forms of care. The strict control provided by these orders is particularly suitable for mentally handicapped offenders, including mentally disordered offenders of the inadequate type, who need help in managing their affairs.

15.3 Our opinion of the usefulness of guardianship orders has been supported by a number of case histories we have considered. Under the regular supervision of the social worker, supported by the authority of the courts, the general behaviour of the subjects tended to improve. Some were helped to find suitable employment, others were given training; the provision of hostel accommodation also had a stabilising effect. With the guidance of the supervising officers the subjects were able to manage their everyday affairs, particularly financial matters, more successfully. Where there was a history of offences there was some success, too, in preventing the subject offending again. Whilst it appeared that the making of a guardianship order did not often substantially affect the management of cases, the extra powers conferred by the court sometimes enabled steps to be taken which otherwise would not have been possible. The point was made in several of the case histories that the shortage of local community resources for the mentally handicapped made handling the cases more difficult: improvements in these resources would greatly enhance the effectiveness of guardianship orders.

15.4 In view of their evident value, we have been surprised to find what little use has been made of guardianship orders for offenders by the courts. Published statistics show that only 11 orders were made in 1971, 4 in 1972, 8 in 1973 and 7 in 1974. Their limited use may perhaps be explained in part by a general lack of understanding of what is involved. Coupled with this may be the reluctance of the social services departments to accept the addition

200

to their already substantial burden of the heavy demands that the law makes in these cases, which, indeed, they may feel they will be unable adequately to comply with. The exercise of powers equivalent to those of a parent takes up much time and seriously taxes scarce manpower resources.

15.5 Sometimes, in cases for which a guardianship order may be equally suitable courts may prefer to make a probation order with a condition of psychiatric treatment. This may be explained simply by the close connection between probation officers and the courts. There is not the same contact between the courts and local authority social service departments, and improved liaison is required. In line with our encouragement in paragraphs 20.1–20.3 for the development of closer relationships among all those involved in the care of the mentally disordered offender, we believe that discussions between the courts and social services departments on the operation of the guardianship provisions would, by exposing areas of difficulty and uncertainty, lead to improved understanding of the nature and value of the order and result in its increased use. It would probably be impractical to appoint a departmental liaison officer, as is the practice with the juvenile courts, but the general arrangements for consultation should be improved. When it appears to the court that a guardianship order may be advantageous in a particular case about which the social services department has not been consulted, the court should adjourn pending the department's report.

15.6 Acceptance by the proposed guardian is an essential pre-requisite for the making of a guardianship order: section 60(4) of the Mental Health Act provides that a guardianship order shall not be made unless the court is satisfied that the local authority (or other person designated by them) is willing to receive the offender into guardianship. This freedom to refuse offenders was criticised by some witnesses, who argued that in every case where an order is proposed there will be evidence by two doctors that an order is warranted on medical grounds. Further, it was pointed out that the probation and after-care service cannot refuse to supervise offenders made subject to probation orders by the courts, nor is the consent of the social services department required before magistrates make a care order for a juvenile. However, we are not in favour of changing the present position, particularly because of the limitations of facilities that local authorities can at present provide, and because the powers conferred on a guardian are so great that they should not be given where the social services department is not satisfied of its ability to exercise them. As regards the comparison with the probation order provisions there is an important difference between the effects of the two orders. The probation officer can bring back to court an offender under his supervision who does not co-operate, but with the adult under guardianship there is no sanction for breach of the order. It is therefore important that the local authority should have the opportunity at the outset of deciding whether it is going to be able to manage the offender satisfactorily. Also, in practice, the probation and after-care service, as we have mentioned above, has the advantage of its close contact with the court, a probation officer invariably being present during proceedings, and it can always represent its opinion that the offender is not suitable for probation. The fact that the consent of the social services department is not required while care orders are made for juveniles is not a convincing argument for abolishing the requirement of consent in guardianship cases, in view of the differing natures of the orders themselves and the wider facilities that local authorities have for dealing with young people in care compared to those for persons under guardianship. We emphasise, however, the desirability of full consultation by the courts with the relevant social service in all cases where it is proposed to make a psychiatric probation order or a guardianship order; and clearly great weight should be attached to the views of the service which would be responsible for carrying out the order.

15.7 We considered a suggestion by the Justices' Clerks' Society that guardianship orders should not require two medical recommendations, since psychiatric probation orders need only one. However, as mentioned above, guardianship orders impose certain obligations and disabilities which are not involved in psychiatric probation orders, and they are imposed compulsorily whereas probation orders are accepted by the offender on a voluntary basis. The requirement of two medical recommendations is in line with that for other compulsory forms of disposal under the Mental Health Act and we do not think that there is any justification for change.

15.8 It is our view that guardianship orders offer a useful form of control of some mentally disordered offenders who do not require hospital treatment; as we have said, they are particularly suited to the needs of subnormal offenders including those inadequate offenders who require help in managing their affairs. Evidently these orders are not being used in many cases for which they would be well suited, and we draw the attention of the courts to their value. We do not think that there is a need for any statutory alteration with regard to the present system of guardianship orders, but we would encourage the development of closer liaison between the courts and the social services departments of local authorities.

GUARDIANSHIP ORDERS

SUMMARY OF CONCLUSIONS

1. The guardianship order is a valuable form of disposal which is at present very little used. There should be closer liaison between the courts and local authorities social services departments with a view to discussing difficulties and improving the working of the present arrangements. (Paragraphs 15.2–15.5 and 15.8.)

2. There should be full consultation by the courts with the relevant social service in all cases where it is proposed to make a guardianship order. Local authorities should continue to have the right to refuse to accept offenders into guardianship. (Paragraph 15.6.)

3. There is no need to change the present arrangements regarding medical recommendations. (Paragraph 15.7.)

CHAPTER 16

PSYCHIATRIC PROBATION ORDERS

16.1 Another form of disposal open to the courts, subject to the agreement of the offender, is the probation order with a condition of psychiatric treatment —conveniently called a psychiatric probation order—made under section 3 of the Powers of Criminal Courts Act 1973, which replaced section 4 of the Criminal Justice Act 1948 (see paragraph 13.3). Increasing use has been made of the order in recent years: 1,527 orders were made in 1971, 1,708 in 1972, and 1,985 in 1973. Where the psychiatric probation order specifies in-patient treatment the offender is admitted to hospital as an informal patient.

(1) The value of the psychiatric probation order

16.2 We have had conflicting evidence as to the value and effectiveness of this form of order. One view is that psychiatric treatment in the best conditions is limited in scope and uncertain in result; and resources are inadequate to the demands made on them. Furthermore we have been told, and we accept, that a patient who comes for treatment as a requirement of a probation order, albeit undertaken voluntarily, is less likely to be motivated to co-operate than a patient who has sought treatment himself. Other evidence has suggested that some offenders who agree readily in court to undergo medical treatment change their minds when free from the pressure of the court situation; in particular alcoholics and drug-addicts, who are orientated towards immediate goals, will often agree to anything to get out of court.

16.3 Little empirical work has been done to gauge the effects of psychiatric probation orders, but according to one study[1] attendance at clinics after psychiatric examination does not seem to decrease the likelihood of reconviction. Reconviction rates are primarily associated with the number of previous convictions, the type of current offence, and work record and marital status. Psychiatric treatment may eliminate a distressing symptom without eliminating criminality. A study by Mrs Woodside of the operation of these probation orders in Edinburgh from 1966 to 1968 was also discouraging.[2] It is possible that in the meantime circumstances may have changed, and we urge that more studies in this field should be carried out.

16.4 We have received a number of medical opinions that are broadly favourable to the psychiatric probation order. The order is a recognition by the court that the offender needs treatment, and gives him the opportunity of receiving it. It enables the court to take a positive step in relation to the offence without inflicting harm, and there is always the hope that it may do good. From their own experience of involvement with probationers some of our members were able to support the value of the psychiatric probation order. Where a team approach had developed, with the doctor and the probation officer playing active, mutually supportive roles in giving the probationer the encouragement he needed, the arrangements had proved effective. They also referred to their experience that a second probation order often succeeded after the first had proved a failure: the probationer

---

[1] D J West and J S Bearcroft in 8 *International Journal of Social Psychiatry* 45.

[2] Moya Woodside in 118 *British Journal of Psychiatry* 56.

seemed in these cases to respond better to his second chance. We have no doubt that courts should continue to be able to make these orders, and we proceed to consider what improvements may be made.

(2) Procedure at the court stage

16.5 An accurate initial assessment by the court of an offender's suitability for this form of disposal is essential. In her report Mrs Woodside pointed out that the success or failure of treatment as a condition of probation is related to careful pre-selection of offenders. The Consultant Forensic Psychiatrists told us that the psychiatric probation order is unlikely to work with the more manipulative personalities. They said that cases in which there is a large element of dishonesty with a mild mental illness, and where there is not a direct connection between the mental illness and the offence committed—for example, mild depression in a shoplifter—are often unsuccessful under these orders, as are alcoholics and drug addicts, for the reasons mentioned in paragraph 16.2 above; and that failure is also likely where an order is made as a result of medical recommendations to the court not based entirely on the needs and suitability of the individual offender but produced in response to other influences, such as suppositions about what the particular court prefers, or the known wishes of the social work agencies.

16.6 The only evidence that the statute requires to be given to the court is that of a duly qualified medical practitioner, and representatives of the probation and after-care service told us that they felt that a psychiatric probation order should be made only when the probation officer and the psychiatrist are in agreement about its appropriateness. They thought that the courts should always consider a social inquiry report as well as a psychiatrist's report. The Conference of Principal Probation Officers were of the view that the reservations that a probation officer might have, arising from his knowledge of the offender, his environment and his social pressures, about the successful operation of a psychiatric probation order, would be relevant in the decision to make an order. They acknowledged that the necessary evidence of mental disorder can be given only by qualified medical practitioners, but they felt that probation officers ought not to be reluctant, as some now are, to express their doubts against the doctor's opinion given in public. We support these views. Clearly, before reaching any decision, the court should give consideration to all the evidence bearing on the likelihood of the success of the order. Since the responsibility for treatment, in its broadest sense, in these cases is to be shared between the doctor and the probation officer, it should also be the normal practice for the court, before making an order, to obtain a social inquiry report on the defendant.

16.7 It sometimes happens that a probation officer has under his supervision a probationer who is subject to an order without a condition of psychiatric treatment but whom he suspects to be in need of such treatment. At present a condition requiring the offender to submit to treatment for his mental condition must be imposed within three months of the probation order being made. There is a difficulty therefore when the probationer's need for psychiatric assessment becomes evident only after three months' supervision, for legally he may not then be returned to court for a psychiatric report and the imposition of a condition of treatment. In many cases probation officers must rely, informally, on the goodwill of medical practitioners for a psychiatric report to be obtained. We propose that the time limit of three months during which the probationer may be returned to court for psychiatric assessment should be removed. The social work members of the inter-disciplinary teams at the forensic psychiatric centres (to which we refer in paragraphs 20.20–20.21 below) will play an important role in assuring liaison between the probation officer and the medical profession in these cases.

16.8 It was put to us in evidence by the Conference of Principal Probation Officers, that there should be part-time psychiatric consultants to the probation and after-care service one of whose functions should be to provide assistance to the service in the supervision of offenders, including those subject to psychiatric probation orders. As we have explained in paragraph 3.17 we do not think that such appointments would be justified; in our view a more suitable answer to the needs of the probation and after-care service is the development of forensic psychiatric services to which probation officers could have access.

16.9 Courts are required by section 2(6) of the Powers of Criminal Courts Act 1973, to explain to the offender the effect of a probation order, including any additional conditions, and that if he fails to comply with it he will be liable to be sentenced for the original offence. Failure to co-operate in treatment will be a breach of the order. It has been put to us that mentally disordered offenders do not always understand what obligations they are accepting under these orders. To some extent this may be attributable to the mental capacity of the offender, and the circumstances in which the matter is explained to him are not likely to help him to absorb what is said to him. But the explanation which the court is required to give is clearly most important and should be made as intelligible as possible. The court should strive to ensure that the defendant has understood the position. The court should also do what it can to ensure that all others concerned are aware of their obligations.

(3) Procedure at the treatment stage

16.10 Psychiatric probation orders cannot be effectively carried out unless a full contribution is made by both the doctor and the probation officer as well as by the probationer himself. Two factors have been brought to our notice which at present tell against the realisation of this aim. The first concerns the position of the doctor, the second the role of the probation officer.

16.11 The doctor who recommends to the court the offender's suitability for treatment (often the Prison Medical Officer) is not necessarily the one who will carry out the treatment, and inappropriate recommendations and failure to respond to treatment can result. To improve the chances of success, we recommend that, wherever possible, the doctor recommending the treatment to the court should subsequently carry out the treatment. This would mean that in his evidence the doctor, besides commenting on an offender's suitability for treatment, would be giving implicitly an indication of his own ability to provide it. Any chance of a difference of medical opinion between the recommending and the treating doctors as to an offender's suitability would also be ruled out. Our proposals[3] for the introduction of centres, linked to hospitals and integrated wherever possible with the proposed secure units, for the

---

[3] Interim Report, paragraphs 9–11; see also Chapter 20 of this Report.

psychiatric assessment of patients for the courts should go some way to achieving this aim. We do not favour the extension of the practice of some courts requiring doctors to give evidence in favour of psychiatric probation orders orally, as this may have the undesirable effect of discouraging doctors from proposing such orders.

16.12   The second point, about the role of the probation officer, is that while the probationer is under treatment as a resident patient the Act (section 3(4)) requires no more than that " . . . the probation officer responsible for his supervision shall carry out the supervision to such an extent only as may be necessary for the purpose of the discharge or amendment of the order". We understand that for the purpose of this function a hospital liaison probation officer is often nominated in the order as the supervising officer; the probation officer in the patient's home area concerning himself only with maintaining contact with the family. We strongly support the view that was put before us in evidence that supervising probation officers need to have continuously close involvement while their clients are in hospital. There should also be continuity of care on the probationer-patient's discharge from hospital. We therefore propose that wherever possible the order should name the home probation officer as the supervising officer. He should work in conjunction with the doctor in carrying out the treatment plan, and we see value in including him in case conferences, where this can be arranged. Not only would this help to avoid any misunderstanding with the doctor over discharge (see paragraph 16.14 below), but regular contact between the probationer-patient and probation officer would be beneficial to their relationship. In addition, the support of the probation officer would be helpful to the successful completion of the medical treatment. Although we are aware that the importance of this supportive role is widely understood by probation officers and that the restrictive statutory instructions referred to above are largely ignored in the interests of establishing a relationship with the patient as early as possible, we would nevertheless stress the need for the close involvement of the supervising officers throughout the course of their clients' period of hospital residence.

16.13   We considered various proposals to improve liaison among the different agencies involved in psychiatric probation order cases by means of regular prescribed reports by the doctor and case reviews by the court or the supervisory service; but we are not convinced of the need to introduce further statutory requirements. Under paragraph 4 of Schedule 1 to the Powers of Criminal Courts Act 1973 it is already a statutory requirement for the doctor to report in writing to the probation officer if he is of opinion:

(a)   that the treatment of the probationer should be continued beyond the period specified in that behalf in the order, or

(b)   that the probationer needs different treatment, being treatment of a kind to which he could be required to submit in pursuance of a probation order, or

(c)   that the probationer is not susceptible to treatment, or

(d)   that the probationer does not require further treatment,

or where the practitioner is for any reason unwilling to continue to treat or direct the treatment of the probationer. The probation officer must then apply to the court for the variation or cancellation of the requirement. Thus, provision already exists for the court to be informed when action by the court is justified, and we do not think it necessary to require the court to review each psychiatric probation order case regularly on the basis of regular medical reports (an arrangement which would be likely to act as a considerable disincentive to doctors to recommend psychiatric probation orders). The suggestion that a psychiatrist might be co-opted to the probation case committee when such cases are under review would also impose on a busy psychiatrist's time, as well as involving him in advising on other doctors' cases. Furthermore, progress reports by the treating doctor to the case committee or to the supervising probation officer might be inhibited by the principles of medical confidentiality, unless the probationer's consent was forthcoming.

(4) Termination of treatment

16.14 Problems seem to arise mainly where treatment is terminated but the probation officer is not notified despite the statutory provisions set out above, or if he is notified the notice given is too short. We have been told that patients subject to probation orders are sometimes discharged from hospital without preparation, after only 24 hours' notice to the probation officer, or even less. Clearly, this is unsatisfactory. Preparation for discharge from hospital and for follow-up is as important in probation cases as for patients subject to hospital orders. It is particularly embarrassing for the probation officer if his client, who has been discharged from hospital without his knowledge, commits another offence. We see no reason why a formal duty should not be imposed on the psychiatrist to notify the probation officer in every case when treatment is terminated. The existing law as set out in paragraph 16.13 above may be thought already to encompass this requirement, but for the avoidance of doubt it might be helpful if the listed contingencies were extended by the addition "and in any event when treatment is terminated", or words to that effect.

16.15 The statutory provision referred to in paragraph 16.13 gives the psychiatrist, in effect, the absolute right to terminate a condition of treatment if he is "unwilling" to continue the treatment, and in practice he will be unwilling if the offender-patient does not keep his appointments or keeps them but does not co-operate in treatment; and similarly for in-patients. We have had suggestions that the attempt to give treatment may sometimes be too readily given up. For example, it has been said that many psychiatrists discharge an offender-patient the moment he becomes unco-operative, instead of persisting in attempts to persuade him to help in solving his problem; and the Justices' Clerks' Society proposed to us that the right given by law to the doctor to discontinue treatment because he is "unwilling" to continue it should be removed, because such unlimited discretion enables him arbitrarily to frustrate the intentions of the court. We think that the first of these comments does not sufficiently regard the pressures on psychiatrists and that, as to the second, no good purpose would be served by requiring a doctor to continue to give treatment in which he can see no value. The Justices' Clerks' Society have also suggested that the ease with which patients can at present evade the treatment condition of the probation order by withholding their co-operation, with the predictable result that the doctor discharges them and the court cancels the condition, is a positive incentive to probationer-patients not to co-operate. As a counter to this, the Society have proposed that if the doctor terminates treatment on the grounds of the patient's refusal to co-operate the probation officer, instead of applying for the variation or cancellation of the treatment requirement, should be able (if he thinks fit) to bring the probationer back before the court under section 6 of the Powers of Criminal Courts Act 1973 for failure to comply with a requirement of the order.

16.16 A difficulty in this is that the court would not normally, in justice, be able to take any action against the offender. The psychiatrist is unlikely to wish to give evidence against him; the patient's failure may be the result of his illness; some forms of treatment are very demanding for the person under treatment, and it cannot be a ground of complaint that he failed to respond to them. It would be unjust to punish the patient for failure of treatment unless wilful non-co-operation has been established. On the other hand, if wilful non-co-operation can be proved it may be right to substitute a prison sentence—for example, for an alchoholic or drug addict who is given to offences, or a sex offender—because the probation order was made upon an assurance that has been broken by the offender. We hope that, with improved liaison between doctors and the probation and after-care service, the doctor will be prepared to testify in appropriate cases to the simple fact that the patient did not co-operate in treatment, so as to support a finding that the requirement has been broken.

(5) Changing the patient's status

16.17 Our attention has been drawn by members of the probation and after-care service to a difficulty which arises where the order of the court specifies in-patient treatment and the probationer is later discharged to out-patient treatment. Amendment of the order is technically required because of the formulation of section 3(2) of the Powers of Criminal Courts Act 1973. Sub-headings (a), (b) and (c) of the subsection prescribe that the treatment to be specified in the order shall be *either* in-patient treatment *or* out-patient treatment *or* treatment "by or under the direction of such duly qualified medical practitioner as may be specified in the order". The difficulty could easily be removed by revision of section 3(2) and we recommend that this should be done.

(6) Conclusion

16.18 We believe that, where they are appropriately imposed, psychiatric probation orders can be made to work well. They are a valuable form of disposal bringing to bear the combination of skills of psychiatry and the probation and after-care service. The power to order a period of residential treatment or out-patient attendance linked with a sanction through the probation and after-care service should continue to be available to the courts. There are some short-comings in the system, but these can mostly be overcome by developing closer co-operation of courts, doctors and probation officers.

PSYCHIATRIC PROBATION ORDERS

SUMMARY OF CONCLUSIONS

1. Views vary as to the usefulness of psychiatric probation orders and there is a need for more research to be undertaken into their effects. We believe

that they can be made to work well, and the shortcomings in the system can mostly be overcome by closer co-operation of courts, doctors and probation officers. (Paragraphs 16.2–16.4 and 16.18.)

2. Careful pre-selection of offenders is essential for the success of psychiatric probation orders. Those assessing the individual offender should have regard strictly to his needs and suitability. As well as a medical opinion the views of the probation officer should be sought, and it should be normal practice for the court to obtain a social inquiry report on the defendant. (Paragraphs 16.5–16.6.)

3. The three month limit for the imposition on a probationer of a condition requiring him to submit to psychiatric treatment should be removed. (Paragraph 16.7.)

4. The legal requirement to ensure that the offender fully understands what obligations he is accepting must be effectively carried out. The court should also ensure that all others concerned are aware of their obligations. (Paragraph 16.9.)

5. The doctor giving medical evidence to the court should, wherever possible, carry out the treatment. (Paragraph 16.11.)

6. We stress the need for the close involvement of supervising probation officers while their clients are in hospital and we recommend that, wherever possible, the order should name the home probation officer as the supervising officer. The supervising officer should work in conjunction with the doctor, and there is value in including him in case conferences. (Paragraph 16.12.)

7. We do not favour the introduction of a system of regular reviews of probation cases, on the basis of reports by the doctor, to improve liaison between the different agencies involved. (Paragraph 16.13.)

8. There should be a formal requirement for the treating doctor to give notice to the probation officer in every case when treatment is terminated. (Paragraph 16.14.)

9. Doctors should be prepared to testify that the patient did not co-operate in treatment, so as to support a finding that the order has been breached and enable the court to substitute a suitable alternative order instead of merely cancelling the medical requirement. (Paragraph 16.15–16.16.)

10. Section 3(2) of the Powers of Criminal Courts Act 1973 should be revised to remove the technical necessity for amendment of the order when a probationer is discharged from in-patient to out-patient treatment. (Paragraph 16.17.)

CHAPTER 17

PROVISION FOR MENTALLY DISORDERED JUVENILES AND YOUNG ADULT OFFENDERS

(1) Hospital and guardianship orders

17.1 The powers of the courts as they apply to juveniles[1] are set out in paragraphs 13.6–13.7. The Children and Young Persons Act 1969 which made radical changes in many respects, did not effect any change in the power of juvenile courts to make a hospital or guardianship order within the meaning of Part V of the Mental Health Act 1959, but—in section 1(3)—consolidated this power which had previously been expressed in mental health legislation. We share the view approved by Parliament in 1969 that the power should be available to the juvenile court to make a hospital or guardianship order in cases diagnosed as suffering from mental illness, psychopathic disorder, subnormality or severe subnormality.

17.2 As regards "psychopathic disorder" we have already discussed in Chapter 5 the difficulties of this nomenclature and the possible substitution of the term "personality disorder" in section 4 of the Mental Health Act 1959. In their evidence the Association of Heads and Matrons of Community Schools pointed out that, applied to juveniles, certain diagnostic labels such as "psychopathic disorder" or "severe personality disorder", by discouraging the hope of growth potential and future learning, are inimical to the development of long-term treatment programmes which could take advantage of any prospects of change there may be. They said that it was important to define and attempt to deal with the problems than to devise and attach diagnostic labels. We agree with these remarks and moreover we note that there are difficulties in making such diagnoses where the personality has not yet crystallised. Whatever the name by which "psychopathic disorder" may eventually come to be known, we have already said (paragraph 5.40) that juvenile offenders under the age of 17 should be excluded from the new proposals we make for persons suffering from psychopathic disorder with dangerous anti-social tendencies. Placement within the prison system is not appropriate for juvenile offenders suffering from mental disorder. Where two doctors are satisfied that a juvenile offender under the age of 17 is suffering from psychopathic disorder and requires treatment in a hospital which is willing to accept him we consider that he should not be deprived of hospital care. This is particularly important in view of the difficulties of providing satisfactory care and containment elsewhere, to which we refer below.

(2) Shortage of adequate facilities

17.3 Evidence has been given to us of the need for more provision in hospitals for juveniles. The Royal College of Psychiatrists informed us that there was a national shortage of doctors wishing to specialise in this field of psychiatric assessment and treatment and that the reluctance of psychiatrists to involve

---

[1] See footnote 16 to paragraph 2.35. In this chapter also we use the word "juvenile" to include children and young persons within the meaning of the Children and Young Persons Act 1969. Where the terms "child" or "young person" are used they are to be interpreted as having the meaning given to them by the Act.

themselves in this work was partly attributable to the lack of treatment facilities. The decision whether a young patient may be admitted to hospital is made by the hospital consultant and, in line with our previous comments in relation to hospital orders generally (see paragraph 14.7), we think this should continue to be so. We recommend that steps be taken by the Department of Health and Social Security to encourage the establishment of more places in hospital for mentally disordered juveniles and we hope that increased facilities will promote greater willingness on the part of consultants to accept them. We envisage that some regional secure units will provide a limited number of beds, on an inter-regional basis, for their investigation and treatment. In our view it is desirable that some forensic psychiatrists should be encouraged to specialise in this work.

17.4   The effect of the shortage of facilities is also felt in the services provided by local authorities. We have been made aware of the difficulties experienced by local authorities in satisfactorily containing disturbed juveniles subject to care orders in community homes for want of secure accommodation. Although further Youth Treatment Centre places are being provided (see paragraph 2.40) the building of the first of the new centres will not be completed until early in 1977. The need for short-term and possibly long-term secure accommodation will remain. A sub-Committee of the Expenditure Committee of the House of Commons is now reviewing the operation of the Children and Young Persons Act 1969 and will doubtless have recommendations to make on this issue.

17.5.   For our part, we recommend that Children's Regional Planning Committees, which are consortia of local authorities with responsibility for the planning of residential provision, should take urgent steps to encourage their constituent local authorities to provide secure facilities for juveniles for the purposes of both treatment and assessment; we understand that priority is being given to increased assessment provision, and we welcome this in view of the location for some remands which courts are now forced to adopt and to which we refer below. It appears that for treatment and assessment purposes together some 400 secure places are likely to be required and local authorities should implement the recommendations of the Children's Regional Planning Committees in deciding where these places should be situated. It will probably be necessary to provide at least one secure unit for boys and one for girls in each regional planning area.

17.6   We endorse the recommendation in advice recently given to local authorities by the Department of Health and Social Security[2] that a secure unit should be attached to existing community homes to provide a gradual transition to more open conditions without interruption of personal relationships with staff and other children. We recognise that the definition in the Departmental circular of a secure unit as "a room, or an area comprising a group of associated rooms and spaces in which special features have been incorporated for the express purpose of presenting a physical barrier to any attempt on the part of a child accommodated in such room or area to leave it without permission" relates expressly to the use of the term in the circular itself but we are concerned that the reference to "a room" may be misunderstood. Whilst there may be occasions on which it is necessary to accommodate

---

[2] Department of Health and Social Security Local Authority Circular (75)1.

a juvenile in a single secure room, the circular goes on to point out that the time he spends there should be very short and a member of staff should keep in constant touch with him. Our own references to secure units relate to the provision of accommodation, which the circular envisages in the longer term, capable of sustaining the range of activities and affording the range of human contacts essential to constructive treatment of 15 or 20 juveniles over a period of 12 months or longer, with the necessary high staffing ratio. Further, a secure unit must do more than simply present physical barriers to the freedom of movement of those contained in it. While close physical security may be required in some cases it is our belief, as we have remarked elsewhere (paragraph 3.6), that effective security can generally be achieved by less than total physical confinement where there is a high level of expert supervision.

17.7 We have been informed that lack of financial resources has impeded the development of secure accommodation for juveniles. While we have hesitated to enter the field of local authority finance, we feel that the need for this secure accommodation is now so pressing and the special consequences of its absence so serious that special action is required. We therefore recommend that local authorities in whose areas Children's Regional Planning Committees plan secure units should be allocated moneys from central funds for the specific purpose of providing this secure accommodation. In putting forward this recommendation we have been gratified to note the Ministerial statement in the House of Commons on 20 June that the Government intend to make available to local authorities financial assistance in the form of direct grants for the purpose of building secure accommodation for seriously disturbed juveniles.[3]

17.8 One consequence of the lack of secure acccommodation in community homes is that some young persons, even as young as 14, have to be accommodated in prison. Section 23(1) of the Children and Young Persons Act 1969 provides for the commitment to the care of a local authority of a young person (14 to 16 years) on remand or committed for trial or sentence who is not released on bail. Under section 23(2) of the Act if a court certifies that the young person is of so unruly a character that he cannot safely be committed to the care of a local authority it may commit him to a remand centre, or, if no place is available in a remand centre, to a prison. In 1974 as many as 3,647 boys and 242 girls awaiting trial were received into custody under certificates of unruliness. Reference to this has recently been made in debate and questions in the House of Commons,[4] and the Home Secretary has announced that the Government are considering with great urgency the possibility of phasing out these remands of girls aged between 14 and 15. We greatly deplore that it should be necessary to commit any young persons to prison in this way, but we recognise that the shortage of secure facilities available to local authorities often leaves the courts with no alternative. We hope that the Government proposals for financial assistance to local authorities for the provision of secure accommodation (see the foregoing paragraph) will be swiftly implemented so that the present unsatisfactory arrangements can be terminated for all young persons.

---

[3] House of Commons Official Report, 20 June 1975, Col. 1838.
[4] House of Commons Official Report, 2 May 1975, Cols. 979–988.
16 June 1975, Col. 377.
19 June 1975, Cols. 1659–1660.

(3) Detention during Her Majesty's Pleasure

17.9 Some evidence put to us has cast doubt on the value of retaining section 53(1) of the Children and Young Persons Act 1933, which provides for the disposal of juveniles convicted of murder, because of the difficulty in placing those sentenced to be detained "during Her Majesty's Pleasure". In our view indeterminacy subject to Ministerial control must be retained for these juveniles, some of whom may be dangerous, although physical security may not always be necessary. The necessary flexibility in disposal should be provided by the Youth Treatment Centres and the secure accommodation in community homes referred to above, when these facilities become fully available.

(4) Borstal accommodation

17.10 Juvenile courts have power to commit offenders of 15 and over to the Crown Court for sentence of borstal training in certain circumstances. Some of our members have visited two borstal establishments, one for boys and one for girls. Bullwood Hall Borstal for girls contains a very high proportion of mentally disordered girls and in our view is performing functions which, if there were no problems of containment, a hospital would appropriately perform. This borstal has notably better facilities than are generally found in hospitals, especially workshop facilities, but it is unfortunate that so relatively new an establishment should be modelled on old-fashioned lines. We are pleased to note that the Prison Department is proceeding with a programme of new building to remedy the shortcomings. Feltham Borstal similarly has a high number of boys who are mentally disordered—the degree of disorder ranging from minimal to extremely severe—and we feel that a hospital placement would often be more appropriate. While we are pleased to note that plans are advanced for the re-development of Feltham, which has a valuable role to play, we think it undesirable to concentrate specialised resources in the South-East and recommend that comparable provision to cater for disturbed boys and girls be made in the North of England.

(5) Custody and control orders

17.11 We have read with interest the Report of the Advisory Council on the Penal System proposing a new pattern of care for the young adult offender aged 17–21, and consider that the custody and control order recommended by the Advisory Council could provide more flexibility in dealing with such offenders suffering from personality disorders than is available under the Mental Health Act.

(6) After-care hostels

17.12 A young offender's problems are not necessarily removed or even diminished on his return to the community after a period of residential care. We endorse the recommendation of the Home Office Working Group on Residential Provision for Offenders within the Community that more after-care hostels should be provided for young offenders with personality problems. Voluntary organisations, with their willingness and ability to experiment, can make a valuable contribution in this field. Co-ordination with local authorities making similar hostel provision would be advantageous.

(7) Supervision orders

17.13 The courses open to the court for the treatment of the mentally disordered juvenile are not solely institutional. The courts have power under section 1(3) of the Children and Young Persons Act to make a supervision order and may attach conditions to the order, including, under section 12(4), a condition of in-patient or out-patient treatment by a psychiatrist, if a medical practitioner so recommends. Section 11 of the Act provides that supervision may be undertaken by a local authority or a probation officer. Section 13, which deals with the selection of the supervisor, enables a court to designate a local authority as supervisor in all cases where it makes a supervision order, but restricts the designation of a probation officer to two cases: where the supervised person has attained an age to be specified by the Home Secretary (at present this age is 13);[5] and, where the supervised person is under that age, if the local authority to be named in the order so request and a probation officer is already exercising, or has exercised, his statutory duties in relation to another member of the household to which the child belongs. In considering whether to exercise their discretion to request supervision by the probation service, we think that the local authority, and the court in making the order, should have in mind the principle enunciated by the Aarvold Committee in another context that "supervision should be undertaken by the person who can bring most to the case in the way of knowledge, expertise and resources".

17.14 We propose that legislation be enacted to remove an anomaly with regard to the requirements for medical evidence under the supervision provisions of the Children and Young Persons Act 1969. This was pointed out to us by the Justices' Clerks' Society and was referred to in *Justice of the Peace* (136 JPN 19). The anomaly concerns section 12 of the Act which brought the conditions for making a supervision order requiring a juvenile to submit to psychiatric treatment into line with those for making a psychiatric probation order in the case of adults under what is now section 3 of the Powers of Criminal Courts Act 1973. As there was no provision in the 1969 Act corresponding to section 3(7) of the 1973 Act allowing the court to receive written evidence from a doctor the strange situation results that a doctor will normally have to be present in court to give his evidence orally before a supervision order can be made, although a hospital order under section 60 of the Mental Health Act 1959 may, by virtue of section 62 of that Act, be made in respect of a juvenile without the doctor attending court. The necessary steps should be taken to remedy this anomalous situation.

PROVISION FOR MENTALLY DISORDERED JUVENILES AND YOUNG ADULT OFFENDERS

SUMMARY OF CONCLUSIONS

1. The power to make a hospital or guardianship order under section 1(3) of the Children and Young Persons Act 1969 should remain available to the courts for juveniles suffering from mental illness, psychopathic disorder, subnormality or severe subnormality. (Paragraphs 17.1–17.2.)

---

[5] See Children and Young Persons Act 1969 (Transitional Modifications of Part I) Order 1970. (SI 1882, 1970.)

2. More places for juveniles should be provided in National Health Service Hospitals. We envisage that some regional secure units will provide a limited number of beds, on an inter-regional basis, for juveniles for both investigation and treatment. As with adults, the decision as to admission should be made by the hospital consultant. It is desirable that some forensic psychiatrists should be encouraged to specialise in work with juveniles. (Paragraph 17.3.)

3. In the field of local authority responsibility, secure facilities for juveniles of both sexes should be provided, preferably attached to a community home in each children's regional planning area; increased assessment provision should be the priority. The matter is the more urgent because for lack of this provision young persons are being committed to prison, which is quite unsuitable. We recommend that central Government should provide funds to local authorities for the provision of these facilities and we welcome the statement by the Government of their intention to make available financial assistance for this purpose in the form of direct grants to local authorities. (Paragraphs 17.4–17.8.)

4. The indeterminacy of detention subject to Ministerial control provided by section 53(1) of the Children and Young Persons Act 1933 must, in our view, be retained for juveniles convicted of murder. (Paragraph 17.9.)

5. Borstals providing psychiatric care for young offenders, both for boys and girls, comparable to those in the South-East, should be established in the North of the country to reduce the isolation of the trainees. (Paragraph 17.10.)

6. The custody and control order proposed by the Advisory Council on the Penal System in their Report on Young Adult Offenders could provide more flexibility in dealing with young offenders between 17 and 21 suffering from personality disorders than is available under the Mental Health Act. (Paragraph 17.11.)

7. More after-care hostels should be provided for young offenders with personality problems. Voluntary organisations especially could make a valuable contribution in this area, preferably in co-ordination with local authorities making similar provision. (Paragraph 17.12.)

8. Where a supervision order is made the supervising officer should be the person who can bring most to the case in the way of knowledge, expertise and resources, whether a local authority social worker or a probation officer. (Paragraph 17.13.)

9. Legislation should be enacted to enable the doctor who gives medical evidence to the court when a supervision order is made under section 12 of the Children and Young Persons Act 1969 to do so in writing. (Paragraph 17.14.)

CHAPTER 18

THE SPECIAL VERDICT

I. PRELIMINARY CONSIDERATIONS

(1) The existing position

18.1   The extent to which mental disorder constitutes a defence to a charge, or a reason for convicting of a lesser offence, depends at present on a complex body of law represented by M'Naghten's case, the defence of diminished responsibility, infanticide, and the doctrine of non-insane automatism. Although in general the law works well enough, there are two reasons for overhauling it.   The first, which in our view is in itself decisive, is that the Law Commission has embarked upon the task of drafting a Criminal Code, and it will be necessary to incorporate in this Code a provision in acceptable language on the subject of responsibility.   The second is that the law has been developed by a series of expedients and compromises which result in a number of anomalies and are in some ways out of accord with present thought.

18.2   We deal here first with the question of complete exemption from responsibility.   As the Royal Commission on Capital Punishment pointed out "it has for centuries been recognised that if a person was, at the time of his unlawful act, mentally so disordered that it would be unreasonable to impute guilt to him, he ought not to be held liable to conviction and punishment under the criminal law".[1]   The Commission regarded it as a fundamental assumption, which it should hardly be necessary to state, that this "ancient and humane principle that has long formed part of our common law" should continue.   Statutory provision recognising complete exemption from criminal responsibility was first made in the Criminal Lunatics Act 1800, which provided for a special verdict—technically an acquittal—of "not guilty on account of insanity", and that in the event of the special verdict being found the accused person should be detained in custody pending and during His Majesty's Pleasure.   This came to mean in the course of time confinement in a mental hospital or an institution for criminal lunatics or mental defectives, control over release resting with the Home Secretary.   Thus the special verdict absolved from responsibility but imposed an indefinite period of control within a mental institution.   This is still the essence of the special verdict.

18.3   The Trial of Lunatics Act 1883 changed the form of the special verdict from formal acquittal to what was popularly though inaccurately referred to as "guilty but insane".   This change was criticised by the Atkin Committee on Insanity and Crime in 1923,[2] by the Royal Commission on Capital Punishment in 1953[3] and by the Criminal Law Revision Committee in 1963.[4]   The Criminal Procedure (Insanity) Act 1964 restored the form of an acquittal by providing for the jury to bring in a special verdict of "not guilty by reason of insanity" in cases where it appears to them that the accused committed the act or made the omission charged but was not responsible according to law for his actions at the time.   The Act also provided for appeal against a special verdict.

---

[1] Cmnd. 8932, paragraph 278.
[2] Cmnd. 2005, pages 11 and 12.
[3] Cmnd. 8932, paragraph 459.
[4] Cmnd. 2149, paragraph 5.

18.4   The criteria to be applied by the jury in reaching a special verdict were laid down by the judges in reply to questions by the House of Lords in M'Naghten's case (1843).   These "M'Naghten Rules" read in their essential portion as follows:

> "The jurors ought to be told in all cases that every man is to be presumed to be sane, and to possess a sufficient degree of reason to be responsible for his crimes, until the contrary be proved to their satisfaction; and that to establish a defence on the ground of insanity, it must be clearly proved that at the time of the committing of the act, the party accused was labouring under such a defect of reason, from disease of the mind, as not to know the nature and quality of the act he was doing, or, if he did know it, that he did not know he was doing wrong".

The judges added that if the accused "labours under [a] partial delusion only, and is not in other respects insane, we think he must be considered in the same situation as to responsibility as if the facts with respect to which the delusion exists were real".

18.5   Almost throughout their existence the M'Naghten rules have been criticised, generally as being based on too limited a concept of the nature of mental disorder.   The Royal Commission on Capital Punishment in 1953 noted that the interpretation of the rules by the courts had been broadened and stretched to make them fit particular cases, to the point where "the gap between the natural meaning of the law and the sense in which it is commonly applied has for so long been so wide, it is impossible to escape the conclusion that an amendment of the law, to bring it into closer conformity with the current practice, is long overdue".[5]   The Royal Commission pointed out that many offenders who know what they are doing and that it is wrong are nevertheless undoubtedly insane and should not be held responsible for their actions.[6]   Another serious difficulty lies in the outmoded language of the rules which gives rise to problems of interpretation.   It is unclear, for example, whether the reference to the knowledge of the accused of the nature and quality of his act should be taken to cover the whole mental element in crime[7] or some narrower concept.   Similarly the 19th century term "disease of the mind" raises the question whether the rules are intended to cover severe subnormality, neurosis or psychopathy.

18.6   But the main defect of the M'Naghten test is that it was based on the now obsolete belief in the pre-eminent role of reason in controlling social behaviour. It therefore requires evidence of the cognitive capacity, in particular the know-ledge and understanding of the defendant at the time of the act or omission charged.   Contemporary psychiatry and psychology emphasise that man's social behaviour is determined more by how he has learned to behave than by what he knows or understands.   For many years a number of mental disorders differing in their clinical characteristics have been recognised and distinguished

---

[5] Cmnd. 8932, paragraph 291.

[6] *Ibid.*, paragraph 295.

[7] A crime does not consist solely of the physical act or omission but normally requires proof of certain elements in the mind of the alleged offender.   These elements vary according to the particular offence, but in general they amount to whether the defendant intended to commit the act or omission in question or acted knowingly or recklessly in respect of the consequences or surrounding circumstances.   The mental element may therefore be lacking in cases of accident, automatism and mistake.

from one another. In some disorders the patient's beliefs are so bizarre or his change of mood is so profound and inexplicable, or he is so changed in manner and conduct, that his condition can only be described as alien, or mad. In such cases it is accepted opinion in civilised countries that he should not be held responsible for his actions.

18.7 Strictly interpreted the M'Naghten Rules would provide that mentally disordered defendant with very limited protection. Just as a person must generally be very mad indeed not to know what he is doing (the nature and quality of his act) when he is killing a man or setting fire to a building, so he must be very mad not to know that these acts attract the unfavourable notice of the police (his knowledge of wrong). For example, if a psychotic patient kills a person whom he believes to be putting thoughts into his mind, or kills him and gives as a reason that the victim is spying on him, or simply kills him because he has an overpowering urge to do so, the M'Naghten Rules, strictly interpreted, will not give him a defence if he admits that he knew that he was killing a man and that murder was a crime.

18.8 The M'Naghten Rules are in part linked with the *mens rea* doctrine, in recognising that evidence of disease of the mind may have the effect of negativing a mental element of the crime. The "knowledge of wrong" test is not an application of the ordinary rules of *mens rea*, however. "Wrong" has been held to mean "legally wrong"[8] and a sane defendant cannot set up a defence of ignorance of the criminal law. Knowledge of the law is hardly an appropriate test on which to base ascription of criminal responsibility to the mentally disordered. It is a very narrow ground of exemption since even persons who are grossly disturbed generally know that murder and arson, for instance, are crimes. It might seem at first sight more attractive to have regard to the defendant's appreciation of what is morally wrong, but the problems in applying such a test to the mentally disordered would be very great. "Knowledge of wrong", as included in M'Naghten, is not therefore a satisfactory test of criminal responsibility.

18.9 At the time of the Royal Commission on Capital Punishment 1949–1953 a plea of insanity represented the only certain way of avoiding the death sentence for a defendant in a murder trial where there was no doubt that he had committed the offence. If the defence failed, he would be no worse off for having tried it; he would be convicted and his prospects of reprieve would not be prejudiced. The fact that a reprieve would result in a sentence of life imprisonment entailing indefinite detention in prison (subject to removal to hospital if the prisoner was found to be in fact insane), while a successful defence of insanity would lead to indefinite detention in a mental hospital, would be unlikely to rob the insanity defence of its obvious attractions for anyone accused of murder who had no other convincing defence. Release in either case would be at the discretion of the Home Secretary. With the introduction, under section 2 of the Homicide Act 1957, of the defence of diminished responsibility in murder cases, which enabled the court to pass any appropriate sentence from life imprisonment to absolute discharge, according to the degree of blame attributable to the offender, another possibility was opened up to defendants which has proved increasingly popular.

---

[8] *Windle* [1952] 2 Q.B. 826.

Then the Mental Health Act 1959 enabled the court to substitute a hospital order for a sentence of imprisonment in all cases where it had a discretion as to sentence. The abolition of capital punishment[9] has gone still further in removing any incentive on the part of the defence to seek a special verdict, and the insanity defence is in fact almost unheard of nowadays. The table at Appendix 9 illustrates the decline in the use of the special verdict in cases of murder and the rise in the use of the defence of diminished responsibility.

(2) Should an "insanity defence" be retained?

18.10 This decline in the use of the special verdict to the point where it is scarcely used at all does not, we believe, indicate that the law need no longer provide for total exemption from criminal responsibility for the mentally disordered offender. Retention of the "insanity" defence in some form has been supported by a large number of those who have given evidence to us, and we share the view that this is right in principle (for the reasons indicated in paragraph 18.2 above). At the same time, we think it important that the court should be empowered in such cases to make appropriate disposal arrangements in the interests of the defendant and of the community at large. This question of disposal is dealt with in paragraphs 18.42–18.45 below.

18.11 The evidence we have received against retaining an "insanity" defence —from, among others, the British Psychological Society—has been directed at the system of criminal trial within which the defence arises. These witnesses were in favour of fundamental changes in the system, to provide what might be termed a "two-stage trial"—that is to say, a procedure under which the external facts of the offence would be considered separately from consideration of the mental condition of the defendant, which would arise only as an incidental to disposal once it was proved that he had committed the criminal act. A two-stage trial has already been advocated in published literature on mentally disordered offenders, but we share the views of those commentators who have thought it impracticable and undesirable.

18.12 Two kinds of two-stage trial have been proposed. According to the first the jury (in a trial on indictment) would find the external facts, and it would then be for the sentencer (the judge) to find what was the defendant's mental state at the time of the act, as one of the matters bearing upon sentence. Under this system, the trial would not be concerned with the notions of guilt and responsibility except insofar as such matters had a bearing on the appropriate measures to be taken to prevent a recurrence of the forbidden act; but we do not think it would be acceptable to remove these questions altogether from the jury. The proposal would in theory render a person who has been involved in a fatal accident through no fault of his own liable to detention for life, in the same way as if he had committed murder; such protection as he would have would rest only on a wise use of discretion by the sentencing tribunal. Sentencers would apparently be left with no guidance on the relative importance that the community attaches to different prohibitions. Some parts of the present law which rest particularly upon proof of intention, such as the law of conspiracy and attempt, would become unworkable.

---

[9] The death penalty for murder was suspended by the Murder (Abolition of Death Penalty) Act 1965 which is to continue permanently in force by virtue of affirmative resolutions of both Houses of Parliament on 16 and 18 December 1969.

18.13   The second form of the proposal is less extreme: it would allow the jury to decide the question of guilt in the first stage and hear and pronounce on psychiatric evidence in the second stage.   This makes the mistake of supposing that the question of guilt can be decided merely by the establishment of the external facts.   All serious offences require in addition a mental element (see footnote [7] to paragraph 18.5).   For example A may take B's umbrella without B's permission: these are the external facts.   But he will not be guilty of theft if he honestly believed that the umbrella was his own.   The question of state of mind, with possible psychiatric evidence bearing upon it, necessarily arises in the first stage and cannot be removed from it.   In consequence, this form of two-stage trial would sometimes lead to the jury having to consider the same psychiatric evidence twice: in the first stage on the issue of guilt in relation to the definition of the offence, and in the second stage on the issue of exemption from responsibility on account of mental disorder.   In these circumstances there is no advantage, and some disadvantage, in separating the trial into two stages, as was found in California when this form of trial was introduced there.[10]

II.   A REVISED SPECIAL VERDICT

(1) Experience of revised formulations in America

18.14   In considering what recommendation we should make, we have found our point of departure in the remark of the Royal Commission on Capital Punishment, to which we have referred in paragraph 18.5 above, that many offenders who know what they are doing and that it is wrong and therefore are not within the scope of the M'Naghten Rules are nevertheless undoubtedly so severely disordered that they ought not to be held responsible for their actions.   The problem we have to deal with is to devise a formula to provide for them.   In other common-law countries efforts have been made to extend the "insanity" defence by interpretation or statutory additions or restatement. For example, the knowledge of wrong test has been widened by asking whether the defendant was so mentally disordered that he was unable to appreciate the reasons why his act was regarded as wrong, or that he was unable to feel that it was wrong.   Among other formulations we have considered have been the "Durham" formula,[11] under which "the accused is not criminally responsible if his unlawful act was the product of mental disease or mental defect"[12], and the proposal in the American Law Institute's Model Penal Code (1959) that the question be whether the defendant, as a result of mental disease or defect[12], lacked substantial capacity either to appreciate the criminality of his conduct or to conform his conduct to the requirements of law.

18.15   The "Durham" formula has created difficulties of interpretation in its application to the unlawful act as the "product" of the mental condition, and in relation to psychopaths whom psychiatrists could testify to be suffering from mental disease or defect.   The expression "mental disease" itself has gone out of general use in this country, and in any case it does not help to distinguish

---

[10] David W Louisell and Geoffrey C Hazard Jnr.   "Insanity as a Defense: the bifurcated trial", *California Law Review*, 49 (1961).

[11] Propounded in *Durham* v *United States* (1954), 214 F2d *862* (*D.C. Circuit*).

[12] In neither case is the term "mental disease or defect" defined, its interpretation being left to the psychiatrists who give evidence to the court in each case.

between minor and major disorders. The author of the "Durham" formula, Judge Bazelon, has described his own reasons for favouring its abandonment in the following terms:[13]

> "In the end, after 18 years, I favored the abandonment of the Durham rule because in practice it had failed to take the issue of criminal responsibility away from the experts. Psychiatrists continued to testify to the naked conclusion instead of providing information about the accused so that the jury could render the ultimate moral judgment about blameworthiness. Durham had secured little improvement over M'Naghten".

A drawback of the Durham formula is that it encouraged psychiatrists to draw inferences which are not for doctors to draw.[14] This was a problem which we had to overcome in devising a new defence.

18.16 The Model Penal Code proposal is open to the same objection as Durham in its reference to "mental disease or defect", but its second limb raises other problems. In particular the test of capacity to conform has to face a well-known philosophical criticism. How can one tell the difference between an impulse which is irresistible and one which is merely not resisted?[15] Let us imagine two patients whose clinical symptoms appear similar, each of whom has been involved with a friend in an argument. Patient A flies into a rage and stabs his friend: patient B does not. If A is prosecuted, a psychiatrist may be ready to testify that by reason of his disease of the mind he was deprived of the capacity to conform to the law, and he will no doubt be influenced by the fact that A did not conform to it. Patient B, not having assaulted his friend, is not prosecuted, so that no court hears psychiatric evidence about his capacity to conform: but presumably a psychiatrist would say that he had such a capacity, since he did not strike his friend. Some would seek to find a way out of this argument. There are offenders whose lack of self-control shows itself not only in a single offence, but also in their response to everyday temptations or frustrations. If patient A had a history of frequent and violent loss of temper, or if under observation after the assault he reacted violently to petty frustrations in the ward, such evidence would support the claim that he is less able than most men to control his temper. If, on the other hand, he was known to be extremely self-controlled, a psychiatrist would be justified in assuming that at normal times he was able to control himself and would have to explain the assault in some other way, for example, by showing that the argument developed in such a way as to give him extreme provocation (as the psychiatric witness did in the Californian case of Gorshen[16]). To this argument the determinist would reply that the fact remains that the man who was normally able to control himself (ie who normally conformed) was not able to control himself on the occasion in question, as is shown by the fact that he did not

---

[13] David L Bazelon, "Psychiatrists and the Adversary Process", *Scientific American* 230 (1974).

[14] Nor is it clear that "Durham" offers any advantages from the point of view of the jury. Research which has been conducted in the USA on the effect of a "Durham" direction to the jury suggests that it is the same as giving no direction at all: a *M'Naghten* direction on the other hand tended to result in a conviction. (Rita James Simon: *The Jury and the Defense of Insanity*, Boston, 1967.)

[15] Cf. the comments of the Royal Commission on Capital Punishment on the concept of "irresistible impulse": Cmnd. 893, paragraph 313–4.

[16] [1959] 51 Cal. 2d 716, 336 P 2d 492. See B L Diamond: The Criminal Responsibility of the Mentally Ill, *Stanford Law Review* XIV (1961–2) 59.

conform. Also, even the psychopath or schizophrenic who is often aggressive is not always aggressive, so that aggression on a particular occasion is not completely explained by the psychopathy or schizophrenia. However this may be, it will be generally agreed that most cases are of the intermediate sort in which neither the circumstances nor the offender's usual behaviour provided the obvious explanation; and in such cases it is usually fair to say that the only evidence of incapacity to conform with the law was the act itself.

(2) Our proposals

(i) Introductory remarks

18.17 In considering our own solution to these problems we have had in mind certain basic requirements which we think must be met by any reformulated "insanity" defence. In particular it is desirable that the defence should:

    (a) avoid the use of medical terms about which there may be disputed interpretations or whose meaning may change with the years; and

    (b) be such as to allow psychiatrists to state the facts of the defendant's mental condition without being required to pronounce on the extent of his responsibility for his offence. Degrees of responsibility are legal, not medical, concepts.

Moreover, to the extent that the question of "insanity" is to remain one for the jury to decide, the defence must—

    (c) avoid the use of words and expressions which may confuse the jury; and

    (d) be capable of being the subject of a clear direction by the judge.

Our recommendations incorporate two elements which we think satisfy these requirements and, taken together as they are intended to be, will form a more satisfactory basis for protecting the mentally disordered from conviction and punishment than is the case under the existing law, while avoiding the difficulties which attach to the alternatives we have discussed. The first element, dealt with in paragraphs 18.20–18.25, covers what may be called the *mens rea* portion of the M'Naghten Rules. The second element confers a specific exemption from conviction upon any defendant who, at the time of the act or omission charged, was suffering from severe mental illness or severe subnormality (paragraphs 18.26–18.36). Such a person is exempted from responsibility on account of his disordered mental state notwithstanding technical proof of *mens rea*.

18.18 The two elements are the basis for a new formulation of the special verdict which, as has been explained in paragraph 18.2 above, is a form of acquittal with particular consequences. We propose that the new formula for the special verdict should be "not guilty on evidence of mental disorder". We suggest this departure from the existing formula ("not guilty by reason of insanity") for two reasons. First, the continued use of the words "insanity" and "insane" in the criminal law long after their disappearance from psychiatry and mental health law has been a substantial source of difficulty, and we attach importance to the discontinuance of the use of these words in the criminal law. We also propose that the use of the term "insanity defence" should be discontinued and replaced by "defence of mental disorder" or "defence of severe mental disorder" as may be appropriate. Secondly, the words "by reason of",

222

with their indication of a causal connection, are not apt for the purposes of the second element of our proposed new special verdict, which does not depend on proof of such a connection. (See also paragraph 18.37 below.)

18.19 Magistrates' courts as well as the Crown Courts should be allowed to return the special verdict. It will then not be necessary to continue the existing power under section 60(2) of the Mental Health Act 1959 whereby magistrates' courts in certain cases, having heard psychiatric evidence, may make a hospital or guardianship order without convicting. At present this provision is sometimes also used by magistrates' courts as a way of dealing with defendants who are unfit to stand trial, but it is inappropriate for this purpose since it requires the court to be satisfied that the defendant did the act charged. We are proposing other means by which magistrates' courts can deal with defendants who are under disability in relation to the trial (paragraphs 10.35–10.40), and we think that under our present proposals for the special verdict there will be no need to make a distinction of principle between the Crown Court and magistrates' courts.

(ii) *The mens rea element*

18.20 To provide the first element of the new defence we recommend that where medical or other evidence is given of mental disorder, within the meaning of section 4 of the Mental Health Act 1959, for the purpose of negativing a state of mind required for the offence (intention, foresight or knowledge), if the jury find that the defendant did the act or made the omission they should return a verdict of "not guilty on evidence of mental disorder". Magistrates should make a similar finding on summary trial. The special verdict would also cover cases where the prosecution are required to negative a state of mind required for a defence (such as belief in the imminence of being attacked), and the evidence of mental disorder helps to confirm the existence (or the possibility of the existence) of that belief.

18.21 We are aware of the reservations felt by psychiatrists as to the possibility of establishing the intention of a defendant by an examination that may take place weeks or months after the act in question. The psychiatrist naturally wishes to report on the state of mind of a patient at the time of examination, not at some previous time. However, it would not be acceptable for the law to provide that psychiatric evidence is inadmissible on the state of the defendant's mind at the time of the crime. So long as psychiatrists are prepared to testify on this question either for the defence or (in rebuttal) for the prosecution, the possibility must be faced that a defendant may win an acquittal by reason of the psychiatric evidence. If the evidence is of mental disorder, then the acquittal must be by the special verdict which gives the court powers of disposal that it would not possess in the event of an ordinary acquittal.

18.22 This proposal may be said to provide for the irreducible minimum of an "insanity" defence. Special consideration needs to be given to intoxication and automatism. A defendant may set up a defence that he had a "black-out" or other state of confused or altered consciousness inconsistent with the mental element alleged against him. If this were regarded as an "insanity" defence success in it would, under existing provisions, lead to a special verdict and mandatory commitment, but several forms of the defence are not regarded as amounting to "insanity". For example, it has long been the law that evidence of intoxication may be given to negative the criminal state of mind, and if as a result of this evidence the jury or magistrates are not satisfied that the mental state existed, the result will be an absolute acquittal. Some decisions make it uncertain how far this rule extends, and there certainly are cases where death is caused, where a manslaughter charge would lie. However, evidence of intoxication can certainly negative liability in some cases; and no one would say that a person who was drunk was therefore "insane". Nor is intoxication regarded as automatism, though the legal result of automatism and intoxication is the same, in that both can negative a necessary mental element. The doctrine of automatism has been applied particularly to acts (including killing) done while sleepwalking, or in a confusional state caused by hypoglycaemia or concussion, or in a state of dissociation. Sometimes injuries inflicted during an epileptic seizure are regarded as resulting from "insanity", sometimes as being merely instances of non-insane automatism. Although psychiatrists certainly distinguish between forms of mental disorder the terms "insanity", "non-insane automatism" and "disease of the mind" are exclusively legal terms, and the sharp divide between "insanity" and non-insane automatism[17] is unknown to medical science. It is a legal distinction, the result partly of an endeavour to construe language in a commonsense way and partly of a desire to spare defendants the stigma that an "insanity" verdict still carries, and to save them from mandatory commitment. The influence of the outcome upon the legal classification is shown by a well-known remark of Lord Denning. Speaking of the distinction between "insanity" (a "disease of the mind") and non-insane automatism, he said:

> "It seems to me that any mental disorder which has manifested itself in violence and is prone to recur is a disease of the mind. At any rate it is the sort of disease for which a person should be detained in hospital rather than be given an unqualified acquittal".[18]

This proposition needs qualification: a condition that would not in common sense be called "insanity" will be put in the class of non-insane automatism notwithstanding that it is prone to recur.[19] In case of doubt, however, the question of future danger may be decisive. We think that it should be an objective in restating the law to clarify the distinction, and some problems would be removed if, as we propose, the word "insanity" were removed from the special verdict, and if the court were given a discretion as to disposal (so that those who presented no danger were not bound to be sent to hospital). We make a proposal on the latter point in paragraph 18.42.

18.23 The rule proposed in paragraph 18.20 would apply to evidence of any mental disorder, except that we propose an express exclusion for evidence of transient states not related to other forms of mental disorder and arising solely

---

[17] An example of a case of "non-insane automatism" resulting in a court appearance might be that of a car driver who caused the death of a pedestrian, having lost control of his vehicle while experiencing an uncontrollable fit of sneezing.

[18] *Bratty* v *Attorney-General for Northern Ireland* [1963] A.C. at 412. (The reference to "violence" was directed to the particular case. The context makes it clear that it was not intended that other forms of mental disorder not manifesting themselves in violence should be excluded as "diseases of the mind").

[19] Cf. *R* v *Quick* [1973] 1 Q.B. 910.

as a consequence of (*a*) the administration, mal-administration or non-administration of alcohol, drugs or other substances or (*b*) physical injury. Evidence falling within this exception would not lead to a special verdict, but would leave the jury to their normal choice between verdicts of guilty and not guilty. The exception would cover some of the cases in which defences of non-insane automatism or based on the intoxication of the defendant are raised. We make the exception because we think that it would generally be regarded as strange and indeed wrong that a person who has committed a criminal act in a state of confusion following concussion, or when his soft drink has without his knowledge been laced with alcohol which caused him to be so drunk that he did not know what he was doing, or, in the case of a diabetic, when he has failed to take his insulin, should be described as having been mentally disordered and be subject to any power of control by the court, even though not mandatory. (We deal in paragraphs 18.51–18.59 below with the subject of voluntary intoxication whether by alcohol or by the consumption of drugs and propose the creation of a new offence with respect thereto.) All other cases now regarded as non-insane automatism would be left to fall under the special verdict. The problem of the future dangerousness of the offender would then be decided not in drawing an artificial line between "insanity" and non-insane automatism (cf paragraph 18.22 above) but by the judge in deciding whether any restrictions or requirements need to be imposed upon the defendant in order to prevent a recurrence. The powers of disposal which we propose in paragraphs 18.42–18.45 below would rule out punishment.

18.24   There remains to be considered the knowledge of wrong test in the M'Naghten Rules discussed in paragraphs 18.7–18.8. This test is simply one indication of the extremity of the "insanity" from which the defendant was suffering. The limited nature of the exemption which it confers has often been commented on. We do not think it would be satisfactory to include it in terms in a modern code, although it will in substance be covered by the broader test of severe mental illness or severe subnormality which we propose as the second element in the new provisions.

18.25   A question that has not been systematically considered by the judges is the relation of M'Naghten to evidence of subnormality. On the one hand, a deficiency of intelligence may be given in evidence for the purpose of persuading the jury that the defendant did not intend or foresee what he would have been assumed to have intended or foreseen, and if the deficiency is not great the result may be an ordinary acquittal and not a special verdict. In *R* v *Hudson*[20] a question arose on a statutory defence of absence of knowledge. The Court of Criminal Appeal said:

"In considering his state of mind, a jury is entitled and, indeed, bound to take into account the defendant himself. There may be cases, of which this is not one, where there is evidence before the jury to show that the defendant himself is a person of limited intelligence or possibly suffering from some handicap which would prevent him from appreciating the state of affairs which an ordinary man might realise. Again that is a matter which, in the appropriate case, would no doubt receive consideration in the summing up".

[20] [1966] 1 Q.B. 448.

Nothing was said on the question whether an ordinary acquittal would be proper in such circumstances. The authorities leave the law in some doubt but it is impossible to imagine that a mentally handicapped person who commits some harmful or dangerous act, like obstructing a railway line, and who escapes conviction because the evidence of mental handicap leaves the jury unconvinced that he knew the consequences of what he was doing, would, under the direction of the judge, be given an ordinary acquittal. In common sense, the distinction between the mental handicap that produces an ordinary acquittal and that which produces a special verdict should reside in the danger of repetition of the act. The rule proposed in paragraph 18.20 is not in terms the same as this: it requires attention to be directed to the question whether the handicap was a form of "mental disorder". This is defined in section 4 of the Mental Health Act to include "arrested or incomplete development of mind". The latter phrase is not itself defined, but it would seem to be wide enough to cover not only all dangerous mentally handicapped people but even, perhaps, the "person of limited intelligence" referred to in the judgment in Hudson. Thus the effect of the rule we propose may be to extend the special verdict to cover persons who would now obtain a complete acquittal. On the other hand we are proposing that the special verdict should no longer carry the consequence of a mandatory commitment to hospital. The trial judge will, under our proposal, be able to give full weight to the question whether the defendant presents a danger to the public when considering disposal.

(iii) *Mental disorder as displacing legal responsibility that would otherwise attach*

18.26 We have so far discussed only the first element of the special verdict which will apply where the evidence of mental disorder caused the jury or the magistrates to be unsure that the defendant had the state of mind required for the offence at the time when the act was committed; he may not, for example, have had the mental capacity to form an intent. Some severe mental disorders, however, do not prevent the sufferer from forming positive intentions and carrying them out efficiently. An instance would be a person who killed someone quite deliberately but under the delusion that he had been ordered by God to do so. We have been concerned to provide adequate safeguards in relation to disposal in such cases, in order to ensure that the offender is not subject to punishment.

18.27 Generally, a defendant who is mentally disordered at the time of sentence will have been disordered at the time of the act. Occasionally this will not be so. A very unlikely type of case may serve to bring out the point of principle. It is theoretically possible, even though unlikely, that a mentally normal person may commit a serious crime, evade justice for several months or years and during that time develop a psychosis before being caught. All that the Mental Health Act 1959 requires the doctor to specify, as a condition of making a hospital order, is that the defendant is presently suffering from one of the named conditions and that the case complies with the other conditions for an order. Yet in the circumstances just outlined it may seem unsatisfactory on grounds of justice (ie equality of treatment between different offenders) to make a hospital order which may result in the offender's symptoms being alleviated so that he is let out on the community after a short time. Logically, supervening mental illness should no more exempt an offender from punishment

226

than supervening physical disease[21]. So it would not seem to be wrong if such an offender were given a prison sentence, with initial transfer to hospital under section 72 of the Mental Health Act for so long as he is ill. In practice, however, it would probably be regarded as humane to make a hospital order and to neglect this refinement of theory.

18.28 The converse case is much more likely: that a person who was mentally disordered at the time of the act has recovered before the trial. Here a hospital order cannot be made. Yet, when compared with the offender who was normal at the time of the act but has become disordered since, he is the very person who in justice should be spared from punishment. At present such a person is subject to punishment unless the case falls within the M'Naghten Rules; but since the court has a discretion as to sentence (even on a charge of murder, if the defendant establishes diminished responsibility), the court may in practice recognise a wider measure of exemption on account of mental disorder than the M'Naghten Rules provide.

18.29 We have given a great deal of thought to the ways in which this practice might be expressed as a principle. In the common-law jurisdictions this has always proved difficult for legislators. The Code Napoléon of 1810 cut the Gordian Knot by providing simply that "Il n'y a ni crime ni délit, lorsque le prévenu était en état de démence au temps de l'action . . ."; and similar provisions are still in force in France and some other countries whose codes derive from the Code Napoléon. The essence of the formula is that it simply presumes absence of responsibility when it is established that the accused was suffering from a sufficiently severe degree of mental disorder (démence) at the time of his act or omission, and thus confines argument to a question of fact which psychiatrists can reasonably be expected to answer. It is true that it is theoretically possible for a person to be suffering from a severe mental disorder which has in a causal sense nothing to do with the act or omission for which he is being tried: but in practice it is very difficult to imagine a case in which one could be sure of the absence of any such connection.

18.30 Accordingly, we propose that the special verdict should be returned if at the time of the act or omission charged the defendant was suffering from severe mental illness or severe subnormality. This formula would not include psychopathic disorder, subnormality or the other abnormal states of mind mentioned in section 4 of the Mental Health Act, nor the transient states excluded under our proposals for the first element of the special verdict. Severe subnormality is defined in section 4(2) of the Mental Health Act 1959 as ". . . a state of arrested or incomplete development of mind which includes subnormality of intelligence and is of such a nature or degree that the patient is incapable of living an independent life or of guarding himself against serious exploitation, or will be so incapable when of an age to do so". Neither mental illness nor severe mental illness is defined in the Act. It is important that what is meant by severe mental illness should be clearly understood, and we now give the argument which led us to find a definition.

---

[21] It was at one period the practice to defer the execution of a felon who became insane after committing his offence, and several rather odd justifications of this were offered: see Nigel Walker, *Crime and Insanity in England* (Edinburgh, 1973), Vol. 1, Chapter 12.

18.31 Mental disorders may be classified according to causes, when these are physical and known; but more often, when they are not physical, or when the causes are uncertain or unknown, they may be classified according to the clinical characteristics by which they are recognised and which distinguish them from one another. The causes of the majority of mental disorders are not known, and modern classifications are clinical characteristics.

18.32 Section V of the International Classification of Diseases (ICD) provided by the World Health Organisation (8th revision 1968) for which there is now an International Glossary[22] recognises three major groups of mental disorders. These are (a) psychoses, (b) neuroses, personality disorders and other non-psychotic mental disorders, and (c) mental retardation (mental subnormality). The psychoses "include those conditions in which impairment of mental functions has developed to a degree that interferes grossly with insight, ability to meet some of the ordinary demands of life, or adequate contact with reality. It is not an exact or well-defined term. Mental retardation is excluded". The group of psychoses includes mental disorders associated with known physical conditions (the organic psychoses, the subcategories of which are classified according to causes), and the large categories of schizophrenia, the affective psychoses (mania and depression) and the paranoid states (collectively the functional psychoses, the subcategories of which are classified according to clinical characteristics, for the causes are unknown).

18.33 Section 4 of the Mental Health Act 1959 provides a classification and some definitions of mental disorder. "In this Act 'mental disorder' means mental illness, arrested or incomplete development of mind, psychopathic disorder and any other disorder or disability of mind". Mental illness is not defined, but subnormality, severe subnormality and psychopathic disorder are. Subnormality and severe subnormality can be equated in the World Health Organisation Glossary with the degrees of mental retardation and psychopathic disorder with certain categories of personality disorder (these have been discussed in Chapter 5). The various forms of mental illness can be equated with the psychoses, but some authorities consider that there are minor forms of mental illness—the neuroses. The ICD, following European tradition, has classified the neuroses as forms of mental disorder associated with or arising from personality disorder. Be this as it may, it is evidence that the psychotic types of mental disorder are major forms of mental illness and are by common consent regarded as severe. The psychotic person, unlike the neurotic, tends to confuse his morbid subjective experiences and fantasies with external reality. There is an impairment of those mental functions upon which insight and understanding depend and an inability to adapt to the ordinary demands of the social environment. This can come about because intellectual capacities are seriously reduced (the group of organic psychoses); because alteration of mood is lasting and profound (the group of manic and depressive psychoses); or because thinking is disordered or perceptions are distorted (the groups of schizophrenic and paranoid psychoses).

18.34 We have considered whether to equate the definition of severe mental illness with the concept of psychosis, but there are two objections. On the one hand there are mild or incipient forms of psychosis, which, while clear enough

---

[22] Glossary of Mental Disorders and Guide to their Classification. 1974, World Health Organisation, Geneva (HMSO).

to enable the clinician to make a diagnosis, would not be regarded as being evidence of severe mental illness in the terms in which we have described it. On the other hand the concept of psychosis, as a general category to embrace all those mental illnesses for which physical causation is already known or is expected to be discovered in the future, may not survive as a medical classificatory term. It is therefore necessary to identify the abnormal mental phenomena which occur in the various mental illnesses and which when present would be regarded by common consent as being evidence of severity. A definition of severe mental illness derived in this way must be comprehensive but also, as far as possible, economical.

18.35 We propose the following definition:

"A mental illness is severe when it has one or more of the following characteristics:—

(a) Lasting impairment of intellectual functions shown by failure of memory, orientation, comprehension and learning capacity.

(b) Lasting alteration of mood of such degree as to give rise to delusional appraisal of the patient's situation, his past or his future, or that of others, or to lack of any appraisal.

(c) Delusional beliefs, persecutory, jealous or grandiose.

(d) Abnormal perceptions associated with delusional misinterpretation of events.

(e) Thinking so disordered as to prevent reasonable appraisal of the patient's situation or reasonable communication with others."

Further explanation of the above sections of the definition is given in Appendix 10.

18.36 We are of the opinion that these tests draw the line of criminal responsibility at a place and in a way to which medical witnesses can testify. But it has to be borne in mind that the mental conditions included in our definitions are of such severity that the causative links between the offence and the defendant's mental condition can safely be presumed; and it is necessary that such a mental condition, which is of itself to carry freedom from criminal responsibility, should be both justifiable to the public and also strictly defined. It is essential to exclude mild or incipient forms of psychosis; it is not a question of severe mental illness suffered to a slight degree. Moreover, the adoption of this definition necessarily turns over the test of criminal responsibility to medical opinion. But doctors are often, and understandably, mainly concerned for the welfare of the patient (in this case the offender), and may forget or even ignore the duty owed to the public in the enforcement of the criminal law. Stretching of the test because it is thought that criminal sanctions or the "stigma" of conviction may be anti-therapeutic must be guarded against. Strict definition in the form we propose is also required because simply to say "severe mental illness", or some general label such as "schizophrenia" would only produce all over again the situation which brought about the failure of the Durham formula (see paragraph 18.15). The psychiatrists would testify to the naked conclusion. Therefore factual tests to which doctors must depose, and on which the jury will determine, must be spelt out so that the jury (and everyone else) can be sure that the tests of legal responsibility are being complied with.

Therefore we also propose that these tests should be incorporated in the statute. To allow for adjustment in the light of future developments in the field of psychiatry or in the meanings of the terms used there should be power for the statutory definition to be revised by statutory instrument in accordance with medical and legal advice.

III. PROCEDURAL MATTERS

(1) The finding of the court

18.37   The result of our proposals is that the jury would be directed to return a verdict of "not guilty on evidence of mental disorder" if (1) they acquit the defendant solely because he is not proved to have had the state of mind necessary for the offence and they are satisfied on the balance of probability that at the time of the act or omission he was mentally disordered, or (2) they are satisfied on the balance of probability that at that time he was suffering from severe mental illness or severe subnormality (as defined by the judge in accordance with the definition in paragraph 18.35 so far as relevant to the evidence in the case).   The judge would be required not to leave (2) to the jury unless the defence is supported by the evidence of two psychiatrists, who must be medical practitioners approved by an Area Health Authority as having special experience in the diagnosis or treatment of mental disorders.   There would be an exception for certain transient states of mental disorder.   We do not propose that the jury should be required to find any causal connection between the act charged against the defendant and the mental disorder.   As we have explained in the preceding paragraph, in cases under (2) the causal connection can safely be presumed from the severity of the mental condition required.   In other cases there will nearly always be such a connection, but the inquiry to establish that it existed would be too difficult to be made.

18.38   For the avoidance of doubt, it should be enacted that a special verdict on one count in an indictment should, while it subsists, be a bar to conviction on any other count relating to the same offence, or of any alternative charge. For example, a special verdict on a charge of murder should be an end of the case; the jury would not be able to convict the defendant of manslaughter; and a special verdict on a charge of wounding with intent should bar a verdict of guilty of unlawful wounding.   The present law is not explicit on this, but in practice a conviction on a lesser charge is never recorded.

(2) The burden of proof

18.39   Under the present law the burden of proving the mental element is normally on the prosecution; but M'Naghten treats the burden of proving the "insanity" defence as resting on the defendant, and it is always assumed that this survives as an exception from the general rule.   It is difficult to understand how this can be.   If the defendant says that he thought he was shooting a fox when in fact he was shooting a baby, the burden of proving that he knew he was shooting a baby must rest on the prosecution, whether the defendant's mistake as to the "nature and quality of his act" was the result of "insanity" or not.   In our view, the burden of proving the requisite mental state should rest on the prosecution, and if the prosecution fail to prove this a verdict of not guilty must follow; but the problem of burden of proof still arises in relation to the choice between an absolute acquittal and a special verdict.   We think that in this situation, that is to say where the mental element has not been proved, the defendant should be entitled to an ordinary acquittal unless the jury are satisfied on the balance of probability that he was mentally disordered. This relates to the first limb of the special verdict (see paragraph 18.20). The second limb concerns the choice between a conviction and the special verdict, where the mental element has been proved but the defendant was suffering from severe mental illness or severe subnormality at the time of the act or omission charged (see paragraph 18.30). Since it would be confusing for the jury if they had to consider a different burden of proof of mental disorder in relation to the two limbs, we recommend that the same rule should be applied to the second limb, so that the jury would be directed to convict unless satisfied on the balance of probability that the defendant was suffering from severe mental illness or severe subnormality.

18.40   In other words, where the jury are satisfied that the defendant did the act or made the omission charged, but the prosecution have not proved the mental element, the special verdict may be brought in by the jury if they find that on the balance of probability the defendant was mentally disordered within the definition of section 4 of the Mental Health Act 1959 at the time; but if the prosecution have proved the mental element, the special verdict may be brought in only if the jury find that on the balance of probability the defendant was severely mentally ill or severely subnormal at the time. Where the special verdict is not brought in, it will follow that in cases where the mental element has not been established by the prosecution the defendant will be acquitted, whereas in those cases where the mental element has been established the defendant will be convicted.

18.41   In a complicated case, particularly one involving lesser included offences or defences of self-defence or provocation, it may be desirable, in view of the instructions that have to be given on the burden of proof, for the judge to request the jury to answer specific questions and to enter the appropriate verdict on the basis of their answers (a "special verdict" as opposed to a general verdict).

(3) Disposal

18.42   As explained in paragraph 18.2 above, the statutory provision which, long before M'Naghten, introduced the special verdict also provided that following upon the special verdict the court must commit the defendant to a hospital to be selected by the Home Secretary, there to remain until the Home Secretary authorises his discharge. In contrast, success in an ordinary defence of lack of *mens rea* leads to acquittal and release. If a defendant argues that he lacked *mens rea* without referring to "insanity", there is authority for saying that the prosecution are entitled to reply with evidence of "insanity", which if accepted will lead to a special verdict and mandatory commitment (paragraph 18.48). We propose that the powers of disposal of the court in the event of a special verdict should be the same discretionary powers as those already recommended for cases of disability in relation to the trial (see paragraph 10.29 above). While it is plainly right that success in an "insanity" defence should lead to a special verdict with consequential powers in the court, the absence of any judicial discretion as to the disposal of the defendant has caused difficulty. There have undoubtedly been cases in the past of people being sent to Broadmoor on an "insanity" defence although they did not present a danger to anyone. Practice has greatly improved, and patients are now wherever possible sent to a local hospital, from which in suitable cases they may be quickly discharged. Even so, there are cases where the medical evidence and the circumstances indicate that hospital treatment is not called for. Under our proposal the court would have power to make a hospital or guardianship order only when the normal requirements for these orders are met, including the appropriate medical recommendations.

18.43 The recommendation of the Criminal Law Revision Committee in their Third Report[23] (referred to in paragraph 10.27 above in connection with disability in relation to the trial) that the court should be empowered to order the immediate release of the defendant if satisfied that his detention in hospital was unnecessary, applied also to cases in which the special verdict was returned. During consideration of the draft Bill appended to the Committee's Report and based on the Committee's recommendations, which became the Criminal Procedure (Insanity) Act 1964, it was felt that there were objections to dividing the responsibility between the Home Secretary and the courts—a view shared by the Lord Chief Justice and the Queen's Bench Judges at that time. This proposal was therefore dropped. Under our recommendation the responsibility for disposal will rest wholly on the court and we think it right that in appropriate cases it should be possible for the court to order an absolute discharge.

18.44 There remain those defendants who receive a special verdict and who need a measure of supervision but who do not need to be sent to hospital. This may be because, although they were mentally disordered at the time of the act, their disorder has remitted or improved by the time of the court hearing so that a hospital order is by then inappropriate. If the test of the special verdict is amended in accordance with our recommendations, it is likely that a number of offenders who at present are dealt with on a defence of diminished responsibility will in future get a special verdict. At present only about half of those who are dealt with as "diminished" are sent to hospitals (see the table in paragraph 19.6), and diminished responsibility applies only where the offence is homicide. Moreover, it is foreseeable that as medical science improved, early relief of severe mental illness may become more frequent. This possible class of offender may therefore be of some material size; yet if they get special verdicts it will not be possible to impose any form of imprisonment, nor a probation order (with or without a condition for psychiatric treatment) for a probation order would lack any possibility of enforcement because the defendant cannot be sent to prison in the event of a breach of conditions. Something akin to a probation order, however, is needed.

18.45 Our proposal is that provision should be made for courts to make an order analogous to a hospital order with restrictions under section 65 of the Mental Health Act, under which the offender would not be detained in hospital but would be deemed to have been so detained. He would be discharged into the community with the status of an ordinary discharged section 65 patient. The normal conditions of after-care and recall to hospital would apply, so that if the supervising officer felt that the offender's mental condition and behaviour warranted such a course he would arrange for him to be "readmitted". It will be necessary to appoint a doctor to act as the responsible

---

[23] Cmnd. 2149, paragraph 34.

medical officer in these cases, who would be willing to accept the offender into hospital in the event of "recall". We would expect this doctor to be one of those giving medical evidence at the court hearing. It would be right for the court to use this power only when no other form of disposal allowed by the special verdict was appropriate.

(4) Instruction to the jury

18.46   It is not the normal practice for the judge to convey to the jury the scope of his powers of disposal, but we considered whether in this context such instruction might be appropriate in order to dispel any misconceptions on the part of the jury. It is possible that for some time to come juries might remain under the impression that the special verdict still automatically entailed committal to a psychiatric hospital, and it would be unfortunate if wrong verdicts came to be returned for this reason. In this special case it is arguable that the judge should be able to tell the jury the extent of his discretion as to disposal. We do not think necessary any statutory requirement to this effect, but it will be open to the judge if he thinks fit to explain the powers he possesses to the jury.

18.47   Since the court is, under our proposal, to be given a discretion as to disposal after a special verdict, we think there would be an advantage in the court being given a discretion also whether to instruct the jury as to the special verdict. (In the same way, magistrates should be given a discretion whether to instruct themselves.) For example, a woman who has been suffering from early dementia may be charged with shoplifting. Evidence is given for the defence that she has been in hospital and that her illness involves episodes of forgetfulness. This evidence is offered for the purpose of procuring an acquittal, and it is obvious that if the jury or magistrates are not satisfied that she intended to steal there should be an ordinary acquittal. Technically, however, the case might be thought to fall within the formula proposed above for the special verdict, since the evidence of dementia would be offered for the purpose of denying *mens rea*. The point could arise equally under the present law, because a woman who offered evidence of early dementia for the purpose of establishing that it was failure of memory on her part to walk out of a supermarket with goods that had not been paid for could, on a strict reading of the law, be regarded as setting up a defence of disease of the mind to show that she did not know the nature and quality of her act. Under our proposal, even if a special verdict were returned, the court would obviously discharge the defendant without conditions. It would be kinder to avoid the special verdict, and this could be done by the exercise of a discretion not to instruct the jury upon it. This would be consistent with the proposals we make in paragraphs 9.16–9.25 to relieve from the ordeal of an unnecessary court appearance persons in need of psychiatric treatment.

(5) Initiative in raising the mental issue

18.48   We do not propose any change in the general principle at present prevailing that the initiative in raising the issue of mental disorder, before verdict, rests with the defence. It would be too prejudicial to the defendant, when he denies committing the act charged, if the prosecution were allowed to adduce evidence that he is mentally disordered, perhaps for the purpose of showing that he is a person likely to have committed such a crime. However, it is the present law that when the defendant sets up a defence of diminished responsibility the prosecution may reply by showing that the case was in fact one of mental disorder[24]: and there is authority[25] for saying that whenever the defendant denies having had the requisite mental element (as when he says that he was intoxicated, or in a state of non-insane automatism, or that he made a reasonable mistake) the prosecution may reply with evidence of mental disorder in order to obtain a special verdict. We think that this is right. If the defendant admits doing the act and contests the case solely on his state of mind, it is right that all the evidence as to his state of mind can be given, and if the evidence is that he was mentally disordered when he did the act there should be a special verdict rather than an ordinary acquittal. The point should be made clear in legislation.

18.49 To facilitate the production by the prosecution of all relevant information as to the mental state of the defendant we propose that whenever the defence intend to adduce psychiatric or psychological evidence on the mental element—whether in relation to the special verdict or the defence of automatism—there should be a requirement that they should give advance notice of their intention to the prosecution, on conditions similar to those on which advance notice is required of a defence of alibi.[26] At present a defendant is not required to give advance notice of a defence of "insanity" or diminished responsibility, or of intention to adduce psychiatric evidence for the purpose of establishing a defence of mistake or accident (ie denying the mental element). It seems to us unsatisfactory that the defence should be able to produce psychiatric evidence of mental state going to questions of responsibility and disposal without having given the prosecution the opportunity to call evidence in rebuttal. If the disorder is serious the prosecution will already know about it and are unlikely to be taken by surprise by the defence. But this is not so where the defence is one of non-insane automatism, such as a state of dissociation. Advance notice is required by law in several American States and we think that it should be required here also, both in magistrates' courts and in the Crown Court. As in the case of the alibi defence we think that the court should have discretion to waive the requirement of advance notice where necessary. Otherwise in relation to proceedings in the Crown Court a time limit of seven days after committal within which notice must be given will not in our view be unreasonably onerous, and in relation to proceedings in magistrates' courts seven days' notice should be given.

18.50 At present the defendant is allowed to plead guilty to manslaughter by reason of diminished responsibility, but not to set up an "insanity" defence by plea. Moreover, if a mentally disordered person pleads guilty the conviction is likely to be quashed on appeal, because of the possibility that the plea was made under a mistake.[27] While possible dangers must be considered, we think that the balance of advantage is in favour of allowing a defendant who is not under disability at the time of the trial to plead "not guilty on evidence of mental disorder". The plea would not be accepted if the court had reason to believe that the defendant may be under disability in relation to the trial; in

---

[24] Criminal Procedure (Insanity) Act 1964, section 6.
[25] *Per* Lord Denning in *Bratty* v *Attorney-General for Northern Ireland* [1963] A.C. at 411-2.
[26] Criminal Justice Act 1967, section 11.
[27] *R* v *Forbes* [1968] 52 Cr. App. R. 585.

such circumstances the court would either determine his fitness to plead or make an interim hospital order (paragraphs 12.5–12.6). Acceptance of the plea would have the same effect as a special verdict. The plea would naturally be accepted if the prosecution and the court were satisfied that the defendant would be likely to receive a special verdict from the jury. In the unlikely event of the defendant being unrepresented the court would, we are sure, either not accept the plea or would accept it only after reading the committal statements or hearing witnesses to establish that the facts charged can be substantiated. Where the defendant is represented the procedure might have considerable value in enabling the hearing to be expedited, so that, if the defendant needs treatment, this may be started at the earliest moment. It may also avoid the giving of unpleasant evidence that may cause grave distress to the witnesses, their relatives, and to the defendant himself. Before such a plea is accepted it will be necessary for the prosecution case to be outlined in open court. The court will need medical reports in order to decide on the proper order to make. The judge may require either or both of the reporting medical practitioners to give oral evidence.

IV. OFFENCES COMMITTED WHILE INTOXICATED

18.51 Since our remit concerns mentally disordered offenders, it could be interpreted to include intoxicated offenders. In general we have not concerned ourselves with drunkenness and drug addiction, but we have made an exception for one topic, partly because it falls within the question of criminal responsibility with which we have been concerned, and partly because a solution of it is necessary for the purposes of the projected criminal code.

18.52 On a charge of an offence, the general principle is that the defendant may give evidence that he was intoxicated at the time, for the purpose of supporting a defence that he lacked the intent necessary for the alleged offence. Although the rule is clearly right on principle, it would, if logically applied, mean that a person who is habitually violent when in drink may escape any criminal charge. Of course, an intoxicated person will generally know well enough that he is making an attack on another, and if so he is subject to conviction; but the evidence of drunkenness may occasionally be sufficient to create a doubt in the minds of the jury or magistrates. The drunkard may also escape conviction on the argument that in his fuddled condition he mistakenly believed that he was being attacked,[28] and in Canada and Australia it has been held that a person charged with rape could give evidence of drunkenness for the purpose of supporting a defence that he believed that the woman was consenting, although no sober person would have believed it. The difficulty does not arise if death has been caused, because a charge of manslaughter does not require proof of an intent to kill or even to attack. Moreover, in order to avert a complete failure of the prosecution the courts have developed the doctrine that the offence of assault does not require a "specific intent" that can be rebutted by evidence of intoxication. However, the phrase "specific intent" has never been defined. The courts recognise that assault requires an intention to apply force to another or (possibly) recklessness as to such force,[29] so that it is illogical to exclude the evidence of intoxication on a charge of assault; and the practice

---

[28] *R v Gamlen* (1858), 1 F. & F. 50.
[29] *Fagan* v *Metropolitan Police Commissioner* [1969] 1 Q.B. 439.

is not immune from attack if an appeal is taken to the House of Lords, particularly because it seems to be directly contrary to section 8 of the Criminal Justice Act 1967.

18.53 In our view, the courts should be given by statute clear power to convict those who become violent when voluntarily intoxicated. The object is not necessarily to punish them. An alcoholic or drug addict may after conviction be persuaded to accept treatment. But not all these offenders are addicts (the violence may be committed on an occasional drunken spree), and in any case powers of punishment are necessary for those who will not accept treatment and who cannot otherwise be controlled.

18.54 We propose that it should be an offence for a person while voluntarily intoxicated to do an act (or make an omission) that would amount to a dangerous offence if it were done or made with the requisite state of mind for such offence. The prosecution would not charge this offence in the first instance, but would charge an offence under the ordinary law. If evidence of intoxication were given at the trial for the purpose of negativing the intention or other mental element required for the offence, the jury would be directed that they may return a verdict of not guilty of that offence but guilty of the offence of dangerous intoxication if they find that the defendant did the act (or made the omission) charged but by reason of the evidence of intoxication they are not sure that at the time he had the state of mind required for the offence, and they are sure that his intoxication was voluntary.

18.55 A dangerous offence for this purpose should be defined as one involving injury to the person (actual bodily harm) or death or consisting of a sexual attack on another, or involving the destruction of or causing damage to property so as to endanger life. A dangerous offence is to be regarded as charged if the jury can convict of it under the indictment.

18.56 "Voluntary intoxication" would be defined to mean intoxication resulting from the intentional taking of drink or a drug knowing that it is capable in sufficient quantity of having an intoxicating effect; provided that intoxication is not voluntary if it results in part from a fact unknown to the defendant that increases his sensitivity to the drink or drug. The concluding words would provide a defence to a person who suffers from hypoglycaemia, for example, who does not know that in that condition the ingestion of a small amount of alcohol can produce a state of altered consciousness, as well as to a person who has been prescribed a drug on medical grounds without warning of the effect it may produce. We do not think it necessary to define intoxication, drink or drug, because this offence would be a fall-back offence, relevant only when the defendant has been acquitted on another charge by reason of evidence of intoxication.

18.57 These provisions would mean that the offence would be one of strict liability (not requiring proof of a mental element or other fault) in respect of the objectionable behaviour, but would require the fault element of becoming voluntarily intoxicated. A mistaken belief in a circumstance of excuse (such as that the victim was about to attack so that the force was necessary by way of defence, or that the victim consented) would not be a defence unless a sober person might have made the same mistake.

236

18.58 We have not found the recommendation of an appropriate penalty altogether an easy matter. If the penalty is too severe it becomes unfair. On the other hand, if it is too light then in cases such as wounding with intent to cause grievous bodily harm (where in everyday experience in the courts the vast majority of defendants blame drink for their actions) the existence of a "fall-back" verdict will encourage time-consuming unsuccessful defences to be run in inappropriate cases. On balance, we have come to the view that on conviction on indictment of dangerous intoxication the defendant should be liable to imprisonment for one year for a first offence or for three years on a second or subsequent offence. It should be left to the judge to satisfy himself that the offence is a second or subsequent one. On summary trial the maximum sentence of imprisonment should be six months. Magistrates who try an information for one of the dangerous offences should be enabled to convict of dangerous intoxication without a fresh information. In considering the scale of punishment, it must be realised that we are not proposing an arrangement whereby drunken offenders obtain the benefit of a reduced punishment. The new offence is needed only when the defendant has been acquitted of the offence originally charged, so that apart from the new offence he would not be subject to any control. There would be no injustice to the defendant in providing for the possibility of conviction of dangerous intoxication as an alternative charge, because the evidence of intoxication would have been produced by him at the trial in answer to the main charge. In our view, it should be made obligatory on the defendant to give the same notice of his evidence of intoxication as we propose in relation to evidence of mental disorder (paragraph 18.49). It should also be provided, as we recommend in paragraph 18.48, that if the defendant gives evidence contesting his state of mind the prosecution may reply with evidence of mental disorder.

18.59 It may well be that the new offence should ultimately be included in a new Offences against the Person Act, but we hope that as an interim measure it will be included in any legislation passed to give effect to our recommendations, should that come before Parliament before the Criminal Law Revision Committee has completed its work on offences against the person.

THE SPECIAL VERDICT
SUMMARY OF CONCLUSIONS

I. Preliminary considerations

1. Provision should continue to be made for exemption from criminal responsibility for mentally disordered offenders but the M'Naghten Rules are not a satisfactory test and in any case a revised formula will be required for inclusion in the Criminal Code which is being drafted by the Law Commission. (Paragraphs 18.1–18.10.)

2. We do not regard as practicable or desirable arrangements for "two-stage" trial, in which the "facts" are pronounced upon first, or the question of guilt is decided, before the psychiatric evidence on the defendant's mental condition is heard. (Paragraphs 18.11–18.13.)

II. The revised special verdict

3. We do not favour solutions based on the "Durham" formula or the American Law Institute's Model Penal Code. (Paragraphs 18.14–18.16.)

4. We propose a new formulation of the special verdict, namely "not guilty on evidence of mental disorder", the grounds for which should comprise two elements: (*a*) a *mens rea* element approximating to the first limb of the M'Naghten Rules ("Did he know what he was doing?"); (*b*) specific exemption from conviction for defendants suffering, at the time of the act or omission charged, from severe mental illness or severe subnormality. (Paragraphs 18.17–18.18.)

5. Magistrates' courts should be allowed to return the special verdict. It will not be necessary to retain section 60(2) of the Mental Health Act. (Paragraph 18.19.)

The first element

6. The jury (or magistrates) should return a verdict of "not guilty on evidence of mental disorder" if they find that the defendant did the act or made the omission charged but (by reason of the evidence of mental disorder) they do not find that the state of mind required for the offence has been proved and they further find that on the balance of probability the defendant was mentally disordered at the time. (Paragraph 18.20.)

7. The first element would apply to any mental disorder but should exclude transient states not related to other forms of mental disorder and arising solely as a consequence of the administration, mal-administration or non-administration of alcohol, drugs or other substances, or from physical injury. All other cases now regarded as non-insane automatism would be within the special verdict. Thus the distinction between conditions which are now legally regarded as "insanity" and those dealt with as "non-insane automatism" would be clearly drawn. (Paragraphs 18.22–18.23.)

8. The M'Naghten "knowledge of wrong" test should not be included in terms in the new special verdict, but it will be covered in substance in the second element. (Paragraph 18.24.)

9. The new formulation of the first element may have the effect of widening the scope of the special verdict to cover certain categories of mentally disordered persons (including the subnormal) who would now obtain a complete acquittal; but under our recommendations the court's discretionary powers of disposal will enable account to be taken of the individual circumstances of each case. (Paragraph 18.25.)

The second element

10. We recommend that statutory exemption from punishment should be provided for defendants who, although they were suffering from severe mental disorder at the time of the act or omission charged, do not come within the compass of the first element because they were able to form intentions and carry them out. We propose that the special verdict in the terms set out in Conclusion 6 above should be returned if at the time of the act or omission charged the offender was suffering from severe mental illness or severe subnormality. We suggest a definition of severe mental illness, which we propose should be incorporated in the statute, subject to the possibility of revision by statutory instrument. (Paragraphs 18.26–18.36.)

238

III. Procedural matters

11. The first and second elements of the special verdict should be combined in one decision to be made by the jury. The judge should not leave the decision on the second element to the jury unless the defence is supported by the evidence of two psychiatrists, who must be medical practitioners approved by an Area Health Authority as having special experience in the diagnosis or treatment of mental disorder. The jury should not be required to find any causal connection between the act charged and the mental disorder. (Paragraph 18.37.)

12. It should be provided by statute that the special verdict should, while it subsists, be a bar to conviction on any other count relating to the same offence or of any alternative charge. (Paragraph 18.38.)

13. In relation to the first element of the special verdict, the burden of proving the requisite mental state should rest on the prosecution. In the choice between an absolute acquittal and the special verdict the defendant should be entitled to an ordinary acquittal unless the jury are satisfied on the balance of probability that he was mentally disordered. In relation to the second element, in the choice between a conviction and the special verdict the jury should be directed to convict unless satisfied on the balance of probability that the defendant was suffering from severe mental illness or severe subnormality. In complicated cases it may be desirable for the judge to request the jury to answer specific questions and to enter the appropriate verdict on the basis of their answers. (Paragraphs 18.39–18.41.)

14. For disposal following a special verdict the courts should have the same discretionary powers as those recommended in paragraph 10.29 for cases of disability in relation to the trial. Hospital or guardianship orders should be made only when the normal requirements for these orders, including medical recommendations, are met. In appropriate cases it should be open to the courts to order an absolute discharge. Courts should be able to make an order analogous to a hospital order with restrictions under section 65 of the Mental Health Act, placing the offender in the community under supervision, for those cases where admission to hospital is not needed but where a measure of supervision with power of "recall" to hospital is required. (Paragraphs 18.42–18.45.)

15. To avoid any misapprehension by the jury that the new special verdict would still, as now, automatically entail committal to hospital, it might be desirable for the judge to explain to the jury his powers of disposal. (Paragraph 18.46.)

16. The initiative in raising the issue of mental disorder, before verdict, should remain with the defence except that where the defendant admits doing the act and contests the case solely on his state of mind (for instance, by claiming that he was intoxicated or in a state of non-insane automatism) the prosecution may reply with evidence of mental disorder in order to obtain a special verdict rather than a complete acquittal. (Paragraph 18.47.)

17. The defence should be required to give advance notice to the prosecution of their intention to adduce medical evidence and raise the mental issue. In Crown Court proceedings notice should be given within seven days of committal, and in magistrates' courts, seven days' advance notice should be given. As with the alibi defence, the courts should have discretion to waive the requirement of advance notice. (Paragraph 18.48.)

18.   A defendant should be able to set up a plea of "not guilty on evidence of mental disorder".   Acceptance of the plea would have the same effect as the special verdict.   Special care should be taken in accepting the plea when the defendant is unrepresented or when it is thought that he might be under disability.   The doctors giving medical evidence may be required to do so orally.   (Paragraphs 18.49—18.50.)

IV.   Offences committed while intoxicated

19.   We suggest measures to deal with people who become violent when voluntarily intoxicated.   We propose that it should be an offence for a person while voluntarily intoxicated to do an act (or make an omission) that would amount to a dangerous offence if it were done or made with the requisite state of mind for such offence.   The offence would not be charged in the first instance but the jury would be directed to find on this offence in the event of intoxication being successfully raised as a defence to the offence originally charged.   We define "dangerous" and "voluntary intoxication" for this purpose.   We suggest penalties for the new offence.   (Paragraphs 18.51–18.59.)

CHAPTER 19

DIMINISHED RESPONSIBILITY AND INFANTICIDE

(1) Introduction

19.1   The doctrine of diminished responsibility had been developed in Scotland for more than a century before its eventual incorporation in the English law of homicide.[1]   The Royal Commission on Capital Punishment 1949–53 considered at some length the proposal that the concept should be introduced into England, but they forbore to make any recommendation on the matter, which they regarded as a general question going beyond their own terms of reference.[2] The Royal Commission's preferred proposal, that in capital cases the jury should be given discretion to find the accused guilty of the offence, but with extenuating circumstances, a finding which would bind the judge to impose a sentence of life imprisonment, was not accepted by the Government of the day, but in a debate on capital punishment in 1956 the Home Secretary undertook to consider the question of diminished responsibility further.   This resulted in section 2(1) of the Homicide Act 1957, which provides that:

"Where a person kills or is party to the killing of another, he shall not be convicted of murder if he was suffering from such abnormality of mind (whether arising from a condition of arrested or retarded development of mind or any inherent causes or induced by disease or injury) as substantially impaired his mental responsibility for his acts and omissions in doing or being a party to the killing."

19.2   The issue of diminished responsibility (as it is called in a marginal note to the section) must be raised by the defence, except that where the defendant contends that at the time of the alleged offence he was insane it is open to the prosecution to adduce or elicit evidence tending to prove that he was not insane but suffering from diminished responsibility.[3]   The onus of proof on the balance of probability also rests on the defence. If the defence is accepted by the jury, a person who would otherwise have been liable to be convicted of murder is liable instead to be convicted of manslaughter, the sentence for which is entirely at the discretion of the court, from life imprisonment down to absolute discharge.

19.3   An earlier and limited example of a special provision for reduced responsibility and the possibility of a lesser penalty (while not necessarily exempting altogether from punishment) is to be found in the Infanticide Act 1938.   This Act, which re-enacted (with amendment) the Infanticide Act 1922, deals with the special case of the woman who causes the death of her child under 12 months and provides that, where the court is satisfied that the balance of her mind has been disturbed by reason of her not having fully recovered from the effect of giving birth to the child or by reason of the effect of lactation consequent upon the birth, she is guilty of infanticide and may be dealt with and punished as for manslaughter rather than murder.   This again means that the sentence is entirely at the discretion of the court.   We discuss the Infanticide Act further in paragraphs 19.22–19.26 below.

[1] See Nigel Walker, *Crime and Insanity in England* (Edinburgh, 1973), Vol. 1, Chapter 8.
[2] Cmnd. 8932, paragraph 413.
[3] Criminal Procedure (Insanity) Act 1964, section 6.

241

(2) Operation of existing provision as to diminished responsibility

19.4 It will be apparent that the extent of the diminished responsibility provision in section 2 of the Homicide Act 1957 largely turns on the meaning to be attached to the phrase "abnormality of mind". The courts are ready to give it the widest possible meaning. In the case of *Byrne*,[4] the then Lord Chief Justice (Lord Parker) defined "abnormality of mind" in the following terms:

". . . a state of mind so different from that of ordinary human beings that the reasonable man [earlier defined as 'a man with a normal mind'] would term it abnormal. It appears to us to be wide enough to cover the mind's activities in all its aspects, not only the perception of physical acts and matters, and the ability to form a rational judgment as to whether the act was right or wrong, but also the ability to exercise will-power to control physical acts in accordance with that rational judgment."

This direction was held to be "authoritative and correct" in *Rose* v *R*[5] and has been followed in subsequent cases. The provision is still not without difficulties, however, and HM Judges expressed the opinion to us in their evidence that section 2 of the Homicide Act embodies a concept which is easier to grasp than to define. They suggested that it "might be broadly, if not wholly accurately in law, expressed by saying that, if the jury think on the evidence before them that the defendant has shown recognisably abnormal mental symptoms and that in all the circumstances it would not be right to regard his act as murder in the ordinary sense, it is open to them to bring in a verdict of manslaughter".

19.5 The wording of section 2, as the Judges readily conceded, is open to criticism from several aspects. "Abnormality of mind" is an extremely imprecise phrase, even as limited by the parentheses and defined by the Court of Appeal (see the foregoing paragraph). "Mental responsibility", a phrase not to be found elsewhere in any statute, has created difficulty both for doctors and for jurors. It is either a concept of law or a concept of morality; it is not a clinical fact relating to the defendant. "Legal responsibility" means liability to conviction (and success in a defence of diminished responsibility does not save the defendant from conviction of manslaughter); "moral responsibility" means liability to moral censure (but moral questions do not normally enter into the definition of a crime). It seems odd that psychiatrists should be asked and agree to testify as to legal or moral responsibility. It is even more surprising that courts are prepared to hear that testimony. Yet psychiatrists commonly testify to impaired "mental responsibility" under section 2. Several medical witnesses pointed out to us that the difficulty is made worse by the use of the word "substantial". The idea that ability to conform to the law can be measured is particularly puzzling. (See the discussion in paragraph 18.16.) Despite the difficulties of the section in relation to psychiatry the medical profession is humane and the evidence is often stretched, as a number of witnesses remarked.[6] Not only psychopathic personality but reactive depressions and dissociated states have been testified to be due to "inherent causes" within the section.

---

[4] [1960] 44 Cr. App. R. 246.

[5] [1961] 45 Cr. App. R. 102 (Judicial Committee of the Privy Council).

[6] Some of the problems presented to psychiatrists by the existence of diminished responsibility as a defence are discussed by Dr W Lindesay Neustatter, "Psychiatric Aspects of Diminished Responsibility in Murder", *Medico-Legal Journal*, 101 (1960), 92–101.

19.6   It would be wrong, however, to suppose that success in a defence of diminished responsibility ensures a lenient disposal.   The table below shows the disposal of those found guilty of manslaughter under section 2 of the Homicide Act 1957 in the four years 1970–1973.

Hospital Order under section 60 of the Mental Health Act 1959 ...	27
Hospital Order together with Restriction Order under section 65 of the Mental Health Act 1959 (all without limit of time)	126
Life imprisonment	40
Other terms of imprisonment	52
Probation	35
Otherwise dealt with	10
TOTAL ...	290

Hospital orders were made in over half the cases and of these the vast majority were made with a restriction order without limit of time.[7]   Imprisonment accounted for a little under a third of the offenders, and almost half of those sent to prison (some 14 per cent of the grand total) were sentenced to life imprisonment.   Thus, over half the total number of offenders (those made subject to a section 65 order together with those sentenced to life imprisonment) were subject to indefinite detention, their release requiring the approval of the Home Secretary.   We were told in evidence by the Home Office that a man imprisoned for life on conviction of manslaughter after a finding of diminished responsibility may in the event be detained longer, because of the doubts cast on his mental condition, than men given a mandatory life sentence on conviction of murder, and we accept the occasional need for this.

19.7   Although the outcome of a successful defence under section 2 is generally a hospital order or prison sentence, cases which have been felt to merit sympathetic consideration have resulted in more lenient disposal.   The main examples relate to killing in compassion or from jealousy.   There have been several cases where a father has killed his severely handicapped infant; he is charged with murder, medical evidence of a reactive depression is given, the verdict is one of diminished responsibility, and a lenient sentence is passed, sometimes involving only a psychiatric probation order.   There have also been cases of morbid jealousy where an elderly woman has killed her husband, rightly or wrongly believing that he is being unfaithful, and where again the sentence, after a verdict of diminished responsibility, has been a probation order.   Sometimes depression and jealousy can properly be diagnosed as mental disorders; but the distinction between conditions which can be so diagnosed and normal depression or normal jealousy may be one of degree only, and the effect of the present law is to put strong pressure on the psychiatrist to conform his medical opinion to the exigency of avoiding a very severe sentence, fixed by law, for a person for whom everyone has the greatest sympathy.

---

[7] As to the duration of detention under hospital orders, see footnote to paragraph 14.17; and as regards hospital orders with restriction orders, see paragraph 7.23.

(3) The case for abolition of diminished responsibility and of the mandatory life sentence

19.8   In setting out the arguments in favour of the concept of diminished responsibility, the Royal Commission on Capital Punishment made two main points:

> "It must be accepted that there is no sharp dividing line between sanity and insanity, but that the two extremes of 'sanity' and 'insanity' shade into one another by imperceptible gradations.   The degree of individual responsibility varies equally widely; no clear boundary can be drawn between responsibility and irresponsibility . . .   The acceptance of the doctrine of diminished responsibility would undoubtedly bring the law into closer harmony with the facts and would enable the courts to avoid passing sentence of death in numerous cases in which it will not be carried out".[8]

With the abolition of capital punishment for murder this last justification has disappeared.   The case for the plea of diminished responsibility now rests largely on the fact that precisely because there is a fixed sentence of life imprisonment for murder there should be some way for the court to avoid it in cases where there is evidence of mental disorder.   Diminished responsibility is a special device for, as it were, untying the hands of the judge in murder cases.   Although it has the subsidiary advantage of avoiding stigmatising as murderers certain individuals who may not be fully responsible for their actions, we think that the need for its continuance depends essentially on whether the fixed sentence of life imprisonment for murder is itself to remain.

19.9   It is true that the suggestion is sometimes made that diminished responsibility should be extended to other offences.   The Royal Commission contemplated the possibility, and a few of our witnesses urged us to consider such a step.   But if this provision is needed only where an offence carries a mandatory penalty, its extension to offences other than murder would not be justified.   The courts have a wide range of powers for dealing appropriately with mentally disordered offenders convicted of offences other than murder, whether by penal sentence or by orders requiring medical treatment.   It is noteworthy that in Scotland, the original home of the provision, it is applied only to murder.

19.10   The penalty for murder is at present under consideration by the Criminal Law Revision Committee in the context of their review of offences against the person.   The Committee published an Interim Report[9] on this subject in January 1973, which concluded, provisionally, that the mandatory life sentence should be retained, subject to further consideration being given to the proposal that in certain tragic cases of murder a judge should be able to make a hospital order, or a probation order, or order a conditional discharge, where he is satisfied that it would be contrary to the interests of justice for the accused to serve any sentence of imprisonment.   In the course of our review we have received a good deal of evidence bearing upon these conclusions of the Criminal Law Revision Committee, and while we acknowledge that the question of the mandatory life sentence is for that Committee, not us, to consider, we are

---

[8] Cmd. 8932, paragraph 411.

[9] Cmnd. 5184.

properly concerned with the implications of the life sentence for the legal provisions on diminished responsibility and infanticide. We think it right therefore to make some observations on this matter.

19.11 The evidence we have received leads us to think that many in the legal profession and other professions associated with the law believe in the abolition of the mandatory life sentence and in giving the courts the widest possible discretionary powers in sentencing. Our impression is that such a change is seldom advocated publicly because of the fear that it will be unlikely to commend itself to public opinion. The main points made to us against the mandatory life sentence for murder are as follows:

(a) There are cases of murder that can be adequately dealt with by a determinate sentence, and it is cruel to give a life sentence if there is no social justification for it. Prison Medical Officers state that this often induces a sense of hopelessness in the prisoner and makes him difficult to deal with.

(b) The use of the life sentence in cases that do not really call for it dilutes what should be the awe-inspiring nature of this sentence.

(c) In support of the mandatory sentence it is said that the trial judge cannot be trusted to decide when it will be safe to let the defendant out.[10] This argument seems quite inconsistent with the fact that when the defendant is mentally unstable he can set up a plea of diminished responsibility and if he is successful in this the judge will have a discretion. If judges may be trusted with discretion with regard to disordered killers who are the most unpredictable kind, then, *a fortiori*, they can be trusted to sentence normal persons who may have killed only in exceptional circumstances of great stress.

(d) To enable the trial judge to show humanity in cases involving mental disorder medical witnesses sometimes have to stretch their conscience in testifying under section 2 of the Homicide Act.

(e) The diminished responsibility provision relates in practice to disposal, a matter for the judge rather than the jury. It may be prejudicial to the defence to have to bring out before verdict matters relating to the mental condition of the defendant, and the prejudice will be all the greater if medical witnesses testifying have to refer in detail to the defendant's unstable past.

(f) Because of the role of the jury in considering the medical evidence the diminished responsibility provision is not available to the man who has a mental disorder within the terms of the section but denies that he committed the act alleged against him. If his defence fails the sentence must be one of life imprisonment, notwithstanding that evidence of diminished responsibility could be given; he has ruled himself out of psychiatric disposal.

19.12 We are in no doubt that in many murder cases a life sentence is inappropriate and may be inhumane. Fairly common examples which, but for the defence of diminished responsibility, would attract a mandatory life sentence are the devoted and respectable husband who kills his wife and

---

[10] Cmnd. 5184, paragraph 16.

children while severely depressed, and the woman recently widowed or undergoing the menopause who kills her children. The defendant may have recovered from the mental disorder before the trial, and this is likely to become increasingly common as medical treatment, aided by new drugs, is developed.

19.13 The Criminal Law Revision Committee have considered the determinate sentence as an alternative to the mandatory life sentence,[11] but the alternative we propose would be complete discretion for the judge whether to impose a life sentence or some other sentence. The life sentence should remain available. (We do not go into the question whether, if the judge does not impose a life sentence, but sentences for a fixed term, there should be a statutory limit on this term, this matter being beyond our terms of reference.)

(4) Solutions
(i) Our first choice
19.14 In the light of these considerations our own decided preference would be for the abolition of the mandatory life sentence for murder and abolition of diminished responsibility. The Criminal Law Revision Committee have, as we have indicated above, expressed their provisional conclusion that the mandatory life sentence should remain. In reaching a final conclusion on the matter we hope that the Committee will take into account the many expressions of opinion we have received against the mandatory sentence from doctors and others concerned with the penal process. We have already communicated some of these arguments (which we list in paragraph 19.11 above) to the Committee but we have thought it appropriate to refer to them in this Report.

19.15 An argument that is sometimes maintained against the abolition of the mandatory life sentence is that such a step would involve accepting the merger of murder and manslaughter in one offence. There would be little justification for having two separate offences, each carrying the same range of penalties, where an allegation of murder necessarily involves an allegation of manslaughter. Public opinion, it is said, would be strongly against such a merger, which, by removing the special stigma attaching to a conviction for murder, might be thought to weaken the protection given to the public against those who kill. We do not accept the premise upon which this argument is based, since it would in our view remain feasible to continue to regard murder and manslaughter as separate offences, just as at present infanticide and manslaughter, while carrying the same penalty, remain distinct. If it were thought necessary to differentiate the penalty, this could be done by making murder punishable with a (discretionary) life sentence, while manslaughter could be punishable either with a determinate sentence up to a statutory maximum or in appropriate cases with a reviewable sentence in accordance with our proposal in paragraphs 4.39–4.45. On the other hand, some manslaughters may be more culpable than some murders which may have mitigating circumstances. This was indeed pointed out recently by Lord Kilbrandon in delivering his judgment in the case of Hyam.[12]

---

[11] Cmnd. 5184, paragraphs 14–19.

[12] "It is no longer true, if it ever was true, to say that murder, as we now define it, is necessarily the most heinous example of unlawful homicide". [1974] 2 All ER 72–3.

19.16   As regards the abolition of diminished responsibility it is sometimes objected that this would leave the stigma of an unqualified conviction of murder for people who at present receive a verdict of manslaughter by reason of diminished responsibility.   This point could be met if on a charge of murder the jury were empowered to return a verdict of murder (or manslaughter) by reason of extenuating circumstances, the extenuation being left undefined by law.   In cases where such a verdict was returned the sentencing powers of the judge would be identical to those for an unqualified conviction of murder (or manslaughter).

(ii) *Our second choice*

19.17   If the mandatory life sentence is in the event to be retained, we would wish to keep section 2 of the Homicide Act in its essentials but we recommend an improvement in the wording.   We point out in paragraph 19.5 above that the present wording of section 2 gives rise to difficulties of interpretation. We propose the following rewording which would remove some of the difficulties but not materially alter the practical effect of the section:

> "Where a person kills or is party to the killing of another, he shall not be convicted of murder if there is medical or other evidence that he was suffering from a form of mental disorder as defined in section 4 of the Mental Health Act 1959 and if, in the opinion of the jury, the mental disorder was such as to be an extenuating circumstance which ought to reduce the offence to manslaughter."

This would be consistent with our approach to the special verdict.   By tying the section to the definition of mental disorder in the Mental Health Act the formula provides a firm base for the testifying psychiatrists to diagnose and comment on the defendant's mental state, whilst it leaves the jury to decide the degree of extenuation that the mental disorder merits.   In theory the omission of the reference to the impairment of mental responsibility would slightly widen the defence but that would not in our view matter because if the judge thought that the disorder was not such as would justify either a medical disposal or a mitigated penal disposal, it would still be open to him to give the life sentence.   Under our proposal in paragraphs 4.39–4.45 it would sometimes be open to the judge to give a reviewable sentence instead of a life sentence.   In such a case the main objection to the section would remain, namely that to examine the issue of mental disorder at length before the jury and then, when they have brought in a verdict of "diminished responsibility", to end up with the same sentence as if there had been a verdict of murder, may be misunderstood.   If the suggested amendment in section 2 is made, the marginal note will need to be reworded to refer to "persons suffering from mental disorder".

19.18   Section 2(2) of the Homicide Act places the burden of proving a defence of diminished responsibility upon the defendant.   This follows the analogy of the defence of insanity under M'Naghten.   We have made fresh proposals with regard to the burden of proof under the reformulated special verdict (see paragraphs 18.39–18.41) and we recommend that the only burden resting on the defendant in the proposed reworded defence of mental disorder under section 2 should be that of adducing evidence to raise the issue.

19.19 Notwithstanding the burden of proof placed upon the defendant by section 2(2), it has been held that on a charge of murder a plea of guilty to manslaughter on account of diminished responsibility may be accepted by the court.[13] In giving evidence before us, HM Judges thought that where the question of diminished responsibility was in issue between the defence and the prosecution it should be decided by a jury, reflecting as they do the views of the public on a matter of great public importance. Where, however, the medical evidence is unanimous in showing plainly that the case is one of diminished responsibility they thought that the present practice of accepting, if tendered, a plea of guilty to manslaughter avoids what might otherwise become an unnecessary trial for murder with all the distress and expense which would inevitably be involved. We accept this view, and we recommend that in addition it should be regarded as a proper practice, where the prosecution are in possession of evidence indicating that a defence under the section can be made out, for them to charge manslaughter in the first instance rather than murder. This could probably be done, for example, where a woman has killed her child in tragic circumstances, the case either falling outside the offence of infanticide (eg because the child is over the specified age) or that offence having been abolished in accordance with our recommendation in paragraph 19.26. The prosecution would be likely to adopt this course only when it is clear that the defence are agreeable to it. If the defence wish to resist evidence of mental disorder the charge should be of murder, as now.

(iii) *Our third choice*

19.20 A less satisfactory alternative, if the mandatory sentence is to remain, is that the provision for diminished responsibility under section 2 of the Homicide Act should go, but on a conviction of murder the judge should have the discretion, where the appropriate medical evidence is forthcoming, to make a hospital order or a probation order with a condition of psychiatric treatment, in place of awarding the life sentence. The judge would still not be allowed to sentence for a fixed term or to give a discharge. However, once the principle of a mandatory sentence is breached there is then no reason for preventing the full exercise of judicial discretion. Also the defendant, who may have been severely disordered at the time of the offence, may have recovered by the time of the trial, in which case a hospital order could not be made and a psychiatric probation order would be inappropriate.

19.21 If the mandatory life sentence and, therefore, some form of the "diminished responsibility" provision are to remain, we recommend that the proposals we have made in connection with the special verdict (see paragraph 18.49) for advance notice to be given by the defence of their intention to adduce psychiatric evidence should also apply in "diminished responsibility" cases.

(5) Infanticide

19.22 We turn now to consider the future of the Infanticide Act 1938, which, as explained in paragraph 19.3, provides a special offence based on the concept of diminished responsibility for the purpose of avoiding a conviction of murder or manslaughter. Although the maximum penalty on conviction of infanticide

---

[13] *Cox* [1968] 1 W.L.R. at 310.

is imprisonment for life, in practice the mother who has killed her child is almost invariably treated very leniently. It seems unlikely that the Infanticide Act would have been passed if the defence of diminished responsibility had been recognised at that time, since the latter defence is so widely interpreted that it would in practice cover all cases of infanticide by a woman whose balance of mind is disturbed. There would be little difficulty, in our view, in regarding such mental disturbance as "arising from . . . inherent causes" within the meaning of section 2(1) of the Homicide Act (or as a form of mental disorder as defined in section 4 of the Mental Health Act under the substitution proposed in paragraph 19.17 above), even though it was precipitated by giving birth. There is, therefore, an argument for abolishing the offence of infanticide in order to rationalise and simplify the law.

19.23 The medical principles on which the Infanticide Act is based may no longer be relevant. The theory behind the Act was that childbirth produced a hormonal disorder which caused mental illness. But puerperal psychoses are now regarded as no different from others, childbirth being only a precipitating factor. Minor forms of mental illness following childbirth are common, but psychoses, which usually occur in the first month, are much less so (between 1 and 2 per 1,000 deliveries). The danger to the infant in the acute stages is well recognised and guarded against in the provisions made for the care of such cases. Mental illness is probably no longer a significant cause of infanticide. Dr D J West, who studied cases where married women had killed their children, found no particular association with this period.[14] The operative factors in child killing are often the stress of having to care for the infant, who may be unwanted or difficult, and personality problems; to some extent these affect the father as well as the mother and are not restricted to a year after the birth.

19.24 Perhaps the most impressive evidence we have had on the subject of infanticide is from the Governor and Staff of Holloway Prison, which is worth quoting at length:

"The disturbance of the 'balance of mind' that the Act requires can rarely be said to arise directly from incomplete recovery from the effects of childbirth, and even less so from the effects of lactation. Infanticide due to pueperal psychotic illness is rare. The type of infanticide where the child is killed immediately after birth and which is usually associated with illegitimate concealed pregnancies is also very uncommon. Most cases of child murder dealt with by the courts as infanticide are examples of the battered child syndrome in which the assault has had fatal consequences and the child is aged under 12 months. A combination of environmental stress and personality disorder with low frustration tolerance are the usual aetiological factors in such cases, and the relationship to 'incomplete recovery from the effects of childbirth or lactation' specified in the Infanticide Act is often somewhat remote. The Act is nevertheless nearly always invoked in cases of maternal filicide when the victim is aged under 12 months, in order to reduce the charge from murder to manslaughter. The illogical operation of the Act is illustrated by the fact that an exactly similar type of case where the victim happens to be over the age of

---

[14] D J West, *Murder followed by suicide* (London, 1965), 147.

12 months can no longer be dealt with as infanticide . . . We consider that the repeal of the mandatory penalty for murder would make the Infanticide Act unnecessary."

19.25 The Infanticide Act is open to other criticisms. When a charge is brought under the Act, the charge by its very nature admits that the woman's act was done while the balance of her mind was disturbed so that this is not in issue, and the outcome is likely to be lenient. But the Act does not extend to the woman who does not succeed in killing her child, but merely injures it; nor does it save her from being charged with and possibly convicted of the murder of an older child killed at the same time as the new baby, since the protection given by the Act is withdrawn the day after the child reached the age of 12 months (although it would be open to her to plead diminished responsibility in respect of such a charge). The Director of Public Prosecutions has expressed anxiety to us on this point.

19.26 The Infanticide Act offers the woman two advantages over the law of diminished responsibility. First, it allows the prosecution to charge infanticide, out of kindness, rather than having to proceed on a charge of murder. In contrast, the prosecution according to the present practice do not charge manslaughter by reason of diminished responsibility, but charge murder and wait for the accused to set up diminished responsibility as a defence. We have already recommended in paragraph 19.19 that the prosecution should feel free to charge manslaughter by reason of mental disorder in a proper case. Secondly, by charging infanticide the prosecution concede the mental disturbance which the woman will not have to prove. It is true that on a charge of murder the defendant may plead guilty to manslaughter, and if this plea is accepted the defendant will not have to prove diminished responsibility. But the judge must assent to acceptance of the plea by the prosecution, which he may not do if he sees no evidence of mental disorder. By charging infanticide the prosecution in effect tie the hands of the judge. If our previous proposal is accepted, the prosecution by charging manslaughter will put the defendant in the same favourable position as that provided by the Infanticide Act. In these circumstances, we see no reason why the Infanticide Act should be continued. There may be argument whether a conviction of manslaughter is more or less stigmatic than one of infanticide, but we do not regard the verbal point as important.

(6) Conclusion

19.27 To sum up, the only substantial justification for maintaining the existing provision for a finding of diminished responsibility appears to us to be the continued existence of the mandatory life sentence for murder. This is the first question to be considered, and our view is that there is a strong case for leaving the judge free to suit the sentence and disposal to the circumstances. Were this change not to be made we think that a section on the lines of section 2 of the Homicide Act relating to diminished responsibility must remain, though the defence would depend on mental disorder and not upon diminished responsibility under the amendment we propose in paragraph 19.17. It would not be necessary to continue the present offence of infanticide, if it is recognised that the prosecution can properly charge manslaughter with mental disorder.

DIMINISHED RESPONSIBILITY AND INFANTICIDE

SUMMARY OF CONCLUSIONS

1. The present provision relating to diminished responsibility is unsatisfactory. (Paragraphs 19.5–19.7.)

2. The provision for diminished responsibility is needed only because the offence of murder carries a mandatory life sentence. Its extension to offences other than murder is not justified. The need for its continuance depends on whether the fixed sentence of life imprisonment for murder is to remain. This is a question for the Criminal Law Revision Committee, but there are strong arguments against the fixed sentence, and because it stands in the way of the recommendations we wish to make within our remit we have thought it necessary to state them. (Paragraphs 19.8–19.13.)

3. Our preferred solution would be the abolition of the mandatory life sentence for murder, and of the provision for diminished responsibility which would then be unnecessary. We have suggested answers to possible objections. (Paragraphs 19.14–19.16.)

4. If the foregoing solution is rejected some form of "diminished responsibility" should remain, but we propose revision of section 2 of the Homicide Act 1957. (Paragraph 19.17.)

5. The burden of proving "diminished responsibility" should be removed from the defendant, who should have only to adduce evidence to raise the issue. The present practice by the courts of accepting a plea of guilty to manslaughter where there is sufficient medical evidence supporting "diminished responsibility" should continue. It should be open to the prosecution, if the defence agree, to charge manslaughter in the first instance where they have evidence to show that a case for "diminished responsibility" can be made out. (Paragraphs 19.18–19.19.)

6. A less satisfactory alternative to revision of section 2 of the Homicide Act would be to repeal it but provide that, on a conviction of murder, the judge should have discretion, where there is appropriate medical evidence, to make a hospital order or a psychiatric probation order in place of awarding a life sentence. He should not be allowed to sentence for a fixed term or give a discharge. (Paragraph 19.20.)

7. If some form of "diminished responsibility" remains, the defence should be required to give advance notice of their intention to adduce psychiatric evidence. (Paragraph 19.21.)

Infanticide

8. We recommend that the special provision for the offence of infanticide should be abolished. Its purposes are now sufficiently covered by the more recent provision for diminished responsibility, while the medical principles on which the Infanticide Act 1938 is based are probably no longer relevant, and the Act is unsatisfactory in a number of respects. Our recommendation that the prosecution should be able to charge manslaughter by reason of "diminished responsibility" in appropriate cases will bring the two advantages of the Infanticide Act within the wider defence: the stigma of a charge of murder will be removed, and the mental element will be accepted from the outset. (Paragraphs 19.22–19.26.)

251

CHAPTER 20

CO-OPERATION AMONG THE PROFESSIONS: FORENSIC PSYCHIATRIC SERVICES

I. IMPROVING CO-ORDINATION AMONG TREATMENT SERVICES

20.1 A great volume of evidence presented to us has stressed the need to develop closer relationships among the various services responsible for treating the mentally disordered offender and to improve mutual understanding. This need is endorsed by the Advisory Council on the Penal System in their Report on the Young Adult Offender. They advocate a fuller use of the arrangements for preparing reports for the courts and lay particular stress on maintaining the closest possible links between psychiatrists and the probation and after-care service. In our discussions about the problems of handling confidential information (which we deal with below) the significant point was made both by representatives of the British Medical Association and by probation and after-care service witnesses that difficulties are most likely to arise where the doctor and the probation officer are not known to one another. Many difficulties could undoubtedly be overcome by more communication and better personal contacts. It seems an obvious thing to say that, for example, courts who think the local hospital unco-operative might usefully arrange to discuss their problems with the hospital doctors, incidentally, perhaps, obtaining insights into the doctors' problems; or that doctors and social workers, who inevitably have many related difficulties in dealing with the same patients, could benefit from considering them together: but often no one takes the initiative and the various minor frictions are allowed to continue.

20.2 Sometimes *ad hoc* local conferences involving all the relevant services might well be found valuable. We have been encouraged by hearing of several examples of positive developments of this kind. The most formalised that has come to our notice is in the Wessex Region where towards the end of 1974 the Regional Health Authority established a Co-ordinating Committee on the Management of the Mentally Abnormal Offender comprising members of the Authority and the judiciary, magistrates, Directors of Social Services and Chief Probation Officers, the Regional Director of Prisons, the Regional Consultant in Forensic Psychiatry, the Regional Specialist in Community Medicine, the Assistant Chief Constable of Hampshire and the Area Nurse (Service Planning) to the Wiltshire Area Health Authority. We understand that it is envisaged that subsequently joint committees at the local practitioner level may be established in the Wessex Areas. In the British Medical Journal on 31 May 1975[1] reference was made to an interesting development in Manchester where a group known as the "General Practitioner and Social Worker Workshop" has been established whose aim is to foster co-operation between social work and general practice. Although not stated to be specifically concerned with mentally disordered offenders, such co-operation cannot be other than constructive and helpful from their point of view. We hope that comparable arrangements designed to foster inter-disciplinary co-operation

---

[1] Pages 501–2.

and smooth out difficulties will be established in as many more areas as possible. An important development has been the establishment under the National Health Service Reorganisation Act of Joint Consultative Committees of representatives from Area Health Authorities and local authorities. The existence of a joint consultative body to provide a forum for discussion and to aid collaboration between statutory authorities is welcome and the establishment under statute of the Committees serves to underline the need that exists.

20.3 But desirable and helpful as are these deliberate methods of improving co-operation, they do not in themselves satisfy the need, as we see it, for the establishment of fully co-ordinated treatment services. We think that this objective should be adopted as a matter of policy, and elaborated in detail with the full involvement of all the disciplines and services concerned. The fundamental question to be determined is, how can the existing facilities, resources and legal powers be used to the best advantage to deal with the medical and social needs of all the mentally disordered patients to be catered for? It may be, for instance, that the optimum results would be achieved by arranging for defined territorial areas to have access to a complete range of facilities, and to be responsible for the treatment of all cases occurring within the area, under agreed policies regarding the location of treatment and transfer between facilities. Another question which needs to be worked out is that of exchanges of staff for training purposes, for example between the prisons and the special hospitals and between special hospitals and local psychiatric hospitals. We have already mentioned (paragraph 3.31 above) the difficulties arising out of incompatible conditions of service which prevent the exchange of staff for training purposes between prisons and National Health Service hospitals. Such issues as these evidently require consideration at national level as well as in the regions.

II. CONFIDENTIALITY OF PERSONAL INFORMATION

20.4 A particular problem connected with improving co-operation among the different services which might be eased in the course of such consultations as we have mentioned is that of communicating confidential personal information about the patient. Fully effective treatment, including the successful resettlement of the patient in the community, requires the sharing between all the different services that are necessarily involved of all information which may be relevant at any stage; but the disclosure of personal information gained in a professional relationship is an issue which gives rise to widespread concern. Moreover, apart from professional considerations of ethical propriety, breach of confidence involves the risk of a legal action for damages. In the medical profession, there may also be the possibility of disciplinary proceedings by the General Medical Council. The reason of policy against disclosure is that patients or clients may become less willing to speak frankly to doctors or social workers if they think that everything they say may be passed on to someone else, without their knowledge and perhaps for purposes detrimental to them. The British Medical Association told us that there were instances of people being refused employment as a result of the misuse of medical information provided in good faith for some other purposes. Even where the patient authorised disclosure serious hardship might result. In a case cited as an example a patient who was being discharged from a special hospital had agreed that information about her previous history could be disclosed to potential employers and landladies; the result was that they all rejected her. On the other hand, in discussion the British Medical Association representatives recognised that disclosure by the doctor would often be in the patient's interests, especially in preventing the misapprehension about his condition which could be brought about by mistaken information being passed over; and the National Association for Mentally Handicapped Children stated in their evidence, with particular reference to subnormal patients, that it had been found essential to their success in open employment that the personnel officer and future workmates should have some understanding of the individual's limitations before he was introduced into the work situation. They saw some advantage in involving the outside agencies, including perhaps the relative or landlady with whom the patient would live in the community, as well as the future employer and the patient himself, in the discussions about discharge, with the agreement of the patient. Nevertheless, the Association recognised that the prejudice against the mentally disordered and even more against those who have committed an offence involves the risk of rejection when these facts are disclosed.

20.5   The British Medical Association, who said that breaches of confidentiality were very rare, officially supported complete confidentiality between doctor and patient, as laid down in their own Code of Ethics which recommends, *inter alia*, that its members do not voluntarily disclose any information about a patient to a third party without the valid consent of the patient or his legal adviser except in circumstances where (*a*) the information is required by law; (*b*) information regarding a patient's health is given in confidence to a relative or other appropriate person in circumstances where the doctor believes it is undesirable on medical grounds to seek the patient's consent; and (*c*) rarely, where the public interest persuades the doctor that his duty to the community overrides his duty to maintain his patient's confidentiality. Discussing with us what constituted the "public interest" the Association expressed the strong feeling that this was a matter of judgment in individual cases. The prevention of the commission of a crime might well be a matter of "public interest" but it depended very much on the gravity of the crime. If the doctor thought that he was dealing with a potential murderer, clearly the authorities should be alerted; but in general the possibility of property offences being committed (with the exception of crimes of the seriousness of arson), would not justify a breach of confidence. In all cases, it was thought, it would be the patient's likelihood of committing in the future a serious offence with irremediable consequences, not any past crime, that should influence the doctor in deciding whether a breach of confidence would be justified "in the public interest". While we recognise the difficulty of the doctor's professional position, we are acutely aware of the risks imposed on society if the doctor remains silent when he has good reason to believe that an offence, other than a trivial one, may be committed by his patient. We feel bound to stress this aspect of the matter, and to suggest that the medical profession might usefully give further consideration to the balance of the arguments, with a view to the possibility of formulating further guidance for doctors in the very responsible exercise of their discretion.

254

20.6   On the question of rehabilitation the Association said that there was a delicate balance between professional ethics and the need to ensure the patient's safe resettlement within the community.   In practice much depended on a satisfactory liaison being established between the individual doctor and the individual social worker.   It was desirable that social workers should be subject to a professional code of ethics, and there had been discussions between the British Medical Association and the British Association of Social Workers on this matter.   We have been informed by the British Association of Social Workers that they have drawn up a code of ethics and a statement on confidentiality which have been approved by their Council and will be presented for ratification at the annual general meeting in the autumn.   This is an encouraging development.   Further talks on an ethical code are scheduled to take place between the British Association of Social Workers and the British Medical Association.   We hope that in these discussions our remarks at paragraph 20.8 below will be borne in mind and that positive results will be forthcoming.   The probation and after-care service organisations were not a party to the original discussions but we have no doubt that they will take note of the outcome of any future talks and consider any implications there may be for the probation and after-care service.

20.7   The local authority representatives informed us that the issue of confidentiality had in the past caused difficulties, but these were gradually being eliminated by improved arrangements and understanding between the medical profession and social workers.   There was a great advantage in having a social worker from the local authority social services department within the hospital. Very similar evidence was given by probation and after-care service representatives who said that the problems, which should not be over-emphasised, tended to arise where the doctor and the probation officer dealing with a particular case were at a distance and not known to one another.   Sometimes information or consultation was withheld through thoughtlessness or inadvertence, rather than as a matter of principle.   Communications between the prison and the outside probation and after-care service had been improved by the appointment of prison welfare officers from the probation and after-care service to serve inside the prisons.   They thought that improvements could still be made in connection with releases from prisons, where even in parole cases there was often little medical information available to the supervising officer;[2] and in medical recommendations to the courts, which were often made without previous consultation with the probation officer, who might after all be made responsible for supervision if the recommendation was accepted. Better contact at the pre-trial stage, it was suggested, would avoid many wrong decisions, and at the release stage the probation officer should be fully informed of any medical findings suggesting dangerousness.

20.8   We note that the Committee on Privacy referred[3] to the dangers to privacy in the spread of medical information from doctors to others such as social workers and administrators, but thought that the answer lay in the professional ethics of those who had responsibility for the patient.   They saw no difficulty of principle in acquainting all such professional persons with the information which they might need to have in the public as well in the patient's

---

[2] Members of the Prison Medical Service are subject to the same ethical restraints as other doctors.

[3] Cmnd. 5012, paragraph 381.

own interest. The Aarvold Committee referred to these comments of the Committee on Privacy in their own Report, and stated that they agreed.[4] While we agree that complete freedom of exchange of information between all those professionally concerned with a patient's welfare is highly desirable, we understand the reservations expressed by the British Medical Association. They feel that there will continue to be a difficulty of principle as long as confidentiality in some professions is not guaranteed by a code of ethics which is enforceable through some kind of sanction. In practice sharing of information does, of necessity, take place, particularly where a good working relationship based on mutual trust and respect is established between the doctor and his colleagues in other professions. The production of an enforceable code of ethics for each profession involved, by providing a firm base for mutual confidence, would go far to help to improve inter-disciplinary co-operation on this matter.

20.9   With regard to disclosure of information to people outside the professional circle, such as relatives, employers and landlords, we agree with the Aarvold Committee's conclusion[5] that decisions about how much information is relevant and should be divulged, and to whom, cannot be governed by any general rule but can only be resolved by the responsible judgment of those concerned with the patient's continuing care; and that where the potential danger to others might be appreciable in the event of relapse the bias should be towards full disclosure of the essential elements of the patient's history, such as the fact of his treatment in a particular hospital and the nature of his offence.   Decisions as to the information to be imparted to non-professional persons should be shared by members of the rehabilitation team, primary responsibility resting with the responsible medical officer while the patient is in hospital, and afterwards with the supervising officer, in full consultation, in each case, with the other members of the team.[6]

20.10   Some evidence put to us was in favour of the patient having a complete right to refuse permission for personal details to be disclosed to any third person; other evidence favoured the patient's consent being sought for the release of personal information to responsible agencies but suggested that the patient's right to refuse should not be absolute, though he should be told what information was being given and to whom.   The Aarvold Committee proposed[7] that the patient should be asked, when discharge was under consideration, for his written consent to the disclosure of relevant information. As witnesses from the Law Society remarked, a factor in the discharge decision must always be the degree of responsibility shown by the patient, and the Aarvold Committee, with their particular concern with restricted patients, thought that failure to co-operate in this respect would be a factor which the Home Secretary would no doubt take into account in his decision about discharge.   The local authority representatives thought that it was generally right to inform a prospective employer or landlady of the patient's background, but that the patient should be told that the information would have to be given.

[4] Cmnd. 5191, paragraph 49.
[5] *Ibid.*, paragraph 50.
[6] *Ibid*. 5191, paragraph 51.
[7] *Ibid.*, paragraphs 50 and 52.

20.11   We think that the patient's consent to disclosure of personal history should normally be obtained, but with regard to offenders who are dangerous in the sense we have defined in paragraph 4.10 above, protection of the public must be the overriding consideration.   If the patient's consent is not forthcoming this may mean that for the protection of other people either he cannot for the time being be discharged or the relevant information must be disclosed without his consent, in which event he should be told what information has been given and to whom.

20.12   We hope that the suggestions we have put forward in these paragraphs will result in the improvement of understanding on the question of the confidentiality of personal information among all those professions concerned. It is a difficult and sensitive matter, but it is one on which agreement must be reached if sound inter-disciplinary co-operation, which necessarily involves close working relationships, is to develop.   Such co-operation is essential if our proposals for forensic psychiatric services, which we now go on to discuss, are to be successfully implemented.

III.   FORENSIC PSYCHIATRIC SERVICES

(1) Functions and structure

20.13   A central feature of fully co-ordinated treatment services would be a network of forensic psychiatric services[8] based, as we suggested in our Interim Report, on secure hospital units in each Regional Health Authority area.

We said:

"9.   [These units] will fulfil a need for non-offender patients while advancing the general cause of the 'open door' policy in psychiatric hospitals by enabling the most difficult cases to be treated in more appropriate conditions; but, by reason of our terms of reference, our main concern is that the units are crucial to the greater flexibility in placement which is needed for mentally abnormal offenders, and to the early relief of the prisons and the special hospitals.   We think it right that offenders and non-offenders should be treated together; they should share all the facilities of the units without any distinction being made between them. At present the services dealing with the mentally abnormal offender are fragmented, and we have received a great volume of evidence urging closer co-operation among them and the more effective use of the scarce professional resources.   By focussing the activities and expertise of the various professions in these centres much can be achieved towards these ends.   The offender in need of treatment will be better served, not least because of improved assessment, which will also be of immense value to the court in deciding what to do with him; and, besides providing reference points to which the probation and after-care service will be able to turn

---

[8] Forensic psychiatry, as its name implies, is the application of general psychiatric principles to the problem of the mentally disordered offender at all stages of his treatment.   Those working in the field of forensic psychiatry will have received a generalist psychiatric training, but they require, in addition, a knowledge of and consideration for the scope and limitations of the legal process as it applies to the mentally disordered offender.   Those doctors who are at present involved with forensic psychiatric work are the special hospital psychiatrists, prison medical officers (many of whom are fully qualified psychiatrists) and the "joint appointees" whose time is shared between working in the National Health Service and the prisons.   (The joint appointments were introduced following the report of the working party on the Organisation of the Prison Medical Service in 1964, see paragraph 20.17 below.)

for the advice which they have told us they often need, the centres will have an essential role in training and research, for which reason they should be closely associated with the universities.

10. Our final Report is likely to have more to say about the need for forensic psychiatric services and the scope of their functions, of which the provision of assessments for the courts will undoubtedly be one of the most important. These assessments will be carried out both on an out-patient basis and during remand in custody in the secure unit. Witnesses closely connected with the courts—magistrates, barristers and the probation and after-care service—have stressed that the courts should always be made aware of mental abnormality in the offenders appearing before them, and that, to this end, they should have ready access to adequate assessments, including, where appropriate, psychiatric, psychological and social reports. In general, the present arrangements for obtaining psychiatric reports are unsatisfactory for a variety of reasons, except in certain favoured places, such as, for example, where appointments of joint forensic consultants have been made between the prison system and the health service. We are strongly in favour of increasing the number of these appointments, as we are of the development of forensic psychiatry generally.

11. It would obviously be in the interests of the most effective use of scarce resources that these assessment services which, like the secure units we are proposing, should be located accessibly in towns, should be integrated wherever possible with the secure units, although assessment centres may also be required in some places where there are no such units."

20.14 The discussions we have had and the evidence we have received since the publication of our Interim Report have strengthened our conviction that the development of forensic psychiatric services is an essential element in dealing with the problem of the mentally disordered offender. We propose that the services should be established within the existing framework of the National Health Service at the Regional Health Authority level, and, wherever possible, their operational centres should be in the new secure units which are themselves to be situated in each hospital region. In this way it will be possible to ensure that the services will be based in or near the large centres of population from which most of their patients will come and where the courts and the University Departments (with both of which the services will be closely associated, the first for purposes of assessment, the second for training and research) are situated. Moreover, establishment at the regional level will make it possible to maintain greater administrative flexibility which is essential in the interests of developing the closest liaison among all those involved in forensic psychiatric work. The organisation of the services should be in line with, and indeed integrated with, the existing hospital and community mental health services of the regions.

20.15 On the treatment level we see the regional secure units as the hospital facility of what will otherwise be a service mainly dealing with patients in the community. The main emphasis in forensic psychiatric services therefore should be on community care and out-patient work. Area psychiatric hospitals should continue to provide a wide range of facilities for forensic patients, including where possible some provision for intensive care short of the security which the regional units will provide. The principle followed should be that treatment should always be provided as close to a patient's home as possible.

(2) Objectives

20.16 Apart from their day-to-day functions, these services would lead towards certain fundamental long-term objectives, namely, the development of closer links between the National Health Service and the Prison Medical Service on the one hand, and on the other hand between the hospital and general practitioner services and the social services, both local authority and probation, in the community.

(i) *Links with the Prison Medical Service*

20.17 As regards the Prison Medical Service it has long been recognised that there is much to be gained through a mutual exchange of knowledge and expertise with the National Health Service. The Report of the Working Party on the Organisation of the Prison Medical Service (1964) proposed that the Prison Medical Service should be expanded substantially, not only to meet the growing demands made upon it but also to allow for secondments and other arrangements for further training and study, and to enable more research to be undertaken. It recommended the establishment of more forensic psychiatric clinics outside the prison system, and the appointment, jointly by the Home Secretary and Regional Hospital Boards or Boards of Governors, of consultant psychiatrists to work part-time in a prison service establishment and part-time in a psychiatric hospital or clinic outside the forensic field and possibly also in a teaching post. It also recommended that there should be joint appointment training posts for forensic psychiatrists at registrar or senior registrar level. The Working Party were of the opinion that "eventually all reports on the state of mind of accused persons should be made by doctors trained and specialising in forensic psychiatry". The Report stated that "ideally, and in the long run, all recruitment should be initially to joint appointment registrar posts", and it was considered that "the highest posts in the Prison Medical Service should be open equally to Prison Medical Officers and to forensic psychiatrists according to ability and experience". Despite the initial difficulties to which the implementation of some of the recommendations of the Working Party has given rise we support the long-term objectives of the Report and urge that continuing effort be made to meet these aims. In particular we are aware that some difficulties have been experienced in establishing satisfactory working arrangements between consultants occupying the joint appointments and their colleagues in the prisons, but we think that such problems are to be expected in the development of new relationships of this kind. To ease these difficulties it is important that the responsibilities and roles of senior doctors working in the prisons and those working jointly in the National Health Service should be clearly defined and understood. If this is done we feel sure that with goodwill and co-operation the difficulties in establishing satisfactory working arrangements can be overcome, particularly in the light of the extended scope of the forensic psychiatric services envisaged in our recommendations.

20.18 We have already stated our opinion that the forensic psychiatric services should be established under the aegis of the National Health Service.

Prison Medical Officers and others working in the prisons should have full opportunity and encouragement to share the work with National Health Service staff. This sharing of work on a basis to be agreed between Regional Health Authorities and the Prison Department (including agreement on any appropriate financial adjustment) would greatly extend the concept and effectiveness of "joint appointments", which in our opinion would be to the advantage of both. We envisage that, as required, junior prison doctors could be seconded to NHS forensic psychiatric services to be trained and qualify as psychiatrists. Formal appointment to forensic psychiatric posts would be made as to other posts within the National Health Service. Prison Medical Officers should be encouraged to accept clinical posts of appropriate status on an honorary basis. We believe that appointments in the forensic psychiatric centres should be made attractive to the Prison Medical Service, as we see great advantages to both services, and above all to the treatment of mentally disordered offenders, in the participation of prison doctors in the work of the National Health Service.

20.19   In this connection, we note that there is no training grade in the Prison Medical Service equivalent to senior registrar in the National Health Service, and consequently secondment of Prison Medical Officers to the National Health Service is not feasible. If these training grades were introduced, the movement of medical officers into and out of prisons would be encouraged and variety of experience fostered, one result being that experience in the Prison Medical Service would be more attractive to doctors who do not wish to adopt it as a life-long career. We would expect the career plan of all forensic psychiatrists to include a period spent working in either a prison service establishment or one of the special hospitals.

(ii) *Links with the social services*

20.20   The second fundamental purpose served by these arrangements, as we noted above, would be to foster closer relationships with the community social services. An essential feature of each regional forensic psychiatric service would be the participation of both local authority and probation and after-care service social workers, who would see themselves as members of a team prepared to give whatever assistance might be required to patients both in the hospitals and in the community. Working within the forensic psychiatric services the social workers would be within an inter-disciplinary group, through which expert advice would be available to officers of the two services in the field when they are confronted with the problems of supervising and supporting mentally disordered offenders. As explained earlier in the Report (paragraph 3.17), we are not in favour of the special appointment of psychiatric consultants to provide advice to the probation and after-care service. We think that membership of an inter-disciplinary group would enhance the processes of consultation, the sharing of information and the giving of advice which all those responsible for the care of patients require and through which clinical and therapeutic decisions can be taken.

20.21   A period spent as a member of the inter-disciplinary treatment team at one of the forensic psychiatric centres would be a valuable experience for members of the two services, and should, we think, be recognised as helping towards professional advancement (as we understand is the case with second-ments of probation officers to the welfare departments of prisons). In our

Interim Report we made the point that the social work staff in regional secure units should be numerically sufficient to allow for the supervision of trainees, who would have much to gain from the experience of working in a secure unit. Forensic psychiatric centres will often be situated in regional secure units, but some may not be; we think that the same remarks apply to these, and that all the centres have an important training role. This role should be as wide as possible, offering training facilities not only to social workers but to doctors, nurses, psychologists and others involved in the treatment of the mentally disordered offender. In particular, we think that nurses should be given the necessary training over and above their normal nursing training to equip them with those social skills for which work in the forensic psychiatric field, with its emphasis on social rehabilitation, often calls.

(iii) *Links with the special hospitals*
20.22 The forensic psychiatric centres should have links with all the special hospitals; at any one time each of the special hospitals would have some patients from the area of each of the forensic psychiatric centres, and vice versa. In the development of forensic psychiatric services the special hospitals have a considerable contribution to make. We foresee them assisting in the training of prison personnel, medical and others, on secondment to them.

(iv) *Co-ordination*
20.23 A most important aspect of the development of forensic psychiatric arrangements is the provision of effective liaison among those working in the forensic psychiatric services, the regional secure units, the assessment centres (if these are not within those units), and the psychiatric hospitals in the Region, as well as with the social services and the remand prisons. To promote the development of these relationships there will be a need for officially recognised co-ordination, which might be brought about by regional committees to advise on planning and policy. Representatives of all those taking part in the services should be appointed to them. In this process of co-ordination the role of the joint consultant forensic psychiatrists will be important.

20.24 In the introduction to this chapter we referred to the need to develop fully co-ordinated treatment services; and earlier in this Report (paragraph 8.1) we indicated the importance of providing continuity of treatment ("through-care") for mentally disordered offenders. Our proposals for establishing forensic psychiatric services would provide the central core for co-ordination of the various treatment services and would facilitate the provision of "through-care", linking treatment in hospitals and prisons with treatment in the community in day treatment units. We agree with the remarks of the British Psychological Society in their memorandum of evidence that the same diversity of professional groups should be available to provide community treatment and after-care as is provided for residential units, and that in the interests of continuity of treatment and supervision the same personnel should be available to follow the offender through the various stages of residential and community treatment, with staffing levels adequate to enable time to be spent in both settings. This, they have suggested, is especially important where social workers are concerned, because of the particular understanding they have of the offender's normal environment, for example at home, in the family, and at work. These recommendations are similar to the proposals put to us by the British Medical Association, which were drawn from Chapter 8 of *The*

Mental Health Service after Unification published by the Tripartite Committee with authorisation of the Royal College of Psychiatrists, the Society of Medical Officers of Health and the British Medical Association. The proposals were quoted in the British Medical Association's memorandum as follows:

"3. We suggest that in large urban areas (population approximately 1,000,000) appropriate multi-disciplinary centres should be established for the specialised long-term support of those suffering from the types of personality disorders under consideration. Each centre would need to be staffed by an adequate number of experienced psychiatrists and social workers, most of whom would probably be full-time. The overall control would be exercised jointly by the authorities responsible for health services and social work services. Essential part-time attachments to the staff would be other psychiatrists (including those from the child psychiatric and mental subnormality fields), social workers, prison medical officers, probation officers, prison welfare officers, disablement resettlement officers, and representatives of voluntary bodies. General practitioners could also usefully be included. We think that at present there is much misunderstanding, to the detriment of the patient, between the various professional experts involved, and that this is primarily due to inadequate communications. It would be the administrator's responsibility to secure co-ordination by means of formal and informal meetings.

4. The essential value of centres would be in their provision of a twenty-four-hour consultation and advice service. They would also be the focal point for continuing medical care and social support. Continuity of contact with the same worker would be an important aim. Close links would have to be established and maintained with all the facilities likely to be used in the area, such as hospitals, hostels and workshops, and also with prisons. The closest possible liaison with special units for the treatment of drug addiction and alcoholism would be necessary. We do not consider that the centres would, as a rule, possess any residential accommodation.

5. The organisation we describe would enable fairly rapid decisions to be made collectively by the multi-disciplinary team, and so patients would receive more consistent care and advice than at present. It would be possible for psychotherapeutic relationship formed within a prison to be continued after the prisoner had returned to the community by giving the prison medical officer the opportunity of continuing the relationship during the crucial resettlement phase. Similarly it should prove much easier than at present to secure continuity of contact between client and the same social worker, whether he be a psychiatric social worker, probation officer or welfare officer.

It is, of course not being suggested that this type of long-term care and support would 'cure' personality disorders, but it should be an advance on what at present obtains. In addition, special skills would be developed, of which at present there is a dearth. Most workers agree that the alleviation of social distress, manipulation of the environment and short-term admission to hospital for crisis situations are essential elements in the management of personality disorders. Such action as was deemed necessary could be agreed upon and implemented at the centre.

Collaboration with courts

6.   Centres such as we advocate would be in a good position to foster closer collaboration between the courts and the helping professions than exists today.   At present courts often have difficulty in obtaining the medical reports which they request quickly enough to warrant the accused being on bail.   Consequently, unnecessarily large numbers of accused people are remanded in custody for medical reports.   In 1968 110,813 male receptions to prison were recorded by the prison department of the Home Office, and 51 per cent of those were in respect of accused men remanded in custody.   Yet the final outcome was that many were dealt with by non-institutional means such as fines or probation, and some, of course, were acquitted altogether.   As regards women in custody for medical examination, it is known that some 80 per cent were sent back into the community after the remand period as the courts did not consider custodial sentences to be necessary.   The inefficiency and injustice of such procedures could be averted if facilities for examinations by forensic psychiatrists, with the help of supporting staff, were provided at the centres."

(3) Conclusion

20.25   As we have already pointed out (paragraph 20.17) the concept of joint psychiatric consultant appointments is not new, having first been advocated in the Report of the Working Party on the Organisation of the Prison Medical Service as long ago as 1964.   A limited number of such appointments have been made in the course of the subsequent decade, but we are aware that to a large extent the hopes surrounding these appointments have not been fully realised.   One or two appointments, where there have been individuals in the services concerned who were determined to achieve results, have brought about a significant improvement in the services in their locality, but in the majority of cases the essential linkage between the National Health Service and the Prison Medical Service has not taken place.   This we attribute largely to the continuing isolation of the Prison Medical Service and in part to a lack of understanding of the potential of these joint appointments.   We believe that the establishment of forensic psychiatric services, as recommended in this chapter of our Report, should achieve the desired objectives more easily than the mere appointment of individual consultants with virtually no supporting organisation, who can only depend on the willingness of the Prison Medical Service to accept them as full members of the team.

20.26   Certain members of our Committee were initially in favour of the integration of the Prison Medical Service with the National Health Service at an early date.   They refrained from so recommending in part because such a recommendation seemed doubtfully within our terms of reference, but also because they were persuaded that our recommendations on the establishment of effective forensic psychiatric services would, if implemented, make a significant contribution towards improving the handling and disposal of mentally disordered offenders.   The entire Committee are of the same opinion and regard the development of such services as a vital element in our recommendations as a whole.

CO-OPERATION AMONG THE PROFESSIONS: FORENSIC PSYCHIATRIC SERVICES

SUMMARY OF CONCLUSIONS

I. Improving co-ordination among treatment services

1. There is a need for close co-ordination among the services involved with the treatment of the mentally disordered offender. This calls for a carefully worked out policy involving the participation of all treating agencies, with close co-operation among them at both national and local level. The establishment in some areas of extra-statutory committees or of informal discussion groups of practitioners with representatives from the relevant services are examples which we hope will be followed elsewhere, and the setting up under the National Health Service Reorganisation Act of Joint Consultative Committees is also an important development. (Paragraphs 20.1–20.3.)

II. Confidentiality of personal information

2. Fully effective treatment, including resettlement in the community, requires the sharing among the services involved of all information which may be relevant at any stage. To safeguard the patient's interests whilst facilitating the sharing of information we urge the production by each profession of an enforceable code of ethics. (Paragraphs 20.4, 20.6 and 20.8.)

3. Disclosure of information to persons outside the treatment team, such as landladies or potential employers, may result in rejection of the patient, and hardship. The decision how much should be told, and to whom, can only be made by the responsible judgment of those concerned with the patient's continuing care, by the responsible medical officer while the patient is in hospital, and afterwards by the supervising officer, all members of the rehabilitation team being consulted. Where there is potential danger to others the bias should be towards full disclosure of the essential elements of the patient's history. We feel bound to suggest that the medical profession should give further consideration to the balance of the arguments with a view to formulating further guidance for doctors. (Paragraphs 20.4–20.9.)

4. The patient's consent to disclosure of personal history should normally be obtained, but protection of the public should be the overriding consideration where the patient is a dangerous offender. If his consent is not forthcoming he may have to continue to be detained, or otherwise if information is disclosed without his consent he should be told what information has been given and to whom. (Paragraph 20.11.)

III. Forensic psychiatric services

5. Forensic psychiatric services are an essential element in dealing with mentally disordered offenders. Their long-term objective would be to develop close links between all those services engaged in providing care for them. The services should be established in each National Health Service region and, wherever possible, should be based on the new secure units. They should be organised at Regional Health Authority level and integrated with the existing hospital and community mental health services. The main emphasis should be on community care and out-patient work, and the principle should be that

264

treatment should always be provided as close to a patient's home as possible. Area psychiatric hospitals will continue to have an important role to play in the treatment of forensic patients. (Paragraphs 20.14–20.16.)

6. To ease the difficulties that have been experienced in connection with the joint appointments it is important that the respective roles and responsibilities of the senior doctors working in the prisons and those working jointly in the National Health Service should be clearly defined and understood. (Paragraph 20.17.)

7. The forensic psychiatric services should be established under the aegis of the National Health Service, but prison doctors should share the work with their National Health Service counterparts, on a basis to be agreed between the Regional Health Authorities and the Prison Department. Junior prison doctors should be seconded to the forensic psychiatric services for training as psychiatrists, and other prison doctors should be encouraged to accept clinical posts of appropriate status on an honorary basis. A training grade equivalent to that of senior registrar in the National Health Service should be introduced into the Prison Medical Service in order to facilitate the movement of doctors into and out of prisons. All forensic psychiatrists should spend a part of their career working in either a prison or a special hospital. (Paragraphs 20.18–20.19.)

8. Close links with the community social services should be fostered. Within the forensic psychiatric centres there should be an inter-disciplinary group working as a team in which local authority and probation and after-care service social workers should participate. Through such a group expert advice would be available to workers in the field and inter-disciplinary co-operation would be enhanced. A period spent as a member of the forensic psychiatric centre team should be seen as an essential step in the career of social workers of both services. The centres would have an important training role not only for social workers but for all those involved with the treatment of mentally disordered offenders, and in particular for nurses. (Paragraphs 20.20–20.21.)

9. The special hospitals should make a significant contribution to the forensic psychiatric services, particularly as regards training of personnel. (Paragraph 20.22.)

10. Co-ordination of all those involved with forensic psychiatric work should be promoted by the establishment of regional committees to advise on planning and policy, with representation from all the services. In the process of co-ordination, the role of the joint consultant forensic psychiatrists will be important. (Paragraph 20.23.)

11. We stress the importance of "through-care" for mentally disordered offenders and the establishment of day treatment units. (Paragraph 20.24.)

12. We believe that our proposals for the establishment of effective forensic psychiatric services will, if implemented, make a significant contribution towards realisation of the long desired strengthening of links between the Prison Medical Service and the National Health Service, and thus towards improving facilities for the treatment of the mentally disordered offender; and we regard the development of such services as a vital element in our recommendations as a whole. (Paragraphs 20.25–20.26.)

SUMMARY OF RECOMMENDATIONS

AND

FINAL REMARKS

Implementation of our Reports

1. We recommend that consideration be given to the feasibility of establishing a national advisory body with representation from all the interests involved to oversee the implementation of those of our recommendations which are accepted, to report where problems are arising and to assist towards solutions. (Paragraph 1.27.)

2. We recommend that the running costs as well as the capital costs of the regional secure hospital units proposed in our Interim Report should be met from Central Government funds. (Paragraph 1.9.)

Action by the police: section 136 of the Mental Health Act 1959

(As regards prosecution of offenders dealt with by the police under section 136, see Recommendation 5 below.)

3. We think that section 136 arrangements should continue to be used to the maximum to ensure that as many as possible of the mentally disordered offenders within the scope of the provision are referred at the outset to the treatment agencies without the need to bring them before the courts. (Paragraph 9.12.)

4. The difficulties that arise in the use of section 136 require administrative rather than legislative remedies. There is a need in some areas for closer co-operation between the police and health authorities to ensure that the statutory provision is operated effectively. (Paragraphs 9.8. and 9.14.)

The prosecuting authorities

5. We think that the police must continue to have ultimate discretion whether to prosecute persons detained under section 136, but that the power should generally not be used unless it serves a useful public purpose, and that this criterion could seldom be satisfied in section 136 cases. (Paragraph 9.15.)

6. Where any apparent offender is clearly in urgent need of psychiatric treatment and there is no question of risk to members of the public the question should always be asked whether any useful public purpose would be served by prosecution. The medical report should be taken into account together with, where possible, a report on the circumstances by a social worker. These remarks apply in cases of homicide or attempted homicide or grave bodily harm as in less serious cases. Chief officers of police should review their policy and practice in the cases for which they have responsibility and the Director of Public Prosecutions should give them guidance in this review. (Paragraphs 9.19–9.20.)

266

7. In general the presumption should be against prosecuting patients already in hospital since this may result in the ordeal of court appearances and the stigma of conviction, with no compensating advantage. Prosecution should be seen as a last resort, and should not be embarked upon where it is not clearly in the interests of the patient or the community. (Paragraphs 9.23–9.24.)

8. Those undertaking medical treatment should be as fully informed as possible and the prosecuting authorities should arrange for any medical and social inquiry reports that may have been obtained to be passed on to the responsible doctor together with a statement of the facts of the charge provided that the person charged admits that he did the act in question. (Paragraph 9.21.)

Information for the courts

(With regard to disability in relation to the trial, see Recommendation 28 below.)

9. We propose that greater use should be made of social inquiry reports as a screening process for mental disorder and to indicate the need for a full psychiatric report. Social inquiry reports should be mandatory in cases involving serious violence or danger to the person. This should include all cases of grave non-sexual offences against the person, all sexual offences on children below the age of 13 or involving violence to persons of any age, and property offences which involve risk to life (for example, arson). (Paragraph 11.4.)

10. Magistrates' courts should in all cases be empowered to seek a medical report on a defendant in relation to disposal following conviction. In other cases a medical report should be sought only when a defence of mental disorder has been raised or where there is a possibility that the defendant may be under disability or when the defence seek a remand to hospital. The same rules should apply to reports on women defendants, but the courts should be particularly vigilant to notice signs of mental disorder in women defendants. (Paragraphs 11.4–11.5.)

11. Doctors who are asked to prepare for the courts psychiatric reports on defendants must be given adequate information both on the reasons why the court has requested the report and on the circumstances of the offence. For cases in the Crown Court they should always see the depositions or statements of witnesses, and where the report is requested after conviction a short transcript of the proceedings should be made available, if this can be obtained in good time. Any other reports on the defendant that are in the court's possession should also be shown to the doctors. (Paragraphs 11.7–11.8.)

12. Where it comes to light in the course of court proceedings that a defendant has received psychiatric treatment a note should be made in the police records of the name of the hospital concerned and the dates when treatment was carried out, if known. No other psychiatric information should be recorded: nor should any information from the police record normally be read out in open court. (Paragraph 11.12.)

Court procedure

(In relation to diminished responsibility, see Recommendations 59 and 61 below. With regard to disability in relation to the trial, see Recommendations 20–38.)

13. The initiative in raising the issue of mental disorder, before verdict, should remain with the defence except that where the defendant admits doing the act and contests the case solely on his state of mind (for instance, by claiming that he was intoxicated or in a state of non-insane automatism) the prosecution may reply with evidence of mental disorder in order to obtain a special verdict rather than a complete acquittal. (Paragraph 18.47.)

14. The defence should be required to give advance notice to the prosecution of their intention to adduce medical evidence and raise the mental issue. In Crown Court proceedings notice should be given within seven days of committal, and in magistrates' courts, seven days' advance notice should be given. As with the alibi defence, the courts should have discretion to waive the requirement of advance notice. (Paragraph 18.48.)

15. A defendant should be able to set up a plea of "not guilty on evidence of mental disorder". Acceptance of the plea would have the same effect as the special verdict. Special care should be taken in accepting the plea when the defendant is unrepresented or when it is thought that he might be under disability. The doctors giving medical evidence may be required to do so orally. (Paragraphs 18.49–18.50.)

Remands to hospital

16. One form of court order should be adopted to cover the following four situations in which the courts should have the power to remand a mentally disordered person to hospital before deciding his ultimate disposal:

   (i) where a medical report is required on a convicted defendant; (Paragraphs 12.2–12.3.)

   (ii) where the defendant requires medical care during a custodial remand; (Paragraph 12.4.)

   (iii) where a period in hospital is required to determine whether a hospital order is appropriate; (Paragraphs 12.5–12.6.)

   (iv) where a defendant is found under disability in relation to the trial. (Paragraph 12.7.)

The order should be available at all National Health Service hospitals (including the special hospitals and the proposed regional secure units), and should provide for the remand of a defendant to a particular hospital for compulsory treatment for a specified period of time. Duration should be of three months maximum where remand is for medical report or care, and of three months initially extendable by one month at a time to a maximum of six months, in other cases. Time spent in hospital on remand should be kept to the minimum required by the circumstances of the case. (Paragraphs 12.2–12.9.)

17. Remand to hospital should be considered only if remand on bail is not feasible. The power to remand to hospital should be exercised only where there is medical evidence that there is reason to suspect mental disorder and there is a hospital place available. Where remand is for a medical report or for care, or in cases of disability, the oral evidence of one medical practitioner will suffice. Where an "interim hospital order" is made two medical practitioners, one of whom should be on the list maintained by Area Health Authorities, should give written or oral evidence. One of the recommendations

should normally be that of the receiving doctor. In uncontested confirmation proceedings where the patient is legally represented the signature of one doctor will suffice. If a restriction order is to be made, the oral evidence of at least one doctor will be required in accordance with section 65(2) of the Act. (Paragraphs 12.10–12.11.)

18. There will sometimes be a need for the secure custody of a remanded mentally disordered defendant. It will be for the courts to decide whether this need will be met by remand to a local psychiatric hospital or a regional secure unit; exceptionally, the security of a special hospital might be required. If no suitable hospital place is available, remand to prison, though generally undesirable, may be unavoidable. All defendants remanded to hospital remain within the jurisdiction of the court. (Paragraph 12.12.)

19. On the resumption of court proceedings following a period of remand the defendant's presence in court will be necessary except where the court is to be advised to confirm an "interim hospital order" and the defendant is legally represented or in a case of disability where it is considered undesirable for the defendant to be present in court (cf. Recommendation 34 below). Proceedings should resume no later than the expiry of the remand period. (Paragraphs 12.13–12.14.)

Disability in relation to the trial

(a) *Preliminary matters*

20. The expression "unfit to plead" is unsatisfactory, and should be replaced by the phrase "under disability in relation to the trial", shortened colloquially to "under disability". (Paragraph 10.2.)

21. The criteria for determining whether a defendant is under disability should be whether he can:

    (i) understand the course of the proceedings at the trial so as to make a proper defence;

    (ii) understand the substance of the evidence;

    (iii) give adequate instructions to his legal advisers;

    (iv) plead with understanding to the indictment.

(Paragraph 10.3.)

22. There is a need to ensure speedy medical attention for the disordered person, whilst establishing the facts of the case without delay. (Paragraphs 10.12–10.15.)

(b) *Crown Court*

23. The question of disability should be decided at the outset of the trial or as soon as it is raised. Where disability has been found and where there is (on medical evidence) a prospect of early recovery the judge may adjourn the trial for up to three months in the first place with renewal for a month at a time up to a maximum of six months. If the defendant recovers within the six month period the normal trial should proceed immediately. A trial of the facts should take place as soon as disability has been found if there is no

prospect of the defendant recovering or as soon during the six month period as he may prove to be unresponsive to treatment, or recovers. (Paragraph 10.19.)

24. The issue of disability should be decided by the judge except if the medical evidence is not unanimous and the defence wish a jury to determine the issue. (Paragraphs 10.20–10.23.)

25. If the defendant is found to be under disability there should nonetheless, at the appropriate time, be a trial of the facts. If a finding of not guilty cannot be returned the jury should be directed to find "that the defendant should be dealt with as a person under disability". This new verdict should not count as a conviction nor should it be followed by punishment. (Paragraphs 10.24–10.25.)

26. The court should have a discretion as to disposal in the event of the new verdict being returned, but an overtly penal disposal should be excluded. (Paragraphs 10.27–10.29.)

27. The defendant should be entitled to appeal against the finding of disability, and against the return of the new verdict. In the event of his recovery after the new verdict being found he should also be entitled to apply for a normal trial. Except in these circumstances, after the trial of the facts there should be a bar to further prosecution. (Paragraphs 10.31–10.32.)

(c) Magistrates' Courts

28. Magistrates' courts should have the power to determine the issue of disability and, where it is found, to order a period in hospital in the same way as the Crown Court. Where there is doubt about the defendant's ability to consent to the summary trial of an indictable offence his representative should be empowered to do so on his behalf (but this should not be binding on the defendant in the event of his recovery and normal trial—see paragraph 10.37). Where it is thought that the defendant may be under disability or unable to give, with understanding, his consent to summary trial magistrates should have the power to call for reports on his mental condition at any stage in the proceedings. (Paragraph 10.35.)

29. The full trial or trial of the facts should take place before a differently constituted court from that which decided on the disability issue. (Paragraph 10.36.)

30. Similar arrangements to those for the Crown Court should apply to the timing and conduct of the trial of the facts, with any appropriate disposal within the competence of the magistrates' courts except a penal disposal. Provision should be made for appeal. In sentencing a defendant who has been found to be under disability and who has subsequently recovered courts should take into account any time he may already have spent in hospital prior to the normal trial. (Paragraphs 10.37–10.39.)

31. In trivial cases the present practice of adjourning the proceedings *sine die* or of not proceeding, where the defendant is plainly disordered and arrangements have been made for his admission to hospital under Part IV of the Act, should continue. (Paragraph 10.40.)

(d) All Courts

32. There should be a statutory requirement for two doctors to give supporting evidence before disability in relation to the trial may be found. In line with the requirements for section 60 orders, at least one of the doctors should be a practitioner approved for the purposes of section 28 of the Act by an Area Health Authority as having special experience in the diagnosis or treatment of mental disorders. (Paragraphs 10.41–10.42.)

33. If counsel is repudiated, the court should appoint an *amicus curiae* whether or not the defendant is present in court. (Paragraph 10.43.)

34. It is important that the defendant should always be present in court at the outset of the proceedings. He should also normally be in court for the trial of the facts, but the court should be free to exercise its existing power to dispense with his presence after plea, provided that certain conditions are met. (Paragraphs 10.44–10.45.)

35. The defendant should not have the right to waive trial of the facts. (Paragraph 10.46.)

36. Provision should be made for a defendant who seems to be under disability to be represented by any solicitor or counsel who is instructed to appear on his behalf, and if there is none, for the court to appoint one. Solicitor and counsel retained by relatives should be assigned under any legal aid order. (Paragraph 10.47.)

37. The law should be amended to enable courts to grant legal aid to a defendant immediately the question of disability in relation to the trial is raised without first requiring a submission of statement of means. Such a statement should be furnished subsequently for the purpose of confirming the legal aid order. (Paragraph 10.48.)

38. If disability is found initially, a social inquiry report on the defendant should normally be obtained to enable the court to consider all possible alternatives to hospital admission. (Paragraph 10.50.)

Proposed reviewable sentence for dangerous offenders

39. We propose that a new form of indeterminate sentence should be introduced, from which release would be dependent entirely on the issue of dangerousness. The sentence would be for offenders who are dangerous, who present a history of mental disorder which cannot be dealt with under the Mental Health Act, and for whom the life sentence is not appropriate. It should be subject to statutory review at regular (two-yearly) intervals. On release the offender should be under compulsory supervision, again subject to statutory review. (Paragraphs 4.39–4.40.)

40. Imposition of the sentence should be restricted to conviction of those offences which caused or might have caused grave harm to others and are either "life"-carrying offences as drawn up in Schedule "A" or non-"life"-carrying sentences as drawn up in Schedule "B" (see Appendix 4) provided that there has already been a conviction of a Schedule "A" offence. Threats (where these are made an offence by statute), together with attempts and

incitement to commit these offences, are included. We have set out strict conditions to be met before the reviewable sentence can be imposed. (Paragraphs 4.41–4.42.)

41. If the offender is simultaneously (or subsequently, while at large) convicted of another offence for which the reviewable sentence is not appropriate, it should be open to the court to impose a determinate sentence for this other offence to run concurrently with the reviewable sentence. (Paragraph 4.43.)

42. The Home Secretary should have the power to authorise the transfer of a prisoner serving a reviewable sentence from prison to hospital under section 72 of the Mental Health Act. In every such case a restriction under section 74 of the Act should be placed on the discharge from hospital of the prisoner. (Paragraph 4.44.)

43. The two-yearly review should be carried out by the Parole Board who, as in other cases, should make recommendations to the Home Secretary. The Home Secretary's powers to accept or reject the Board's recommendations should be the same as in relation to determinate sentences. Release should be on licence of unlimited duration, but the conditions should be subject to a two-yearly review, with the possibility of their eventual removal. (Paragraph 4.45).

The special verdict

44. Provision should continue to be made for exemption from criminal responsibility for mentally disordered offenders but the M'Naghten Rules are not a satisfactory test and in any case a revised formula will be required for inclusion in the Criminal Code which is being drafted by the Law Commission. (Paragraphs 18.1–18.10.)

45. We propose a new formulation of the special verdict, namely, "not guilty on evidence of mental disorder" the grounds for which should comprise two elements: (*a*) a *mens rea* element approximating to the first limb of the M'Naghten Rules ("Did he know what he was doing?"); (*b*) specific exemption from conviction for defendants suffering, at the time of the act or omission charged, from severe mental illness or severe subnormality. (Paragraphs 18.17–18.18.)

46. Magistrates' courts should be allowed to return the special verdict. It will not be necessary to retain section 60(2) of the Mental Health Act. (Paragraph 18.19.)

47. The jury (or magistrates) should return a verdict of "not guilty on evidence of mental disorder" if they find that the defendant did the act or made the omission charged but (by reason of the evidence of mental disorder) they do not find that the state of mind required for the offence has been proved and they further find that on the balance of probability the defendant was mentally disordered at the time. (See Recommendation 45, the first element.) (Paragraph 18.20.)

48. The first element would apply to any mental disorder but should exclude transient states not related to other forms of mental disorder, and arising solely

272

as a consequence of the administration, maladministration or non-administration of alcohol, drugs or other substances, or from physical injury. All other cases now regarded as non-insane automatism would be within the special verdict. Thus the distinction between conditions which are now legally regarded as "insanity" and those dealt with as "non-insane automatism" would be clearly drawn. (Paragraphs 18.22–18.23.)

49. The M'Naghten "knowledge of wrong" test should not be included in terms in the new special verdict, but it will be covered in substance in the second element. (Paragraph 18.24.)

50. We recommend (the second element) that statutory exemption from punishment should be provided for defendants who, although they were suffering from severe mental disorder at the time of the act or omission charged, do not come within the compass of the first element because they were able to form intentions and carry them out. We propose that the special verdict in the terms set out in Recommendation 45 above should be returned if at the time of the act or omission charged the offender was suffering from severe mental illness or severe subnormality. We suggest a definition of severe mental illness, which we propose should be incorporated in the statute subject to the possibility of revision by statutory instrument. (Paragraphs 18.26–18.36.)

51. The first and second elements of the special verdict should be combined in one decision to be made by the jury. The judge should not leave the decision on the second element to the jury unless the defence is supported by the evidence of two psychiatrists, who must be medical practitioners approved by an Area Health Authority as having special experience in the diagnosis or treatment of mental disorder. The jury should not be required to find any causal connection between the act charged and the mental disorder. (Paragraph 18.37.)

52. It should be provided by statute that the special verdict should, while it subsists, be a bar to conviction on any other count relating to the same offence or of any alternative charge. (Paragraph 18.38.)

53. In relation to the first element of the special verdict, the burden of proving the requisite mental state should rest on the prosecution. In the choice between an absolute acquittal and the special verdict the defendant should be entitled to an ordinary acquittal unless the jury are satisfied on the balance of probability that he was mentally disordered. In relation to the second element, in the choice between a conviction and the special verdict the jury should be directed to convict unless satisfied on the balance of probability that the defendant was suffering from severe mental illness or severe subnormality. In complicated cases it may be desirable for the judge to request the jury to answer specific questions and to enter the appropriate verdict on the basis of their answers. (Paragraphs 18.39–18.41.)

54. For disposal following a special verdict the courts should have the same discretionary powers as those recommended in paragraph 10.29 for cases of disability in relation to the trial. Hospital or guardianship orders should be made only when the normal requirements for these orders, including medical recommendations, are met. In appropriate cases it should be open to the courts to order an absolute discharge. Courts should be able to make an

order analogous to a hospital order with restrictions under section 65 of the Mental Health Act, placing the offender in the community under supervision for those cases where admission to hospital is not needed, but where a measure of supervision with power to "recall" to hospital is required. (Paragraphs 18.42–18.45.)

55. To avoid any misapprehension by the jury that the new special verdict would still, as now, automatically entail committal to hospital, it might be desirable for the judge to explain to the jury his powers of disposal. (Paragraph 18.46.)

Offences committed while intoxicated

56. We suggest measures to deal with people who become violent when voluntarily intoxicated. We propose that it should be an offence for a person while voluntarily intoxicated to do an act (or make an omission) that would amount to a dangerous offence if it were done or made with the requisite state of mind for such offence. The offence would not be charged in the first instance but the jury would be directed to find on this offence in the event of intoxication being successfully raised as a defence to the offence originally charged. We define "dangerous" and "voluntary intoxication" for this purpose. We suggest penalties for the new offence. (Paragraphs 18.51–18.59.)

Diminished responsibility and infanticide

57. The present provision relating to diminished responsibility is unsatisfactory; our preferred solution would be the abolition of the mandatory life sentence for murder, and of the provision for diminished responsibility which would then be unnecessary. We have suggested answers to possible objections. (Paragraphs 19.5–19.16.)

58. If this solution is rejected some form of "diminished responsibility" should remain, but we propose revision of the wording of section 2 of the Homicide Act 1957. (Paragraph 19.17.)

59. The burden of proving "diminished responsibility" should be removed from the defendant, who should only have to produce evidence to raise the issue. The present practice by the courts of accepting a plea of guilty to manslaughter where there is sufficient medical evidence supporting "diminished responsibility" should continue. It should be open to the prosecution, if the defence agree, to charge manslaughter in the first instance where they have evidence to show that a case for "diminished responsibility" can be made out. (Paragraphs 19.18–19.19.)

60. A less satisfactory alternative to revision of section 2 of the Homicide Act would be to repeal it, but provide that on a conviction of murder, the judge should have discretion where there is appropriate medical evidence, to make a hospital order or a psychiatric probation order in place of awarding the life sentence. He should not be allowed to sentence for a fixed term or give a discharge. (Paragraph 19.20.)

61. If some form of "diminished responsibility" remains, the defence should be required to give advance notice of their intention to adduce psychiatric evidence. (Cf. Recommendation 14 above). (Paragraph 19.21.)

62. We recommend that the special provision for the offence of infanticide should be abolished. Its purposes are now sufficiently covered by the more recent provision for diminished responsibility, while the medical principles on which the Infanticide Act 1938 is based are probably no longer relevant, and the Act is unsatisfactory in a number of respects. Our recommendation that the prosecution should be able to charge manslaughter by reason of "diminished responsibility" in appropriate cases will bring the two advantages of the Infanticide Act within the wider defence: the stigma of a charge of murder will be removed, and the mental element will be accepted from the outset. (Paragraphs 19.22–19.26.)

Appeals

(With regard to disability in relation to the trial, see Recommendations 27 and 30 above.)

63. We recommend that the Court of Appeal should be able to make the following substitutions only if the appellant gives his consent: a hospital order for a sentence of imprisonment; a sentence of imprisonment for a hospital order: a reviewable sentence for a fixed-term sentence. (Paragraphs 13.22–13.26.)

Treatment—disposal by the court

64. The guiding principle in disposal of mentally disordered offenders by the courts is that they should be sent wherever they can best be given the treatment they need: generally treatment by the health services is appropriate. If it is necessary to impose a prison sentence on a mentally disordered offender the court should not hold out to him the prospect that he will receive medical treatment in prison. (Paragraphs 13.10–13.12.)

Treatment—co-operation among the professions

65. There is a need for close co-ordination among the services involved with the treatment of the mentally disordered offender. (Paragraphs 20.1–20.3.)

66. Fully effective treatment, including resettlement in the community, requires the sharing among the services involved of all information which may be relevant at any stage. To safeguard the patient's interests whilst facilitating the sharing of information we urge the production by each profession of an enforceable code of ethics. (Paragraphs 20.4, 20.6 and 20.8.)

67. The decision how much information should be disclosed to persons outside the rehabilitation team and to whom can only be made by the responsible judgment of those concerned with the patient's continuing care, by the responsible medical officer while the patient is in hospital, and afterwards by the supervising officer, all members of the rehabilitation team being consulted. Where there is potential danger to others the bias should be towards full disclosure of the essential elements of the patient's history. We feel bound to suggest that the medical profession should give further consideration to the balance of the arguments with a view to formulating further guidance for doctors. (Paragraphs 20.4 and 20.9.)

68. The patient's consent to disclosure of personal history should normally be obtained, but protection of the public should be the overriding consideration where the patient is a dangerous offender. If this consent is not forthcoming he may have to continue to be detained or otherwise if information is disclosed without his consent he should be told what information has been given and to whom. (Paragraph 20.11.)

Forensic psychiatric services

69. Forensic psychiatric services should be established in each National Health Service region and, wherever possible, should be based on the new secure units. They should be organised at Regional Health Authority level and integrated with the existing hospital and community mental health services. The main emphasis should be on community care and out-patient work and the principle should be that treatment should always be provided as close to a patient's home as possible. (Paragraphs 20.14–20.16.)

70. To ease the difficulties that have been experienced in connection with the joint appointments it is important that the respective roles and responsibilities of the senior doctors working in the prison and those working jointly in the National Health Service should be clearly defined and understood. (Paragraph 20.17.)

71. The forensic psychiatric services should be established under the aegis of the National Health Service, but prison doctors should share the work with their National Health Service counterparts, on a basis to be agreed between the Regional Health Authorities and the Prison Department. Junior prison doctors should be seconded to the forensic psychiatric services for training as psychiatrists and other prison doctors should be encouraged to accept clinical posts of appropriate status on an honorary basis. A training grade equivalent to that of senior registrar in the National Health Service should be introduced into the Prison Medical Service in order to facilitate the movements of doctors into and out of prisons. All forensic psychiatrists should spend part of their career working in either a prison or a special hospital. (Paragraphs 20.18–20.19.)

72. Close links with the community social services should be fostered. Within the forensic psychiatric centres there should be an inter-disciplinary group working as a team in which local authority and probation and after-care service social workers should participate. Through such a group expert advice would be available to workers in the field and inter-disciplinary co-operation would be enhanced. A period spent as a member of the forensic psychiatric centre team should be seen as an essential step in the career of social workers of both services. The centres would have an important training role not only for social workers but for all those involved with the treatment of mentally disordered offenders, and in particular for nurses. (Paragraphs 20.20–20.21.)

73. The special hospitals should make a significant contribution to the forensic psychiatric services, particularly as regards training of personnel. (Paragraph 20.22.)

276

74. Co-ordination of all those involved with forensic psychiatric work should be promoted by the establishment of regional committees to advise on planning and policy, with representation from all the services. In the process of co-ordination, the role of the joint consultant forensic psychiatrists will be important. (Paragraph 20.23.)

75. We stress the importance of "through-care" for mentally disordered offenders and the establishment of day treatment units. (Paragraph 20.24.)

76. We believe that our proposals for the establishment of effective forensic psychiatric services will, if implemented, make a significant contribution towards realisation of the long-desired strengthening of links between the Prison Medical Service and the National Health Service, and thus towards improving facilities for the treatment of the mentally disordered offender; and we regard the development of such services as a vital element in our recommendations as a whole. (Paragraphs 20.25–20.26.)

Consent to treatment

77. Where a patient's condition does not prevent him from appreciating what is involved we do not think it justifiable to impose treatment (other than nursing care) without his consent. There are three exceptions to the general rule. Treatment may be given without consent (a) where it is not hazardous or irreversible and is the minimum necessary to prevent the patient behaving violently or being a danger to himself or others; or (b) where it is necessary to save his life; or (c) where (not being irreversible) it is necessary to prevent him from deteriorating. Where by reason of his disability the patient is unable to appreciate what is involved, despite the help of an explanation in simple terms, the treatment may be given; but special considerations apply to treatment involving irreversible procedures (see Recommendation 79 below). (Paragraphs 3.50–3.54.)

78. It is essential that the nature of the treatment proposed, and the prospects of success, together with the implications in relation to his prospects of release, should be carefully explained to the patient. Needless to say prospects should not be held out to the patient unless they are genuine and fully justified by the prognosis. (Paragraphs 3.55 and 3.56.)

79. In view of anxieties expressed to us about irreversible procedures we propose that, where these are involved, in addition to the consent of the patient (where the patient is capable of giving it), a second psychiatric opinion independent of the treating hospital or prison should be obtained, unless delay would be likely to endanger life; and the nearest relative (or guardian, if there is one) should also be consulted if this can be done within a reasonable time. (Paragraph 3.56.)

80. In view of the obscurity of the legal position with regard to the compulsory treatment of detained patients we recommend that consideration should be given to clarifying it when the Mental Health Act is under review, to conform to the requirements we have indicated. (Paragraphs 3.57–3.59.)

Provision for inadequates

(As regards provision of hostels see Recommendation 85.)

81. Consideration should be given to the possibility of the National Health Service playing a greater part in the provision of shelter for "inadequates". (Paragraph 6.6.)

82. Hospitals and other specialised institutions should provide for the medical treatment of "inadequates", including alcoholics and drug takers, where this is required. We note the disappointing lack of progress in providing detoxification centres, as recommended by the Working Party on Habitual Drunken Offenders in 1971, and hope that the new Advisory Committee on Alcoholism will be able to suggest ways of overcoming the difficulties. (Paragraph 6.7.)

83. There is a great need for local authorities to provide more long-term supportive accommodation for single homeless people, many of whom are "inadequates", regardless of whether they are offenders. (Paragraph 6.8.)

84. Although there are objections of principle to placing in penal institutions men for whom the courts do not consider a penal sanction is appropriate, prison provides them with in some respects a suitable (and, in many cases, familiar) environment. It may be that special arrangements could be devised for them. The Home Office should consider this. (Paragraphs 6.11–6.12.)

Accommodation in the community

(As regards juveniles see Recommendations 134 and 137.)

85. We urge a substantial increase in the provision of general hostel accommodation and greater co-ordination among the various bodies, both statutory and voluntary, who provide and administer hostels for discharged offenders. The provision of "after-care" hostels by voluntary organisations under the Home Office scheme for the rehabilitation of offenders and, in future, by the probation and after-care service, is of particular importance for the support of the inadequate mentally disordered offender. Government reception centres also have an important contribution to make. The new probation homes for adults seem a hopeful development and plans should be made for a quick expansion of this provision if they prove successful. (Paragraphs 6.9–6.10 and 8.11–8.19.)

Guardianship orders

(With regard to juveniles, see Recommendation 132 below. On a finding of disability in relation to the trial see Recommendation 26 above. On the return of a special verdict see Recommendation 54 above.)

86. The guardianship order is a valuable form of disposal which is at present very little used. There should be closer liaison between the courts and local authorities social services departments with a view to discussing difficulties and improving the working of the present arrangements. (Paragraphs 15.2–15.5 and 15.8.)

87. There should be full consultation by the courts with the relevant social service in all cases where it is proposed to make a guardianship order. Local authorities should continue to have the right to refuse to accept offenders into guardianship. (Paragraph 15.6.)

Psychiatric Probation Orders

88.   Careful pre-selection of offenders is essential for the success of psychiatric probation orders.   Those assessing the individual offender should have regard strictly to his needs and suitability.   As well as a medical opinion the views of the probation officer should be sought, and it should be normal practice for the court to obtain a social inquiry report on the defendant.   (Paragraphs 16.5–16.6.)

89.   The three month limit for the imposition on a probationer of a condition requiring him to submit to psychiatric treatment should be removed. (Paragraph 16.7.)

90.   The legal requirement to ensure that the offender fully understands what obligations he is accepting must be effectively carried out.   The court should also ensure that all others concerned are aware of their obligations. (Paragraph 16.9.)

91.   The doctor giving medical evidence to the court should, wherever possible, carry out the treatment.   (Paragraph 16.11.)

92.   We stress the need for the close involvement of supervising probation officers while their clients are in hospital and we recommend that, wherever possible, the order should name the home probation officer as the supervising officer.   The supervising officer should work in conjunction with the doctor, and there is value in including him in case conferences.   (Paragraph 16.12.)

93.   There should be a formal requirement for the treating doctor to give notice to the probation officer in every case when treatment is terminated. (Paragraph 16.14.)

94.   Doctors should be prepared to testify that the patient did not co-operate in treatment, so as to support a finding that the order has been breached and enable the court to substitute a suitable alternative order instead of merely cancelling the medical requirement.   (Paragraphs 16.15–16.16.)

95.   Section 3(2) of the Powers of Criminal Courts Act 1973 should be revised to remove the technical necessity for amendment of the order when a probationer is discharged from in-patient to out-patient treatment. (Paragraph 16.17.)

Treatment in hospital and subsequently

(a) Treatment under section 60 hospital orders

(See also for juveniles Recommendations 132 and 133 below.   In cases of disability in relation to the trial, see Recommendation 26 above.   Following a special verdict, see Recommendation 54 above.)

96.   No general distinction should be made between offenders and non-offenders in the question of eligibility for hospital treatment.   Mentally disordered offenders should be put into the treatment situation which is best suited to their treatment needs, with proper regard for the requirements of safety.   (Paragraphs 3.3–3.8.)

97. Regard should be paid to the provisions in section 28(4) of the Mental Health Act (relating to the proscription of certain persons from making recommendations for the admission to hospital of non-offenders) and to the principle which underlies them. The matter may be important where the defendant objects to an order being made, and in such cases particular care should be exercised in this connection. (Paragraphs 14.2–14.4.)

98. One of the medical recommendations should normally be that of the doctor who will receive the patient, but there may be circumstances in which it would be unnecessary or inconvenient to insist on such a practice. (Paragraph 14.5.)

99. In all cases where it is proposed to make a hospital order on the ground that the defendant is suffering from subnormality one of the medical recommendations should be that of a specialist in subnormality. (Paragraph 14.6.)

100. It is essential that the consent of the receiving doctor should be obtained before a hospital order is made. (Paragraph 14.7.)

101. We propose that section 40 of the Mental Health Act 1959 should be amended to allow the responsible medical officer full discretion to decide, at any time during the operation of a hospital order, whether to seek the recall to hospital of a patient who has absconded. (Paragraphs 14.13–14.16.)

102. In the absence of compulsory after-care for hospital order cases doctors should use trial leave to test a patient's ability to live in the community, but this power should not be used to maintain control over patients indefinitely. (Paragraphs 7.3 and 8.4.)

(b) *Importance of after-care for hospital order patients*

(On co-operation among the services involved, see Recommendations 65–67 and 72–76 above.)

103. It is desirable, and we believe essential, practice for the responsible medical officer to satisfy himself that the best after-care arrangements possible in the circumstances have been made before a patient is discharged. Where, exceptionally, he regards after-care as unnecessary or impracticable we hope that he will officially record his reasons. (Paragraph 7.2.)

104. Mental Health Review Tribunals should, as they may, adjourn hearings until they are satisfied that, so far as is practicable, suitable after-care arrangements have been made. (Paragraphs 7.4–7.10.)

105. If satisfactory after-care arrangements for hospital cases are to be made it is important that there should be close co-operation between hospitals and outside agencies. (Paragraph 8.6.)

106. Responsibility for the after-care of discharged offender hospital patients should be given to the person who can bring most to the case in the particular circumstances, including considerations of public safety, regardless of whether he or she belongs to the local authority social services department or the probation and after-care service. (Paragraph 8.7.)

(c) *Section 65 restriction orders*

107. There should be a statutory requirement that the consent of the doctor to receive a restricted patient should be obtained before a restriction order is made. We hope that such a statutory right of refusal would not be used by doctors indiscriminately. (Paragraphs 14.21–14.22.)

108. We propose that section 65(1) should be revised to make it clear that the intention of the restriction order is to protect the public from serious harm. (Paragraph 14.24.)

109. We think that restriction orders should invariably be made without limit of time and that the power to make orders of limited duration should be removed from the statute book. (Paragraph 14.25.)

110. The responsible medical officer's decision as to the restricted patient's suitability for discharge should be based on continuing inter-disciplinary assessment of the patient. Co-operation, including free exchange of information, among all those involved with the patient after discharge is necessary to ensure his successful rehabilitation. (Paragraphs 4.17–4.18, 4.30 and 7.12.)

111. To improve the protection given to the public we propose that the procedures instituted in 1973 for the special assessment of certain section 65 patients should be modified and extended to cover all restricted patients in the special hospitals. The advisory body should not only be involved in the discharge and transfer decisions in these cases, but should continue to be concerned with former special hospital restricted patients subsequently as regards the grant of leave and their eventual discharge from local hospitals or secure units, and throughout their period of supervision, including the question of recall, if it arises. It should also be open to the Home Office or the responsible medical officer to consult the advisory board in any case where an independent opinion would be helpful in making a decision about a restricted patient who has not been transferred from a special hospital. (Paragraphs 4.19–4.25.)

112. These proposals for extending the work of the advisory board will probably require its reconstitution. It will be for the Government to consider the composition of the new board, after the normal processes of consultation, but we think it would be valuable to include a senior doctor with experience of special hospital work. Supporting staff will be required. The board should discuss each case with the responsible medical officer before deciding what advice to tender to the Home Secretary. (Paragraph 4.23.)

113. Public safety is an essential consideration in deciding the discharge of potentially dangerous people, and responsibility for this decision in respect of patients subject to a restriction order should remain with the Home Secretary, who is publicly accountable. (Paragraphs 7.14–7.16.)

114. To ensure that section 65 patients, most of whom are subject to an order made without limit of time, are not detained longer than necessary, we recommend that regular annual reports on such patients should be submitted to the Home Secretary by the responsible medical officer. (Paragraphs 7.25 and 14.25.)

115. We support proposals for the appointment of a guardian or patient's friend to watch over the interests of individual patients, and propose that statutory provision should be made for this. Paragraphs 7.26–7.28.)

116. We endorse the view that special hospital patients should, wherever practicable, go to a local psychiatric hospital or a hostel as a first stage in rehabilitation. As local hospitals are sometimes reluctant to take patients from the special hospitals, we recommend that these transfers should be for a trial period in the first instance with ready re-admission to the special hospitals if needed. The proposed regional secure units will have an important role to play in taking some patients from the special hospitals, and special hospitals should readily re-admit patients transferred to the secure units should the need arise. (Paragraphs 4.26–4.29.)

117. With regard to the recall to hospital of a discharged restricted patient the supervising officer must have discretion as to the degree of possible risk to the public that may be acceptable. Where he thinks that recall is necessary the presumption on the part of the hospital should generally be in favour of accepting the patient, even if only for a brief period of observation. (Paragraph 4.31.)

118. Before the discharge of any restricted patient agreement should be reached between the consultant and the Home Office as to the circumstances in which the consultant would be prepared to recommend recall to hospital. To deal with the problem of the discharged restricted patient whose behaviour gives cause for alarm but who is refused urgent re-admission to hospital, we propose that there should be provision for his emergency admission for up to 72 hours to a "place of safety", which would normally be a regional secure unit, when these are available, but meanwhile should be the hospital of a local remand prison or remand centre, on the direction of the Home Secretary. (Paragraphs 14.28–14.31.)

119. The standards adopted by the Home Office as general guides for deciding when supervision should be withdrawn are reasonable, but where there is a medical expectation of recurrence of the mental disorder supervision should be extended for more than the usual period related to the gravity of the offence. If our proposals for the modification and extension of the Aarvold arrangements are implemented, the removal of supervision will be a matter for the advisory board to advise upon in those cases which come within their continuing purview; otherwise, the existing board's advice should be sought in cases classified as requiring special care in assessment. (Paragraph 4.32.)

120. Where the advice of a Mental Health Review Tribunal is to discharge a restricted patient, we stress that all consultations should be carried out with the greatest sense of urgency. (Paragraphs 7.19–7.22.)

Psychopaths

121. Dissatisfaction with the concept of psychopathic disorder has led many witnesses to suggest that "psychopathic disorder" should be removed from the definitions of mental disorder in section 4 of the Mental Health Act. This is outside our remit because of the effect on Part IV, but in view of the evidence

we have received and the consideration we have given to the whole subject we have made what we hope may be some helpful observations on the implications of this course. (Paragraphs 5.19–5.26.)

122. Some treatment methods for psychopathic disorder practised in this country which are claimed to have some success are not suitable for the more aggressive psychopathic offender when they can be provided only in the open conditions of local psychiatric hospitals. These offenders are generally sent to prison. Modification of their social behaviour is the object of treatment of these cases and the penal system should continue to receive them. (Paragraphs 5.37–5.38.)

123. Controlled research and experiment are necessary to determine what conditions and treatment regime produce the most encouraging results, but our view is that a long-term training regime designed to encourage the natural process of maturation would be likely to have success. We envisage this training programme being carried out in special units within the prison system. (See further at Recommendation 125 below.) (Paragraphs 5.38–5.39.)

124. We propose an amendment to section 60(1) of the Mental Health Act to make clear the responsibility of the prison system to deal with dangerous anti-social psychopathic offenders where there are no indications of justification for admission to hospital. The amendment should not apply to juveniles under the age of 17; they should not be sent to prison. It should continue to be possible to transfer psychopaths from prison to hospital under section 72. (Paragraphs 5.40–5.42.)

125. We put forward proposals for the training and treatment of dangerous anti-social psychopaths on a voluntary basis in special units within the penal system and have suggested the type of regime we think may prove successful. A start should be made on an experimental basis and research should be "built in" from the outset. A scientifically valid pilot research study should be set up with the help of the Medical Research Council; initially this might be carried out in existing prison accommodation. (Paragraphs 5.43–5.57.)

Prisons
(With regard to "inadequates" see Recommendation 84. In relation to juveniles see Recommendation 134. As to the need for borstals providing psychiatric care in the North of England, see Recommendation 136.)

Medical resources
(On the relationships of the Prison Medical Service to the National Health Service see Recommendations 70, 71, 74 and 76.)

126. There is need for a vigorous and substantial up-grading of the medical resources in the prisons, including physical facilities and staff complements and specialised psychiatric training. All aspects of the problem require to be tackled with urgency, determination and a massive injection of money. (Paragraphs 3.28–3.32.)

127. Priority should be given to improving the general level of psychiatric provision in the prisons, and to establishing experimental training units for psychopathic offenders. (Paragraphs 3.33–3.35.)

Treatment of Sexual deviants

128. We recommend that more resources should be made available for research into behaviour therapy and other forms of treatment for patients suffering from sexual deviation. Such deviants should be included within the scope of section 72 of the Mental Health Act to permit their transfer from prison to hospital in the event of effective treatments becoming available. We share the anxiety of witnesses that sexual offenders in the prisons should be safeguarded against victimisation. In this we think that the attitudes of the staff are of great importance and the prison authorities should give as positive a lead as they can. (Paragraphs 3.24–3.27.)

Transfers to hospital

(In connection with the reviewable sentence see Recommendation 42.)

129. We recommend that the scope of section 72 of the Mental Health Act should be widened to enable prisoners suffering from any form of mental disorder to be transferred to hospital. Certain consequential amendments would be required in other parts of the Act. (Paragraph 3.45.)

130. We urge in this connection, as we have in others, that the local NHS hospitals should accept the responsibility of playing a larger part in the treatment of mentally disordered offenders than many now do, to provide the flexibility which the treatment arrangements in the Act were intended to have, and to ensure that adequate medical treatment is not denied to people who need it. (Paragraphs 3.48–3.49.)

131. Prisoners transferred to hospital under section 72 should have a right of application to a Mental Health Review Tribunal for an early hearing at what would have been their earliest date of release. At this time, also, the Home Secretary should review the need for the continuation of section 74 restrictions if these have been imposed. (Paragraphs 3.41–3.44.)

Juveniles

(See also Recommendation 124 above.)

132. The power to make a hospital or guardianship order under section 1(3) of the Children and Young Persons Act 1969 should remain available to the courts for juveniles suffering from mental illness, psychopathic disorder, subnormality or severe subnormality. (Paragraphs 17.1–17.2.)

133. More places for juveniles should be provided in National Health Service hospitals. We envisage that some regional secure units will provide a limited number of beds, on an inter-regional basis, for juveniles for both investigation and treatment. As with adults, the decision as to admission should be made by the hospital consultant. It is desirable that some forensic psychiatrists should be encouraged to specialise in work with juveniles. (Paragraph 17.3.)

134. In the field of local authority responsibility, secure facilities for juveniles of both sexes should be provided, preferably attached to a community home in each children's regional planning area; increased assessment provision should be the priority. The matter is the more urgent because for lack of this provision young persons are being committed to prison which is quite unsuitable. We recommend that central Government should provide funds to local authorities for the provision of these facilities and we welcome the statement by the Government of their intention to make available financial assistance for this purpose in the form of direct grants to local authorities. (Paragraphs 17.4–17.8.)

135. The indeterminacy of detention subject to Ministerial control provided by section 53(1) of the Children and Young Persons Act must, in our view, be retained for juveniles convicted of murder. (Paragraph 17.9.)

136. Borstals providing psychiatric care for young offenders, both for boys and girls, comparable to those in the South-East, should be established in the North of the country to reduce the isolation of the trainees. (Paragraph 17.10.)

137. More after-care hostels should be provided for young offenders with personality problems. Voluntary organisations especially could make a valuable contribution in this area preferably in co-ordination with local authorities making similar provision. (Paragraph 17.12.)

138. Where a supervision order is made the supervising officer should be the person who can bring most to the case in the way of knowledge, expertise and resources, whether a local authority social worker or a probation officer. (Paragraph 17.11.)

139. Legislation should be enacted to enable the doctor who gives medical evidence to the court when a supervision order is made under section 12 of the Children and Young Persons Act 1969 to do so in writing. (Paragraph 17.14.)

Research

140. We draw attention to the need for more research in connection with mentally disordered offenders, and the importance of planning evaluative studies to be "built in" to any new regime or form of treatment. The initiative in identifying profitable areas of research should more often come from those responsible for the operation of the system, including the Government Departments, the criminal courts and the various services, especially where operational research is concerned. (Paragraphs 1.22–1.25.)

(As to research into the treatment of psychopaths, see Recommendation 125, and as regards research into the treatment of sexual deviants, see Recommendation 128.)

Final Remarks

In conclusion we wish to record that we are particularly grateful to our Secretariat for the care and attention which they have lavished not only on us personally but on this massive report as a whole.

Our thanks are due in particular to Mr A W Glanville of the Home Office, our Secretary, and to Miss M Purvis of the Department of Health and Social Security, our Assistant Secretary, who have shown great ability in mastering an infinite amount of detail and in keeping contact with the many interests concerned, whether medical, psychiatric, forensic or otherwise. We have been much struck by their competence, and together they have made a most effective team.

We are also obliged to Mr R W Hurd, Miss A E Johnson, Miss D J Pirie, Mrs J Scroxton, Mr G Sutton, Mrs R E Thomas, Miss S M West and Mr L P Wright all of whom have made effective and appreciated contributions towards the organisation and completion of our work.

BUTLER (*Chairman*)

DAVID CROOM-JOHNSON (*Vice-Chairman*)

DOUGLAS I ACRES

STEPHEN BROWN

RONALD BUTT

DENIS HILL

DEREK HODGSON

MARGARET RICHARDSON

KENNETH ROBINSON

STANLEY SMITH

NOEL TIMMS

NIGEL WALKER

ALAN WESTON

JESSIE M WHITE

GLANVILLE WILLIAMS

A W GLANVILLE (*Secretary*)

M PURVIS   (*Assistant Secretary*)

MEMBERSHIP OF THE COMMITTEE ON
MENTALLY ABNORMAL OFFENDERS

The Rt Hon the Lord Butler of Saffron Walden KG CH (Chairman)

The Hon Mr Justice Croom-Johnson DSC VRD (Vice-Chairman)

Dr D I Acres MRCS LRCP MRCGP DMJ(Clin) JP

Mr Stephen Brown QC*

Mr Ronald Butt

Professor Sir Denis Hill FRCP FRCPsych

Mr W D T Hodgson QC

Mr W M Moelwyn Hughes JP*

Mrs M A Richardson JP

The Rt Hon Kenneth Robinson

Dr Stanley Smith FRCP DPM FRCPsych

Professor Noel Timms

Councillor Mrs J M White

Dr Nigel Walker*

Dr W A Weston MRCPsych DPM

Professor Glanville Williams QC FBA

---

* Mr Hughes resigned from the Committee on grounds of ill-health on 25 September 1972.
Dr Nigel Walker was appointed Wolfson Professor of Criminology on 1 October 1973.
Mr Stephen Brown was appointed a Judge of the High Court in August 1975.

A. EVIDENCE

(1) The Committee received written and oral evidence from:

Association of Municipal Corporations
Bar Council
British Medical Association
British Psychological Society
Conference of Principal Probation Officers[1]
Consultant Forensic Psychiatrists
Professor Sir Rupert Cross[2]
Department of Health and Social Security
Mr C W French
Professor T C N Gibbens
Grendon Prison Staff
His Honour Judge Hines
Home Office
Howard League for Penal Reform
HM Judges of the Queen's Bench and Family Divisions of the High Court of Justice
Justices' Clerks' Society
Law Society
Magistrates Association
National Association of Chief and Principal Nursing Officers
National Council for Civil Liberties
National Association for Mental Health
Prison Medical Service
Prison Officers Association (including the Broadmoor Branch)
Royal College of Psychiatrists
Dr P D Scott

(2) Others who submitted written evidence included:

Association of Chief Police Officers
Association of Directors of Social Services
Association of Heads and Matrons of Community Schools
Association of Managers of Approved Schools
Association of Police Surgeons
Boards of Visitors
British Association of Social Workers
British Epilepsy Association
British Society for the Study of Mental Subnormality
Broadmoor Hospital Medical Advisory Committee

---

[1] Since re-designated the Conference of Chief Probation Officers.
[2] Oral evidence only.

Central Council of Probation and After-Care Committees
Chief and Principal Nursing Officers of the Special Hospitals
Confederation of Health Service Employees
County Councils Association
Director of Public Prosecutions
Free Church Federal Council
Institute for the Study and Treatment of Delinquency
Institution of Professional Civil Servants
International Commission for Human Rights
National Society for Mentally Handicapped Children
National Association of Probation Officers
Parole Board
Police Federation
Prosecuting Solicitors' Society
Psychologists and Social Workers in the Special Hospitals
Royal College of Nursing
Royal London Aid Society Limited
Scottish Prison Officers Association
Society for Individual Freedom
Thursday Cellar Club Management Committee
Trades Union Congress

We also received written submissions from several Children's Regional Planning Committees, Local Authority Social Services Departments, local Magistrates' Benches, Mental Health Review Tribunals and Regional Hospital Boards. Numerous other people wrote to us either individually or in conjunction with or on behalf of colleagues or contributed to our Report in other ways. These included in particular members of the legal, medical and social work professions, the Universities in this country and overseas, patients in hospitals, including the special hospitals, some prisoners and members of the general public.

We have also received helpful information from the Council of Europe and from Commissions and Committees engaged in similar tasks overseas, in particular from the Law Reform Commission of Canada, the Interdepartmental Committee on Mentally Ill and Maladjusted Persons in the Irish Republic, and the Swedish Committee on Abnormal Offenders.

B. VISITS

(1) Members of the Committee have paid the following visits in the United Kingdom:
Parkhurst Prison
Grendon Prison
Styal Prison
Wakefield Prison
Holloway Prison
Bullwood Hall Borstal
Feltham Borstal
Broadmoor Special Hospital
Rampton Special Hospital
Moss Side Special Hospital
All Saints Hospital, Birmingham (Midland Centre for Forensic Psychiatry)

Highcroft Hospital, Birmingham
Fulbourn Hospital, Cambridge
St Mary Abbott's Hospital, Kensington
St John's Hospital, Lincoln
Horton Hospital, Epsom
Prentice Unit, Royal Western Counties Hospital
Garth Angharad Hospital
St Charles Youth Treatment Centre, Brentwood
Oxford Probation and After-care Service and the Ley Clinic, Oxford
Leeds Reception Centre
Camberwell Reception Centre
Liverpool Day Training Centre
Leeds Social Services Establishments

(2) Members of the Committee have visited and had discussions with representatives of the following Continental establishments or organisations:

SWEDEN   National Forensic Psychiatric Clinic, Uppsala
Rehabilitation Units at Ullerakers Hospital, Uppsala
National Board of Health and Welfare
Swedish Committee on Mentally Abnormal Offenders
Regional top security prison, Akersberg

DENMARK   Institute of Forensic Psychiatry, Copenhagen
Herstedvester Treatment Centre

HOLLAND   Department of Justice
Psychiatric Observation Clinic and Selection Institute, Utrecht
Co-operating Probation and After-Care Services at Hertogenbosch
Mesdagkliniek, Groningen
Van der Hoevenkliniek, Utrecht

THE AFTER-CARE OF SPECIAL HOSPITAL PATIENTS

by Dr D I ACRES

The following study was carried out under the auspices of a Cropwood Fellowship at the Institute of Criminology at Cambridge. The patients studied were all the 17 women and 75 men released from the three Special Hospitals during 1971, who had been detained as the result of a court order, and who had been discharged directly into the community (i.e. not to a National Health Service hospital).

This brief summary presents a few of the more important findings of the research, which involved interviews with nearly 300 persons during 1974. The period studied from a statistical standpoint was the 2 years following discharge, but subsequent information was recorded separately.

The following table shows the whereabouts of the patients at the time of the interview with them or with their supervising officer. On average this was just under three years from the date of discharge:

Present whereabouts		Total No.		Percentage	
Deceased		4		4·34	
In institutions:					
Prison	12			13·04	
Special Hospital	16			17·39	
NHS Hospital	2	30		2·17	(32·6)
Living in the community:					
In own home or in lodgings	49			53·26	
In a hostel	2			2·17	
Living in at work	2	53		2·17	(57·6)
Not known		5		5·43	
		92			

Thus at this time about one-third of the patients had found their way back into institutions, and over a half were reasonably well settled in the community.

Discharge procedure

The pattern of discharge varied between the three Special Hospitals, as can be seen from the following table:

Special Hospital	Number (and %age) released by the Responsible Medical Officer		Number (and %age) released by the Mental Health Review Tribunal	
Broadmoor	32	(86·5)	5	(13·5)
Moss Side	0	(Nil)	14	(100)
Rampton	11	(26·9)	30	(73·1)
Totals	43	(46·7)	49	(53·3)

Re-conviction statistics

The study of the after-care of Special Hospital patients was intended primarily as a descriptive one, though certain statistical factors emerged during its course. In the following tables where re-conviction rates are given it should be made clear that these are crude figures from which comparisons should not be drawn since the different sub-groups had different antecedent histories. It is intended to make a detailed study of these figures before the publication of the completed report.

Marital status

At the time of admission to hospital 68 patients (73·9%) had a settled sexual relationship, but at the time of interview this had fallen to 55 (59·8%).

Legal category

The authority for the detention of the 92 patients was as follows, and against each is the average stay in the Special Hospital:

Legal Category		No. of patients	% age of sample	Average stay in months
s. 60 MHA 1959 (Hospital Order)	...	30	32·6	42·5
s. 72 ,, (Trans. prison) ...	...	20	21·7	46·5
s. 65 ,, (Restn. Order) ...	...	32	34·8	50·6
s. 4 CP(I)A 1964 (under disability)	...	2	2·2	37·5
s. 71 MHA 1959 ("HMP") ...	...	1	1·1	72·0
Others	...	7	7·6	197·7
Totals		92	100·0	58·7

The distribution of the various legal categories between the three Special Hospitals was as follows:

Legal Category	Percentage of the category (with Nos. in brackets)			
	Broadmoor	Moss Side	Rampton	Total
Hospital Orders	13·3 (4)	30·0 (9)	56·7 (17)	100 (30)
Transfer from prison ...	25·0 (5)	25·0 (5)	50·0 (10)	100 (20)
Restriction Orders	75·0 (24)	nil	25·0 (8)	100 (32)
Under disability	100·0 (2)	nil	nil	100 (2)
"HMP"	100·0 (1)	nil	nil	100 (1)
Others	14·3 (1)	nil	85·7 (6)	100 (7)

Principal psychiatric diagnosis

Attention has been drawn in the Report (see paragraph 2.14) to the differing populations of the three Special Hospitals, and these were reflected in the sample studied. Broadmoor admitted most of the patients suffering from mental illness, about a third of the psychopaths, and no subnormals. Moss Side's 14 admissions were equally distributed between subnormality and psychopathy, with no mentally ill patients. Rampton received two-thirds of the subnormals, about half the psychopaths, and only a few mentally ill patients, as follows:

Diagnosis	Percentage of each group (with Nos. in brackets)			
	Broadmoor	Moss Side	Rampton	Total
Mental illness	78·6 (22)	nil	21·4 (6)	100 (28)
Subnormality and severe subnormality	nil	33·3 (7)	66·7 (14)	100 (21)
Psychopathy	34·9 (15)	16·3 (7)	48·8 (21)	100 (43)

Expressed in different terms, the distribution of the diagnoses between the three hospitals was as follows:

Diagnosis	Percentage of the discharges within each group in relation to each hospital:		
	Broadmoor	Moss Side	Rampton
Mental illness	59·5	nil	14·6
Subnormality and severe subnormality	nil	50·0	34·2
Psychopathy	40·5	50·0	51·2

Predictably the reconviction rate for mentally ill patients was the lowest, and for those suffering from subnormality the highest, viz:

Diagnosis	Not reconvicted	Reconvicted	Total	% re-convicted*
Mental illness	23	5	28	17·9
Subnormality and severe subnormality	7	14	21	66·7
Psychopathy	20	23	43	53·5
Totals ...	50	42	92	45·7

Sentencing court

Having regard to the type of offender that one might expect to encounter in a Special Hospital, it was of interest that almost exactly a third of the patients studied had been admitted direct from a magistrates' court. A few more came from courts of assize, and about a quarter from quarter sessions and crown courts (old terminology).

Residence and family contacts

Where the patient was not living with a relative at the time of interview, enquiry was made as to whether reasonable contact was maintained with members of the family. In only 14 instances (15·2 % of the total sample) was there no meaningful contact of this sort.

Having regard to the fact that patients discharged from Special Hospitals suffer the dual disability of being labelled as "criminals" and "mentally disordered", the sample showed a surprising stability in respect of accommodation. 20 of the sample did not move during the 2 years following discharge, and 50 % did not move more than twice. At the other end of the scale 8 moved 9 or more times and 1 over 15 times.

The reasons for changes of residence were not always easy to discover, particularly where they had been frequent and there was little or no contact with a supervising officer. Only 12 landlords or landladies were interviewed, as in general patients were reluctant to give their consent to their being seen.

The following table gives some indication of the reasons for change of residence:

Moved house with landlord	...	...	...	...	11
Left to join family ...	...	...	...	...	20
Left because of better accommodation ...		...	...	76
Asked to leave because of record		...	...	...	4
Asked to leave because of behaviour	...	...	...	124
			Total	...	235

*For the figures in this column see *Re-Conviction Statistics* on page 292.

It is interesting that 4 moves (involving 1 move for each of 4 patients) were attributed to the landlord or landlady hearing of the record of admission to a Special Hospital, whereas 124 moves were attributable to bad behaviour. This appears to be something of an indication of the veracity of the patients, since it would be natural to ascribe moves to previous record rather than current behaviour.

Participation by the family doctor

The part played by the family doctor in the after-care of the patients studied was most variable. 33 patients had had no contact with a general practitioner during the two years, and 36 had only known their doctors since discharge. On the other hand, 12 family doctors had known their patients for more than 10 years, and had a detailed knowledge of them and their families. In these cases it was evident that they were playing an important part in their rehabilitation.

Some of the general practitioners interviewed had developed special skills in dealing with mentally disordered offenders, and those who were also police surgeons seemed at a particular advantage.

Taken overall the average number of contacts of each patient with their doctors averaged 4·3 per annum, not far from the national average. 26 felt that they had good relationships with their doctors, though about the same number saw the relationship as unsatisfactory for one reason or another, and 5 described their attitude to their doctor as hostile.

There were good working relationships between the GP and the supervising officer in 22 instances, and only minimal contact in a further 30. A rapport between the GP and the psychiatrist only appeared to have been established in 7 of the 20 instances in which patients received help from both.

12 family doctors felt that there was a good working relationship with the Special Hospital, and a further 16 considered that there was need for greater contact. It was interesting that amongst this latter group there was a high proportion that claimed that they had received no information from the hospital at all, though on studying the patient's record a letter was discovered in each instance.

Psychiatric care

This was provided in 29 cases, including 20 of the 32 restriction order discharges. Whilst all of this group had had psychiatric help arranged, in 12 cases for varying reasons, generally lack of co-operation on the patient's part, no contact was made.

Psychiatric care was provided for 20 of the 43 discharges initiated by the Responsible Medical Officer (40·8%) and in 9 of the 49 discharges by a Mental Health Review Tribunal (18·4%). No doubt this situation arose largely from the lesser opportunity to arrange after-care where the patient had to be discharged quickly after a tribunal decision.

Female patients received psychiatric supervision in a slightly higher proportion of cases (35·3%) than men (30·7%).

18 of the 29 patients described their relationships with their psychiatrist as satisfactory, 9 as not meaningful, and 2 as hostile. In the 26 instances in which the patient received both psychiatric and probation or social work care, just over half seemed to be at a useful level. None was described as hostile.

294

Social work and probation supervision

59·8% of the sample had had some form of supervision prior to their admission to the Special Hospital, and in a number of instances on 2 or more occasions. The break-down was as follows:

Probation without conditions	44·6%	(41)
Probation with conditional residence	8·7%	(8)
Probation with conditional treatment	2·2%	(2)
Social worker statutorily	17·4%	(16)
Social worker voluntarily	1·1%	(1)
Other	3·3%	(3)
No previous supervision	40·2%	(37)

On discharge supervision was arranged as follows:

By a probation officer as a condition of discharge ...	23·9%	(22)
By a probation officer voluntarily	7·6%	(7)
By a social worker as a condition of discharge	15·2%	(14)
By a social worker voluntarily	42·4%	(39)
None	10·9%	(10)

The choice of supervising officer appeared to have been related to a certain extent with previous contacts, so that an existing rapport could be utilised. There was, however, a marked variation between the 3 hospitals, Broadmoor nominating nearly twice as many probation officers as social workers, with Moss Side and Rampton making use of more than 5 social workers for each probation officer.

There can be no doubt that the supervising officer played a vital role in the after-care of the patients studied. 68% described their relationships with their supervising officer as satisfactory, and only 2% showed hostility.

Many of the officers appear to have been chosen for their experience or their suitability for dealing with this very demanding group of clients. Even so, only about a dozen officers had had any previous experience of Special Hospital patients. One or two of these had had very great experience indeed, and had developed remarkable skills. There appeared to be meagre facilities for training and supporting these officers, a matter which merits some consideration, for some felt very unsupported in their demanding task, even though 67% appear to have enjoyed a good relationship with the Special Hospital. Only one expressed any feelings of hostility, and a number paid tribute to the speedy help given them by the hospital in a crisis situation. Almost without exception the officers welcomed the idea of a regional unit where advice could be obtained more quickly, and a relationship developed prior to discharge. Many felt unheeded in the release decision.

On average each patient was seen at home 12 times by the supervising officer, and 19 times at the office. Local authority social workers tended to concentrate on home visits and probation officers on interviews at the office, though in almost every instance both types of contacts were established. This appeared important, since valuable background information was likely to be forthcoming at home, and in many instances a more relaxed atmosphere for interview could be achieved away from domestic interruptions.

In addition to the above contacts there were innumerable telephone conversations with patients and with others concerned in their after-care. Whilst it proved difficult in many cases to distinguish between contacts initiated by the patient and those at the behest of the supervisor, on average there seemed to be at least 3·5 voluntary contacts during the period studied.

At the time of interview 41 (50%) of those who had been placed under supervision were still receiving it. Of the remaining 41 contact had been terminated as follows:

Discharge made absolute and supervision stopped on the
initiative of the officer ... ...   1 (2·4%)
Discharge made absolute and supervision stopped on the
initiative of the patient ... ...   1 (2·4%)
Patient moved away and contact lost ... ... 19 (46·3%)*
Patient stopped attending ... ...   2 (4·9%)
Supervision discontinued by officer because of impracticability   2 (4·9%)
Recalled (12) or died (4) ... ... 16 (39·1%)

In 52 instances (63·4%) contact was maintained without interruption for the full period, and in a further 8 (9·8%) the loss of contact was for less than a month. For the remainder contact was lost for varying periods up to a year.

The effect of supervision after discharge is very hard to assess, though there is some evidence to suggest that statutory after-care is more successful than voluntary, that those under the supervision of a probation officer have slightly fewer reconvictions than those cared for by social workers, and that both do better than those without either form of help.

The statistics are as follows:

Type of Supervision	Nos. re-convicted	Nos. not reconvicted	Total Nos.	Percentage reconvicted**
Probation officer	12	17	29	41·4%
Social worker	24	29	53	45·3%
No supervision	6	4	10	60·0%
	42	50	92	45·7%
Statutory by PO or SW ...	12	24	36	33·3%
Voluntary by PO or SW ...	24	22	46	52·2%
No supervision	6	4	10	60·0%
	42	50	92	45·7%
PO statutorily	8	14	22	36·4%
PO voluntarily	4	3	7	57·1%
SW statutorily	4	10	14	28·6%
SW voluntarily	20	19	39	51·3%
No supervision	6	4	10	60·0%
	42	50	92	45·7%

In addition to the above, it is noticeable that the 36 patients who were reconvicted and received after-care supervision had an average of 18·9 contacts with their supervising officers, compared with 27·1 contacts for those who were not reconvicted.

Employment

Detailed information with regard to employment after discharge was obtained in 88 of the 92 cases. Many obtained employment within a few days, and after a month 59·1% had obtained work. The figures for 3 months and 6 months after discharge were 71·6% and 79·5% respectively. 17% did not obtain employment within the 2 years studied.

*See Annex "A" and Annex "B".
**For the figures in this column see *Re-Conviction Statistics* on page 292.

The number of employments obtained during this period were as follows:

Unemployed	17·0%
1 or 2 jobs	40·9%
3 or 4 jobs	22·7%
5 or 6 jobs	13·7%
7 or 8 jobs	2·3%
9 or 10 jobs	—
11 or 12 jobs	2·3%
Over 12	1·1%

In addition to the 17% who remained unemployed throughout the period, 22·7 were unemployed for periods up to a month, 50% less than 6 months, and 61·4% for less than a year.

The 73 who obtained employment changed their jobs a total of 178 times during the 2 years, an average of 2·4. The reasons for change:

Dismissal for bad behaviour	63
To obtain a better job	62
Dismissal for bad work	21
Left because work uncongenial	14
Dismissed because of fresh offence	4
Left because of attitude of fellow employees	3

Reconvictions during the two years following discharge

In each instance careful enquiry was made into the question of reconvictions during the 2 years under investigation. Usually this was undertaken by the supervising officer, but on occasion it was necessary to consult the prison record or the Criminal Record Office.

Number of reconvictions	% and (No.)
Nil	54·3% (50)
1	21·7% (20)
2	10·9% (10)
3	4·3% (4)
4	3·3% (3)
5	1·1% (1)
6	1·1% (1)
7	1·1% (1)
8 or more	2·2% (2)
Total ...	100·0% (92)

In spite of the history of admission to a Special Hospital, nearly two-thirds of the cases were disposed of in magistrates' courts, the exact figures being as follows:

Magistrates' Court	64·5% (60)
Quarter Sessions	5·4% (5)
Crown Court (old)	3·2% (3)
Crown Court (new)	25·8% (24)
Assizes	1·1% (1)
Total ...	100·0% (93)

Of the 60 cases disposed of in the magistrates' courts, 55 were property offences, 4 were for assault occasioning actual bodily harm, and one was for robbery. In one of the ABH cases the court returned the patient to the Special Hospital, and when he appeared again he was remitted to the Crown Court, where a fresh hospital order was made. The other three cases of ABH were all in respect of the same individual, who was returned to the Special Hospital on the first 2 occasions and imprisoned on the third. The robbery case was returned to the Special Hospital.

It is of interest that a fair number of patients had served prison sentences prior to admission to the Special Hospital and upon subsequent reconviction were again sentenced to imprisonment. All of these were either psychopathic or in a few instances subnormal. In one instance a patient suffering from a psychopathic disorder served 24 separate prison sentences before being admitted to a Special Hospital, subject to a restriction order. He was detained there for nearly 4 years, and 4 months after his release appeared before a magistrates' court, where he was placed on probation for 2 years for theft. After a further 2 months he was sentenced to a total of 18 months' imprisonment for a similar offence and breach of probation. Since then he has received 4 further prison sentences.

The disposal of the various offences was as follows:

Prison	35·5%	(33)
Return to Special Hospital	2·1%	(2)
Fresh Restriction Order	5·4%	(5)
Fresh Hospital Order	5·4%	(5)
Probation order without conditions	7·5%	(7)
Probation order with conditions	7·5%	(7)
Fine	20·4%	(19)
Absolute or conditional discharge	15·1%	(14)
Bound over	1·1%	(1)
Total ...	100·0%	(93)

For the following offences:

Murder	1·1%	(1)
Rape	1·1%	(1)
Other sexual assault	2·1%	(2)
Non-sexual violence against the person, not involving a property offence	11·8%	(11)
Violence against the person, involving a property offence	2·1%	(2)
Property offence	63·5%	(59)
Other	18·3%	(17)

The one case of murder was a cause célèbre.

Reference has already been made to the variation in the method of discharge between the 3 Special Hospitals, releases from Moss Side during the period studied being entirely by a Mental Health Review Tribunal, and those from Broadmoor being over

86% on the recommendation of the Responsible Medical Officer. The reconviction rate for the two groups of patients shows a similarly marked variation, as will be evident from the following table:

			No.	Recon.	% recon.*
BROADMOOR					
Discharged on the recommendation of	RMO		32	9	28·1%
do.	MHRT		5	2	40·0%
	Totals		37	11	29·7%
MOSS SIDE					
do.	RMO		0	0	—
do.	MHRT		14	11	78·6%
	Totals		14	11	78·6%
RAMPTON					
do.	RMO		11	4	36·4%
do.	MHRT		30	16	53·3%
	Totals		41	20	48·8%
ALL HOSPITALS					
do.	RMO		43	13	30·2%
do.	MHRT		49	29	59·2%
	Totals		92	42	45·6%

These figures are very much affected by the differing populations of the three hospitals and that mentally ill patients have a lower rate of reconviction than other groups, with subnormals the highest. Nevertheless the figures pay tribute to the prognostic ability of the Responsible Medical Officers.

The foregoing is a very brief summary of some of the facts which are of particular reference to the work of the Committee on Mentally Abnormal Offenders. The full study is to be published by The Academic Press Ltd.

Thanks are due to the many patients, probation officers, social workers, doctors, psychiatrists, Special Hospital staff, prison officers, and others who co-operated whole-heartedly in the study, together with senior officers at the Home Office and Department of Health and Social Security. Amongst the many who assisted with advice and encouragement I am particularly indebted to Professor Nigel Walker and Dr Donald West of the Institute of Criminology, who enabled this study to be undertaken under the auspices of a Cropwood Fellowship.

---

*For the figures in this column see *Re-Conviction Statistics* on page 292.

AN ANALYSIS OF PATIENT MOVED AWAY AND CONTACT LOST (see page 296 of Summary)

Sex	Legal category	Principal psychiatric diagnosis	Changes of residence	Involvement of GP	Involvement of psychiatrist	Type of supervision	Changes of employment	Unemployment during 2-year period	Offence leading to admission	Reconvictions during 2 years following discharge	
F	60	Psychopathy	6	Nil	Nil	Social worker voluntary	—	Unemployed throughout	Malicious wounding	Nil	
F	60	Subnormality	5	Slight	Moderate	,,	—	,,	Trespass on railway	Nil	Admitted to hospital under section 29 twice
F	60	Psychopathy	1	Extensive	Nil	,,	1	One month only	Burglary	Nil	Moved with husband and not thought necessary to continue supervision
M	65	Mental illness	1	Slight	Extensive	Social worker statutorily	—	Unemployed	Housebreaking	Nil	Admitted to mental hospital
M	72	Psychopathy	2	Nil	Nil	Social worker voluntary	6	Nil	Possessing offensive weapon	Nil	
M	6th Sch.	Severe subnormality	2	Nil	Extensive	,,	1	One month only	Attempted rape	2 drunk and disorderly	Admitted to mental hospital
M	60	Psychopathy	10	Slight	Extensive	,,	11	Over a year	Larceny	3 theft	Admitted to mental hospital
M	60	Psychopathy	11	Extensive	Moderate	,,	5	18 months	Taking and driving away	2 property offences	Admitted to hospital 4 times then prison

Sex	Age	Diagnosis						Then prison	violence		Prison
M	72	Psychopathy	1	Nil	Nil	voluntary	1	Then prison	Rape	1 violence	Prison
M	60	Subnormality	20+	Frequent change	Nil	"	20+	—	Indecent assault	8 theft and violence	All dealt with non-custodially
M	72	Psychopathy	5	Nil	Nil	"	5	Nil	Assault	1 GBH	Re-admitted to special hospital after 2-year period
M	60	Psychopathy	1	Moderate	Nil	Probation officer voluntary	3	Slight	False fire alarms	7 inc. arson	Admitted to mental hospital
M	65	Psychopathy	9	Nil	Nil	Probation officer statutorily	1	22 months	Wounding with intent to murder	3 offensive weapons etc.	Prison
M	60	Mental illness	2	Nil	Nil	Social worker voluntary	2	6 months	Indecent exposure	2 ABH	
M	72	Mental illness	3	Moderate	Nil	"	2	Nil	Indecent assault	Nil	
M	65	Psychopathy	?	Nil	Nil	"	?	?	Larceny	6 all property	Prison
M	72	Mental illness	5	Moderate	Nil	"	1	3 months	Malicious damage	Nil	

A SYNOPSIS OF THE CIRCUMSTANCES ASSOCIATED WITH THE
PATIENT MOVING AWAY AND CONTACT LOST
(see page 296 of Summary)

Of the 19 persons so noted supervision was as follows:

Probation Officer Statutorily	...	...	1
Probation Officer Voluntary	...	...	1
Social Worker Statutorily	...	...	1
Social Worker Voluntary ...	...	...	16

In the majority of instances contact was lost through imprisonment (5 cases), or admission to a mental or Special Hospital (8 cases).

9 of the 16 cases were reconvicted during the 2-year period, 5 of them for violent offences.

SCHEDULES OF QUALIFYING OFFENCES FOR THE REVIEWABLE SENTENCE

SCHEDULE A

Offences which would qualify irrespective of the offender's previous convictions, if any

NOTE: All these offences carry life sentences under the present law[1] but not all "life"-carrying offences are included in this Schedule.

Common law offences:

> False imprisonment (to cover kidnapping)
>
> Murder and attempts thereat (the penalty for murder is provided by the Murder (Abolition of Death Penalty) Act 1965, section 1)
>
> Manslaughter (penalty provided by the Offences Against the Person Act 1861, section 5)
>
> Rape (penalty provided by 2nd Schedule of the Sexual Offences Act 1956)

Statutory offences:

Criminal Damage Act 1971

Arson and criminal damage endangering life	Sections 1, 4

Explosive Substances Act 1883

Causing an explosion likely to endanger life	Section 2

Firearms Act 1968

Possessing firearm with intent to endanger life ...	Section 16*
Use of firearm to resist arrest	Section 17(1)*

*As amended by the Criminal Justice Act 1972.

Hijacking Act 1971

Hijacking aircraft	Section 1

Offences against the Person Act 1861

Shooting or attempting to shoot, or wounding with intent to do grievous bodily harm	Section 18
Attempting to choke etc or using chloroform etc in order to commit any indictable offence	Sections 21, 22
Causing bodily injury by explosions, or causing explosions or throwing corrosive fluids etc with intent to do grievous bodily harm	Sections 28, 29
Doing certain things with intent to endanger railway passengers	Sections 32, 33

Protection of Aircraft Act 1973

Destroying, damaging or endangering aircraft ...	Sections 1–3

Sexual Offences Acts 1956 and 1967

Buggery in circumstances carrying life imprisonment but not where the victim was over 16 and consented ...	Section 12 and the 2nd Schedule
Sexual intercourse with girl under 13	Section 5 and the 2nd Schedule
Incest with a girl under the age of 13	Section 10 and the 2nd Schedule

---

[1] The Schedules should be read as including attempts to commit the scheduled offences, and threats to commit where these are a statutory offence, also incitement to commit such offences.

Theft Act 1968
Robbery and assault with intent to rob ...   .   Section 8
Burglary, aggravated   ...   .   Section 10

SCHEDULE B

Offences which would qualify if the offender had on a previous occasion incurred a conviction for a Schedule A offence

NOTE: Offences included in this Schedule are *non*-"life"-carrying, but may involve serious sexual molestation or the risk of serious harm to the person.

Children and Young Persons Act 1933
Ill-treatment of a child   ...   .   Section 1

Explosive Substances Act 1883
Offences involving explosives and carrying 14 years'
   imprisonment or more ...   .   Sections 3, 4

Firearms Act 1968
Offences involving firearms and carrying 10 years'
   imprisonment or more   ...   .   Sections 17(2), 18

Indecency with Children Act 1960
Indecency with a child   ...   .   Section 1

Offences against the Person Act 1861
Inflicting bodily injury with or without a weapon   ...   Section 20
Poisoning offences carrying 5 years' imprisonment or
   more   ...   .   Sections 23, 24
Offences involving explosives and carrying 14 years'
   imprisonment   ...   .   Section 30

Prevention of Crime Act 1953
Carrying an offensive weapon in a public place   ...   Section 1

Sexual Offences Acts 1957 and 1967
Buggery in circumstances not carrying life imprisonment
   (excluding buggery with a consenting partner aged 16
   or older) ...   .   Section 12 and the
                                                               2nd Schedule
Indecent assault   ...   .   Sections 14, 15, 16

1. Extract from the British Glossary to the 1968 Revision of the International Statistical Classification of Disease

301. Personality disorders

This category refers to a group of more or less well defined anomalies or deviations of personality which are not the result of a psychosis or any other illness. The differentiation of these personalities is to some extent arbitrary and the reference to a given group will depend initially on the relative predominance of one or other group of character traits. This category includes what is sometimes called "psychopathic personality".

.0 *Paranoid*

This group includes two broad groups of personality anomaly: (1) certain sensitive, vulnerable people who react excessively to some of the average daily experiences of life with a sense of subjection and humiliation, and who tend to blame others for their experiences, and (2) personalities of a more aggressive and robust quality, excessively sensitive to what they conceive to be their rights, vulnerable to any violation of these and extremely tenacious in their defence, which is maintained persistently. The common factor in both types is an excessive tendency to self-reference and suspiciousness. The so-called over-valued idea or "idée fixe" may be prominent in these individuals.

.1 *Affective (cyclothymic)*

This group includes individuals with persistent anomalies of mood—either a predominantly gloomy and depressed attitude to life or the opposite features, namely, a perpetual satisfaction with life, an unshakeably optimistic view of circumstances, and an enhanced zest for life and activity. These characteristics frequently alternate in the same individual, but one or the other attitude often predominates.

.2 *Schizoid*

This group includes individuals whose emotional anomaly takes the form of conspicuous aloofness, shyness and reserve. Such individuals tend to be notably introspective and sometimes show marked eccentricity of conduct.

.3 *Explosive*

These individuals show marked instability of mood with particular liability to sudden outbursts of irritability, anger, aggression, and impulsive behaviour. They are not otherwise prone to anti-social behaviour and their affective relationships to their fellow-men between such outbursts may be unremarkable.

.4 *Anankastic (obsessive-compulsive)*

This group is characterised by a strong sense of personal insecurity, which shows itself in various typical ways: excessive caution and conscientiousness; there is also stubbornness and inflexibility, conformism, perfectionism, meticulous accuracy and the need to check repeatedly in an attempt to ensure this. The ethical standards of these individuals are commonly high and any lapse from these by themselves is visited by severe self-condemnation. The essential traits are timidity, rigidity often with extreme self-control, and an excessive tendency to ambivalence and doubt. This category includes obsessional personality.

.5   Hysterical

This group includes individuals with shallow, labile affectivity, and over-dependence on others.   They crave love and attention, though unreliable and unsteady in their personal relationships.   Under stress they may develop hysterical symptoms.   They tend to over-dramatise situations.

.6   Asthenic

These individuals show a lack of mental vigour in the broadest sense, which may manifest itself in the intellectual or emotional spheres.   With this is often associated a general lack of resilience to the normal demands of life.   Many so-called passive-dependent individuals are examples of this personality structure.   It is evident that this personality is signalised by its negative rather than its positive characteristics. What is sometimes called "inadequate personality" is to be included here.

.7   Antisocial

This term should be confined to those individuals who offend against society, who show a lack of sympathetic feeling, and whose behaviour is not readily modifiable by experience, including punishment.   They are affectively cold and callous.   They may tend to abnormally aggressive and seriously irresponsible conduct.   This category includes those individuals who are classified in the Mental Health Act 1959 (England and Wales) as suffering from "psychopathic disorder".

.8   Other

.9   Unspecified

2.   Extract from the World Health Organisation Glossary of mental disorders and guide to their classification (1974)

301.   Personality disorders

Includes deeply ingrained maladaptive patterns of behaviour generally recognisable by the time of adolescence or earlier and continuing throughout most of adult life, although often becoming less obvious in middle or old age.   The personality is abnormal either in the balance of its components, their quality and expression, or in its total aspect.   Because of this deviation or psychopathy the patient suffers or others have to suffer and there is an adverse effect upon the individual or on society. It includes what is sometimes called psychopathic personality, but if this is primarily due to malfunctioning of the brain, it should not be classified here but as a non-psychotic mental disorder associated with a physical condition (309).   When the patient exhibits an anomaly of personality directly related to his neurosis or psychosis, eg, schizoid personality and schizophrenia or anankastic personality and obsessive-compulsive neurosis, the condition should be classified under the neurosis or psychosis in evidence.

Excludes non-psychotic mental disorders associated with physical conditions (309).

Inclusion term
   Character neurosis

301.0   *Paranoid*

Includes a personality disorder in which there is excessive sensitivity to setbacks or what are taken to be humiliations and rebuffs, a tendency to distort experience by misconstruing the neutral or friendly actions of others as hostile or contemptuous, and a combative and tenacious sense of personal rights.   The patient may be prone

306

to jealousy or excessive self-importance. Some such persons may feel helplessly humiliated and put upon; others, likewise excessively sensitive, are aggressive and insistent. In all cases there is excessive self-reference.

Excludes paranoid states (297); schizophrenia, paranoid type (295.3); involutional paraphrenia (297.1); acute paranoid reaction (298.3).

Inclusion terms
Fanatic personality
Paranoid traits
Paranoid personality (disorder)

301.1 *Affective*

Includes a personality disorder characterised by lifelong predominance of a pronounced mood, which may be persistently depressed, persistently elated, or alternately elated and depressed. During periods of elation there is unshakeable optimism and an enhanced zest for life and activity, whereas periods of depression are marked by worry, pessimism, low output of energy, and a sense of futility.

Excludes affective psychosis (296); depressive neurosis (300.4); neurasthenia (300.5); manic-depressive psychosis, circular type (cyclothymia) (296.3).

Inclusion terms
Cycloid personality
Cyclothymic personality
Depressive personality

301.2 *Schizoid*

Includes a personality disorder in which there is withdrawal from affectional, social, and other contacts, with autistic preference for fantasy and introspective reserve. The patient's behaviour may be slightly eccentric or indicate avoidance of competitive situations. Apparent coolness and detachment may mask an incapacity to express feeling.

Excludes schizophrenia, simple type (295.0); latent, borderline, and pseudoneurotic schizophrenia (295.5); residual schizophrenia (295.6); schizophrenia, schizo-affective type (295.7).

301.3 *Explosive*

Includes a personality disorder characterised by instability of mood with liability to intemperate outbursts of anger, hate, violence, or affection. Aggression may be expressed in words or as physical violence. The outbursts cannot readily be controlled by the affected persons, who are not otherwise prone to antisocial behaviour.

Excludes antisocial personality disorder (301.7); hysterical neurosis (300.1); nonpsychotic mental disorders associated with epilepsy (309.4); psychosis associated with epilepsy (293.2).

Inclusion term
Aggressive personality

301.4 *Anankastic*

Includes a personality disorder characterised by feelings of personal insecurity, doubt, and incompleteness leading to excessive conscientiousness, stubbornness, and caution. There may be insistent and unwelcome thoughts or impulses, which do not attain the severity of those seen in obsessive-compulsive neurosis. The patient feels a need to check repeatedly in an attempt to ensure perfection and meticulous accuracy. Rigidity and excessive doubt may be conspicuous.

Excludes obsessive-compulsive neurosis (300.3); phobic neurosis (300.2).

Inclusion terms
Compulsive personality
Obsessional personality

301.5 *Hysterical*

Includes a personality disorder characterised by shallow, labile affectivity, dependence on others, craving for appreciation and attention, suggestibility, and theatricality. There is often sexual immaturity, eg, frigidity or over-responsiveness to stimuli. (Under stress hysterical symptoms (neurosis) may develop.)

Excludes hysterical neurosis (300.1).

Inclusion term
Histrionic personality

301.6 *Asthenic*

Includes a personality disorder characterised by passive compliance with the wishes of elders and others, and a weak, inadequate response to the demands of daily life. Lack of vigour may show itself in the intellectual or emotional spheres; there is little capacity for enjoyment.

Excludes neurasthenic neurosis (300.5).

Inclusion terms
Dependent personality
Inadequate personality
Passive personality

301.7 *Antisocial*

Includes a personality disorder characterised by disregard for social obligations, lack of feeling for others, and impetuous violence or callous unconcern. There is a gross disparity between behaviour and the prevailing social norms. Behaviour is not readily modifiable by experience, including punishment. People with this personality disorder are affectively cold and may be abnormally aggressive or irresponsible. Their tolerance to frustration is low; they blame others or offer plausible rationalisations for the behaviour that brings them into conflict with society.

Excludes explosive personality disorder (301.3).

Inclusion terms
Amoral personality
Dyssocial personality

301.8 *Other*

Includes personality disorders of other specified types.

Inclusion terms
Asocial personality
Eccentric personality
"Haltlose" personality type
Immature personality
Passive-aggressive personality
Psychoneurotic personality

301.9 *Unspecified*

Includes personality disorders of unspecified type.

Inclusion terms
Pathological personality NOS
Personality disorder NOS
Psychopathic constitutional state
Psychopathic personality (disorder)

Patient's rights of application to the Mental Health Review Tribunal

Patients admitted on a hospital order or transfer direction without an order restricting discharge, or transferred from guardianship under Part V of the Act, may apply to the Tribunal on the following occasions:—

(a) at any one time within six months from the date of the hospital order or transfer direction or (if under age 16 when admitted) from the 16th birthday. (*Section* 63 (4));

(b) at any one time within six months after a transfer from guardianship or (if under age 16 when transferred) after the 16th birthday. (*Section* 41 (5));

(c) if the patient is re-classified as suffering from a form or forms of mental disorder different from the form(s) recorded at the time of admission, he will (if aged 16 or over) be informed that this has been done, and may apply to the Tribunal within the 28 days after being so informed. (*Section* 38);

(d) after any renewal of the authority for detention—the patient (if aged 16 or over) may apply to the Tribunal at any one time in the period for which the authority is renewed. Renewals may take place (for any patients who need to stay in hospital as long as this) at the end of the first and second years, and thereafter at two-year intervals; the arrangements are slightly different for patients transferred from guardianship. Patients to whom this applies will be informed at the time. (*Section* 43.)

Nearest relative's rights of application to the Mental Health Review Tribunal

(a) In the case of a patient admitted on a hospital order or transfer direction under Part V of the Act, without an order or direction restricting discharge, at any one time in the twelve months beginning with the date of the order or direction, and at any one time in any subsequent period of twelve months. (*Section* 63 (4).)

(b) In the case of a patient transferred from guardianship, the nearest relative retains the right to apply at any one time in successive periods of twelve months which he held before the transfer; the transfer does not alter these periods.

(c) If the patient is re-classified as suffering from a form or forms of mental disorder different from the form(s) recorded at the time of admission and is aged 16 or over, the patient and the nearest relative will be informed and either or both may apply to the Tribunal within 28 days after being informed. (*Section* 38.)

Extract from the Home Office Consolidated Circular to the Police on Crime and Kindred Matters

SECTION IV

Disposal of mentally disordered persons

27. The following paragraphs 27A to 28C explain the procedures under which the police may be concerned in the removal to hospital or a place of safety of persons who are suffering from mental disorder.

Provisions of the Mental Health Act 1959

27A. Under section 25 of the Act a person who suffers from one of the forms of mental disorder referred to in section 4 (mental illness, severe subnormality, subnormality and psychopathic disorder) may, if his mental condition warrants it and if he ought to be detained in the interests of his own health or safety or for the protection of other persons, be admitted to hospital for observation with or without medical treatment for a period not exceeding 28 days. In an emergency, a person may be admitted to hospital for observation under section 29 of the Act, but the period for which he may be detained is limited to three days unless the provisions of section 25 are subsequently complied with. Section 26 of the Act provides for admission and detention for treatment for a longer period, but it applies to a person who suffers from subnormality which is not severe or from psychopathic disorder only if he is under 21; and if such a person is so admitted he may not be detained beyond the age of 25 unless his doctor considers that if released he would be likely to act in a manner dangerous to others or to himself (section 44). In addition to these powers for the detention of patients otherwise than as offenders, section 60 of the Act provides that, where a person is convicted of an offence punishable with imprisonment, the court may order his admission to and detention in a particular hospital if it is satisfied that he suffers from mental disorder of a degree warranting such a course, that admission to hospital is appropriate, and that the necessary arrangements for his admission have been made. In this case no age limits apply to the detention of persons suffering from psychopathic disorder or subnormality.

27B. Section 40 of the Act provides that a patient who is liable to be detained in hospital but is absent without leave may be taken into custody and returned by a constable (among other authorised persons).* Sections 135 and 136 make further provision for constables to take into custody and to remove to a place of safety persons at liberty who are already liable to be detained under the Act or appear to be suffering from mental disorder and to be in need of care. Detention under sections 135 and 136 may not exceed 3 days.

27C. An effect of the provisions described in paragraphs 27A and 27B above is that a person aged 21 or over who suffers from subnormality or psychopathic disorder and who is not already liable to be detained, may not be detained compulsorily in hospital for longer than 3 days (sections 29, 135 and 136) or 28 days (section 25). Such a person can be admitted to hospital for compulsory detention for a longer period only if a court, on conviction of an offence, makes an order under section 60 of the Act. How the statute affects a particular person when he is removed to hospital from police custody may not be known to the police at the time of his removal because they do not know the particular form of disorder from which he is suffering.

---

*See also paragraph 11 of Section X of this circular.

Offences by persons suffering from mental disorder

28. If a person who commits an offence not punishable by imprisonment is in obvious need of psychiatric treatment, he will be removed by a constable, usually to hospital under section 136, and it will generally be unnecessary to charge him. Where a person has committed a more serious offence and may be a danger to others it may be necessary to consider charging him later, see paragraph 28A below. Where a person who has committed an offence not punishable with imprisonment has been charged but not brought before the court before his urgent need of psychiatric treatment becomes apparent, the services of a medical practitioner should be sought and, on his making the necessary recommendation, the mental welfare officer should be consulted so that he may consider whether to make an emergency application under section 29 of the Act for the admission of the accused person to hospital.

Exchange of information with hospital authorities

28A. Where the conduct of a person removed to hospital has been such as to suggest that he may be a danger to others, all information known to the police about his mental condition and about the circumstances in which he came to police notice should be brought to the personal attention of the medical officer responsible for the patient's treatment in hospital. This should be done in writing, preferably at the time when the patient is removed to hospital, though preparation of a written report should not be allowed to delay the patient's removal. The responsible medical officer should also be given the name and address of the officer in charge of the police sub-division from which the patient was taken to hospital. The hospital authorities will notify this officer if the patient is subsequently found not to be suffering from mental disorder or (if an adult) to suffer from sub-normality or psychopathic disorder uncomplicated by mental illness or severe sub-normality so that he cannot be compulsorily admitted to hospital under section 26 of the Act, and is being discharged or is discharging himself, or having been admitted as an informal patient is not liable to be detained. The hospital authorities will also give their opinion whether the patient is likely to benefit from treatment in hospital and whether he is likely to be violent in the foreseeable future; and say whether they are willing to accept the patient for further treatment. When the police receive this information they should also make it available to the sub-division in which the patient lives (if different). Chief officers of police may then wish to consider whether, taking into account all the circumstances of the case and the provisions of sections 26 and 60 of the 1959 Act, it would be appropriate to take further action with regard to any offence which the person is thought to have committed.

28B. The fact that a notification has been received from a hospital in accordance with paragraph 28A above need not prevent the person concerned being referred again to hospital under section 135 or 136 on a subsequent occasion if it appears that urgent medical treatment or examination is necessary.

Arrangements for removal to hospital

28C. Persons dealt with under section 135 or 136 may be lodged temporarily in a police station which is one of the places designated in the Act as "a place of safety". Local health authorities have been advised that if a person is removed to a police station as a place of safety on the authority of a warrant issued under section 135(1) of the Mental Health Act, he should not remain there longer than the period (normally a matter of hours only) which may be needed for the mental welfare officer to make arrangements for his removal elsewhere. Local health authorities and hospitals have also been asked, when action is taken on a warrant issued under section 135(2) and the patient is apprehended, to arrange for his removal as soon as possible to the place where he is liable to be detained. A person who is removed by a constable under section 136 from a place to which the public have access should normally be taken direct to a hospital. If this is not practicable, the assistance of the mental welfare officer should be sought immediately.

311

HOME OFFICE

Whitehall, London, S.W.1.

28 June 1973.

The Clerk to the Justices

Sir

HOME OFFICE CIRCULAR NO 113/1973

MEDICAL REPORTS TO COURTS

I am directed by the Secretary of State to say that in the light of a case involving murder and suicide by a person who had received treatment in a mental hospital following a court order, he has been considering whether the arrangements for supplying information to doctors who are asked to provide medical reports to courts can be improved.

2. As you know, when medical reports are requested on an accused person remanded by a magistrates' court under section 26 of the Magistrates' Courts Act 1952, the court is required by Rule 23 of the Magistrates' Courts Rules 1968 to send to the institution to which the accused is committed (or at which he will be examined, if on bail) a statement of the reasons why the court thinks an enquiry ought to be made into his physical or mental condition, and of any relevant information before the court. In Home Office Circular No 265 of 1968 a suggested form was recommended for the conveyance of this information both in these circumstances and where medical reports are called for on remand under section 14(3) of the 1952 Act; and Home Office Circular No 107 of 1971 it was suggested that it would be helpful if courts could make available to reporting doctors copies of any medical, probation or other reports in their possession. The particulars to be given about offences were considered by the Working Party on Magistrates' Courts whose 2nd Report (Wording of remand and committal warrants) was circulated on 20 December 1971 under Home Office reference MAG/71 4/28/4.

3. While the Secretary of State considers the existing procedure to be generally satisfactory, he is anxious to ensure that examining doctors are furnished with all available information likely to be of value to them, particularly where the report required is on the defendant's mental condition. With this in mind a revised version of the form recommended in Home Office Circular No 265 of 1968 has been prepared and is attached.

4. It is especially important that the examining doctor should be fully informed of the reasons which led the court to request the report. Due explanation of these will greatly assist the doctor to relate his report to the points in which the court is interested. If, for example, the court requires a medical opinion about some physical condition which might affect the disposal of an offender, particulars of the alleged disability should be stated. Similarly, if the court has found reason to consider the mental condition of the accused, it is of great assistance if a brief description can be given of any behaviour which may have given rise to this question.

5. The revised form indicates that the required information may often best be conveyed by attaching a copy of the report or statement in the court's possession. Much useful information about the previous medical history of the offender (where known), his past conduct and his present home circumstances will no doubt often be contained in the antecedent and social enquiry reports submitted to the court.

6. It is also important that the court should always provide adequate particulars of the circumstances of the offence, especially where its nature suggests that the offender may possess dangerous or violent propensities. If statements of the facts are in the court's possession copies could be provided where appropriate and convenient. This information may have an important bearing on the recommendation a doctor may make if he considers that the offender needs treatment for mental disorder.

7. The offender's address (or the location of the offence if he is of no fixed abode) is needed to identify the hospital at which he should be treated, if this should be considered necessary. It is also helpful to have the name and station of the police officer concerned in the case, so that the examining doctor may, if he considers it necessary, refer to him for supplementary information about the circumstances of the case.

8. The Secretary of State recognises that courts will not always be in possession of the full facts, particularly as to the background to an offence to which the accused has pleaded guilty, and that they are able to pass onto the examining doctor only such relevant information as may be available to them. He appreciates too that often the entries under the various headings in the recommended form can only, and need only, be quite brief. He feels sure, however, that courts will understand the importance, in the interests both of ensuring the most appropriate treatment of the offender and the protection of the public, of providing the examining doctor with all relevant information to enable him to make an informed clinical assessment and to identify any unusual feature in a case.

I am, Sir,

Your obedient Servant,

(Sd) A. J. E. BRENNAN

REMANDS FOR MEDICAL REPORTS

Remands in custody under S. 14(3) or S. 26, Magistrates' Courts Act 1952

Statement of reasons for medical inquiry (Rule 23)

Name of defendant...

Court.. Date..

Offence...

Section under which remand is ordered...
....

Dear Sir,

This defendant has been remanded for a medical report. To assist the Medical Officer I give below the information available.

1. Type of report (eg on physical or mental condition or suitability for particular treatment).

2. Reasons which led the Court to request the report.

3. Previous medical history of offender and family history, so far as known.*

4. Particulars of circumstances of offence (including, if the offender is of no fixed abode, the place where it was committed, if known).*

5. Previous conduct, including previous convictions, if known.*

6. Address and home circumstances of offender.*

7. Name and station of police officer concerned with case.

8. Name and telephone number of any probation officer appointed to or having knowledge of the case.

Yours faithfully,

Clerk to the Justices.

The Governor,
HM Prison,
....

---

*Where the required information can best be conveyed by attaching a copy of a report or statement in the court's possession, all that need be entered here is "See attached....................."

HOME OFFICE
Whitehall, London, S.W.1

28 June 1973.

The Chief Officer of Police

Sir

HOME OFFICE CIRCULAR No 112/1973
MEDICAL REPORTS TO COURTS

I am directed by the Secretary of State to say that, in the light of a case involving murder and suicide by a person who had received treatment in a mental hospital under a court order, he has been considering whether the arrangements for supplying information to doctors who are asked to provide medical reports to courts can be improved.

2. Where a medical question (especially the possibility of mental disorder) is likely to be a factor in the disposal of a case, the courts have power to remand the accused, either in custody or on bail, for a medical report to be prepared by a prison medical officer or some other doctor. When this is done, the court provides the doctor who is to examine the accused with such relevant information about the case as is available.

3. In some instances the doctor who has to assess the case may need more detailed information about the accused or his offence than is in the possession of the court. For example, where the question of psychiatric treatment for the offender is under consideration, it may be important for the doctor to know whether the offence involved violence, and if so to what degree, but if the accused pleads guilty only brief details may be given in court. It is thought that any additional information which examining doctors might require would usually be known to the police officer concerned in the case.

4. The Secretary of State would therefore be grateful if you would assist in this situation by arranging to make available to examining doctors, on request, such information as you possess and they ask for about the circumstances of offences and offenders in cases where courts call for medical reports. Courts are being asked to notify the examining doctor, when a medical report is requested, of the name of the police officer concerned in the case. The particulars required would broadly be those which would be given in court if necessary, and it will be appreciated that members of the medical profession are alive to the requirements of confidentiality. It is expected that doctors will make enquiries in this way only in a small proportion of all cases in which medical reports are made, and normally by telephone.

I am, Sir,

Your obedient Servant,

(Sd) A. J. E. BRENNAN

Fig. 2.

'MURDERERS' FOUND 'GUILTY BUT INSANE', 'INSANE ON ARRAIGNMENT',
OR OF DIMINISHED RESPONSIBILITY, 1947-63

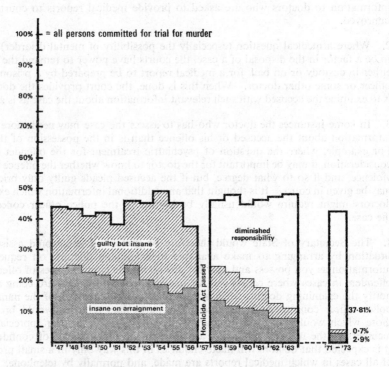

Percentages are shown as sliding three-year averages for 1946–1973. They are also
shown cumulatively: thus in 1946–8 the percentages found 'insane on arraignment' or
'guilty but insane' *together* averaged 44 per cent.

Derived from Nigel Walker, *Crime and Insanity in England* (Edinburgh 1968),
Vol. 1, p. 159, with the addition of the figures for 1971–1973.

316

NOTES ON THE DEFINITION OF SEVERE MENTAL ILLNESS

(i) Mental illness and mental disorder are here used as in the Mental Health Act (1959), and the latter term as also used in the International Classification of Diseases (8th revision), Section V (1968).

(ii) The characteristics in category (a) refer to the essential features of the group of organic psychoses for which, when chronic or progressive in nature, the term "dementia" is commonly used. The term "delirium" is commonly used for *acute* organic psychoses which have a short course, and in which the characteristic features described in category (a) are not so evident because of clouded consciousness, gross mental confusion and disturbing hallucinations. Such cases would be unlikely to have the necessary mental element required for an offence.

(iii) The essential feature of the group of affective psychoses is the severe and lasting disturbance of mood which is either towards depression or towards elation and excitement. Since such changes occur as minor variants of the disorder, severity is recognised when, as a result of the altered mood, the patient is either prevented from making any appraisal (because of elation and excitement) or makes (usually because of depression) a delusional appraisal of his situation, his past or future, or that of others. (It is probable that the word "lasting" in "lasting change of mood" is unnecessary for psychiatrists since "mood" is not applied by them to transient changes in emotion. "Lasting" is included to avoid the risk that courts might interpret the word "mood" in a non-technical sense).

(iv) The three types of delusional belief given in category (c) are those which, when the presenting or only pathology, are characteristic of the paranoid psychoses. They are also common in the schizophrenic psychoses. Delusions of other types are common in all the psychoses.

(v) Abnormal perceptions (illusions and hallucinations) occur in normal people, and also in many forms of mental disorder, as well as in certain brain diseases not associated with mental disorder. The essential characteristic of abnormal perceptions (category (d)) which occur in the psychotic disorders is that they are associated with, or lead to a misinterpretation of real events which has the quality of delusional belief.

(vi) Disorder of thought, referred to in category (e), is often the outstanding characteristic of schizophrenic psychosis. It is also one of the most fundamental aspects of the disorder, and refers both to the disorder in the patient's thought processes and to the patient's awareness of his self and his psychological separateness and identity from other people. In this latter respect thought disorder is well described as a disorder of "ego boundaries", the capacity to identify thoughts, feelings and impulses as being the patient's own. Thus the patient may be unable to communicate adequately because his thought processes are interrupted or diffuse, undirected or inconclusive and the associations of thought bizarre or illogical; or he experiences a sense of being under external control either in thought, feeling or action, or his thoughts taken from him, or spoken aloud, broadcast or known to others.

INDEX

319

324

Printed in England for Her Majesty's Stationery Office by Oyez Press Limited
Dd141833   K28   10/75